ADVANCE PRAISE

"Just when you think you've read and heard everything there is to know about the CIA, JFK, and the mob, along comes Thomas Maier with this meticulously researched and nuanced report that sets the record straight in some areas and breaks new ground in others. *Mafia Spies* reads like a thriller but it's all true. I found it gripping from page one. And important. The events reported on here changed history and give us better understanding of current times."

—Michael Connelly, #1 *New York Times* bestselling author
and creator of the critically-acclaimed series *Bosch*

"*Mafia Spies* is one of those stories that is truly more amazing than fiction, about an unlikely alliance between America's best and worst. The tale is told at a relentless pace and makes great reading."

—Scott Turow, bestselling author of *Presumed Innocent,*
The Burden of Proof, Identical, Innocent and more

"*Mafia Spies* brings history to life in epic, page-turning fashion. The depth of Thomas Maier's research is astounding, as are the famous characters and fantastical events that quietly changed US history."

—Martin Dugard, *New York Times* bestselling co-author of
Killing Lincoln, Killing Kennedy, Killing Jesus, and others written
with television personality Bill O'Reilly

"From CIA secret labs creating assassination tools first dreamed up by Ian Fleming in his James Bond novels, to poisoned cigars, exploding cats, Frank Sinatra, and two of the most well-connected mafioso in gangland history, Thomas Maier's *Mafia Spies* is a revealing look into one of the most outrageous spy tales of the twentieth century. If you are unfamiliar with Sam Giancana and Johnny Roselli, and their connection to everyone from low-life mob hucksters to JFK, this is a book that will open your eyes to a world of political intrigue that reaches into the depths and heights of mid-twentieth century American culture. Maier's knowledge of politics and of gangland lore is impressive, and he uses it here to great effect in *Mafia Spies*, a work that reads like a novel but is, amazingly, a nonfiction tale of mobsters working for the CIA to assassinate Fidel Castro. If Mario Puzo were more interested in journalism than fiction, this unrelenting page turner is the book he would have written instead of *The Godfather*."

—Ed Falco, *New York Times* bestselling author of *The Family Corleone*

"The United States doesn't order foreign leaders killed. Unless it does. And it did in 1960 when the CIA took the unthinkable step of recruiting two Mafiosi—Sam Giancana and John 'Handsome Johnny' Roselli—to murder Cuban Premiere Fidel Castro. The existence of this misbegotten plot was exposed in the 1970s during Senate hearings after the assassination of JFK, but we've been denied a full accounting until now. Drawing upon documents recently released by the National Archives, Thomas Maier spins a vigorously picaresque tale of the hoodlums and their handlers as they make run after failed run at the Cuban premiere with such lunatic ploys as exploding cigars and contaminated scuba gear. Castro's crack intelligence network in Miami allowed him to dodge every bullet. The strength of Maier's account is that he delivers such richly detailed profiles of the players that they seem to unfold in three dimensions. Often frightening, at times hilarious, this is a cautionary tale for anyone thinking it might be a good idea to 'outsource' intelligence operations. *Mafia Spies* is a bracing read and I enjoyed it thoroughly."

—Teresa Carpenter, Pulitzer Prize winner and author of four books, including *Mob Girl: A Woman's Life in the Underworld*

"This story exposes a dark chapter in America's history, when the CIA teamed up with murderous Mafia hitmen in an ill-fated assassination plot. Thoroughly reported and masterfully written, Maier delves deep into a world of political intrigue and underworld brutality. It's a riveting, must-read."

—Shelley Murphy, co-author of the *New York Times* bestseller *Whitey Bulger: America's Most Wanted Gangster and the Manhunt That Brought Him to Justice*

"Meticulously researched and sourced, *Mafia Spies*, the compelling history of the pact between the CIA and Mafia to assassinate Fidel Castro, reads like a bestselling thriller. Thomas Maier's swashbuckling story-telling takes you into a clandestine, paradoxical world where gangsters were patriots, spies were hapless bureaucrats, and political deception and murder were the prevailing currencies. For those who study US foreign and domestic intelligence practices during the second half of the last century, this is a must-read."

—Libby Fischer Hellmann, author of *High Crimes* and *Havana Lost*

"*Mafia Spies* shows how the CIA and the Mafia colluded in a wild 1960s scheme to kill Fidel Castro, covered it up for years, and eventually paid an awful price. Investigative reporter Thomas Maier reveals many new aspects of America's most extensive and shocking spy scandal. As a real-life drama, this non-fiction book blends the mob violence and intrigue of *The Godfather* with the CIA thriller-like quality of TV's *Homeland*."

—Gerard Ryle, director of the International Consortium
of Investigative Journalists, 2017 Pulitzer Prize winner,
"The Panama Papers"

"This is Thomas Maier's epic story of the CIA and the mobsters recruited to assassinate Fidel Castro in the 1960s. Maier's spotlight sweeps across America, casting its sharp focus from Frank Sinatra and the Rat Pack to the lesser stars and starlets of Hollywood to Havana and finally to the White House itself. Maier's prodigious storytelling ability recreates a shocking moment in US history with unprecedented detail and drama, from the bungled attempt to assassinate Fidel Castro to the real possibility that John Kennedy himself was caught in the same seedy web."

—Peter Eisner, author of *MacArthur's Spies*,
former *Washington Post* deputy foreign editor,
and co-author of *The Shadow President*

MAFIA SPIES

THE INSIDE STORY OF THE CIA, GANGSTERS, JFK, AND CASTRO

THOMAS MAIER

Skyhorse Publishing

TO JOYCE AND HER SONS,
THE BEST GANG OF ALL.

Skyhorse Publishing books may be purchased in bulk at special discounts for sales promotion, corporate gifts, fund-raising, or educational purposes. Special editions can also be created to specifications. For details, contact the Special Sales Department, Skyhorse Publishing, 307 West 36th Street, 11th Floor, New York, NY 10018 or info@skyhorsepublishing.com.

Skyhorse® and Skyhorse Publishing® are registered trademarks of Skyhorse Publishing, Inc.®, a Delaware corporation.

Visit our website at www.skyhorsepublishing.com.

10 9 8 7 6 5 4 3 2

Library of Congress Cataloging-in-Publication Data is available on file.

Cover design by Paul Qualcom
Cover photo of Johnny Roselli: John Rosselli after being released from jail, 1948, Los Angeles Times Photographic Archives (Collection 1429). Library Special Collections, Charles E. Young Research Library, UCLA.
Cover photos of Sam Giancana, JFK, and Fidel Castro: Wikimedia Commons

Print ISBN: 978-1-5107-4171-3
Ebook ISBN: 978-1-5107-4172-0

Printed in the United States of America

CONTENTS

PHASE III: THE PATRIOTIC ASSASSIN

PHASE IV: THE PRICE OF EVERYTHING

AUTHOR'S NOTE—
FOR YOUR EYES ONLY

"And ye shall know the truth,
and the truth shall make you free"

—JOHN 8:32 (BIBLICAL PASSAGE INSCRIBED
ON A STONE WALL AT THE CENTRAL INTELLIGENCE AGENCY
HEADQUARTERS IN LANGLEY, VIRGINIA)

S pying, at its very coldest, discerns between truth and lies. Unfortunately, truth often emerges slowly.

Much of what happens in this book—a non-fiction narrative about gangsters Johnny Roselli and Sam Giancana and their fateful involvement with the US Central Intelligence Agency in trying to assassinate Cuban leader Fidel Castro—wasn't known to the public until years, sometimes decades, after its occurrence.

The original 1960s Castro murder conspiracy remained a secret for fifteen years, until Congressional hearings in the mid-1970s revealed the spy agency's basic plot. More spy details were released publicly in the years to come.

But the recently declassified files about the 1963 assassination of President John F. Kennedy, released in batches by the National Archives in 2017-2018, were the biggest help for this book. As I reported for *Politico* in February 2018, these documents from the CIA, FBI, and other agencies provided many new details about the spy agency's Cuban activities. Overall, this glacial disclosure of truths, revealed over the past half century, makes a historical narrative like this one necessary and especially timely today, when the difference between truth and lies is never so apparent.

In putting together this book, lies of various size and sort posed the greatest obstacle. Virtually every major character engaged in some form of deception, half-truths, fabrication, and outright falsehood. Mobsters like Giancana and Roselli used aliases to disguise their true identities. Politicians sought "plausible deniability" to evade responsibility for their lethal actions. And double agents, "cut outs," and master spies routinely evaded the truth, including one former CIA director who eventually pled *nolo contendere* to perjury.

Judging the veracity of each character's assertions was undoubtedly my greatest challenge in coming up with a reliable non-fiction account of their public and private lives. As a result, the more than nine hundred footnotes listed at the back of this text rely primarily on sworn court testimony, Congressional hearings, CIA, FBI, and other government documents, oral histories in presidential libraries as well as published accounts in books, magazines, and major newspapers.

As a window into this complex story, *Mafia Spies* follows the joined fates of Roselli and Giancana, the two Mafia buddies forever linked by their unlikely role as "patriots," in what became the most extraordinary spy mystery in American history.

—Thomas Maier, Long Island, New York, April 2019

CAST OF CHARACTERS

THE TWO GANGSTERS AND THEIR TARGET

Sam Giancana—Boss of Chicago's Mafia organization called "the Outfit," with lucrative casinos and other illicit businesses around the world. He and long-time mob pal Johnny Roselli agreed to help the CIA assassinate Cuban Communist leader Fidel Castro as a way of gaining favor with US officials.

Johnny Roselli—The mob's charismatic fixer in Hollywood and Las Vegas, who befriended many entertainment figures and countless women. He acted as the main "patriotic" go-between with the Mafia, the CIA, and Cuban exiles wanting to kill Castro.

Fidel Castro—The Cuban revolutionary leader who seized power in 1959. During the Cold War, Castro ousted American Mafia figures from their Havana casinos and turned his Communist nation into a Soviet ally. In return, Castro became the target of a CIA assassination plot that recruited Giancana and Roselli as his avenging killers.

THE CIA

Allen Dulles—The CIA's first director secretly approved the Castro murder plot in the final days of the Eisenhower administration and curried favor with the Kennedys until the 1961 Bay of Pigs invasion fiasco forced his departure.

William King Harvey—Touted as the American "James Bond," this tough-talking CIA agent oversaw the Castro assassination plan and became Johnny Roselli's faithful friend.

Robert Maheu—The private eye who acted as a "cutout" middleman between the CIA and the two mobsters, while also serving as a frontman for multi-millionaire Howard Hughes in Las Vegas.

Richard Bissell, Richard Helms, Sheffield Edwards—Top CIA officials who knew of the Mafia involvement in the plan to overthrow Castro's government.

Dr. Sidney Gottlieb—A scientist whose CIA lab created numerous poisons, guns, and "James Bond"-like killing devices meant for Castro.

John McCone—The CIA director morally opposed to assassination who was deliberately kept in the dark about the Castro plot by his minions.

THE WASHINGTON POWER BROKERS

Dwight D. Eisenhower—Two-term president in the 1950s who oversaw the Cold War against the Soviet Union and approved the overthrow plan of the Cuban leader in 1960.

John F. Kennedy—As Ike's successor, he inherited the CIA's disastrous "Bay of Pigs" invasion plan and took blame when it failed yet favored aggressive covert action against Castro. JFK's 1963 assassination prompted widespread rumors of a conspiracy, and whether the Warren Commission should have known about the Mafia-CIA plot against Castro.

Robert F. Kennedy—Former Senate rackets investigator and US Attorney General during his brother's term, RFK personally oversaw the government's anti-Castro efforts after the failed Bay of Pigs invasion.

Arthur M. Schlesinger Jr.—Historian and JFK aide who discounted claims that either JFK or RFK knew of the CIA's murder plot against Castro.

Jack Anderson—Investigative reporter who helped expose in the 1970s the involvement of Roselli and Giancana in the CIA's Castro assassination plot a decade earlier.

Lyndon B. Johnson—Successor to the slain JFK, he didn't learn of the CIA's Mafia plot against Castro until well into his presidency.

THE WOMEN IN THEIR LIVES

Judy Campbell—Voluptuous California divorcée whose succession of controversial affairs with Roselli, Frank Sinatra, JFK, and Giancana were chronicled in numerous FBI investigative reports and eventually caused a national scandal.

June Lang—Unlike so many other Hollywood actresses attracted to Johnny Roselli's "bad boy" charm, she married the mobster. Johnny demanded June quit her film career, and they soon divorced.

Angeline Giancana—Sam's adored wife whose early death left him as a widower with three daughters. Giancana viewed his religious "madonna"-like wife at home very differently from the other outside women with whom he had affairs.

Antoinette Giancana—Sam's erratic, hot-tempered oldest daughter much like himself. Her memoir provided glimpses into her father's personal life.

Donna Reed, Lana Turner, Betty Hutton, Jeanne Carmen, and Virginia Hill—Johnny Roselli's Casanova-style romances and dating included these Hollywood actresses and well-known women.

Phyllis McGuire—Sam's famous girlfriend, part of the singing McGuire Sisters. Sam's intense jealousy for McGuire prompted the bugging of a rival's hotel room by CIA operatives.

Marilyn Monroe—Famous actress who knew Roselli and his entertainment friends. Her tumultuous 1962 visit to Cal-Neva resort in Nevada, owned by Sinatra (and secretly by Giancana), set in motion the events that led to her suicide.

Marita Lorenz—A former lover of Castro, Lorenz was recruited by CIA operatives to entrap the Cuban leader in a hotel room and poison him.

Carolyn Morris—In the 1970s, Giancana considered marriage again, courting this fashionable blonde divorcée from Palm Springs, California, nearly twenty years Sam's junior.

THE INVESTIGATORS

J. Edgar Hoover—The longtime FBI director didn't know initially about the CIA's recruitment of mobsters against Castro—or the infidelities of JFK with Giancana's girlfriend—but once he did, he wielded the information like an anvil.

William Roemer—Like an avenging angel, the Chicago FBI agent became Giancana's nemesis, listening to hours of private conversations through hidden devices in the Outfit's headquarters.

Richard Cain—This "double agent" was a soldier for the Mafia, working secretly for Giancana, while also a corrupt Chicago cop, an investigator for the sheriff, and a freelance spy for the CIA against Castro.

Frank Church —US Senator whose mid-1970s hearings revealed many of the deepest secrets of the CIA's plot against Castro during the Eisenhower-Kennedy years. His demands for Giancana and Roselli's testimony had fateful consequences.

Earl Warren—US Supreme Court Justice who presided over the official 1964 probe into the JFK assassination, though commission member Allen Dulles, the ex-CIA director, never revealed what he knew about the Castro murder conspiracy.

THE CUBANS

Tony Varona—A corrupt former Cuban official strongly opposed to Castro who maintained friendships in Miami with both mobsters and Cuban exiles hoping to "liquidate" the Communist dictator.

Juan Orta—A "double agent" inside Havana who supposedly was going to slip poison pills to Castro at the behest of Mafia figures and the CIA.

Rolando Cubela—Originally a Castro ally, Cubela claimed he wanted to defect. The CIA tried to convince him to kill Castro, but he was probably a double agent.

G-2 (or DGI)—Created during the Cold War, Cuba's intelligence service, also known as Dirección General de Inteligencia, became one of the most effective spy agencies in the world. Several spymasters ran this agency, but the real boss was Castro.

Manuel Artime—A beloved figure among the Cuban exiles and favorite of the Kennedys, he led the ill-fated 1961 Bay of Pigs invasion. Once a rebel with Castro, he strongly opposed Cuba's turn to Communism.

THE ENTERTAINERS

Frank Sinatra—One of America's best-known stars, he campaigned for JFK in 1960, introduced him to girlfriend Judy Campbell and befriended Giancana, Roselli, and other Mafia figures. He invested with Giancana in Cal-Neva casino resort until Nevada authorities learned of the mobster's secret interest.

The Rat Pack—Sinatra's showbiz pals included Dean Martin, Sammy Davis, and Peter Lawford, JFK's brother-in-law. They were friendly with Sinatra's mob pals and sometimes performed at their request.

Dan Rowan—A TV host and comedian, Rowan courted singer Phyllis McGuire, which prompted Giancana's jealousy and a secret bug placed in his hotel room by CIA operatives.

Monte Proser—A front man for a talent agency and nightclubs controlled by members of the Mafia, including Johnny Roselli, in Hollywood, New York, and Las Vegas.

Harry Cohn—Powerful Hollywood movie mogul and close friend of Johnny Roselli.

Howard Hughes—Movie tycoon and wealthy aviator, he employed private eye Robert Maheu and wound up learning of the CIA's secret Castro assassination plot. With the help of Roselli and Maheu, Hughes later bought several Las Vegas casinos.

THE OTHER GANGSTERS

Tony Accardo—Longtime boss of Chicago's Outfit who picked Giancana as his successor but later regretted his decision.

Santo Trafficante Jr.—Florida don who joined Giancana and Roselli in the CIA plot but may have been a "double agent" for Castro.

Sam "Mad Sam" DeStefano—Psychopathic killer who was known as a violent enforcer of Giancana's dictums.

William "Action" Jackson—A mob "juice" loan shark who was butchered by Giancana's gang after being spotted talking with FBI agent Roemer.

Marshall Caifano—Chicago hitman who moved to Vegas to help oversee casinos with Roselli, while flattered his wife had an affair with Giancana.

Willie Bioff—Former Chicago mobster who turned informant in the Hollywood extortion case that sent Roselli and other gangsters to jail. Later murdered when he was discovered in Vegas hiding under an alias.

Jimmy Fratianno—California hitman and long-time friend of Roselli who became an FBI informant.

PHASE I:
PLAN OF ACTION

"There is nothing more necessary than good intelligence to frustrate a designing enemy, and nothing that requires greater pains to obtain."
—GEORGE WASHINGTON, FUTURE US PRESIDENT
AND GENERAL IN THE REVOLUTIONARY WAR,
IDENTIFIED IN SECRET SPY PAPERS AS CODE NUMBER 711

"There are a lot of killers. You think our country's so innocent?"
—PRESIDENT DONALD TRUMP, 2017

CHAPTER 1:

OVERTURE—
"THE GREAT GAME"

"When everyone is dead, the Great Game is finished. Not before."
—RUDYARD KIPLING, AUTHOR OF *KIM* (1901),
CONSIDERED THE FIRST MODERN SPY NOVEL

At a closed-door Congressional hearing in June 1975, gangster Johnny Roselli testified about his role as a "patriotic" assassin for the Central Intelligence Agency, a top-secret operation full of spies, sex, and unresolved mystery.

With wavy hair and steely blue eyes, Roselli looked like a successful businessman—a "strategist" as he preferred to be called—or more like the Hollywood B-movie producer he once was. No run-of-the-mill hoodlum, he wore dark designer sunglasses, dressed in a blue blazer with a polka-dot silk hankerchief in its breast pocket, and carried a smooth leather attaché case. Murder never looked so good.

Surrounded by senators in rapt attention, Roselli offered an assortment of lies and deceptions, sprinkled with a few moments of truth. And when he finished his performance, he confidently stood up, closed his briefcase, and disappeared through a back exit.

Outside, photographers and inquisitive reporters awaited him, like a street gang ready to pounce. Flashing camera lights blinded him.

Few photos existed of this mystery witness in shades. Most were mugshots. None captured Roselli's personal charm, the debonair sense of danger that made women swoon and fellow gangsters refer to him as "Handsome Johnny."

At this shock of public recognition, Johnny's body stiffened. His affable grin tensed. He'd spent his whole life, both in business and personal affairs, avoiding such moments.

As that rarest of "spooks"—a Mafia hitman turned top-secret spy—Roselli preferred the shadows. He never wanted to be in the spotlight, exposing his many deceptions.

Even his name "Johnny Roselli" was a phony, one of several aliases he used to avoid revealing his real identity.

Keeping his head down along a Washington street, Roselli hustled away from the Capitol, shunning the paparazzi eager to splatter his face across the next day's front pages. They chased after this stylish mobster, hoping for more insights about his highly classified government mission.

Under oath that afternoon, Roselli had fielded questions about the biggest secret in CIA history, kept under wraps for more than a decade. As America soon learned, Roselli and his long-time friend, Chicago mob boss Sam Giancana, were two central characters in an elaborate CIA scheme to assassinate Cuba's young Communist leader Fidel Castro during the 1960s.

Poison pills, exploding cigars, lethal James Bond-like gadgets, midnight boat raids from Florida with Cuban exiles carrying bombs and long-range rifles—a veritable army of undercover spies, double agents, and "cutout" handlers—were all part of this ill-fated campaign emanating from the White House.

Historically, the CIA's murder plot against Castro marked America's first foray into the assassination business. Kipling's celebrated "great game"—the tradition of gentlemen spies engaged in gathering intelligence—had been now transformed into the killing games of covert operations, carried out by gangsters and other CIA surrogates.

Not even Roselli's charm could mask this ugly truth when asked about his mission's intent.

"To assassinate Castro," he growled matter-of-factly in his deep whiskey-soured voice.

As each detail unraveled before a startled nation, the saga of Giancana and Roselli—two Mafia pals working for the CIA—seemed like a murder mystery and a spy novel all rolled into one.

This complex morality play of Cold War paranoia offered America a bizarre reflection of itself—shattering the heroic Hollywood image of "good guy" agents fending off foreign evil-doers. Instead, this true-life story revealed the much murkier and violent reality of modern espionage by those charged with defending the United States from harm.

As Roselli rushed away from the Senate hearing, reporters peppered him with questions about Giancana's fate and concerns for his own safety. A Washington acquaintance later asked if he feared retaliation because of his testimony.

As always in times of crisis, Johnny never lost his cool.

"Who'd want to kill an old man like me?" he replied.

The unholy marriage of the CIA and the Mafia first became known to the American public in the mid-1970s, amid congressional hearings into the agency's misdeeds and a growing national paranoia about the 1963 assassination of President John F. Kennedy.

For more than a decade, the plot to kill Castro was known only to a few. President Lyndon Johnson didn't learn about it until his fourth year in office. By enlisting Giancana and Roselli, the CIA "had been operating a damned Murder Inc. in the Caribbean," Johnson complained. Many troubling questions went unanswered— such as why the Warren Commission examining JFK's killing was never told of the agency's Castro conspiracy with the Mafia. Full of his own theories, Johnson predicted: "It will all come out one day."

Yet this spy tale remained an enigma for years, including the mysterious fate of Roselli and Giancana. Not until 2007 did the CIA finally admit that Allen Dulles, its legendary director a half-century earlier, was responsible for offering a sizable bounty to the two gangsters in exchange for Castro's head. "The documents show that the agency's actions in the early 1960s still have the capacity to shock," the *Washington Post*'s Glenn Kessler said of that long-surpressed internal CIA report known as "The Family Jewels."

More pieces in the puzzle emerged in 2017, when the National Archives released thousands of files about the JFK assassination, kept secret in full or part for decades. Many pertained to the CIA's Cold War crusade against Castro. Like strands in a ball of yarn, these individual documents revealed a complicated tale far greater than Americans ever realized at the time. Together, they provide the most comprehensive picture yet of America's first confirmed attempt at state-sponsored assassination of a foreign leader.

These files also help illuminate Giancana's and Roselli's shadowy world, which included CIA spies and handlers, beautiful Hollywood women, "Rat Pack" entertainers like Frank Sinatra in Las Vegas, fellow Mafioso in Chicago, Cuban exile commandos in Miami, J. Edgar Hoover's snooping FBI, and the zealous anti-communism of White House officials in Washington. They reveal the many passions, ambitions, and conflicting loyalties among these two outlaw friends, a sort of modern-day *Butch Cassidy and the Sundance Kid*, who rode on planes instead of horses for their getaways.

Giancana and Roselli, at the height of their careers, controlled a multi-million-dollar Mafia empire unprecedented in the annals of American crime—arguably bigger than the five families of New York's La Cosa Nostra combined. Giancana—the gruff, traditionalist mob boss, a widower with three daughters—dreamed of exporting his Midwest criminal enterprise to Latin America. And Roselli, known for his Casanova style, served as the mob's smooth-talking man in Hollywood before overseeing its casinos in Las Vegas.

The two began as young Turks for Al Capone's Chicago gang, long before their CIA mission. They had a history of working together, running gambling palaces in Cuba and Nevada and exerting the mob's will in myriad ways.

With a drink in hand or a woman on their lap, the two Mafia pals could be found in places like the Boom-Boom Room at Miami's Fontainebleau Hotel, where the CIA scheme to kill Castro was hatched in September 1960. Although they cited "patriotic" reasons for accepting this assignment, Giancana and Roselli had their own motivations for eliminating the bearded dictator.

When he came to power, Castro closed down the Mafia's very lucrative casinos in Havana, costing the two gangsters dearly. They still hoped to revive the swank San Souci resort that they had run in Cuba with Spanish-speaking Mafia boss Santo Trafficante Jr. The JFK files suggest Giancana and Roselli believed that cooperating with the government in such a high-risk venture as Castro's assassination would earn them a kind of "get out of jail free" card that would keep the feds off their backs as they pursued their criminal activity at home. And for a time, their arrangement seemed to work.

Through the prism of these two mobsters, a much larger portrait emerges of America's top spying agency spinning out of control when the nation most needed its vigilance. Documents show how the CIA conducted a covert war against Castro from a secret camp next-door to the Miami Zoo; how it developed James Bond-like killing devices at the behest of the Kennedys who loved the Bond novels; and how three different CIA directors lied about this secret murder plot, so it would never be learned by the public. This undercover quest turned southern Florida into a secret war zone and became a wild whack-a-mole hunt for Castro inside Cuba, all without success.

When Fidel Castro finally died in November 2016—not from an assassin's bullet but peacefully asleep in his bed at age ninety—the world was reminded of all the fear he once provoked and why Cuba remains a solitary rogue nation stuck in time.

Instead of being a promised savior, Castro had turned his once prosperous homeland into an armed Communist camp. He enforced his rule with firing squads and merciless prisons. By inviting Russian nuclear weapons into his nation as a way of protecting his despotic regime, he helped incite the 1962 Cuban Missile Crisis with its threatened Armageddon between the United States and Soviet Union. Aware of the plots against him, Castro publicly vowed revenge—what experts called "blowback"—to those who wanted him dead.

Documents describe how Castro's spy agency and its double agents in Florida "penetrated" the CIA operation far more than US officials realized; conspired to blow up New York City in a 9/11-like attack; and managed to keep "El Comandante" from getting killed despite numerous CIA-sponsored attempts. Obituaries about Castro mentioned these repeated assassination tries, but they provided little or no explanation about how he'd managed to avoid getting killed.

As Cuba now re-opens itself to the world, this spy tale serves as a Rosetta Stone for understanding all the Cold War hatred and violence that existed for decades—and is still very much with us. The CIA's Mafia scheme against Castro shows how easily US espionage and law-enforcement agencies were corrupted more than a generation ago, with government-sanctioned murder justified on claims of national security. Talk of assassination pervades this "great game" just as it does in our Trump era, with Russian-trained spies left for dead, rumors of "*kompromat*" and presidential indiscretion, and worries of a new Cold War. Though unfamiliar to many today, this story of espionage and violence offers many important lessons at a time when Americans fear their trusted institutions could again go astray.

In the end, the Castro conspiracy became a Mephistophelian bargain—a promise to do whatever it took to get rid of Cuba's Communist strongman. Giancana and Roselli expected that their actions against Castro, if not rewarded by the US government, at least would keep them free from future prosecution.

Yet danger pervaded every day of their lives, until its vengeful consequences finally caught up with them.

CHAPTER 2:

A STRANGE KIND
OF GENIUS

"Intelligence is probably the least understood and the most misrepresented of the professions."

—ALLEN W. DULLES, THE CRAFT OF INTELLIGENCE

On a wall at his headquarters, a wide map of the world loomed over Allen Dulles, like some Herculean burden he'd carried on his shoulders for years as director of the Central Intelligence Agency.

From his Foggy Bottom offices in downtown Washington, DC, Dulles carefully guided America's civilian espionage organization, created in 1947 from the wartime Office of Strategic Services. Allen had the good fortune to share the same worldview as his older brother, Secretary of State John Foster Dulles. He also enjoyed the confidence of President Dwight D. Eisenhower, who appreciated the CIA's dangerous mission.

"Here is one of the most peculiar types of operation any government can have," Ike explained, "and it probably takes a strange kind of genius to run it."

Dulles didn't fit the trench-coat stereotype of a spy. An honors graduate of Princeton University trained in diplomacy and corporate law, Dulles appeared like an Ivy League professor, with his white hair, dangling mustache, wire-rimmed glasses, avuncular style, and ever-present smoking pipe.

Yet the intrigue of spying was always in his blood. As a young man traversing the globe, Dulles read *Kim*, and was swept up in Kipling's novel about the "Great Game" of espionage. "Its mystery and folk wisdom stayed with him for the rest of his life," biographer Peter Grose observed, "long after the business of spying became more threatening than an artful game."

The adventurousness of spying appealed to young Dulles, born with a clubfoot. Even as an older man, Dulles would speak patriotically, almost romantically, about the importance of espionage (and later died with a copy of Kipling's *Kim* at his bedside).

Since his appointment in 1953, Dulles had successfully contained the ominous threat of international Communism, both with traditional tools of spycraft and other methods quite unconventional. While placing agents strategically around the world, he approved provocative top-secret programs. This included mind-control interrogation using hypnosis and drugs, and the development of high-flying U-2 spy planes— some of which were shot down but eventually proved crucial in spotting hidden Soviet arms in places like Cuba.

During the Cold War, Dulles remained unapologetic about employing necessary evils to keep America safe from harm. "There are few archbishops in espionage," Dulles replied about the morality of employing a spy. "He's on our side and that's all that matters. Besides, one needn't ask him to one's club."

Historians describe Dulles as an enigma—a man of deep and often conflicting impulses, with sharp differences between his image and his true nature. "Dulles was a master of bureaucratic infighting, adept at the arts of polite exchange when murder was in his blood," concluded CIA chronicler Thomas Powers.

The paradox of Dulles could be found all around Washington. "Allen was genial in the extreme, with twinkling eyes, a belly laugh, and an almost impish deviousness," recounted Tim Weiner in his history of the CIA. "But he was also a duplicitous man, a chronic adulterer, ruthlessly ambitious. He was not above misleading Congress or his colleagues or even his commander-in-chief."

At Georgetown parties, Dulles would hobnob about international relations with senators and journalists. Afterwards he'd go home with women other than his wife Clover. ("I don't feel I deserve as good a wife as I have," he admitted to Clover in one letter, "as I am rather too fond of the company of other ladies.")

The worldly spymaster enjoyed numerous affairs with female colleagues, including upper-class spy Mary Bancroft at the end of World War II, before Dulles took over the CIA. "We can let the work cover the romance—and the romance cover the work,"

Dulles assured Bancroft, a Boston Brahmin, whom the long-suffering Clover eventually befriended.

To the public, Dulles talked endlessly about the CIA's vigilance against foreign enemies. Although his agency was sworn to secrecy—so much so that the CIA's spending and number of employees were largely unknown to Congress—Dulles enjoyed the media's limelight, appearing on the cover of *Time* magazine. (Privately, he could record every conversation with microphones hidden in his office ceiling).

By October 1957, Allen Dulles reached the zenith of his power in Washington. He'd overseen a number of successful covert operations designed to resist Communist expansion, including coups in Guatemala and Iran. Each move was like a chess piece in a grand strategem within his mind.

As a sign of his influence, Dulles convinced Congress to build a brand-new CIA headquarters across the Potomac River in then-rural Langley, Virginia. It would be a fitting tribute to his legacy, where the agency would make its home for decades to come. Nestled on a 258-acre college-like campus, the new building eventually would be dedicated with a biblical verse from the New Testament: *"And you shall know the truth, and the truth shall make you free."*

Preaching that national security should be above politics, Dulles intended to be CIA director when his beloved edifice opened in a few years, unveiled by a new president elected in 1960.

But on October 4, 1957, everything changed for Dulles.

On that day, the Soviet Union launched a tiny satellite called Sputnik I. The spheroid in the sky marked the beginning of the Space Age. This startling development in the Cold War sent shivers through the American body politic.

For years, the public had been obsessed with communism, a so-called "Red Scare" stoked by fervent anti-Communist politicians such as Senator Joseph McCarthy of Wisconsin. Sputnik appeared only two years after the Soviets had developed their own hydrogen bomb. Fears ran rampant of future Russian spy satellites overhead, of nuclear missiles raining from the sky. Politicians complained of a "bomber gap" between Soviet rocket technology and Yankee know-how that failed to stay ahead.

Around this time, Dulles lost his main political ally, his older brother, who developed cancer and died. Vice-President Richard Nixon worried Sputnik's political fallout might hurt his 1960 White House chances. Unfairly or not, it seemed the CIA had

been asleep during the Soviet Union's Sputnik invention and H-bomb development—
and Dulles was to blame.

Like a beleaguered batter up at the plate, Dulles faced more unexpected trouble
from a new Soviet *political* satelite—Cuba—only ninety miles from the Florida
coastline.

Within a matter of months, Fidel Castro's band of guerilla fighters won their revolutionary campaign against President Fulgencio Batista's corrupt government. The
fiery rebel leader railed against the CIA and American business interests which he
said undermined his country's future. By 1959, Castro grabbed control of the island
nation and vowed to never let go.

At first, Castro demurred whether he was a mere socialist or a full-fledged Communist. But Cuba soon became an ally of the Soviet Union and the closest Marxist
nation to the United States. Famously, Castro shut down the Mafia-owned casinos in
Havana, stirring the bloody anger of gangsters such as Roselli and Giancana.

Eisenhower became quite unhappy. Although the president and his advisors
couldn't decide "if Castro was a Communist or not, they nevertheless wanted to be
rid of him and the danger he presented," recalled biographer Stephen Ambrose.

Over time, this presidential demand would help transform the CIA—from its original 1947 purpose as a studious collector of foreign intelligence to the armed and
dangerous covert branch of the White House. Though the agency was relatively new,
Eisenhower recognized espionage had been always part of the Republic. At one
White House meeting, Ike recalled reading a George Washington letter to a guest
inviting him to dinner so he could give him a confidential spy mission. "The President observed that spying seems to be nothing new," recorded a memo of that
meeting.

Now in this tense showdown, with a Cuban desperado sponsored by the Russians,
America wanted a sheriff who would set things right in the Caribbean. "We believed
the world was a tough place filled with actual threats of subversion by other coun-
tries," a CIA official involved in the assassination program later explained. "The Russians had cowboys around everywhere, and that meant we had to get ourselves a lot of
cowboys if we wanted to play the game."

The CIA under Dulles faced an unprecedented challenge from the Communist world. They couldn't shoot Sputnik from the sky. But perhaps they could find
some way of eliminating Castro. The agency's charter didn't sanction political

assassination. But its director, ever a practical man, would find a solution—even if it involved drastic measures, like recruiting their own cowboys from the outside.

Aware of the rising national fears, Dulles knew that if he didn't solve this Castro problem, there would be little chance that he would last in the job he loved. Or preside over the long-awaited opening of his cherished project—the CIA's brand-new headquarters at Langley.

CHAPTER 3:

AIMING FOR FIDEL

"Condemn me. It does not matter. History will absolve me."

—FIDEL CASTRO, 1953

T he mounting pressures on Dulles and the CIA to do something—*anything*—about Castro came from numerous sources within the United States. Perhaps the greatest motivation, however, came from the actions of the Cuban dictator himself.

During two trips to America, first in April 1959 and again the following year to visit the United Nations, Castro made sure his personal charisma and revolutionary zeal were on full display. The American press ate it up, naïve and often ignorant about Castro's growing despotism.

In New York, the Cuban leader—clad in green fatigues, Army cap, and chewing a cigar—greeted a massive crowd at Central Park like a hometown hero. He fed a caged tiger at the Bronx Zoo, lunched with Wall Street bankers, and enjoyed a rousing dinner in Harlem. He lectured a convention of newspaper editors and downplayed the influence of Communism in his government. Surrounded by news photographers at his hotel, he posed with smiling schoolchildren wearing curly fake black beards just like Castro.

"The young man is larger than life," enthused the *New York Times*. Castro even traveled to nearby Princeton University—alma mater of the Dulles brothers—where he received a standing ovation.

Eisenhower refused to meet with the thirty-one-year-old Cuban leader. Instead he dispatched his vice-president, Richard Nixon, who became famous during the 1950s McCarthy era as a fervent anti-Communist. Nixon and Castro conversed for more than three hours.

"This man has spent the whole time scolding me," Castro complained. Equally unimpressed, Nixon informed the CIA he favored "goon squads" to halt Castro's advance. Dulles later sent the GOP's budding 1960 presidential candidate a seven-page report, entitled "What We Are Doing in Cuba." It included plans to embarrass Castro and adulterate his food with drugs, like LSD, to make him appear irrational.

Security was high during the Castro trips for fear of assassination. Dozens of New York City detectives and police barricades at Central Park protected Castro after a man carrying a homemade bomb was arrested. The press portrayed Castro as a brave man with a target on his back. A few months earlier, Havana authorities had halted another murder plot by a Chicago man allegedly offered $100,000 by supporters of the deposed Cuban leader Batista.

Pointing at America, Castro warned of "counter-revolutionary" forces that were determined to do him in. "We are prepared to take counter-measures," he vowed to a Havana crowd. Admirers lionized the tall dynamic revolutionary, likening him to America's George Washington. They claimed Castro "could outfight, outrun, out-swim, outride and outtalk any man in Cuba."

But the flattering news coverage surrounding Castro glossed over the escalating violence and increasing repression by his government, largely dictated by Fidel and his younger brother, Raul. Thousands of Cuban refugees—many from a once thriving middle-class—flocked to Miami and surrounding Florida to avoid persecution and possible death as political enemies of Castro's anti-democratic rule.

These exiles hated Castro and his Latin brand of Marxism for ruining their lives and beloved country. Behind Fidel's smiling socialism, they said, was a bloodthirsty tyrant who killed his way to the top.

Once in power, Castro's forces offered blindfolds and firing squads to those who opposed his Communist government, even some who had shared in his fight against the corrupt Batista. Rather than reform, Castro put into place "a highly effective machinery of repression," the Human Rights Watch later concluded in 1999, including torture of political prisoners, inhumane jails, and widespread suppression of the press and other forms of free expression. During these years, the estimated number of Castro's political opponents who were executed ranged from several hundred to more than a thousand.

Those who fled to Miami lost nearly everything. Bitterly, they promised revenge. "Castro will fall within six months," predicted Manuel Antonio de Varona, the last premier in a democratic Cuba before Batista, in 1960. He rallied exiles into a small volunteer army called *Frente Revolucionario Democrático* (FRD), based in Florida and underwritten by the CIA. "Tony Varona," as his Yankee patrons called him, vowed his organization would "destroy the Castro myth—that Premier Castro is 'a great liberator.'"

This impromptu war against Castro, however, created many unforeseen difficulties for Dulles and his spy agency. Guerilla fighting, terrorist bombs, and propaganda campaigns like Fidel's visits had changed the traditional warfare of nation-states. Gone was the old distaste for snooping and covert "black ops" actions expressed a generation earlier when Secretary of State Henry Stimson declared, "Gentlemen do not read each other's mail." Now in a world of thermonuclear bombs and hordes of refuges fleeing Castro, Dulles and his lieutenants wondered how much of their assassination "plan of action" would be legally, if not morally, permissible if the president approved it.

CIA officials, sifting though the 1947 National Security Act that created their agency, looked for legalistic ways to get around old restrictions. They found an obtuse phrase—allowing for "other functions and duties related to intelligence affecting the national security"—and suitably twisted it to their liking. Dubiously, they now interpreted that phrase as a way to shoot, poison, or bomb objectionable foreign leaders, not only in Cuba but also in places like the Congo and Dominican Republic.

But the war against Castro also extended within American borders, rather than just a faraway land. Growing into the largest CIA operation of its kind, the Cuban Project, as the overthrow of Castro's government became known, would be run largely out of southern Florida, breaking the old rules that barred domestic spying.

The practical and moral paradox of this new world was strikingly evident during Castro's second New York visit in 1960 to the United Nations. While the local police spent a king's ransom for security measures to protect Castro, the CIA was secretly trying to assassinate him.

The killing device, carefully prepared by the agency's technicians, was an exploding cigar. At the Waldorf Astoria, a luxury hotel where Castro was staying, a CIA agent asked New York City's chief inspector Michael J. Murphy to purposely place a box of cigars, including the loaded one, near the Cuban leader so he would smoke it. When lit, the cigar would blow off Fidel's head. Murphy couldn't believe his ears and refused. For the moment, the agency dropped its murderous plans.

But Dulles soon learned that the nation's top leaders were more agreeable to such a scheme than a city cop. By 1960, even liberals considered Castro too dangerous. "For the first time in our history, an enemy stands at the throat of the United States," warned Sen. John F. Kennedy, the leading Democratic candidate for president. "There is no doubt of the Communist-orientation of the Castro government. They are our enemies and will do everything in their power to bring about our downfall."

Pressed to be "more aggressive" by Eisenhower and his ambitious vice-president Nixon, Dulles considered several proposals from his staff to please the White House. Though accounts vary, Col. J. C. King of the CIA's Western Hemisphere division was apparently the first to suggest assassinating the troublesome Cuban leader. Deputy Director for Plans Richard Bissell, the agency's rising star, offered a similar killing plan. This Yale-educated former professor suggested "thorough consideration be given to the elimination of Fidel Castro," with methods, he later testified, dreamed up by his deputy, Col. Sheffield Edwards, Chief of Security.

With a wink and a nod, Eisenhower eventually gave the green light to the CIA's assassination plans at a January meeting of his "Special Group" of military and security advisors. "Castro's regime must be overthrown," the group decided. Ike, the commander of D-Day and other great battles during World War II, stressed the need for secrecy. "The great problem is leakage and breach of security," he warned. "Everyone must be prepared to swear that he had not heard of [the plan] . . . Our hand should not show in anything that is done."

Historians later had trouble deciphering Eisenhower's exact role in this CIA go-ahead because of the lack of documentation. Those involved understood the need for "plausible deniability"—a general way of "protecting" the president's reputation through denial, regardless of the truth. If a sensitive mission went awry, Dulles believed his duty was to fall on his sword and take the blame.

"I have always felt the director should naturally assume full responsibility for anything his agency has done," Dulles later explained, "and wherever he could shield or protect the president in anyway, he should do it."

But Bissell, in a private 1965 speech at CIA headquarters made public in 2014, underlined the president's deciding role in all such sensitive matters. "Throughout Eisenhower's period in office, these things always went to him," Bissell said. "They were always taken to him by Dulles" and other top CIA officials.

By mid-1960, the assassination scheme had made its way down the Washington chain of command. From Ike to Dulles, from Bissell to Edwards, and eventually to an agreeable CIA case officer named James P. O'Connell. His job, simply put, would be to help find assassins and make the plan work.

That wouldn't be easy. It was agreed among the CIA's brass that no one in the agency would directly fire a gun. Instead, these Ivy league-educated spies and West Point-trained colonels wanted Mafia figures to be recruited to kill Castro in "gangster type action"—a bloody, bullet-ridden mess that would be untraceable to the CIA and especially the White House.

Careful not to tell others, those who knew of this plot convinced themselves that the risks posed by Castro far outweighed any legal or moral niceties.

"I hoped the Mafia would achieve success," admitted Bissell, one of the CIA's top masterminds. "My philosophy during my last two or three years in the agency was very definitely that the end justified the means, and I was not going to be held back."

As O'Connell testified years later, Bissell asked Edwards "whether we had any assets" that could oversee this murder plot. Edwards replied that he had a seasoned go-between in mind—one with agency clearance, who had worked with them before and could be trusted.

When the CIA gave the sensitive task to O'Connell that summer of 1960, the instructions couldn't be clearer. "The thing was to get rid of Mr. Castro—there was no question of what the assignment was," O'Connell recalled. "Colonel Edwards doesn't mince words, he will just tell you."

The need for secrecy was stressed. Unlike most CIA ventures, O'Connell noticed this mission wouldn't have a code name or cryptonym, at least not initially.

Then Edwards mentioned the name of the outside handler—the "cut-out"—he wanted for this top-secret mission, a person familiar with organized crime types. The name was also familiar to O'Connell, a former FBI agent, who had worked before with this middleman.

"Get in touch with Bob Maheu," Edwards directed. "You know he's been out in Las Vegas quite a bit, and they have got a bunch of characters out there. I am sure that they would have somebody that might be able to handle the assignment."

And thus, like some unguided missile or a long shot bet at a Las Vegas crap table, the government-sanctioned murder plot against Fidel Castro began.

CHAPTER 4:

THE CUTOUT

"Deadly poisons are often concealed under sweet honey."

—Publius Ovidius Naso, "Ovid"

As a top-secret cutout for the Central Intelligence Agency, Robert Maheu prided himself on getting the job done, whatever its risk or complexity. This freelance spook knew when to hide in the shadows, perform a dirty trick or, if necessary, exert a little muscle.

A balding, rubbery-jowled man with an ingratiating countryclub manner, Maheu began his career after World War II in J. Edgar Hoover's FBI, where he claimed to have investigated counterintelligence cases and learned the importance of electronic listening devices. He knew the value of a good poker face in undercover work. With money he won in a friendly crap game against his fellow FBI agents, Maheu later opened his own private detective firm in Washington, DC.

For the right fee, Maheu favored clients with "special problems" that he could fix or make go away. A native New Englander, Maheu adopted the sly syrupy approach of Boston pols who advised never to write when you can speak, never speak when you can nod, and never nod when you can wink.

One of Maheu's earliest and most valued clients was the CIA. Friends such as James O'Connell put Maheu on a $500 a month retainer as a cutout. It was the agency's term for a go-between, insulating spies from one another or shielding superiors from any culpability. "Over the years, he (Maheu) has been intimately involved in providing support for some of the CIA's more sensitive operations," the agency later acknowledged.

Secret cutout matters for Maheu were usually kept on a "need to know" basis, with only a small inner circle aware of its existence. The daring expertise of Maheu's "off the books" assignments for the CIA reportedly inspired the 1960s television show "Mission Impossible." In one dispute involving Saudi Arabia, the agency hired Maheu to put a compromising wiretap inside the New York office of Greek shipping magnate Aristotle Onassis, leading to the desired result.

Another such "impossible" task, records say, called for the "procurement of feminine companionship" to please a foreign potentate during his official Washington visit. In this ruse, Maheu connived with the CIA to produce a phony "porno" film in Los Angeles to prevent Indonesian leader Achmed Sukarno from siding with the Communists. This sexual stunt—accompanied by a CIA-sponsored revolt by Indonesian rebels—would be a prelude to the violent and even more elaborate Castro drama to follow.

Maheu's Hollywood handiwork was orchestrated under the direction of O'Connell and his boss, Colonel Sheffield Edwards, head of the CIA's Office of Security. As leverage for sexual blackmail, the agency wanted to create a made-up surveillance film, simulating a real-life carnal encounter. The gritty film was constructed from an undercover photo taken inside a Kremlin bedroom with Sukarno and a blond-haired woman who happened to be a Soviet secret KGB agent.

Sex was an important weapon in the Soviet spy game. The Russians employed this alluring female "honeytrap"—the commonly-used term—as a way of compromising Sukarno into becoming an USSR ally. Such intimate blackmail was as old as time, from Samson and Delilah in the Bible to stories of German spy Mata Hari in World War I.

Tweedy CIA officials were generally hesitant to trade in sex. But the Soviet spy agency notoriously aimed its honeytraps at selected and usually unwitting targets. The Russians called it "*kompromat*," a shorthand translation for "compromising material." In this case, however, the phony CIA film was designed to keep Sukarno on the American side.

After much preparation, Maheu arranged for a late-night filming of actors portraying Sukarno and the Soviet woman inside a LA movie set, made up as a replica of the Moscow bedroom. Eventually, the CIA secretly released to the media only a few selected frames from the phony film as a way of embarrassing Sukarno and convincing him the Soviets could not be trusted.

No one was the wiser about the CIA's production, including Sukarno, eventually forced from power in 1967. "I don't think it's stretching things too much to say that, in its own way, my little film marked the beginning of his end," Maheu boasted decades later.

In 1959, Maheu repeated his matchmaker magic for the CIA by arranging for B-movie actress Susan Cabot (*Kiss of Death* and *The Wasp Woman*) to secretly rendezvous with Jordan's then twenty-three-year-old King Hussein at a Long Island beach house. "We want you to go to bed with him," government agents instructed Cabot. As they say in Hollywood, the rest was Kismet, but kept hush-hush for the next several decades, according to a secret CIA memo released in 2017.

A few months after this escapade, CIA men Edwards and O'Connell approached Maheu, their can-do intermediary, with a new assignment again involving a foreign potentate. But this time, the plan called for drastic actions that, Maheu said, gave him great pause. Instead of sex, it involved murder.

Couched in their spy terminology, Maheu's two CIA friends said the agency wanted him to serve as their cutout in arranging with the Mafia to assassinate the Cuban leader Fidel Castro. This extermination, they explained, would be part of a US strategy to weed out Communism before the infestation spread throughout Latin America. All they had to do was spray around a few bullets.

Maheu tried not to show his initial shock. "Though I'm no saint, I am a religious man, and I knew that the CIA was talking about murder," he recalled.

In the name of patriotism—and earning a few bucks—Maheu was happy to arrange a few dirty tricks or hidden surveillance for the Agency. But he'd attended enough classes as a devout young man at Holy Cross College in Massachusetts, the Jesuit answer to secular Harvard, to understand the difference between venial and mortal sins.

"In my mind, justified or not, I would still have blood on my hands," Maheu recalled. "The deal carried a pretty big price tag. I kept thinking about my family. What kind of danger would it put them in? If anything went wrong, I was the fall guy, caught between protecting the government and protecting the mob, two armed camps that could crush me like a bug."

Edwards and O'Connell listened to Maheu's concerns. Both CIA officials admitted to sharing at first the same moral reservations. They argued killing Castro would be part of a "just war"—though undeclared—signed off by the highest level of government.

"They said it was necessary to protect the country," Maheu recalled. "They used the analogy of World War II: if we had known the exact bunker that Hitler was in during the war, we wouldn't have hesitated to kill the bastard. The CIA felt exactly the same way about Castro."

Maheu, the usually gung-go undercover spy, remained uncertain. "I have to think about it, think very deeply," he told his CIA handlers. "I'll give you my answer tomorrow."

That night inside his suburban Virginia home, where he lived with his wife and children, Maheu didn't go to bed at the usual time. Instead, he stayed up all night in his downstairs recreation room, wrestling with his conscience. "I considered myself a reasonably good Catholic," he recalled, "and I did not like the idea of getting involved with murdering anybody."

To soothe his frayed nerves, he listened to string orchestra music. But mostly, Maheu wondered if he was willing to become an assassin.

CHAPTER 5:

SPRUCE GOOSE AND BROWN DERBY

"There are moral as well as physical assassinations."

—VOLTAIRE

Robert Maheu and his CIA handlers didn't disclose very much to each other, not at this early stage of their assassination game plan. Spying—like the sleight of hand among high-stakes poker players—demanded discretion, if not outright deception. No one showed all their cards.

For his part, Maheu had no idea how his efforts figured into the larger US strategy to overthrow Fidel Castro's regime. Lowly cutouts weren't privy to the high-level discussions of superiors like CIA director Allen Dulles and those insulated figures around him.

Nor did the CIA know fully the considerations crossing Maheu's mind. Along with his eternal soul and how assassination might be judged someday at the pearly gates, Maheu suffered a more earthly concern:

He worried what Howard Hughes might think.

As one of the world's wealthiest men, Hughes was Maheu's prized client. The private investigator feared losing his hefty compensation from Hughes, a notoriously secretive man, if he got caught up in the Castro controversy, already igniting headlines around the world.

Maheu's strange arrangement with Hughes seemed like its own form of corporate espionage. In the mid-1950s, the multi-millionaire hired Maheu to be "his eyes, his ears, and his mouthpiece," though the two never met in person. Instead, they communicated by telephone or through other go-betweens.

Hughes was a true enigma, a real-life Gatsby figure. Once handsome and vibrant, Hughes gained fame as a self-made aviator turned Hollywood producer in the years before World War II. He was known for his flying "Spruce Goose"—then the largest plane ever built—and for dating beautiful actresses such as Jane Russell, Jean Harlow, and Ava Gardner. With his aeronautical eye for detail, he even designed a special bra for the well-endowed Russell to wear in one of his films.

With age, however, Hughes turned increasingly from an eccentric genius into a paranoid recluse. Rather than deal with the outside world himself, Hughes paid Maheu to be his fixer.

The former FBI agent kept embarrassments out of the press—like the blackmail attempt by a greedy minister who claimed his female parishioner had a sinful affair with Hughes. Maheu also maintained a watchful eye on actress Jean Peters, a long-time Hughes paramour who eventually became his wife. Despite his own wanderings, Hughes was a jealous and possessive sort, demanding to know about any man who might approach his beautiful actress-wife when he wasn't looking.

Maheu's employment with the multi-millionaire began with a blind phone call from a lawyer who turned out to be working for Hughes. The lawyer asked Maheu to check out rumors that Jean Peters's first husband, Texas oilman Stuart Cramer, was a CIA operative. Maheu made a call to his CIA contact, "Big Jim" O'Connell, who checked it out and confirmed Cramer's agency connections.

"The whole thing probably took me an afternoon, most of which was spent waiting for Jim to call me back," recalled Maheu, picking up an easy fee. Hughes also paid Maheu for keeping tabs on actress Ava Gardner—another Hughes obsession—while she stayed at the Cal-Neva Lodge in Nevada during her divorce from entertainer Frank Sinatra.

As a fixer, Maheu was part of a rare clandestine breed. In postwar America, grey-flanneled corporate executives retained men like Maheu—private investigators, lobbyists, PR specialists, and lawyers with revolving door ties to the government— to make problems go away or gain a "hidden hand" advantage over competitors. Probably more than most, Hughes placed a premium on secrecy. In hiring Maheu, Hughes was impressed with his sleuthing for shadowy business clients, such as Greek shipping tycoon Stavros Niarchos, as well as his connections to "the intelligence community"—a euphemism for the CIA.

Eventually, Hughes provided a huge retainer for Maheu to move his Washington-based firm out to the West Coast. It was enough money to buy a beautiful new home and two Cadillacs. The exclusive deal required Maheu to give up most of his other clients.

By enlisting in the CIA plan against Castro, Maheu worried about endangering his sizeable private fees as much as his moral or patriotic concerns. As FBI records noted, Maheu was "reluctant to become involved in the operation since he thought it might interfere with his relationship with his new client, Howard Hughes."

Yet to Maheu's surprise, when he fleetingly mentioned the CIA's Cuba invitation, Hughes gave his blessing. After all, the industrialist was already allied with the spy agency. During the 1960s, Hughes would help several CIA fronts and covert operations, including an $800-million attempt to recover a sunken Soviet submarine in the Pacific with one of Hughes' underwater devices.

Perhaps Hughes didn't understand the lethal intent of Maheu's mission. There was no mention of Castro's name, nor poisons or possible gunfire either. Maheu kept things strictly on a need-to-know basis.

Hughes knew only one thing for sure—having the government secretly in your corner was always good for business.

Like Maheu, the CIA had its own unspoken agenda. Though agency higher-ups spoke vaguely about "gangster" involvement, O'Connell and Shef Edwards specified that the CIA wanted Maheu to recruit his friend, Johnny Roselli, for their assassination plan. They felt Roselli was the kind of man who could be trusted with such a risky assignment.

Maheu first met Johnny a few years earlier when a mutual friend, Washington powerhouse lawyer Edward Bennett Williams, suggested he ask for Roselli's help in getting a room in an overbooked Las Vegas hotel. Magically, the closed doors opened up. Everyone in Vegas seemed to know Johnny.

"He was able to accomplish things in Las Vegas," Maheu recalled, "and nobody else seemed to get the same kind of attention."

Roselli and Maheu became fast friends, the kind of strange but comfortable alliance between a gangster and a detective who frequently straddled both sides of the law. They shared many lunches in Vegas, and Los Angeles, and even spent one Thanksgiving at Maheu's home in Virginia. "We built a solid friendship over the years—so solid, in fact, that my children took to calling him 'Uncle Johnny,'" recalled Maheu.

Roselli was very different from Maheu, the avuncular family man. With his sensuous eyes and gleaming smile, Roselli appeared like an aging movie star, like those matinee idols he'd known in Hollywood. Johnny moved confidently and spoke with a deep-toned voice, full of authority. Though middle-aged, he appeared slim and fit, like a fighter with a bantamweight physique. His full head of dark hair then featured only a glimmer of silver.

Johnny always showed up meticulously dressed, usually from the finest clothiers in Beverly Hills. The ladies particularly appreciated his manly style and charm. "But it was his eyes that people remembered best, cool and blue-gray, 'dancing and delightful,' as one friend recalled, or flashing and steely in anger," his biographers described. "His confidence and presumption of power proved irresistible to many women."

Before moving out to the West Coast, Maheu hosted a Maine-style clambake in his Virginia backyard—filled with lobsters, steamers, and booze—for an old FBI buddy whom the Eisenhower administration was sending to Ireland as ambassador. Social occasions were important for Maheu's consulting firm. They allowed government officials such as Senator Styles Bridges, an influential Republican, to mingle with Maheu's friends and business acquaintances. Maheu invited his two CIA handlers, Shef Edwards and Jim O'Connell, whom he now considered pals. At the last minute, when Roselli called to say he was staying in town, he also received an invite to this 1959 clambake.

In Maheu's backyard, Shef Edwards cornered Roselli. They talked for a while, though the plans against Castro weren't discussed. Instead, Edwards tried to take his own measure of whether Roselli could be recruited as an asset. While Maheu often bloviated as a natural con man, this understated mobster seemed almost humble, with no urgent need to impress.

Over the next several days, Edwards and the CIA checked out Roselli's background further. "They independently learned that Johnny had access to the highest levels of the Mafia," Maheu recalled. "And that's when the Company came to me, to see if I could get Johnny interested in the Cuban situation."

The two CIA handlers, O'Connell and Edwards, overcame Maheu's reluctance about the assassination plot by appealing to his friendship as well as his sense of patriotism. "Bob was a pretty sharp guy, and he just didn't want to get involved in a thing like that," recalled O'Connell. "But he took it on merely because he felt he owed us a commitment."

Setting aside his qualms, Maheu agreed to become the cutout in the government's murder plan. Like some modern-day Paul Revere, he felt an urgency to protect his fellow countrymen from the looming threat of Castro in nearby Cuba.

"If it saved even one American life," Maheu explained later, "I decided, it was worthwhile."

Around Labor Day 1960, Johnny Roselli met with Maheu for lunch at the Brown Derby in Hollywood.

The celebrated eatery, literally topped with a huge derby-like roof, was a place where Roselli conversed for years with entertainers, businessmen, and underworld figures. Its cushioned booth seats were made of red leather, with framed caricatures of movie stars hanging from the walls. On Oscar night, the Brown Derby served as a prized location for parties after the awards were handed out.

As always, Johnny strode in like he owned the joint. He presented himself splendidly, enough so the spit shine on his shoes reflected the lights above.

Beforehand on the telephone, Maheu said he wanted to get together to discuss a business proposition. At the restaurant, however, Maheu was full of small talk and didn't get around to the main topic until coffee was served.

Typically, Maheu began with a lie—a cover story suggested by his CIA handlers, O'Connell and Edwards. Maheu told Johnny that he represented a group of international businessmen, thrown out of Cuba by the communist takeover. They wanted Castro dead. "This was a story that Shef and I conjured up," O'Connell later testified. "We had to have some story."

The CIA knew Maheu had other real-life "clients of an international nature," and figured their phony cover story would sound plausible to Roselli. According to this ploy, O'Connell recalled, "the international investors were quite unhappy about their money going down the drain as a result of Castro taking over, and they had put together an amount of $150,000 which would be made available to carry out the ultimate mission."

Their cover story didn't fly with Roselli. From the clambake and their previous conversation, Johnny knew Maheu's firm worked for the CIA. Almost immediately, he suspected this plan derived from the government.

"I am not kidding—I know who you work for," Roselli insisted.

Between friends, Maheu quickly gave up the ruse. There was no sense in trying to fool Johnny, not if he was asking for his help. For all of Maheu's gifts at bluster and high-minded earnestness, Roselli saw right through his deception. With an acute sense for smelling a rat, Johnny had detected plenty of schemes in the past far less obvious. It was an essential tool for survival in the Mafia.

Changing tack, Maheu acknowledged the private investors angle was a phony but stressed the CIA's plan to kill Castro was genuine. As Maheu explained, the assassination attempt would be a cutout operation financed by the CIA with the $150,000 bounty. "When I presented Roselli with the proposition, I made it clear that anything we talked about was strictly confidential," Maheu recalled.

Under the CIA's original murder-for-hire scheme, Roselli and his mob associates would eliminate Castro with gunfire—gangster-style, just like the St. Valentine's Day massacre during the Al Capone days in Chicago. They'd rely on their old gambling contacts in Havana to set up the unsuspecting Communist dictator. All the while, Maheu would serve as the happy intermediary between the CIA and Johnny's bloodthirsty crew.

The whole game plan must remain top-secret, Maheu insisted, made to look like a private hit job with "total deniability" for the government.

Roselli's smile grew as he listened to this fantasy. Finally, he burst out laughing. "Me? You want *me* to get involved with Uncle Sam?" Roselli chortled. "The feds are tailing me wherever I go. They go to my shirt maker to see if I'm buying things with cash. . . . They're always trying to get something on me. Bob, are you sure you're talking to the right guy?"

The US government indeed wanted him, Maheu assured. The agency had carefully checked him out. They wanted to enlist Roselli as a crucial mercenary in their assassination squad. The CIA would give Johnny free reign to eliminate Castro, the man who'd cost the Mafia millions when he shuttered their Havana casinos and other gambling joints.

"It's up to you to pick whom you want, but it's got to be set up so that Uncle Sam isn't involved—ever," Maheu said. "If anyone connects you with the US government, I will deny it."

Inside their Brown Derby booth, Johnny remained hesitant. Could this all be a strange set-up, designed to catch him accepting a hit job? As tourists and Hollywood players passed by, Roselli tapped his fingers nervously on the table while Maheu outlined the stunningly brazen plan, underlining the seriousness of the agency's commitment.

Putting together a team of assassins would require Roselli to consult with his Mafia bosses, gain their approval, and take on tremendous risks. Even if the CIA approved of their actions, there was no guarantee the FBI or some other law-enforcement agency wouldn't come cracking down on their heads.

Though he couldn't make any guarantees for the government, Maheu personally assured Johnny that he'd look the other way if Roselli relied on other Mafioso or other illegal methods to attack Castro. He wanted to make Johnny as comfortable as possible, to gain his trust as a friend who would keep his secrets.

"I won't ever reveal the content of any private conversations," Maheu vowed. "It's none of my business."

Roselli stared at Maheu, contemplating the offer. There was interest in his eyes.

"I would have to be satisfied that this is a government project," Johnny finally replied.

Despite the initial phony cover story, Maheu certified the CIA's commitment. "It comes from high level sources," he replied. To further verify, he'd even be willing for Johnny to meet his immediate CIA handler.

Though he didn't know for sure, Maheu surmised aloud that killing Castro was undoubtedly part of a bigger US plan for regime change in Cuba, ridding the island of its Communist curse. And to seal the deal like a good negotiator, Maheu emphasized the huge reward—roughly $1.1 million in today's dollars—which the CIA would gladly pay.

Johnny brushed aside the offer. Money wasn't necessary, he said, not if it was a matter of national security. He spoke about his loyalty to America, how much the country meant to him.

Maheu was surprised by the refusal but eventually came to understand Roselli's motivations.

"Many people have speculated that Johnny was looking for an eventual deal with the government, or some sort of big payoff," Maheu recalled. "The truth, as corny as it may sound, is that down deep he thought it was his "patriotic' duty."

While that may be so, Maheu also realized Roselli faced more pragmatic concerns as well.

For the past several years, Johnny had enjoyed the confidence of several Mafia powers in Los Angeles, Havana, Miami, and Las Vegas. The Mafia in America was at its height in 1960 and individual territories and fiefdoms were carefully guarded and protected. A national commission ensured that disputes between various ruling dons did not get out of hand and ruin La Cosa Nostra's enormous sources of revenue.

Under its unforgiving rules, the national commission needed to be informed of this secret CIA killing plan that, in effect, would restore the Mafia profitable franchises in Cuba and regain millions in lost gambling revenue. If he pulled off this remarkable caper, Roselli knew he'd be hailed as a hero within the mob. He wouldn't have to worry about money again.

But first, Roselli had to answer to his main boss—Sam Giancana, the head of Chicago's sprawling organized crime empire. The Chicago Outfit arguably had the most clout in Las Vegas, and Roselli reported to Sam directly.

These two gangsters had worked together for years and shared many friends and good times. A sense of loyalty existed between them, a rare commodity in Mafia circles where trust could lead to tragedy. They also held the same ambitious view for the future, expanding organized crime internationally and multiplying the take from a cornucopia of businesses—some criminal, others legal.

Most times, Giancana listened to Roselli's ideas and adopted them. But Sam was mercurial and aggressive. He didn't always agree. A plan like this one might strike Giancana as foolish or not worth the risk. His endorsement was another wild card in this top-secret CIA assassination plan.

At the Brown Derby luncheon, Roselli didn't explain to Maheu the full complexity of his world in the mob, just as Maheu didn't explain his shadowy relationship to the CIA's hierarchy. Maheu apparently assumed Roselli could launch a deadly assault on a foreign leader all on his own, without getting permission.

Roselli sipped his coffee and agreed to cooperate. But he left the restaurant that day without mentioning one essential fact: Without Giancana's approval, Johnny couldn't go forward.

CHAPTER 6:

MOONEY

"The Outfit, as you should know if you had a proper education, is how Chicagoans refer to the crime syndicate. Or the Cosa Nostra, or the Mafia, or whatever they call it in New York and the movies."

—MIKE ROYKO

Sam Giancana's crime empire was big enough to rival General Motors, U.S. Steel, or any other conglomerate in mid-twentieth century America. Experts estimated more than a billion dollars, virtually all untaxed and collected secretly, emerged each year from its far-flung illicit enterprises.

Giancana presided over a smorgasbord of rackets and mayhem. Its breathtaking scope ranged from Chicago's bookies and one-armed bandits in Las Vegas casinos, to a host of other suspect ventures in Florida, California, the Midwest, Mexico, and elsewhere in Latin America.

More than a thousand henchmen associated with Giancana's organization greased, bribed, threatened, or killed for small fortunes. Though generally homicidal by nature, they offered a full plate of criminal specialties including loan-sharking, robbery, extortion, narcotics, prostitution, union embezzlement, corrupt cops, and judges on the take.

Sam took a piece of everything, pocketing an estimated $40 million annually himself in 1960s dollars. Because of its unified control, the Outfit, as Chicago's Mafia was known, possessed more clout than any of New York's five crime families.

"Sam Giancana is the chief executive, the boss of all bosses, the man responsible for the day-to-day success of the operation," observed writer Ovid Demaris in the 1960s. "In terms of leadership, this makes Giancana the most powerful arch criminal in the world."

Mike Royko, the Bard of Chicago's newspapers, recognized this pervasive grip on the city's life. "For years, the Mafia has thrived in Chicago," wrote the streetwise newspaper columnist. "It has done so well that it has placed its own people in the judiciary, the police department, the state legislature, the Congress of the United States and even in the Chicago City Council."

Giancana, like his contemporary Johnny Roselli, came of age as a young gangster in the 1930s Mafia world shaped by Chicago's Al Capone (America's most famous gangster nicknamed "Scarface").

"Shit, I knew Sam (Giancana) when he was driving for Jack McGurn," Roselli recalled, referring to "Machine Gun Jack" McGurn, Capone's associate and "public enemy" linked to the St. Valentine's Day Massacre. In that notorious incident, seven rival gang members were lined up against a wall and shot by Capone's Outfit.

Both Sam and Johnny were then young tigers in "the Outfit," an organization guided by what ethologists and other animal experts call "territoriality," with its violence triggered by aggressive turf-guarding at the scent of oncoming enemies. In a perverse way, their association with other well-known criminals and atrocities like the St. Valentine's Day shootings brought instant credibility and fearful respect among their peers.

Over the next decade, Roselli served the Outfit's interests in Hollywood, as Giancana worked his way up as a hoodlum in the city's Italian-American ghetto known as The Patch. By inclination, Johnny liked to work alone. But Sam showed his organizational skill and money-making ability by becoming a captain in the mob, leading a tough assemblage of fellow killers and enforcers. "It gives him a little more leverage, if anybody gets out of line," Roselli explained about Sam's dominating urge to be boss. "I never wanted to be a *capo* [head of a gang]. You've got too many mouths to feed."

A tautly built man with a hair-trigger temper, Giancana slugged, shot, and butchered his way to the top. Violence came naturally to him, a child of the streets with a sixth-grade education. From the tragedies of life, he developed a hard shell. Shortly after his Sicilian parents immigrated, his mother Antonia died from an infection, leaving his laborer father distraught. Sam was only two, but family members said the little boy turned sullen with her death.

Eventually Sam grew up with a stepmother who was later killed on a roadway, trying to shield his younger brother from an oncoming motorist. The driver sped away. Perhaps to hide his pain years afterward, Sam fabricated a different account. He claimed to his children that it had been his natural mother Antonia who'd been run over by a car trying to protect him. Somehow in Sam's mind, this lost maternal figure, idolized from youth, had sacrificed her life to save his own.

Full of anger, young Giancana turned from a street urchin into a gangland thug. He became deeply cynical about the easy money and threatening power derived from a life in organized crime. When many men volunteered to serve in World War II, Army doctors rejected Sam from the draft as a "constitutional psychopath" with anti-social tendencies. Years later, Giancana admitted he faked it. "Who wouldn't pretend he was nuts to stay out of the army?" he explained.

While money was important in the Outfit, Giancana realized violence was the true coin of the realm, the most effective method of enforcing one's domain. His gang's instruments of terror included machine guns, hidden bombs, baseball bats, ice picks, power tools, and metal vises to squeeze or break victims—the more violent, the better.

At his most vicious, Giancana's eyes glazed over in such a killer's stare that he was called "Mooney"—meaning "crazy"—a moniker that Sam grew to like for the fear it engendered. His death toll, by some estimates, would reach more than a hundred victims. Though he went to jail for lesser offenses, including bootlegging, he would be accused of murder three times but never convicted.

Initially, Giancana began as a "wheelman"—the driver of getaway cars—nimbly weaving through streets and alleyways as police chased from behind. He eventually became the driver for Paul Ricca, the Outfit's boss after the notorious Capone was sent to prison for tax evasion. Both Ricca (nicknamed "The Waiter" by the press) and his successor Anthony ("Big Tuna") Accardo experienced similar tax headaches with the law. By 1956, Tony Accardo was kicked upstairs in the Outfit's hierarchy, as a retired *consigliere* along with Ricca, and Giancana assumed his place as top day-to-day boss.

Within the Outfit, Giancana's reputation stemmed largely from the violent way he took over the "policy wheel" rackets in Chicago's predominantly black South Side. Sam impressed Accardo by being the first in the Outfit to recognize the huge cash flow potential from this street lottery. (Policy "wheels" were circular devices from which winning numbers were drawn.)

Giancana scared away several "Negro" policy racketeers with threats of murder, including one who fled to Mexico. His gang eventually attempted to kidnap Ted Roe, the ruling South Side policy king, by pushing his moving car to the curb. A gun battle erupted, with a spray of bullets killing "Fat Lenny" Caifano—the brother of one of Sam's top mob lieutenants, Marshall Caifano. Police charged Roe with murder, but Roe successfully pled self-defense.

Back on the streets, Roe hired a policeman as an unofficial bodyguard and carried a pistol. The millionaire African-American policy king proudly flashed his wealth by driving a Cadillac, living an expensive lifestyle, and, most memorably, giving out money "Robin Hood" style to the poor. But Roe remained wary of Giancana's gang.

"I know they're going to kill me, but I would like to take one of them with me when they do," Roe told associates. "I never have and never will hide from the hoods."

Meanwhile, Giancana vowed revenge for Fat Lenny's death. It arrived a year later on a warm summer's night in August 1952.

"Roe!" a voice called out, as he unlocked his car, parked near his apartment. When Roe turned, assassins hiding in the shadows killed him with twelve-gauge shotgun blasts. The sheer force ripped Roe's face and slammed his body into a tree.

Police questioned Marshall Caifano, a former boxer with a cauliflower ear, about the murder. "He denied knowing Roe, and also denied knowing Sam Giancana, another hoodlum suspected of having a part in the abortive kidnap plot," reported the *Chicago Tribune*, in one of Sam's first mentions in the press. No one was ever charged with Roe's death, which cemented Giancana's hold on the policy rackets for the Outfit.

At age forty-eight, Sam took on the top job in Chicago's mob. By stepping aside into self-imposed retirement, Accardo assumed Giancana's wild tendencies would simmer as the new manager of their ever-widening criminal empire.

Accardo, a former Capone gunman, had proven to be a corporate chieftain at heart. He resided in a palatial twenty-two-room mansion in suburban River Forest, living off his ill-gotten gains the way CEOs do with stock options and dividend checks. Accardo carefully built the financial foundation for Chicago's mob without a lot of bloodshed—at least compared to his predecessors. Throughout his tenure, Accardo avoided the flaunting, flashy style of Capone and the national notoriety of a St. Valentine's Day Massacre. He learned inviting scrutiny from federal prosecutors led to eventual ruin.

"Keep your head down," Accardo advised Sam, his most prescient message in passing the mantle.

Accardo had reason to believe Giancana might follow his advice. Although a gang leader by day, Sam had kept up appearances for many years as a family man, going home most nights to his beloved wife Angeline and three daughters in suburban Oak Park. He cut his own lawn in summer and shoveled snow in winter.

Sam adored Angeline, a devout Roman Catholic, and treated her like a madonna, though he often had a girlfriend on the side. Matrimony was a sacrament to him, just as the church taught, despite his many transgressions.

"A man's got to marry a virgin, not a slut," Sam admonished his younger brother Chuck.

Because Angeline's middle-class family had warned her about marrying Giancana, a convicted felon, he always viewed her as a much-desired prize, another affirmation of his ambitions. He attended mass with Angeline, and even helped her run a big charity fundraiser called "Night of the Stars" at Chicago Stadium. It featured several entertainers including Frank Sinatra, who counted Giancana among his Mafioso friends.

Although Sam had been hardly an ideal husband, he never stopped idolizing Angeline. At home, his wife dealt primarily with their three daughters, including the oldest, Antoinette, whose wayward behavior reminded Sam of himself. But Giancana's family life was soon shattered by tragedy. During a 1954 Florida trip, Angeline died suddenly of a cerebral embolism following an argument with Antoinette. Sam was crushed and blamed his daughter.

Virtually everyone at her funeral would "say with all sincerity that Mooney had treasured Ange more than any other woman," his brother Chuck recalled. Antoinette noticed her father's stark reaction. "Sam was morose, disconsolate, no longer interested in what happened around him," Antoinette remembered. "Mother was gone and there was no one left for him to please."

As the Outfit's new boss, Giancana looked to places other than hometown Chicago for answers. Rather than play it safe, as Accardo advised, tending to ten-cent policy games and other local rackets, Giancana aggressively expanded the Outfit's distant businesses in Las Vegas, Hollywood, and Cuba. These new projects held out the promise of fantastic financial returns, much more than cautious men like Accardo might envision.

Giancana's travels introduced him to a more complex world of people, including beautiful women he hoped might fill the hole in his heart left by Angeline's death. And in this new phase of middle-aged life outside of Chicago, there was no one Sam depended upon more than his longtime friend, Johnny Roselli.

CHAPTER 7:

THE VEGAS STRIP

Las Vegas, with its millions in free-flowing cash, beckoned to Sam Giancana like a siren's song. Old-time crooks in Chicago seemed blind to this lucrative gem in the desert. But Giancana's "policy wheel" bonanzas at home impressed the Outfit's elders enough to become out-of-town investors in this boulevard of casinos known as "the Strip."

Giancana's interest dated back to at least 1953 when he flew to Los Angeles with boss Tony Accardo to see another booster of this venture, Johnny Roselli. Gambling was already a big moneymaker for the Outfit in Cuba, but Sam and Johnny wanted to make sure they had their piece of the future in Las Vegas.

As the Outfit's man in Hollywood, Roselli planned to drive his two visitors out to Vegas, where they intended to extend their influence.

"Sam asked me to concentrate on Vegas," Johnny recalled. "They had plenty of cash to invest and they wanted to get into some of these gambling joints."

Roselli had been friendly with Bugsy Siegel, the New York mob's driving visionary force behind the development of Las Vegas, until Siegel was fatally shot inside the Beverly Hills home of his girlfriend Virginia Hill.

With Bugsy's untimely demise, Roselli recognized a newfound opportunity—both in Vegas and, for a time, in dating Virginia Hill. However, the initial inspection tour, meant to impress Chicago boss Tony Accardo, didn't fare so well.

Once they landed in Los Angeles, Sam and Tony jumped into a car driven by Johnny, but undercover detectives followed them. The cops finally approached them at Perino's Restaurant, a fancy French-Italian eatery in Beverly Hills. It was one of Johnny's favorite hangouts, featuring starry customers such as Cary Grant and Bette Davis. Inside, tables and booths were covered in pink with a single rose.

Before they could eat, the cops frisked Giancana and Accardo, discovering $12,000 in their pockets. The two Chicago hoodlums were ordered to return home.

Two years later, however, Roselli placed the perfect bet in Las Vegas when Tony Cornero, owner of the half-built Stardust Hotel, mysteriously dropped dead.

Roselli quickly alerted Giancana and Murray Humphreys, the Outfit's longtime fixer and moneyman, who recognized the opportunity and sprung into action. When finished, the Stardust promised to be the largest gambling resort in Vegas for "low rollers"—with the most guest rooms, the biggest lobby, the most massive swimming pool, and a crowd-pleasing drive-in movie theater in the back.

The Stardust fell into trouble when Cornero—a man of vision called "Mr. Lucky"—ran out of good fortune. He'd previously built a floating casino called the "SS Rex" off the coast of Los Angeles until local authorities stopped him. Cornero later survived an assassination attempt by gunmen at his home when he tried to invest in Mexico.

On the day he keeled over from a heart attack—reportedly provoked by a Mickey Finn in his glass while playing craps—Cornero was deep in debt. He wanted a loan from Moe Dalitz, the mob's frontman at the upscale Desert Inn, and his partner, Meyer Lansky, the Miami-based crime boss.

Humphreys and Roselli, the Outfit's smoothest negotiators, brokered an investment deal in which it shared the Stardust with other Mafia brethren. Thanks to a huge influx of cash from Chicago, the Stardust soon opened its doors with Dalitz at the helm. Giancana's men, especially Roselli, made sure to get their share of the "skim"—the part of the casino profits stolen by the mob and never reported to tax authorities.

"I'm now *the man* in Vegas," declared Roselli, usually not one to boast. "I got the Stardust for Chicago . . . [At the Stardust] I'm pulling fifteen, twenty grand under the table every month. They're skimming the shit out of that joint. You have no idea how much cash goes through that counting room every day. You, your family, your uncles and cousins, all your relatives could live the rest of their lives in luxury with just the pull out of there in a month."

———

Until the Stardust purchase, Roselli had spent most of his life in Hollywood. With both shrewdness and force, he pushed the Chicago mob's interests in movies, nightclubs, and labor unions. His biggest pal in the Outfit, Giancana, marveled at how Johnny fit in with the showbiz crowd "quicker than you could hum a few bars of 'Anything Goes.'"

In this land of make-believe, no one had more to hide than Roselli, a man of many secrets and identities.

He was born Filippo Sacco in Esperia, Italy on July 4, 1905. With his mother Maria, he came to America six years later—his entry apparently illegal, so that he worried all his life about being deported. They joined his father Vincenzo already working as a shoemaker in Boston's North End, with its many Italian immigrants. Young Johnny strove to be accepted as an American. "I stopped talking Italian because of the beatings I received in school," he remembered.

A life of crime seemed the fastest method of becoming rich in a country that venerated millionaires. "When Christ died on the cross, the closest man to him was a thief, and that's good enough for me," he proclaimed. During Prohibition, Roselli relied on bootlegging to raise himself above a grifter. "I was a young fellow with very little education," he later testified. "Just buying and selling a little liquor here and there, trying to do anything I possibly can to make a living."

Violence became part of this mix. FBI records indicate Roselli, under the name Philip Sacco, was charged with larceny and selling heroin. He reportedly killed the informant who implicated him before fleeing Boston. Sacco landed in Chicago, taking on a new name and identity. His new last name was inspired from a book mentioning Cosimo Rosselli, a fifteenth century Italian painter, who helped decorate the Vatican's Sistine Chapel. Johnny's choice of pseudonym begged a question: What form of devotion or delusion motivates a gangster to adopt the surname of an artist known for painting scenes of the Nativity and The Last Supper? Or did Roselli simply recast himself the way Hollywood picked out stage names like John Wayne, Marilyn Monroe, or Cary Grant?

Whatever personal insights this identity change might suggest, Roselli took care to hide his origins. No questions about his past were tolerated. He forged birth records to make it appear he'd been born in the Windy City. Over time, he'd use other aliases, including spelling variations of Roselli with a double "s," to cover his tracks.

Yet no matter how carefully Roselli masked himself in stylish clothes and ill-gotten wealth, scrubbed away any hint of an accent in his voice, the fear of being found out—exposed as an illegal immigrant without proper papers—never left him.

In Depression-era Chicago, Roselli became a soldier in the Capone gang and quickly a driver for the boss himself. After a bout of tuberculosis, Johnny was sent to the warmer climate of Los Angeles, as the Chicago gang's shakedown artist in the burgeoning movie industry. Roselli reported to local Mafia boss Jack Dragna, but he never lost touch with his original sponsors, who got a piece of all his deals.

In Hollywood, Johnny proved a natural. He dealt with producers and film executives, accustomed to fakery and assumed names, who knew that behind his slick ingratiating demeanor was a well-dressed killer.

"You either click with people or you don't," Roselli explained. "The secret is not to look in their eyes. You pick a spot on their forehead and zero in. That way you don't blink, you don't move. It intimidates the hell out of them."

On any given day, Johnny could be found at the Santa Anita racetrack, the Bel-Air Country Club, and his favorite nightclubs and eateries like Ciro's and the Brown Derby. He dated Hollywood celebrities such as Lana Turner, Donna Reed, Betty Hutton, and many other women. Actress Ann Corcoran once kept Johnny's clothes and some money in a trunk so police wouldn't find them while he was on the lam.

Beautiful women came and went from Johnny's West Hollywood apartment and his place at the Garden of Allah complex on Sunset Boulevard, where so many Hollywood entertainers resided in Spanish-style villas. The Garden of Allah—with its palm trees, huge swimming pool, and Bohemian air—suited Roselli's tastes. It offered a world far different from his earlier hardscrabble existence.

In 1940, Roselli eloped with June Lang, a blue-eyed, strawberry blonde-haired actress and dancer. A justice of the peace married them in Yuma, Arizona. Her given name was Winifred June Vlasek from Minneapolis, Minnesota. In Hollywood, June performed as a wholesome leading lady in such films as *Bonnie Scotland* with Laurel & Hardy and *Wee Willie Winkie,* a Shirley Temple adventure film directed by John Ford. Through the magic of studio hair and make-up, she could appear platinum blonde or sultry dark. Three decades later, a Hollywood fan magazine still raved, "To this very day, she [Lang] remains one of the truly great beauties Hollywood ever produced."

For women like Lang, there seemed an exciting "bad boy" appeal to Johnny, whose suave sophistication complemented his tough masculinity. Roselli wasn't like the self-absorbed pretty boy actors she dated, or the movie biz execs, including Howard Hughes, who wanted to procure rather than seduce. Headstrong, June pursued her relationship with Johnny in the troublesome way women sometimes ignore obvious warning signals about men and their longterm prospects.

When Johnny entered her life, Lang had been in a smorgasbord of forgettable films, with names like *Stage Door Canteen* and *Footlight Serenade,* looking for her big break as a headlining star. Perhaps she believed Johnny, with his various Hollywood contacts, could help her. Certainly, he'd been generous with other women he met in nightclubs and studio lots. But in his uncomfortable role as a husband, Roselli possessed different ideas about marriage. Wanting June to concentrate solely on his needs, he shut down her acting career.

"It was Johnny who made June quit the movies; possibly with some sense of social superiority, he made her break connections with cinema folks," a Chicago newspaper later reported. Imagine June's surprise when she realized her new husband wanted her in the kitchen baking lasagna just like any other Mafioso wife, an obedient matronly presence such as Angeline Giancana. As a man about town, Johnny may have acted courtly and quite solicitous to the starlets he dated, but it was quite another matter at home.

Their marriage soon began to fall apart. Friends in Hollywood were aghast that June had wed a Mafioso, albeit one as seemingly charming as Roselli. Even if love was blind, it seemed hard to believe June didn't know her bethrothed was a gangster. A newspaper story about their wedding made no mention of Johnny's occupation, except to describe him as a former "bodyguard for Harry Cohn, head of Columbia Pictures."

The relationship between the Hollywood mogul and his mobster buddy was a great deal more than that. Cohn later described Roselli as his "good friend," often playing tennis at the apartment complex where they lived and socialized together. The gruff Columbia studio chief wore a ruby ring given to him by Roselli, as "blood brothers" and committed pals.

Johnny appreciated Cohn's acerbic self-made reputation. As a Hollywood powerhouse, Harry relied on street instincts rather than formal education in appealing to the public. "I have a foolproof device for judging a picture," he determined. "If my ass squirms, it's bad; if my ass doesn't squirm, it's good."

Their circle of friends included Jonie Taps, another Columbia producer, who enjoyed stories of Cohn's malaprops, like the time he criticized the script for a swashbuckling film about British royalty. Cohn wondered why it would use such hackneyed phrases as "Yesiree" and "Nosiree," sounding like the Bowery Boys from New York's Lower East Side. Looking at the offending dialogue, the movie's producer shook his head at Cohn. "Harry," he said, recognizing the phrase meant for kings, "that's 'No *sire*' and 'Yes *sire*.'"

Around the studio, Roselli's ominous presence was a reminder that Columbia's top boss enjoyed pushing people around like a despot. Cohn insisted on a casting couch, demanding sex from starlets and others he could bully. Mess with Cohn and Johnny might make you regret it. When Cohn died of a heart attack in 1958, comedian Red Skelton quipped about the well-attended funeral, "It only proves what they always say—give the people what they want to see and they'll come out for it."

Cohn wasn't the only studio executive cultivated by Roselli as a mob fixer in Hollywood. His other friends included Louis B. Mayer of MGM and particularly Pat Casey, a key negotiator for the studios. "I represented, we might say, the picture industry," Roselli later testified. "I have always had some knowledge of the picture business."

Fatefully, Roselli dealt with Willie Bioff, another Chicago mobster sent to Los Angeles to corrupt the Hollywood unions. Contrary to Johnny's style, Bioff was a loud-mouthed ruffian and former pimp. He once tortured his female prostitutes with dry ice internally to gain their compliance.

After gaining union power through beatings and fatal shootings, Bioff and his partners launched a plan to extort money from Hollywood's top studios, including Warner Bros., MGM, and Cohn's Columbia, by threatening a mass worker shutdown. He pulled the same scam with movie theater owners around the country. "I had Hollywood dancing to my tune," boasted Bioff.

When federal prosecutors indicted Bioff for tax evasion, he sought a lighter sentence by implicating other Chicago mobsters, including bosses Paul Ricca, Frank Nitti, and their fixer in Hollywood, Roselli. Johnny got into legal trouble by trying to help his pal Harry Cohn avoid a strike at Columbia and was indicted along with the other Chicago mobsters. Their trial didn't go well. After hearing Bioff's devastating testimony, Nitti committed suicide rather than spend his remaining years in jail.

Johnny's life seemed in an irretrievable spiral downwards. Roselli, Ricca, and the others were sentenced to ten-year prison terms in the Hollywood extortion case. That same year, Roselli's actress wife June Lang divorced him on grounds of mental cruelty. By then, Fox movie studio had dropped Lang's contract to avoid being associated with the "criminal element." June claimed she didn't know of Johnny's history before she married him. Among their Hollywood friends, she had complained bitterly of the controlling demands of a husband now behind bars.

Eventually, the Chicago Outfit helped Johnny get out of jail early. Through his political contacts, Chicago's Murray Humphreys eventually negotiated a backroom deal to get Roselli and the fellow gangsters paroled after only three years.

Released beforehand, Willie Bioff changed his name and fell out of sight. Johnny swore he'd kill Bioff if he ever found where the government's incriminating witness was hiding.

The Hollywood extortion case continued to haunt Johnny. In October 1950, he answered questions about Bioff before a special US Senate panel investigating organized crime in America. With a fuzzy memory, Johnny didn't disclose much at the closed-door hearing in Chicago headed by Sen. Estes Kefauver. Fleetingly, Roselli acknowledged knowing Giancana's then-boss Tony Accardo, Chicago mobster Charles Fischetti (a friend of singer Frank Sinatra), and to once sharing a table at New York's Copacabana nightclub with then top crime boss Frank Costello.

But Johnny carefully guarded the biggest secret—his real identity. He falsely testified he was born in Chicago. He gave a wrong date of birth. He lied about distant cousins living in the Windy City. And when asked about meeting Al Capone as a young man, Roselli replied facetiously (and perhaps crudely) that he'd been introduced through an uncle named "Anthony D'Kunta."

"I think you are trying to give this testimony of yours a quick brush over," Rudolph Halley, the Senate panel's chief counsel, finally complained in frustration.

"I am on the truth's side, Mr. Halley," Johnny assured.

For much of the early 1950s, Roselli tried once again to build up his power and influence in Hollywood. He worked as an "associate producer" employed by his colorful pal Bryan Foy (eldest of "The Seven Little Foys" troupe) at a small studio called Eagle Lion. Luckily for Johnny, Harry Cohn also remained a loyal friend despite their past legal difficulties.

As a mob catalyst, Johnny performed special tasks, big and small. During this time, he reportedly helped convince Cohn to give Marilyn Monroe her first contract at Columbia's studio. Monroe was friendly with another actress, Jeanne Carmen, who dated Roselli. A voluptuous blonde B-movie actress, Carmen was a Monroe look-alike who also happened to be an ace golfer. She helped Johnny scam wealthy men he met on the links who made large wagers they couldn't lose to a beautiful girl like Carmen. They were shocked when Carmen hit a ball two hundred yards. During this time, Roselli was enamored with Monroe and may have dated her too. As a favor, Johnny's influence was enough to prevail on Cohn to sign up Monroe even after she refused the Columbia mogul's sexual advances.

Roselli also convinced Cohn to hire singer Frank Sinatra, then down on his luck, for a supporting role in the film *From Here to Eternity*, which later won Sinatra an Oscar. Johnny had a smooth way of delivering ultimatums.

"Harry, I need your help," Roselli said. "Either give Frank the role or I will have you killed." No horse's head was needed as inducement in this real-life exchange.

When the Outfit moved into Las Vegas, first with the Stardust and then with a percentage stake in other casinos such as the Desert Inn, Roselli made sure he got his share. Expanding from Hollywood, Roselli successfully developed casino gambling as a huge money-maker for the mob inside America's new capitol of unabashed hedonism. Johnny seemed well suited for the job.

"Nothing happens without my say so," Roselli explained. "I keep it low key. Nothing flashy. I settle beefs but everything's done in a gentlemanly manner. I tip good, I gamble here and there, just spreading the good will around. Play lots of golf, eat good food . . . . I'm fucking all these broads, not chorus girls, but the stars. You've never seen nothing like it. This Vegas has more broads than anyplace I've ever seen."

To help keep an eye on things, Sam Giancana dispatched another Outfit ambassador, Marshall Caifano—the brother of slain Fat Lenny—to provide muscle when needed in Vegas.

One of Caifano's first tasks was to get rid of Louis "Russian Louie" Strauss, an underworld gambler who had welched on his debts. Caifano enlisted Jimmy "The Weasel" Fratianno, Roselli's favorite hitman in Los Angeles, to help strangle and bury "Russian Louie" somewhere in the desert. After Strauss's demise, delinquent gambling debtors would joke with gallows humor, "I'll pay when Russian Louie hits town."

But Caifano's biggest payoff on the Strip was in discovering snitch Willie Bioff. Like a moth to a flame, the government's key informant in the Hollywood extortion scandal found a new job handling entertainment at The Riviera, then a Vegas casino also controlled by organized crime. Willie did little to disguise himself except to use his wife's maiden name for his new alias, "William Nelson." In 1955, while walking through a clothing store inside the Desert Inn casino, Caifano recognized Bioff and alerted the Outfit bosses.

As it turned out, the clothing store's owner was Sen. Barry Goldwater, the future 1964 Republican presidential nominee, who was friendly with this convicted mobster with the phony name. "Bioff seemed a pleasant individual and asked me out golfing and to his home," Goldwater later recalled in his memoir. "My wife and I saw nothing wrong in it." Bioff also gave a $5,000 donation to Goldwater's campaign and vacationed with him in Las Vegas at the mob-run Riviera.

In plotting revenge, Roselli and Giancana were loath to see blood spilled on the Vegas Strip. Any violent incident would upset visiting customers and the constant money flow streaming into their casinos. Thus, the ending for Willie Bioff, like the disposal of Russian Louie, turned into an out-of-town affair.

While in Phoenix, Arizona, Bioff spotted a metal device under his car. Based on previous experiences, he assumed it was a "bug"—some sort of government listening device. Unsure, he called his lawyer and asked what to do. The lawyer instructed him to come over to his office as soon as possible.

Bioff got in his car and, when he turned the ignition key, it blew up.

"There is no doubt in my mind that Willie Bioff was repaid for being a traitor and an informer on my father's friends," Antoinette Giancana later concluded.

As further warning, the Mafia bosses sought retribution from Gus Greenbaum, the former Chicago mobster who ran the Riviera and knew Bioff's real identity when he gave him the job. Over the next several months, Greenbaum became sloppy, developing a taste for narcotics and high-priced prostitutes. Even worse, the Chicago bosses caught him skimming from their casino profits.

Johnny handed Gus an ultimatum—either quit now or suffer the consequences.

"This goddamn town is in my blood," Greenbaum replied defiantly, sealing his fate.

A few days after Thanksgiving 1958, Greenbaum and his wife were found dead in their Phoenix house. Both had their necks slashed, nearly decapitated with a butcher knife.

No one was ever charged. Johnny expressed satisfaction with this Mafia justice. "Chicago got that stoolie Willie Bioff, who testified against us," Roselli concluded. "He was hiding out in Phoenix and chumming around with Senator [Barry] Goldwater and Gus Greenbaum. I did forty-three months because of that stoolie."

By adding millions in revenue from Las Vegas and Hollywood, Chicago's mob empire became exponentially larger and more powerful. With so many domestic outlets, Giancana and Roselli now turned their attention to even greater expansion in Cuba, where they would spread their brand of lawless capitalism the way the United States feared Communism's creep throughout the Caribbean.

CHAPTER 8:

HAVANA'S ALLURE

On sultry winter nights in the late 1950s, the Sans Souci nightclub and casino sizzled with action. While joints in Chicago were covered in snow, visiting American tourists basked in the warm glow of Latin music, sumptuous dinners, and sensuous floor shows.

Nearly naked dancers in colorful feathered costumes, big-name entertainers like Tony Bennett, and elaborate production numbers with voodoo themes were all part of Havana's allure for Sans Souci customers.

"It's like stepping into a movie set of what Hollywood thinks a tropical nightclub should be like," a visitor explained to the press.

Most of all, there was gambling at the Sans Souci. On any night, guests dropped hundreds of dollars, sometimes thousands, at tables for roulette, blackjack, craps, and other games of chance.

Located along Havana's outskirts, the Sans Souci was run by the Chicago Outfit. Sam Giancana's criminal enterprise pumped more than a million dollars into turning this old Spanish villa into a state-of-the art gambling center. While the White House and CIA viewed Cuba primarily in geopolitical terms, the Mafia calculated it in terms of dollars and cents.

To ensure the best return on investment, Giancana sent Johnny Roselli temporarily to oversee the Sans Souci's management. In Las Vegas, Johnny always made sure the boys back in Chicago received their due profits. Roselli visited their new place in Havana like a visiting ambassador. On the floor, he escorted around big spenders and influential figures, like actor George Raft, always with a beautiful girl on his arm.

At the Sans Souci, Giancana and Roselli relied on Santo Trafficante Jr., a second-generation gangster based in Tampa, with sizeable interests in other Havana casinos and resorts. Trafficante supervised their resort as well as the popular Hotel Capri and the Hotel Nacional, a mob favorite. This quiet and cunning man was the Mafia's local power in Cuba. He could be easily underestimated. The *gangsterismo* Trafficante appeared almost professorial with his grey conservative suits, close cut hair, thick eye-glasses with brown tortoise-shell rims, and unflaggingly reserved manner.

Trafficante "displays none of the mobster flare for the sensational," a 1960 FBI memo observed. It quoted a 1958 *Life* magazine article describing this suspected killer/narcotics kingpin as "scholarly looking, as if he might be around Havana to complete a PhD in Sociology." A FBI informant later labeled Trafficante as "a very unusual personality, who appears to have considerable influence, but it is the type of person that 'one can never feel close to.'"

On his visits to Havana, Roselli worked harmoniously with Trafficante. He treated him like a friend and a valued co-conspirator, squeezing every cent from the Sans Souci. Although the Outfit was an absentee owner many miles away, Sam and Johnny believed Trafficante understood who was ultimately in charge.

"Down there, when Santo wants to clear anything, he goes to Chicago," Roselli explained.

Based on their success in Havana's swank casinos, Johnny and Sam later enlisted Trafficante's help in the CIA's campaign against Castro. Both would be guilty of mis-reading Trafficante—with his conflicting loyalties and boundless capacity for treach-ery—far more than they ever realized.

———————

Since Prohibition in the early 1930s, Havana's gambling palaces had provided a rich source of income for the Mafia, a decade before the first major Las Vegas casino opened its doors. Because Cuba was considered an "open territory," various mob gangs from New York, the Chicago Outfit—as well as Florida's Trafficante and Miami-based gang-ster Meyer Lansky—controlled portions of the betting action. Indeed, in the 1950s, Cuba's president Fulgencio Batista appointed Lansky as a "gambling reform" advisor.

Havana's casinos were notoriously corrupt, so much that the Mafia-owned places run by Trafficante and others were considered, ironically, the most honest. "For gam-blers, particularly the high rollers who were the lifeblood of any casino, having an American mob-connected casino manager was reassurance that the games were untainted by loaded dice, shady blackjack dealers, and rigged roulette wheels," histo-rian Peter Moruzzi said about these pre-Castro days.

Disputes in Havana over money or power were settled up north by a loose national commission of organized crime bosses who operated with little opposition from either the US or Cuban governments. However, that delicate balance was upset in 1957, when Albert Anastasia, a particularly violent New York mobster, demanded more profits from the Cuban casinos. He wasn't accustomed to being told no.

Infamously, Anastasia ran "Murder Inc."—the killers-for-hire enforcement arm of the national Mafia. Authorities claimed he was responsible for some four hundred murders without being convicted. During a cantankerous Havana trip, Anastasia made his demand for more casino profits known. Soon afterwards, Trafficante traveled to New York City for a follow-up meeting.

The two mobsters met in October 1957 at Anastasia's suite inside the Warwick Hotel, ostensibly for some settlement agreement. Santo arrived with a few Cuban associates. After listening to Anastasia's request for a half-ownership in a newly built Havana gambling palace, they shook hands on what seemed a new deal.

Two days later, Anastasia received his real answer. While in the nearby Park Sheraton Hotel barbershop for a haircut and shave, Anastasia was murdered by two unknown assailants. His killers wore long coats, fedoras, and bandanas over their faces.

Police found Anastasia's bloodied corpse on the barbershop floor. Forensics showed that Anastasia, with a warm towel across his brow, tried to stop the attack. Bullets cut through his head, hip, and left hand. Detectives discovered the murder weapon in a subway garbage can.

That same morning, Trafficante checked out of his guest room at the Warwick. The quiet Florida mobster headed back directly to Havana without being questioned.

At first, the gory headlines of Anastasia's murder suggested a local gangland squabble. A month later, however, the American public learned that his death had much deeper consequences, illustrating the Mafia's mighty place in society.

On November 14, 1957, a national commission of top organized crime bosses, including Chicago's Sam Giancana and Tony Accardo, met inside a lavish stone mansion in Apalachin, NY. The rustic estate was 150 miles north of Manhattan. The purpose was to smooth over unrest caused by Anastasia's murder and to maintain their flourishing businesses in Cuba, Las Vegas, and elsewhere without further bloodshed.

Curious state police conducted a surprise raid. They encircled the Apalachin home of hoodlum Joseph Barbara after hearing of many "price is no object" hotel reservations by visiting wiseguys and of fancy cars with out-of-state license plates parked nearby.

The secretive Apalachin meeting revealed that the Mafia was more than just a group of gangs scattered across the country. They were more like a criminal consortium, a confederation of mob chieftains, capable of ironing out their differences instead of reverting to constant warfare. "The point is that these bosses don't have an ounce more power than any other boss," Roselli explained. "That's what the commission's all about. All bosses on the commission also have equal power."

When the cops made their move, Giancana was enjoying a steak luncheon around a barbeque pit. Most of the attendees inside the eighteen-room hilltop mansion, including Vito Genovese and Carlo Gambino, were arrested. But a dozen gangsters ran away, including Giancana and Accardo. Sam later described the wild scene to Roselli.

"I ran like I was doing the 100-yard dash in the Olympics," Giancana recalled to his pal. "I made the woods in the back by going out the back door, and I stayed there and watched them pull everyone in. When it was all over . . . when it was dark and safe . . . I got the hell outta there."

Police caught Trafficante. He gave them an alias of "Louis Santo." They listed his occupation as "operator of the Sans Souci night club, Havana." Frank DeSimone, Johnny's former lawyer turned new Los Angeles mob boss, was also arrested during the raid. DeSimone later received six months on contempt of court charges for refusing to testify about Apalachin's purpose.

That evening, Giancana hitch-hiked with another mobster from the chilly upstate New York woodlands to downstate Long Island. Two days afterward, Sam wound up in Chicago, still appalled by his shabby treatment. He swore there would have been no police raid if the mob commission met in Chicago instead of the boonies of rural New York. "I tore up a $1,200 suit on some barbed wire and ruined a new pair of shoes," he fumed.

Over time, "Apalachin" proved a turning point for *La Cosa Nostra*, up until then a largely secret organization. Most Americans had no idea that any national commission of Mafia bosses existed and wielded such clout. Even the press seemed surprised and suddenly awakened.

On its front page the next day, the *New York Times* published a large story about this gangland "convention," which the US Attorney in New York, Paul W. Williams, attested was "further proof of the existence of a criminal syndicate organized across state lines." Williams estimated this organized crime empire collected an unfathomable $2.2 billion annually from narcotics, gambling, and extortion.

For Giancana, the Apalachin fiasco also marked a turning point. After months of evading a subpoena to testify about the event, Sam was forced to appear in 1959 before a US Senate investigation panel known as the "Rackets Committee," examining organized crime. Authorities now identified Giancana as one of America's top crime bosses, Chicago's successor to Al Capone.

Before cameras and lights, Sam wore dark glasses and a hairpiece to cover his balding scalp. He wasn't a naturally handsome man like Roselli. But he had a certain roughhewn vanity and sartorial flair whenever he appeared in public.

Sam laughed as he repeatedly invoked his Fifth Amendment rights. He refused to answer questions that might incriminate him.

"Are you going to tell us anything or just giggle?" asked chief counsel, Robert F. Kennedy, whose brother, Senator John F. Kennedy, was a committee member. "I thought only little girls giggled."

Giancana wasn't amused.

———————

The adverse publicity surrounding Apalachin also held a profound effect on the FBI's longtime director J. Edgar Hoover and his army of G-men, the slang term for government agents popularized in gangster films. For years, America's top lawman had downplayed the very real existence of a Mafia. Instead of a national syndicate of crime bosses, Hoover preferred to chase the perceived threat of domestic Communism, as he had since the start of the Cold War.

The embarrassing revelations from Apalachin forced Hoover to redirect his energies. "With the exposure of this new menace, he [Hoover] could choose to take agents and throw them into a fight against organized crime," recalled William F. Roemer Jr., a Chicago FBI agent who'd become Giancana's chief nemesis in this fight against the Mafia. "Not only was this dangerous group undefeated, no law enforcement agency had yet to come to grips with them and taken them on."

The Apalachin conclave and Anastasia's murder also underlined the mob's ongoing concerns about Cuba's future. When Fidel Castro overthrew the Batista government in 1959, the bearded guerilla leader in green fatigues condemned the shadowy Americans in silk suits who'd supported the corrupt dictator.

"We are not only disposed to deport the gangsters but to shoot them," Castro told a cheering crowd.

In Havana, Castro viewed mobsters as capitalist oppressors and promised reform.

Many Westerners were sympathetic to his revolution, like novelist Graham Greene, who'd been appalled by police brutality and torture during Batista's rule. "The murder of hostages by the government is an almost daily occurrence—bodies are found flung out by the wayside," Greene wrote to a friend in the British Parliament. "As one Cuban said to me, there is hardly a family in Havana who has not lost one member at the hands of the Secret Police."

In the zeal of Castro's revolutionary takeover, Sans Souci and other mob-owned casinos were torched and ruined. Trafficante was detained temporarily at the Trescornia prison where he claimed to be nearly killed by a firing squad.

"They're going to execute me—I'm on the damn list," Trafficante pleaded with his attorney Frank Ragano from prison.

Eventually, Trafficante was released, apparently through a bribe and the help of Fidel's brother, Raul Castro. The exact details of this Houdini-like escape from prison was never made clear. Whether friend or foe, however, Trafficante's relationship with the Castros and the new Cubans in charge would remain mysterious for years. .

Giancana hated to lose the Sans Souci and his other Cuban investments. Castro's ban on American-owned businesses included Sam's shrimp boat business, which netted a huge amount of revenue yearly. Havana was a long-time winter haven for Sam— away from the pesky scrutiny of American law-enforcement—and a place where he kept a *pied-a-terre* apartment with a local girlfriend.

"That rotten bastard, he stole millions of dollars from us," Sam said about Castro. "I can't wait to kill the fucker."

Reacting to his friend George Raft, the ex-actor who became an official greeter at one of Trafficante's mob-run casinos, Johnny was even more graphic.

"You give me a couple of guys with machine guns, we could go down there and take over the whole island," Roselli vowed.

Johnny and Sam soon received their opportunity for revenge against Castro, to reclaim the Sans Souci and the whole island nation of Cuba for the Mafia. That chance came with the CIA's assassination offer relayed by Bob Maheu in 1960. The two mobsters realized the US government wanted to get rid of the new Communist despot in Havana as much as they did, but for different reasons. And the feds were willing to pay for it.

Although getting involved with the government carried its own risks to their future, Roselli and Giancana decided to go ahead and enlist in the CIA's not-so-secret war against Castro.

CHAPTER 9:
AT THE PLAZA

After their Brown Derby lunch in California, Robert Maheu set up another meeting with Johnny Roselli in early September 1960 at the Hilton Savoy Plaza Hotel in New York City. This grand hotel, with scores of out-of-towners milling about, was a perfect place to talk freely.

As a cutout for the CIA, Maheu's job was to build confidence and calmly hold the nervous hands of fellow spies. Maheu had reassured Jim O'Connell, the agency's direct contact with him, that the CIA's conspiracy to kill Fidel was moving along as planned. In turn, O'Connell reassured his superiors. This CIA chain of command—insulated in "full deniability"—reached all the way to the White House.

There were other hands to hold. Certainly Maheu felt it necessary to keep his top private client, multi-millionaire Howard Hughes, convinced of his full-time devotion. He didn't want to appear too swept up in government skullduggery.

But at this point in the top-secret conspiracy, Maheu believed it most important to reassure Johnny Roselli, keeping this suspicious mobster fully engaged as a newly-recruited spy.

At their amiable Brown Derby chat a few weeks earlier, Roselli said he wanted more than just Maheu's assurances. Johnny insisted on meeting someone official from the CIA, proof that this highly risky plan had the agency's approval.

In his glib manner, Maheu swore he wasn't "pulling any punches." He insisted on being "totally up front" about the deal. But apparently there remained an air of uncertainty in Roselli's mind. No way could Johnny get the Mafia's cooperation if this CIA offer wasn't rock solid.

For their second talk in New York, Maheu lived up to Roselli's demands by convincing O'Connell to join them. A true Company man, O'Connell insisted on maintaining the original ruse—claiming that displaced "industrials" were behind the assassination plan and not the CIA. This pretense was insisted upon by O'Connell's bosses, Sheffield Edwards and Richard Bissell. They believed Roselli wouldn't be any wiser.

O'Connell, a tall husky Irishman who looked like a neighborhood cop, pretended he wasn't a CIA agent. He introduced himself as "Jim Olds."

"We may know some people," Roselli said, playing along. O'Connell didn't know that Maheu had already conceded the CIA's role to Johnny during their first conversation at the Brown Derby.

At the Hilton Savoy Plaza, neither Maheu nor Roselli informed O'Connell that his contrivance wasn't needed. They let "Jim Olds" explain himself without comment.

Johnny didn't object to this play-acting because he recognized O'Connell's face from the clambake in Maheu's backyard, when he chatted with his boss, Shef Edwards. To Roselli, O'Connell's very presence at the Hilton Savoy Plaza confirmed the CIA's involvement.

Despite this faulty introduction, the hotel conversation turned out successfully. All three agreed the Mafia's prior connections with Cubans in Havana's gambling underworld would be invaluable to their assassination plot against Castro.

At the insistence of "Jim Olds," Roselli agreed to a future meeting in Florida, where he promised to introduce the CIA agent and Maheu to a man named "Sam Gold" who "knew the Cuban crowd."

Only when the subject of money came up did Roselli give the slight glimpse that he knew the CIA was behind this mission. After "Jim Olds" repeated the offer of a $150,000 bounty for Castro's killing, Johnny quickly shunned payment.

"Roselli made it clear he did not want any money for his part and believed Sam would feel the same way," O'Connell later testified.

The Hilton Savoy Plaza meeting between Roselli and two CIA representatives finished well. Their conspiracy would move ahead to its next step.

While in Manhattan, Johnny caught up with Giancana, already in town for a romantic date as well as mob business. Sam was staying at the Hampshire House on Central Park South, a short distance from the Hilton Savoy Plaza. "He was going with this young lady in New York, and I did meet with him, and I had dinner with him," Roselli recalled.

The two mobsters agreed among themselves to carry on with the CIA plan. Why not see what advantages a foreign assassination plan might engender for them with the government? they figured. One benefit was obvious: If Castro was killed, the Sans

Souci might be back in business soon, along with their other money-making investments in Cuba.

Yet Sam remained more skeptical about the scheme's chances of success than
Johnny. Perhaps this doubt was why Giancana never informed the Mafia's national
commission about the plan, as he would be expected to do, particularly in the wake
of the Apalachin fiasco. Though they were trusted pals, Giancana could pull rank on
Roselli and even disparage him to other underlings outside of his earshot. Sam never
trusted anyone fully, an occupational necessity in his dangerous role as a gang leader.

Johnny's pitch to become spies proved convincing, however. Giancana indicated
he'd be willing to meet with the CIA's men in Florida as Roselli promised. The mob
boss, who evaded the World War II draft by feigning insanity, seemed amused by
Roselli's sense of patriotism.

"Give Johnny a flag and he'll follow you around the yard," Sam laughed.

Back at CIA headquarters in Washington, O'Connell's bosses also were pleased. In
their tight administrative circle, good news about his progress spread quickly—from
O'Connell and his superior Director of Security Shef Edwards, to Deputy Director
Richard Bissell and the CIA's longtime chief Allen Dulles.

Roselli seemed an ideal undercover spy. "We were just trying to find somebody
who was tough enough to be able to handle the job, but not mention Mafia specifically," O'Connell recalled. With their agency code words and obtuse espionage language, the CIA men took great care not to admit—even among themselves—that they
were dealing with killers. As the CIA's Inspector General later found, "The objective
clearly was the assassination of Castro although Edwards claims that there was a studied avoidance of the term in his conversation with Bissell."

An economics professor by training, Bissell let expediency overcome whatever
moral qualms he had about the killing plan. A seemingly level-headed man who
peered at the world through thick horn-rimmed glasses, Bissell had never known
failure of any sort. A graduate of Groton in 1928 and Yale in 1932, Bissell's career
march upwards, from the Ford Foundation to the CIA, seemed unstoppable. As a
clubby member of the influential "Georgetown Set" of Washington politicians and
journalists, he cultivated many friends with Ivy League pedigrees who predicted Bissell someday would succeed Dulles. Eliminating Castro would be another feather in
Bissell's cap, with little regard for its consequences.

"His extraordinary mind was fatally flawed, and his confident enthusiasm for ambitious projects crossed the threshold of recklessness," historian Evan Thomas observed. Bissell's son later agreed. "There had to be a piece of him that was cold to do what he did," Richard Bissell III said in 2013. "When you are in the business of getting a foreign leader out of a job—or killed—you have to be."

For Bissell, it seemed perfectly logical to retain the heirs of Murder Inc. to conduct a bloody obliteration of Castro—and then, diabolically, get the press to blame it on the Mafia rather than the government. The CIA deputy wanted to keep an organizational distance from the ugly deed. "Bissell got calls from the Mafia, but he wouldn't take them," his secretary Doris Mirage recalled. "I don't even know how they got his inside number."

Bissell preferred not to deal with Johnny Roselli and his ilk. "I had no desire to become personally involved in its implementation, mainly because I was not competent to handle relations with the Mafia," Bissell admitted.

When they briefed Dulles on O'Connell's progress, Bissell and Edwards avoided any "bad words" such as "Mafia" or "assassination," as Edward recalled. They kept their wordplay in the most elemental A-B-C terms. "A" meant Maheu. "B" was Roselli. And "C" was for their intended target in Cuba.

During the debriefing, Dulles merely nodded his understanding and approval. He said nothing and made no objections. Through this oblique exchange, Dulles maintained his "plausible deniability," but also gave his implicit blessings. Edwards interpreted the director's sphinx-like nods as "tacit approval to use his own judgment."

Bissell, like a puppetmaster pulling the strings, remained supremely confident that their top-secret plan would never be exposed outside their tight circle of conspirators. As he recalled: "I knew it was serious. I knew these were Mafia leaders. And I knew they were in a position to make very damning revelations about the agency. But we thought it was all under control."

One person who, most notably, didn't know of the CIA's recruitment of organized crime figures was the FBI's Director J. Edgar Hoover. America's top lawman didn't like to be kept in the dark about any government secrets in his terrain. And when he finally did find out, he usually reacted with vengeance, hoping to save face and make up for lost time.

Following double-barrel embarrassments about the Mafia from the Apalachin "convention" and the US Senate Rackets Committee hearings in the late 1950s, Hoover ordered his agency to launch a "Top Hoodlum Program"—designed to identify, investigate, and prosecute the nation's leading mobsters. FBI squads were set up in New York, Chicago, and other key places, where they learned about the nefarious activities of men like Giancana.

Starting in July 1959, William Roemer and other young FBI agents planted a listening device inside the Chicago Outfit's downtown headquarters, based in a tailor shop on North Michigan Avenue serving as a front. They called the device "Little Al," a sarcastic homage to Capone.

Roemer, a tall, broad-shouldered graduate of the Notre Dame Law School and a former heavyweight boxer, pursued the Mafia with an archangel's zeal. "I thank God to this day that I had competent associates and that the good faith of my objective allowed me to succeed with the mission," Roemer observed. "If it hadn't, I hate to think where I might be today . . . or where the FBI would be in the crusade against the mob."

Almost immediately, the microphone placed behind a radiator by Roemer yielded remarkable information.

For starters, the FBI found out many Chicago cops and judges accepted bribes from Giancana's organization, providing protection from any pursuit by local law-enforcement. They learned fixer Murray Humphreys wasn't a doddering old geezer retired and out of touch—as local Chicago detectives claimed—but rather the Outfit's key overseer of graft to politicians and nefarious deals with Roselli in Las Vegas.

Shockingly, they heard the verbose Humphreys brag about how he'd arranged a decade ago for the early parole of Roselli, Paul Ricca, and other convicts in the Hollywood Extortion case with a bribe to Attorney General Tom Clark in the Truman administration. Humphreys handed over the cash himself to an intermediary. Clark was promised even better things if he went along. "Finally a deal was made: if he [Clark] had the thick skin to do it, he'd get the next appointment to the Supreme Court," said Humphreys, noting that Clark did get his seat on the bench. When he learned of this secret recording, Hoover insisted on hearing it himself.

Although the FBI gathered a lot of information about the Chicago mob, Hoover remained in the dark about the CIA's involvement with Giancana and Roselli. While "Little Al" picked up Humphreys and other mobsters, FBI agents realized Giancana conducted most business at the Armory Lounge, a suburban Forest Park restaurant that served as his personal clubhouse. Several months would pass before the FBI installed a second listening device and heard the voice of Giancana talking about a plot against Fidel Castro.

The delay was caused by a legal delicacy surrounding the listening devices. Installing bugs, like wiretapping telephones, was considered illegal behavior by the courts and was formally disavowed by Hoover and the FBI. No prosecutions could be based on what was learned from these tapes. Secretly, the law-enforcement agency allowed Roemer's "black bag" installation of the Chicago microphones only as a way of catching up to the Mafia's very advanced criminal activities and perhaps preventing future crimes.

If Roemer and any of the other G-men were caught with the bugs, the FBI would disavow any prior knowledge. In heroic terms, Roemer considered himself a good guy willing to bend, if not break, the law to eradicate evils from organized crime figures like Sam Giancana.

"Had my colleagues and I been caught by either the mob or by the authorities, we would have been thrown to the wolves," Roemer explained about his undercover activities, unofficially sanctioned by higher-ups. "I would certainly be fired from the Bureau, probably convicted of at least breaking and entering, disbarred from the legal profession, perhaps serve time in prison, certainly be very much disgraced, and in the future be seriously impaired from earning a living at my chosen profession—law enforcement."

In this respect, top FBI officials were similar to their counterparts in the Central Intelligence Agency—they both demanded "plausible deniability" for the actions taken in their name.

Ironically, the only person outside the CIA's Foggy Bottom circle who learned of the Castro murder plot in its early stages was Howard Hughes, courtesy of his fixer Bob Maheu. Previously, Hughes seemed to have no problem with CIA moonlighting, perhaps because Maheu kept the mission's precise details to himself. He never mentioned Castro's name.

But as Maheu flew around the country—spending time with Johnny Roselli in Los Angeles, New York, and then headed to a meeting in Miami—Hughes started complaining. As Maheu's top paying client, he demanded to know why Maheu's attention was so diverted.

On the phone from Miami, Maheu felt compelled to reveal one of the nation's biggest secrets. Maheu admitted he was working with the CIA to "dispose of Castro in connection with a pending invasion of Cuba."

The eccentric industrialist, sitting naked in the "germ-free zone" of his Beverly Hills bungalow, acquiesced. Killing Castro, Hughes said, sounded to him like "a pretty good idea."

CHAPTER 10:

FONTAINEBLEAU

"James Bond, with two double bourbons inside him, sat in the final departure lounge of Miami Airport and thought about life and death."
—IAN FLEMING, OPENING LINE FROM *GOLDFINGER*

The next step in the Castro assassination plot took place at the Fontainebleau, a bold white hotel stretched along Miami Beach. In the early 1960s, it seemed an ideal setting for both Hollywood spy fantasies and real-life mobsters.

Opening scenes for the movie *Goldfinger*—based on Ian Fleming's novel about secret agent James Bond—featured brassy music and a sweeping shot of the Fontainebleau's outdoor pool. Frank Sinatra also filmed scenes for movies at the Fontainebleau and broadcast a live 1960 TV extravaganza, *Welcome Home Elvis*, from the hotel.

With millions watching in America, Elvis sang Frank's hit "Witchcraft" while Sinatra crooned "Love Me Tender," a Presley trademark. Critics noted the odd pairing between the young king of rock-and-roll returning from the Army and the middle-aged Rat Pack master of swing music. "In that moment, Sinatra is welcoming Presley to the Great Showbiz Fraternity," observed biographer James Kaplan, "and at this crucial hinge point in his career Elvis is headed straight to Hollywood and Vegas."

That same year, the Fontainebleau hosted another odd pairing.

Far from the media's glare, Johnny Roselli and Sam Giancana became freelance spies in the service of the Central Intelligence Agency, volunteer conspirators against Fidel Castro. Their late September 1960 meeting took place when Roselli told Robert Maheu and their CIA handler Jim O'Connell to meet him at the hotel.

The Fontainebleau was a sentimental favorite for Giancana. A year earlier, as the father of the bride, Sam hosted two hundred people in a huge reception at the hotel for the marriage of his daughter Bonnie. A string orchestra and red-coated waiters in white gloves attended to this affair. Sam was a constant visitor to the hotel. "Giancana was on location during the entire filming of the movie *A Hole in the Head* where they stayed at the Fontainebleau," the FBI reported about that 1959 Sinatra film.

Inside the Fontainebleau's large showroom, or its lounge known as the Boom-Boom Room, the name "Giancana" was golden, whispered as a close friend of Sinatra.

"People would fall over themselves to make sure he [Sam] had a ringside table and was ushered back to see the entertainers," recalled Giancana's oldest daughter, Antoinette. "In fact, it was at the Fontainebleau where Sam introduced me to Frank Sinatra in his suite."

Giancana didn't use his real name when he first met Maheu, the CIA's go-between. In the Boom-Boom Room, Roselli introduced his pal to Maheu as "Sam Gold," one of Giancana's favorite aliases. Johnny also used a phony "cover" name for this trip— "John Rawlston." Maheu was impressed with "Sam Gold," though none the wiser about the true identity of Roselli's pal.

"He didn't come off as thuggish," Maheu recalled about this "Sam Gold" introduction. "You could tell, he wanted attention and he got it. When he walked down the hallway, you could just sense his power. He didn't have to say a word. It was just how he carried himself."

During the conversation with Maheu, Giancana nodded at another figure in the room. He called him "Joe" who also knew "the Cuban crowd." In fact, it was Santo Trafficante Jr., the high-level Florida mob boss who had worked with Johnny and Sam in running Cuba's now closed Sans Souci. "Joe" joined their table. He was introduced as someone who "could serve as a courier to Cuba and make arrangements there."

Inside a Fontainebleau suite, the CIA's representatives and Johnny's mysterious friends talked discreetly about ways of murdering Castro. Maheu said his agency bosses thought a mob-like rubout was best—a blood-splattering public event that would shatter Cuba's allies and rally the Cuban exiles looking to restore a US-friendly government.

"Sam Gold" nixed that idea. Gunfire would be too messy, he argued. Too difficult to find an assassin willing to commit to what would surely be a suicide mission. Instead, Giancana proposed a "potent pill, which could be placed in Castro's food or drink."

The two mobsters pushed hard for "something lethal that could be done without any fanfare—they didn't want a thing like an ambush or a shootout or anything like that," O'Connell later recalled. "They wanted it to look like the guy just passed away from natural causes." In other words, a scenario similar to poor "Mr. Lucky," who dropped dead at the Stardust from a presumed Mickey Finn.

With this pharmaceutical approach, there would be no fingerprints on a murder weapon. All involved could deny their culpability. Sam and Johnny seemed confident a Cuban spy—probably one they knew from the old days in Havana's underworld—could be recruited for this subtle but lethal task.

The CIA's two ambassadors at the Fontainebleau, Maheu and O'Connell, were agreeable to this scheme. They promised final approval after they returned to Washington and debriefed their higher-ups.

Trafficante said little, if anything, at this meeting. But the longtime Florida hitman noted the government's eagerness to exterminate the Marxist in Havana. "The thing that I got is that anything that could have been done to assassinate Castro or eliminate his associates or overthrow the Government of Cuba short of an atomic bomb, everything was permissible," Trafficante recalled.

Maheu claimed he had no idea of the true identities of Johnny's two acquaintances or their Mafia prominence. That day at the Fontainebleau, Maheu was the only one who used his real name. The CIA handler O'Connell continued to use his own cover name as "Jim Olds," which Johnny found tiresome. While playing cribbage near the beach, Johnny urged the CIA spy to come clean.

"Look Jim, I know who you are," Roselli said, showing his cards. "You are not kidding me. You are with the Central Intelligence Agency. I don't want you to confirm that."

At that moment, O'Connell didn't give up his phony moniker. Nor did Maheu offer the real identity of "Jim Olds."

"You don't have to tell me if it is true," Roselli whispered, in his smoky baritone. "I understand your situation. But I am very happy that that is the situation. Because I really didn't have any heart in it until I was convinced that this was the US Government."

Then Johnny confessed to the CIA man, as he did earlier with Maheu, how much he felt he owed America. This spy mission would be his payback. There wouldn't be any disposal fee by Roselli and his friends for getting rid of the Cuban leader. And they would pay their own expenses at the Fontainebleau or any place this conspiracy would take them.

"He [Roselli] never took a nickel," recalled O'Connell, the CIA handler. "He said, 'No, as long as it is for the government of the United States, that is the least I can do.'"

Several days later, while still in Florida, O'Connell received an urgent call from Maheu. It would prove the first of many unexpected surprises in their CIA-Mafia alliance.

Astonished, Maheu said he spotted photos of Roselli's two mysterious friends from the Fontainebleau. They appeared inside *Parade* magazine, a Sunday newspaper supplement distributed around the nation. It featured the FBI's list of America's top 10 gangsters and included their pictures.

"Sam Gold," Maheu read aloud, was really Sam Giancana, "the Chicago chieftain of the Cosa Nostra and successor to Al Capone." And the seemingly shy, green-eyed man named "Joe" was actually Santo Trafficante Jr., "the Cosa Nostra boss of Cuban operations."

O'Connell realized his cutout was as ignorant as he was about their recruits. "Maheu claimed that this was the first time that he was aware who we were actually dealing with," he later attested.

As a dutiful CIA handler, O'Connell quickly reported the news about Giancana and Trafficante to CIA security chief Shef Edwards, the next link in the spy agency's chain of command. He spoke "cryptically" over the telephone to Shef. He was careful again not to use the words "Mafia" or "assassinate."

"They are Johnny's close friends," O'Connell explained. "I told him [Edwards], we were using some high-powered people here, which really neither Maheu or myself knew. And I assume he reported that to [CIA Deputy Director Richard] Bissell."

Shef didn't seem upset or nervous that the Agency was using top killers posted by the FBI. "This is probably what we could have expected," Edwards replied.

O'Connell pushed forward like a good soldier with the Cold War plans against Castro, just like he would in any war.

"You have to consider the perspective of the times," O'Connell explained. "I was in World War II. And I was told that there was an enemy, and I was told that I was supposed to do it in the interest of national defense support. And I felt that this was coming from a higher up, and in their wisdom and judgment, this was the way to go. I was just doing as I was directed."

During this same period, the Fontainebleau was home to another matter of intrigue—a "love triangle," as Hollywood might say, that would remain secret for years but have a disturbing impact on how the American public eventually learned of this CIA assassination conspiracy.

Kept carefully under wraps, this drama involved a beautiful twenty-six-year-old woman named Judy Campbell, with long raven-like black hair and eyes as deep and blue as the Fontainebleau pool. Campbell certainly fit the description in a FBI report by undercover agents who spotted Roselli at the Fontainebleau "in the company of a good-looking girl."

Plenty of pretty women could be found at the Fontainebleau—dancing on stage, milling with drinks in the smoky Boom-Boom Room, or sunbathing in bikinis around the outdoor pool and cabanas. That weekend, Campbell was the special female guest of the hotel's headliner, Frank Sinatra.

During this warm winter jaunt to the Fontainebleau, the singer introduced Judy to his good friend "Sam Gold." It was the same alias Giancana used with the CIA men.

"I didn't know then that Sam was the Chicago Godfather," recalled Campbell, "but I did know he was important to Frank because of the way Sinatra acted around him, bowing and scraping and being so deferential."

Sinatra had been introduced to Campbell by Johnny Roselli. The Mafia's man-about-town first met Judy as a teenage bride in the early 1950s, living on a family inheritance, "hanging around the studios" in Hollywood, and in a tumultuous marriage to struggling actor William Campbell, ten years her senior. There was a sweetness to this natural beauty that caught Johnny's eye.

Campbell, born Judith Immoor, grew up in an affluent family in Pacific Palisades, California, and attended Catholic schools. She was the daughter of a successful architect who knew several Hollywood celebrities, including comedian Bob Hope and Bert Lahr, who played the Cowardly Lion in *The Wizard of Oz*. She briefly dated the handsome young actor Robert Wagner before getting married at age eighteen to Campbell.

The young couple resided around the corner from Roselli's place in Los Angeles. As an actor, William Campbell caught a few breaks—including singing beside Elvis Presley in the film *Love Me Tender*. But mostly, he seemed relegated to B-movies and horror flicks while battling alcoholism at home. When Judy finally divorced Campbell, Johnny started dating her occasionally before moving on to other women.

"Beautiful," as Roselli described her to a friend. "Looks like Liz Taylor, but nicer, a real sweet kid. Comes from a good family, lots of class."

Over the next few years, Judy Campbell changed from a wholesome ingénue to a sultry divorcée often found in nightclubs. Roselli and other powerful men in her life passed along Campbell as a party girl intent on a good time. Like other gorgeous women from Hollywood who visited Vegas, she became the dazzling accoutrement for an evening or a companion for the night. Whether she was paid for any of these encounters would remain a source of conjecture.

In 1959, at Puccini's restaurant in Beverly Hills, Roselli helped Judy meet Sinatra. The singer soon invited her on a Hawaiian vacation. They were joined by Sinatra's friend, Peter Lawford, and his wife, Patricia Kennedy Lawford, the sister of soon-to-be presidential candidate John F. Kennedy.

Lawford, a thin-framed foppish British actor, was part of Frank's "Rat Pack" group that also included entertainers Dean Martin and Sammy Davis Jr. The name "Rat Pack" was originally coined by their friends, actors Humphrey Bogart and his wife Lauren Bacall, after a night of Vegas drinking. Lawford didn't have the Runyon-esque characteristics of his other showbiz pals but possessed the right political credentials.

During this time, the "Rat Pack" made a motion picture called *Ocean's 11*, filmed in Las Vegas at several hotel casinos, including the Sands and the Desert Inn. The now classic caper film—about a Vegas heist one night inside five casinos—captured the cool "bad boy" aura projected by Sinatra, an associate of real-life mobsters whose attitude he reflected on screen.

After a day of shooting, the Rat Pack performed nightly at the Sands to standing-room-only crowds. While many casino dwellers wore cowboy hats, these high-flying entertainers showed up in mohair tuxes and black satin shoes. The indefatigable performers stayed fresh until 2 a.m. Then they relaxed in a sauna, grabbed a few hours sleep, and went back to filming the next day.

Their intense marathon partying was filled with laughs, Jack Daniels or gin, and friendly showgirls. Someone asked Giancana to call Los Angeles for "an outside girl," and soon Roselli's beautiful brunette friend, Judy Campbell, showed up. Judy could be seen sunbathing poolside at "the D.I," where Frank made sure all her drinks and poolside were comped. She was no longer the teenage bride projecting innocence but rather a woman quite familiar with the pleasures of the world.

After *Ocean's 11*, Judy remained in the picture. At the Sands, during a February 1960 campaign swing, JFK visited Lawford, his actor brother-in-law. The newly declared presidential candidate attended a few evening shows with Frank and the Rat Pack.

With his gleaming teeth, wave of auburn hair, and inveigling smile, Kennedy appeared like another pleasure-seeker in Vegas rather than the seemingly prudent senator known to the public. Vocalist Eddie Fisher traveled in the same circles with Sinatra and was struck by this party-loving politician so different from his sober image. "I used to think he [JFK] was more interested in gossip than in Russian missiles," Fisher remembered.

From the stage, Sinatra and his fellow performers pointed to Senator Kennedy and declared him an honorary member of their gang.

"What'd you say his name was?" Dino asked kiddingly, to knowing guffaws from the audience.

Inside a private Sands suite, Kennedy later entertained Judy Campbell and began their long-term affair. Behind closed doors, another side of Kennedy's complex persona emerged, far different than how he appeared on the Capitol floor. Ignoring the obvious risks, the senator began seducing the young woman. Their conversation ranged from the mysteries of politics to their shared Catholicism.

"When you talked to Jack, he talked *just* to you," explained Campbell, mesmerized by his presence. "He was endlessly curious about everything and everybody. He loved gossip. That night he did not want me to leave his side."

The following month at the Plaza in New York, Judy Campbell and the married forty-two-year-old senator spent a leisurely night together, while his presidential campaign staff prepared anxiously for the New Hampshire primary. The potentially explosive liaison would continue for several more months, eventually documented by a trail of FBI reports, telephone records, and other evidence.

Playing match-maker was Sinatra, friendly with Giancana and Roselli as well as the future president.

"They seemed to have a genuine mutual admiration society; Frank was in awe of Jack's background and his power as President, and Jack was mesmerized by Sinatra's swinging lifestyle," Campbell later recalled. Sinatra would soon record a campaign song for Kennedy adapted from his hit tune "High Hopes."

In March 1960, Sinatra arrived again at the Fontainebleau, this time for the Elvis

TV special. For kicks, Frank brought along Judy Campbell. At a private party, he introduced the nubile young woman to his friend named Sam.

After Judy met Giancana, the middle-aged mobster began wooing her with gifts and pleasantries. She described it as more a courtship between a self-assured older man and younger woman adrift, rather than a lustful fling with the expectation of sex. Though hardly handsome, Sam somehow exuded an appealing confidence borne of power and money. When asked what he did for a living, Giancana would explain, "I own Chicago. I own Miami. I own Las Vegas."

Soon Judy Campbell was having affairs with both the princely JFK and the beastly Mafia chieftain—an extraordinary turn of events. Campbell later claimed to carry notes and a suitcase full of money between Giancana and the Kennedy campaign, something doubted by critics and never proven. "I feel like I was set up to be the courier," she recalled. "I was a perfect choice because I could come and go without notice, and if noticed, no one would've believed it anyway."

But Judy Campbell correctly suspected she was now caught in the middle of something far beyond her grasp. She'd become the bait in a trap, the glittering, sensuous lure used by calculating men to ensnare and compromise another. The two mobsters had delicately orchestrated this triangular affair—with Sinatra as the procurer and Campbell as an unwitting Mata Hari—in a way a seasoned spy might envy.

With more influence than ever before, Giancana and Roselli anticipated a rosier future for their criminal empire. By taking bold unprecedented steps, these two friends gained advantages far greater than if they were still small-fry hoodlums in Chicago. They now possessed scandalous insider knowledge about Kennedy's sex life, enough to ruin his career. And under the veil of top-secret national security, the two ambitious gangsters agreed to be unpaid assassins in the government's covert war against Castro's regime in Cuba.

As if holding two winning casino chips, Sam and Johnny expected a big boost soon in the cash flow for their underworld operations, with an early demise for Castro and an easing of the FBI's recently stepped-up investigations of the Mafia.

And if they weren't pleased, they could always ask their pal Frank Sinatra to intervene with the Kennedys.

PHASE II: COVERT OPERATIONS

"Covert operations can rarely achieve an important objective alone."
—THE CIA's COVERT OPERATIONS STUDY GROUP, 1968

"The modern patriotism, the true patriotism, the only rational patriotism, is loyalty to the Nation all the time, loyalty to the Government when it deserves it."

—MARK TWAIN

CHAPTER 11:

THE SECRET WAR BEGINS

With the CIA's backing, Rolando Masferrer was among the first Cuban exiles to attack, hoping to topple Fidel Castro's newly formed government. Masferrer was a fervent anti-Communist, a former Batista ally friendly with mobster Santo Trafficante Jr. from their days together in Havana's casinos.

Fond of wearing cowboy hats, the dashing rebel organized a private army that trained at a Florida ranch owned by Howard Hughes before launching into the Atlantic. In October 1960, Masferrer's Tigers, as they were dubbed, were sent out in four small boats, with a total of twenty-six men, headed for the Cuban shoreline of Oriente Province.

Onboard was Bobby Fuller, a young former US Marine, whose family once owned a farm in the Cuban countryside before Castro confiscated it. This ragtag militia on the high seas was united in their hatred for Fidel.

But when their boats neared, Castro's forces were ready for them. While some invaders escaped, Fuller and several others were captured. The young American faced a firing squad the next day.

"He was shot and killed after being tortured by having his blood drained from his body," said his daughter Lynita Fuller Caskey years later. "His body was thrown into an unmarked mass grave in an unknown location."

Back in Florida, Masferrer kept up his violent anti-Castro activities for years afterward. But Castro's spies eventually gained their own covert revenge—blowing up Masferrer with a car bomb planted in his garage.

As US leaders gradually realized, America's secret conflict against Castro in the 1960s wouldn't be like any traditional warfare they had known. Instead of marching armies, rolling tanks, and hand-to-hand combat in open battlefields, this contest of wills depended on guerilla fighting and espionage in the streets.

Often the most intense sabre-rattling took place around Miami rather than in Havana. Southern Florida overflowed with thousands of newly displaced Cubans, ready to seize their homeland back from Castro. Many were armed and angry, organized into various paramilitary groups financed by Uncle Sam.

Some exiles, encouraged by veteran CIA agents like E. Howard Hunt, became freelance fighters sent into Cuba on sabotage missions. With patriotic bloodlust, these young warriors swore to end Castro's tyranny, regardless of the dangers.

"I learned of hundreds of people, labeled as agitators, who disappeared without a trace, others who were festering in dungeon-like prisons because they had uttered a few words against Castro," recalled Hunt, who later became infamous for his role in the Watergate break-in. Too often, Hunt said, Cuban dissenters "had been lined up against a wall and shot as a lesson to others."

Throughout early 1960, CIA planes flew loads of armaments, technical gear, and espionage equipment into Cuba. These undercover "black flights" dropped their cargo by parachute at designated spots, meant for pick up by "stay behind" spies and double agents.

Too often the risky missions failed. The first CIA cache of weapons landed seven miles from its target. When a double agent inside Cuba finally arrived to recover it, he was caught and shot.

Anti-Castro fighters exacted their own gruesome toll through a series of attacks. On March 4, the French freighter *La Coubre*, carrying arms and explosives for Cuba's military, blew up in Havana's harbor. At least seventy-six people were killed, with dozens more injured. Castro quickly accused US-sponsored spies of causing the terrorizing blast. He later executed an American, William Morgan—once favorable to Castro's revolution—for allegedly playing a role in the massive explosion.

"We have the conviction that it was the imperialistic United States which assassinated the Cuban workers," Castro told a large crowd honoring the dead. Newspapers around the world carried his words. A stark black-and-white photo of Che Guevara, Castro's top aide called to the explosion scene, would later become iconic as "Guerrillero Heroico" (Heroic Guerilla Fighter).

From his revolutionary days in the jungle, Castro knew how to use publicity as a weapon to gain sympathy against the American spy agency that prized silence. He'd eventually create Radio Havana as a way to spread propaganda both at home and abroad. More significantly, as a fledgling Communist dictator hanging on to power, Castro learned to fight back challenges to his rule by creating a spy agency of his own.

At his request, the Soviet Union immediately sent five top intelligence experts to teach its methods and oversee training.

Since its own Communist revolution in 1917, no one in the world seemed more devoted to spying than the Russians. In the grand chess game of *realpolitik*, Soviet leader Nikita Khrushchev wanted to establish himself as a provocative player in the Western Hemisphere "theater" of Cuba, comparable to the US role in Berlin. "He completely believed . . . that socialism should triumph in Cuba and the entire world," one of Khrushchev's diplomats later recalled.

Under the guidance of his newfound Russian allies, Castro quickly established his brutal G-2 foreign intelligence force. This secret agency, modeled on the Soviet KGB, tracked foreign spies and often murdered political opponents. It reflected the deep paranoia within Cuba. "All week long Havana rang with feverish alarms against 'U.S. aggression' and 'invasion,'" *Time* magazine observed in the Cuban capitol. "As newspaper, radio and TV commentators beat the drums, the country went on a virtual war footing."

After an attempt on Castro's life by insiders, bloody retaliation followed against more than a hundred dissidents. Unsure of the next attack, Castro moved around frequently—undetected from house to house, place to place—obsessed with enemies both real and imagined. Years later, a visiting American asked him what it was like to be the target of so many killing attempts. "Do you have a sport?" Castro replied. "Well, avoiding assassination is a sport for me."

In this shadowy conflict, the CIA hadn't much success toppling Castro. Instead of its old methods of intelligence-gathering, the agency relied increasingly on covert actions, such as the midnight assaults by angry exiles willing to return to Cuba in small armed groups, hoping that might be enough to overturn Castro's iron grip on their homeland. In these early skirmishes, they were often shot or captured by Fidel's security forces. More than twenty men, including three Americans, were executed for counter-revolutionary activities.

By mid-1960, CIA Director Allen Dulles and his top deputy Richard Bissell came up with a different top-secret strategy for Cuba, demanded by that old warhorse Dwight D. Eisenhower in the twilight of his presidency. Ike wanted results, not more failure. The agency had "received a thorough education in the difficulty of establishing an effective guerilla organization," Bissell later wrote. "There had been a number of successful small infiltrations of supplies and people by boat, but generally these detachments were picked up within forty-eight hours and never heard from again."

As a result, Bissell and his boss Dulles called for a new two-pronged course of action: a full-fledged invasion by an army of Cuban exiles and an assassination of Castro himself. Historians later called it the most ambitious covert operation in US history.

Before the CIA men left the White House meeting where Cuba was discussed, Eisenhower reminded them of the secrecy surrounding their operation. Unfortunately, the CIA plans were not much of a secret in Miami's loquacious Little Havana. "Cubans don't know how to keep secrets," Bissell complained.

While still intent on a large-scale invasion, Dulles and Bissell increasingly focused on the much smaller, secret Castro assassination plan concocted by Johnny Roselli and Sam Giancana and their Cosa Nostra connections. If the Cuban exiles didn't eliminate Castro, perhaps these professional killers would. Whatever reservations there might be about using Mafioso were now gone.

"I am quite certain he [Shef Edwards] said, 'This has the approval of the DCI [Director of Central Intelligence],'" recalled O'Connell, the agency's handler relaying the lethal go-ahead plans from headquarters to middle-man, Bob Maheu.

For now in 1960, the CIA's best hope of eliminating Castro—at least until a full-out attack could be launched on the island of Cuba—seemed an alliance with the two mobsters.

Although he liked the Fontainebleau as his headquarters, Johnny Roselli realized most efforts to get rid of Castro were taking place outside of Miami Beach, in the small Cuban neighborhoods surrounding the city or along the Florida Keys.

While Spanish was the native tongue of Cubans, many exiles understood Johnny's streetwise English. At first, Roselli claimed he was "a Wall Street guy out for Castro." He used favorite aliases, such as "John Rawlston" and "J. A. Rollins," and didn't reveal his status as a US-sanctioned assassin. As he slowly learned, these daring young freedom fighters also thought of themselves as patriots. Many who ventured into Cuba were never seen again.

"They would lose men there [inside Cuba] but I would not know who they were, and they would never supply me with the names," recalled Roselli about these secret exile raids launched from Florida. "They were killed or captured and shot at sunrise, or whatever method he [Castro] used at the time."

In Miami, CIA handler Jim O'Connell spent more time than he anticipated helping Roselli with his Castro plans. Their cutout, Bob Maheu, was an early no-show. Despite being paid by the agency for his services, Maheu had returned temporarily to Los Angeles to deal with his other master, Howard Hughes.

Maheu promised to come back after a short absence. His flim-flammery, playing both sides against the middle, was clearly on display. Before he left, Maheu gave Johnny a confidential CIA telephone number for O'Connell in Washington, just in case he needed it. But the agency's security chief, Shef Edwards, instructed O'Connell to remain in Miami as a "babysitter" for Roselli, until their middleman returned.

"I was sort of holding Roselli's hand," said O'Connell. He recalled Maheu was "getting an awful lot of static from Hughes, who couldn't understand why he was spending so much time in Miami."

Luckily, the staid CIA handler and the hip mobster got along without Maheu. Roselli, always well dressed, teased O'Connell that he needed a wardrobe makeover for their new assignment. The big burly Irishman didn't fit in with the colored pastels and sharply-fitting clothes of Miami.

On a lark, Johnny convinced the CIA spy to go shopping at a downtown mall containing one of Roselli's favorite haberdasheries.

"To humor him I went along" to the store, O'Connell recalled. Johnny bought him a "very fancy silk shirt." Several haberdashery employees knew Roselli and were glad to see him.

The CIA handler soon found out the other reason for their visit.

Toward the rear of the store, O'Connell followed along as Roselli entered through a door into a large, lavishly-appointed backroom that "looked like a club of some sort." Instead of clothing supplies, as O'Connell expected, he discovered a group of older men actively engaged in some gambling activity, most likely bolita.

As they passed through, Johnny introduced several of the men by their first names. Each greeted Roselli and then went about their business. "They were just a sea of faces as far as I was concerned," O'Connell said.

After they left, Roselli reminded his CIA handler of the tanned leather-skinned man with green eyes and dark horn-rimmed glasses sitting in a specific place in the haberdashery's fancy backroom. O'Connell vaguely recognized the weathered face and green eyes.

"That's Joe, our courier," Johnny said. He identified him as "Joe Pecora," an alias used by Santo Trafficante Jr.

Roselli provided no further clues about the stranger.

Unimpressed, O'Connell kept walking away. It wasn't until years later that he realized the importance of Trafficante to the CIA's covert mission and to the fate of Roselli and Giancana.

CHAPTER 12:

BOLITA DREAMS

Bolita, the Spanish term for "little ball," helped build Santo Trafficante's organized crime kingdom in Florida.

A game of chance, Bolita customers usually bet on what winner would be plucked from a bag of a hundred small numbered balls. Like the illegal policy rackets up north, Bolita appealed traditionally to hard-working, low-income workers, many of whom migrated from Cuba.

Found in Latin saloons and behind storefronts, the game was easily rigged. Cheating abounded. But Bolita remained popular and, through bribes to police, out in the open in Miami and Tampa.

"The cops played Bolita and so did priests," recalled Trafficante's longtime attorney Frank Ragano. "It was a way of life in Tampa, and entertainment, and almost no one thought there was anything wrong in the Bolita operators making money out of the game."

For decades, Bolita provided a huge and steady source of income for the Mafia family first run by Trafficante's father and later inherited by his ambitious namesake son. By the 1950s, the junior Trafficante raked in "more than a million" annually from bolita.

As a top Mafia don in Florida, Santo Trafficante Jr. traded in gambling, racketeering, extortion, prostitution, and drugs. Though he appeared conservative in manner and appearance, a closer look showed Santo preferred hand-tailored suits, ate at Miami's best restaurants, and paid with hundred dollar bills. Those wishing to do business in his organized crime universe were told to "see the man with the green eyes."

Trafficante had plenty of blood on his hands, including a likely role in Anastasia's Manhattan barbershop murder. In 1953, when an old rival tried to kill Trafficante and push him out of the Bolita market, retribution came swiftly. The rival's throat was slit. His wife found his dead body inside their Tampa home. No one was ever charged.

That same year, Trafficante bought an interest in the Sans Souci, one of Havana's top casino nightclubs, where he'd become associates with Sam Giancana and Johnny Roselli.

Law-enforcement officials suspected Trafficante—though sympathetic to Cuban refugees in Miami—played both sides with Castro. Some wondered if Trafficante might be a double agent, taking advantage of Cold War tensions for his own profit.

"Fidel Castro has operatives in Tampa and Miami making heavy Bolita bets with Santo Trafficante Jr.'s organization," warned a Federal Bureau of Narcotics report.

But publicly, Trafficante showed the customary antipathy toward Castro. After the Havana casinos were closed and he spent time in a Cuban jail, Trafficante appeared bitter toward the Cuban dictator. When approached by his two fellow mobsters, Roselli and Giancana, with their murder scheme, Trafficante reacted favorably. Even if he had mixed feelings, he played along as a patriot waving the flag.

"At the time I think that it [the assassination plan] was a good thing because he [Castro] had established a communistic base 90 miles from the United States," Trafficante later testified. "And being that the Government of the United States wanted it done, I'd go along with it, the same thing as a war. I figured it was like a war."

Despite what Roselli told the CIA, Trafficante was more than a mere "courier" in their plan. At age forty-six, Santo had spent much of his life in Havana, travelling back and forth from his Tampa home base. He spoke Spanish fluently and knew many friends and former casino employees still living in Cuba.

"Santo Trafficante Jr. was perhaps the most important of the three [mobsters], for it was his men, both in Miami and Havana, who were supposed to carry out the murder," George Crile III later observed in the *Washington Post*. "He [Trafficante] had built a large organization there and still had a number of associates in Castro's Havana. Moreover, his professional experience made him ideally suited for assassination work."

With millions at stake in the narcotics trade, Trafficante remained poker-faced and ever-watchful. Trafficante's style was different from the two mobsters from the North. He wasn't as blustery as Giancana from the Windy City, nor a smooth glad-hander as Roselli perfected in Hollywood and Vegas.

Despite his underworld training, Trafficante claimed it didn't seem odd that a Mafiosi like Roselli was cooperating with the US government, working as an undercover spy with a go-between like Robert Maheu.

"I don't know why—it didn't seem strange at all," Trafficante said of Roselli. "I think he was a fellow that, if he told you something, he wasn't going to lie. I thought he was a very classy individual . . . . I took it that that meant that him and Mr. Maheu trusted me enough to want to do something for the country."

Though Santo's patriotic motives were hardly pure, his utility as an assassin was never in doubt.

Within a short time, Trafficante excited his mob partners—and their CIA overseers in Washington—by saying he could contact a well-placed spy in Havana with access to the highest reaches of Cuba's government. And if given the right opportunity, this mole was willing to poison Castro.

An old dull-looking Chevrolet car pulled up to the hotel where Roselli and Robert Maheu were staying in October 1960. After several weeks away, Maheu had finally returned to Miami, glad to be back after tending to Howard Hughes in Los Angeles. The two men climbed into the Chevy and were driven away to an important meeting.

FBI agents, keeping an eye on gangsters at the Fontainebleau, apparently had no idea of Johnny's sudden departure. The hotel wasn't helpful either when the G-men asked about the whereabouts of guest Sam Giancana. Its manager "volunteered no information and answered all questions tersely with no elaboration," a FBI memo recounted. "He advised that it was not hotel policy to make records available to law enforcement in the absence of a subpoena."

Driving the old Chevy was its owner, Santo Trafficante. He preferred more modest vehicles than the flashy cars used by Roselli and Giancana, who liked to be seen in a Cadillac. Trafficante and his passengers rode across the Venetian Causeway, connecting Miami Beach to the mainland, only a few miles from the Fontainebleau.

During his time away, Maheu had informed the CIA of the two mobsters' plans to poison Castro, rather than use noisy firearms. The agency didn't flinch. The killing methods really didn't matter to the CIA as long as the deed was done.

"Hell, we would not care if they went to the devil himself," Maheu laughed, summarizing the Agency's reaction. "This thing has got to happen."

Maheu looked forward to his secret meeting with top Cuban exiles in Miami, especially a man later given the codename "Mr. Y." The CIA had high expectations for this meeting, though they ordered Jim O'Connell, the agency's handler, not to join this gathering. If murder and other crimes were to be discussed, it was better that the government's man not be involved directly. Instead Maheu would be the CIA's representative at this meeting, just as Roselli represented Giancana who was out of town and presumably in Chicago running the Outfit's business.

During the car ride, Trafficante didn't discuss much. Privately, he'd chatted already with Sam and Johnny about their intentions to kill Castro. Trafficante decided there was no need for small talk with Maheu.

But with Santo as his "interpreter," Roselli had great confidence in Trafficante's ability to handle sensitive matters with the Cuban exiles. "I spoke the language, he didn't, and he had to deal with Cuban people," Trafficante later said of Roselli. "I thought he figured he could trust me."

The car arrived at the Miami home of Tony Varona, the former Cuban prime minister and a leader of the anti-Castro movement. Short, squatty, and pugnacious, Varona was an outspoken critic of the Communist rule in his homeland. He stressed his fledgling organization's need for more ammo, rifles, machine guns, and battle-ready boats.

Inside Varona's residence, several prominent Cuban exiles—eager to learn how the United States might get rid of Castro—listened intently to Maheu's rallying call. With his big bald head, protruding potbelly, white shirt and tie, Maheu looked like a typical suburban father figure featured on black-and-white American TV. Rather than honestly admit for whom he was working, Maheu claimed he was a businessman from New York.

"The subject was the destruction of Castro, the communists," Trafficante recalled. "Mr. Maheu told them he was going to get all the help he could get."

At Varona's home, Roselli and Maheu met the mysterious figure recommended by Trafficante. His name was Rafael "Macho" Gener, a Cuban memorable for his reddish hair. Gener first met Trafficante while working at the mob-run casinos in Havana. Gener rented an apartment from him there. When Trafficante was held in a Cuban detention center for four months following Castro's takeover, Gener helped him get free. Trafficante felt a debt of gratitude to Gener. He willingly vouched for him when Roselli wondered whether Gener could be trusted to help carry out their plan.

Roselli asked "if I knew about him, knew what kind of man he was," Trafficante recalled about Gener. "I told him I thought he was a good man, he was against Castro anyhow, and that is about it."

The meeting at Varona's home lasted for a few hours. But the CIA's scheme to poison Castro wasn't discussed directly.

Instead that discussion occurred shortly afterwards, at the home of another top Cuban exile leader—Jose Aleman. This chubby-faced son of a former top Cuban official had lost a fortune in Cuban investments when Castro's Communist regime came to power. Roselli and Maheu traveled again with Trafficante to this meeting at Aleman's home. And once more, Santo provided the Spanish-English translation.

Both the Florida Mafia don and Gener seemed comfortable with Aleman, whom they had known for years back in Havana. In the hush-hush lexicon of CIA memos, Aleman would be referred to as "Mr. X" while Gener was known as "Mr. Y."

During this meeting, the specifics of the Castro poisoning scheme were thoroughly reviewed and considered. Under the plan, Gener would secretly transport lethal pills to Cuba and get them into the hands of Juan Orta Cordova, a disaffected official in Castro's government. Orta was willing to do the job—slip the CIA-prepared poisons into the Cuban leader's food—as soon as possible, Gener assured.

Maheu promised the CIA's secret spy lab in Washington would supply the pills. Undoubtedly, Trafficante's mention of a US bounty of $150,000 also sweetened the plot for these desperate Cuban exiles.

Given the shared hatred for Castro in Aleman's home that day, it seemed the fatal moment would arrive very soon. Aleman owned a Miami hotel where he allowed many of his poor fellow exiles to stay, and vowed to commit his remaining funds to Castro's ouster. But Aleman didn't tell his guests all his secrets.

Certainly they didn't know Aleman was an informant for the FBI. Aleman provided information about Trafficante's narcotics and bolita operations as well as about his fellow expatriates from Havana. As a FBI memo explained: "Informant [Aleman], who is a Cuban exile, has furnished extremely valuable information regarding criminal activities of the Cubans in exile here in Miami."

The CIA also apparently didn't know much about Trafficante's hidden motives. A FBI missive later sent to the agency pointed to Trafficante and warned that "efforts were being made by U.S. racketeers to finance anti-Castro activities in hopes of securing gambling, prostitution, and dope monopolies in Cuba in the event Castro was overthrown."

Trafficante apparently didn't realize Aleman—the man he vouched for with Roselli—was informing on him to the feds. A subsequent FBI memo said Trafficante told Aleman he had "clients who wanted to do away with Castro and that they would pay big money for the job." Aleman was "very receptive," it said, because the American bounty would mean he'd "be able to buy his own ships, arms and communications equipment." But FBI officials still knew little about the CIA's intentions.

Ironically, as the conspirators left Aleman's home after their meeting, all agreed the success of the Castro killing depended on secrecy and a little bit of luck. The poison plan with "Macho" Gener and Juan Orta would take many more weeks of preparation and probably not happen until a new US president took office in early 1961.

How much confidentiality would remain with this assassination plan was anyone's guess. In Miami, plenty of Castro spies and double agents were eager to learn such a secret.

Roselli's trusted interpreter, Trafficante—a Mafioso with seemingly no other agenda—assured Johnny not to worry. The CIA's middleman Maheu didn't detect a rat, certainly not one who spoke a language other than his native English. These would-be assassins needed to wait patiently for the CIA's lab to come up with foolproof poison pills and for the agency higher-ups to give a final green light.

In the meantime, Sam Giancana went ahead with his own plans to kill Castro. He wasn't waiting for anyone's permission.

CHAPTER 13:

LIE DETECTORS

Inside the top-floor restaurant of a Los Angeles high-rise building, several stories above Wilshire Boulevard, Johnny Roselli broke bread with his old friend, hitman Jimmy "The Weasel" Fratianno, fresh from his prison release.

For a time in fall 1960, Roselli returned from Florida to his regular gangster life on the West Coast. He wanted to keep an eye on the thriving gambling business in Vegas, and to catch up on his own private affairs in Hollywood. Fratianno, beaten down from his years behind bars, marveled at his friend's good fortune. He noticed Roselli seemed most enthusiastic about his activities in Miami.

"I've got a little more than luck going for me," explained Roselli, looking tanned and fit. "You know, something came up, and—if it works out—we'll have the fucking government by the ass."

With little prompting, Roselli revealed how he, Sam Giancana, and Santo Traffi-cante Jr. had been recruited into the CIA's plan to kill Cuba's leader. "The government wants us to clip Fidel Castro," he said. "What do you think of that?"

Fratianno, a Mafia "made" man like Roselli, seemed more worried than pleased. Didn't this violate the rules of the Mafia's national commission? The Weasel asked if they had the commission's permission to work with government officials on this assassination conspiracy.

"Fuck the commission," Roselli snapped. "Look, Sam's on the commission, he's taken full responsibility. I cleared it with him. So he tells Santo what he wants, Santo's in the clear. Now, if we don't pull it off, nobody's the wiser. If we do, then we've got the power . . . If somebody gets in trouble and they want a favor, we can get it for them. You understand?"

Trading favors with the government was always the main consideration for both Giancana and Roselli. From the outset, Sam went along willingly with the CIA men and their wild scheme against Castro for this purpose. Roselli told Maheu that Sam was his "backup," as if playing some secondary role.

But in fact, as Johnny's Mafia boss in Chicago, Giancana launched his own separate effort to eliminate the foreign leader. He did it without the need for CIA approval, Cuban exile cooperation, or concern for Cold War foreign policy. And best of all, Giancana's selected assassin, Richard Cain—an American who spoke Spanish—was someone he had personally trained and trusted like a son.

Cain, a Chicago police officer with an apt surname, soon became Giancana's secret weapon. A cocky fireplug of a man with curly slicked-back hair, Cain started his law-enforcement career in a dubious but telling way. He bribed a recruiting captain to ignore the five-foot nine-inch height restriction for his police job. Fond of exaggerating his own exploits, Cain was enamored by wiseguys he met on the street. Soon Cain became a "bagman" for Giancana, paying off other cops and politicians. In return, Sam matched his police salary.

Cain was a near perfect blend of detective skills and criminality. In 1960, Cain resigned from the police force after one suspect in his care was allegedly murdered. While on furlough, Cain also was arrested for electronically eavesdropping on the city's Commissioner of Investigation, though that case went nowhere.

Eventually, Cain started a security firm in midtown Chicago called Accurate Laboratories. It featured his unique talents as a wire tapper, lie-detector operator, and the ability to write and speak in Spanish. His business card touted *"Investigations, Guard Services, Undercover Operatives and Polygraph Examinations."*

Cain's odd jobs included tasks for the CIA. "The way he told it—which was vaguely—he worked with the Central Intelligence Agency training Cubans for the Bay of Pigs invasion and worked for the State Department in tracing the flow of American money into Communist hands," the *Chicago Tribune* later reported.

In October 1960, soon after Giancana and Roselli met with CIA operatives, Cain applied for a passport to visit the Caribbean from Miami. Sam gave him sources in Havana and Mexico City to rely on. While in Miami, Cain provided illegal bugging equipment for Cuban exiles running their own spy operations. He also visited a CIA office in Chicago and offered to brief them on his "foreign ventures." Congressional investigators later suggested this agency visit was "a practice Giancana may have promoted in an effort to gain possible leverage."

Cain, once a crooked local cop, now became an international spy. With information from his listening devices, Cain warned the CIA about double agents working for Castro in Florida and how they'd infiltrated the anti-Castro opposition groups. For the next three years, he would share sensitive information with the CIA. Yet his primary loyalty to Giancana never wavered. Those who later traced Cain's activities concluded he was a lone wolf, answering to Chicago more than Washington.

"Several of Cain's activities during the fall of 1960, together with his past experience, support the proposition that if Giancana was involved in any Cuban affairs, specifically an assassination of Castro independent of the CIA plot, he would have recruited Cain to assist him," a House of Representatives panel concluded.

Michael Cain, his half-brother and later biographer, was even more definitive. "Dick Cain was a logical person for Sam to turn to; he was fluent in Spanish and he knew his way around Cuba," he wrote in 2007. "This was a golden opportunity for Dick. It had all the elements of an activity that could hold his interest. It was dangerous, it involved espionage, and it was potentially lucrative."

That fall in 1960, presumably with the help of Roselli, Cain met with Cuban exile leader Tony Varona in Miami. Under the cover of darkness, Cain somehow managed to sneak into Cuba more than once. On one trip, he traveled as a couple with an unidentified woman, their intent to poison Castro.

Congressional investigators later suggested the woman was "a mistress of Castro," recruited by Trafficante "because of his numerous contacts in the Cuban gambling and prostitution circles." Those plotting against Fidel hoped to take advantage of his wandering eye. During Castro's lifetime—unknown to his admiring public but not his two wives—the tall charismatic leader had numerous affairs and mistresses.

Though Cain and this particular mistress arrived safely inside Cuba, their assassination attempt failed. The two spies couldn't figure a feasible way to plant the toxic tablets somewhere, so the Cuban leader might ingest them. Cain claimed to have gotten as close as Castro's office, as he later told his family in a fanciful account.

In Cain's version, his female spy companion was captured and later shot. But heroically, he managed to get away in a narrow escape.

During that time, a similar apocryphal story emerged about Marita Lorenz, a former Castro mistress who had acted as a CIA spy against her ex-lover.

Lorenz first met the Cuban leader in 1959 on her wealthy German father's large ship, which had pulled into Havana Harbor for a visit. Lorenz's family invited Castro aboard as a dinner guest. With her striking eyes, curly black hair, and girlish figure, Marita immediately captured Fidel's attention.

Castro regaled her family with revolutionary stories. He recounted his success as a guerilla fighter in the Sierra Maestra, the mountain range where Castro formed the 26th of July Movement, the brigade that overthrew Batista. Since then, he had transformed himself from a liberating man of the people into a self-absorbed autocrat boasting of his power. Gazing out at Havana's shoreline from the boat, Fidel raised his arms up and proclaimed, "I am Cuba."

Marita fell in love with the charismatic dictator. Castro convinced the young woman to stay in Cuba. She moved into a Havana apartment with him and later became pregnant, though no child was ever born. "Because of his [Castro's] reaction to the pregnancy, she turned against him," surmised a government memo about her.

FBI records say Lorenz first met Johnny Roselli in 1959 at the Riviera Hotel in Havana, the splendid resort where Giancana once owned an interest along with Meyer Lansky and other American gangsters. At the time, Marita was a faithful member of the 26th of July Movement. But ultimately, Marita would leave Havana, feeling bitter like so many refugees from Castro's dystopia.

After she fled to Miami, Lorenz was cultivated as a "honeytrap" double agent by another enigmatic figure, Frank Fiorini. He was later better known as Frank Sturgis, one of the convicted burglars and wire tappers in the 1972 Watergate break-in. Fiorini "was an amazing individual who could and did pop up in the strangest places when you least expected him," recalled fellow Watergate conspirator, E. Howard Hunt, then working for the CIA in Miami.

Unlike Lorenz, Fiorini was attracted to Castro for money rather than love. As an American mercenary during the early days of Castro's guerilla campaign, Fiorini trained Cuban soldiers and shipped loads of weapons as a gunrunner from Miami. With a square jaw and broad shoulders, Fiorini had the determined look of a middle linebacker. Once in power, Fidel named him gambling czar as a reward. In this role, Fiorini became friendly with Trafficante and other casino owners before their ouster.

But when Castro declared himself a Communist, Fiorini, feeling betrayed, became a CIA informant. Eventually, Castro's G-2 intelligence agents learned of his disloyalty. Fearing for his life, Fiorini returned to Miami, where he became active in the anti-Castro resistance. Undoubtedly, Fiorini heard about the money to be made as an assassin. Along with the CIA's offers, there were rumors of a one million dollar bounty for Castro's demise by Meyer Lansky and other former mob casino owners.

After meeting Marita in Miami, Fiorini realized her value as a double agent. "She was pure gold," he said. "And I cultivated her until she was ready to poison Castro." Eventually, he convinced her to see Castro again in Havana. She'd pose as a lover seeking reconciliation while actually pursuing Fidel's death as an assassin. If she didn't kill Castro first, Fiorini threatened, the dictator's Communist spies floating around Florida would take her out.

During this time, Marita was introduced to other would-be Castro assassins. "I met (Johnny) Roselli at the Fontainebleau (Hotel)," Lorenz later told *Vanity Fair* magazine. "He was a nice, flashy guy who treated women nicer than the guys I worked with—because he was Italian. He worked for Sam Giancana and they worked with us because the mob guys hated Fidel because of him closing the casinos."

By January 1960, Marita arrived at the Hotel Habana Libre, the new name for the old Hilton, and went to her suite to await Fidel's arrival. She'd visited Havana a few weeks earlier as a way of warming up Castro and lowering his defenses.

Before she left Miami, Fiorini provided two poison pills prepared by the CIA. Lorenz hid them in a jar of cold cream. But when she opened the jar in her Havana suite's bathroom, she discovered the pills had dissolved accidently.

"I couldn't find the capsules. They had melted," she recalled. "It was like an omen. . . . I thought, 'To hell with it. Let history take its course.'"

When Castro entered the room, he sensed her unease. He asked why she had left so quickly with her first visit. Then he put his finger on it.

"Are you running around with those counter-revolutionaries in Miami?" he demanded.

Marita tried to remain calm but her nervousness showed too much. She said yes.

Castro, playing with his cigar, leaned back onto the bed.

"Did you come here to kill me?" he asked.

Marita stood near the bed, not in it.

"Yes, I wanted to see you," she replied.

"Do you work for the CIA?" he prodded further.

"Not really," she said. "I work for myself."

According to Lorenz, the tired Cuban leader rolled over, pulled out his .45- caliber revolver, and gave it to her. If she wanted to kill him, now was her chance.

Thoroughly disarmed by their exchange, Lorenz instead opened the chamber and removed the bullets.

"He didn't flinch," Lorenz later recalled. "He was so sure of me. We made love."

The next day, she returned to Miami, one of many unsuccessful attempts to assassinate Castro and undermine his government.

CHAPTER 14:

LISTENING DEVICES

For Bob Maheu, a shrewd judge of human nature, understanding Sam Giancana's psyche was far more difficult than his pal Johnny Rosclli's. Whereas Roselli displayed an affable, even-temperedness, Giancana often flashed various sides of his impatient, volatile personality.

One afternoon, while relaxing around the Fontainebleau's pool, Maheu watched Giancana suddenly become infuriated with a young wise guy trying to impress with his toughness. Until this point, Maheu had never seen Giancana use a foul word.

"Without even looking at the punk, Giancana grabbed his necktie and yanked him close," Maheu recalled.

Giancana stared menacingly at this junior hoodlum.

"I eat little boys like you for breakfast," he growled. "Get your ass out of here before I get hungry." Maheu realized this wasn't gangster movie dialect but apparently the real way Sam talked on Chicago's streets.

Another time in the Fontainebleau's nightclub, Maheu watched Giancana become blue and sentimental. Whenever he heard the Sinatra song, "You're Nobody 'Til Somebody Loves You"—Sam's eyes filled with tears. Clearly, the song reminded him of someone special. When Maheu asked about it, Giancana brushed his emotions away.

"Someday I'll explain it to you . . . " he mumbled.

Sam never did.

Florida was the place where his beloved wife Angeline had died years earlier. Certain sentimental moments wouldn't allow Sam to forget her memory. For many months after Angeline's death, Sam left her clothes in their closets and dressers, as if she might come home again.

"He could not bring himself to get rid of anything that was hers," remembered his oldest daughter Antoinette. "He was constantly morose. He traveled frequently back and forth to Florida because that was where Momma died . . . For a time I really feared for him."

Giancana's life as a middle-aged man, now with married daughters on their own, seemed empty, despite the number of showgirls and easy women he met with Johnny in Vegas. He seemed a man lost without a wife to come home to, no matter how often he might roam. Hanging out with Johnny—so different in his approach to women— was part of his search. Perhaps Sam felt he might discover, with Roselli's help, the answer to the old Freudian question, "What does a woman want?" or some Ponce de Leon fountain of youth through frequent affairs.

His dalliance in 1960 with Judy Campbell seemed calculated and insincere, more a chance to compromise a politician than something heartfelt. Yet that same year, in the smoke-filled casinos of Las Vegas, Sam found the next idyllic love of his life— Phyllis McGuire, a beautiful nationally-known entertainer. He would nickname her "Wonderful."

A minister's daughter, Phyllis appeared like a talented real-life Barbie doll, with her blonde bouffant hairdo and innocent demeanor. On America's television screens, she and her two sisters—the singing McGuire Sisters—projected a wholesome image. They appeared often on *The Ed Sullivan Show,* crooning their hits "Sincerely" and "Sugartime" in perfect harmony.

To Sam, Phyllis was a woman he could adore—and aspire to—just as he once did with Angeline. "He had been running around with other women since Momma's death, but none had held a strong attraction for him, at least one that lasted," Antoinette recalled. "Phyllis was different."

Their introduction was hardly innocent. Like other entertainers who gambled while in Vegas, Phyllis ran up a large casino debt at the Desert Inn, where the McGuire sisters were appearing. Sam was enamored by McGuire's prettiness and "damsel in distress" predicament. He impressed her greatly by telling Moe Dalitz, manager of the Desert Inn, to "eat" the expense. Sam exerted his clout as boss of the Chicago mob, which regularly shared in the "skim" of revenue from mob-controlled casinos like the Desert Inn.

"When I met him I did not know who he was," said McGuire, who'd suffered a bitter divorce two years earlier. "I didn't find out until sometime later who he was. And by then, I was already in love."

Sam lavished gifts and jewelry on McGuire. Her friends warned Phyllis that this older man killed people for a living. She wasn't bothered a bit.

"I didn't know what they were talking about," McGuire recalled. "I just knew that I liked the man. His wife had passed away and he was very nice to me. And if he had done all those things they said he did, I wondered why in God's name he was on the street and not in jail."

Although the couple spent time together in Las Vegas and New York, they were often apart. Sam never discussed his business affairs, including his flights to Miami on a secret CIA mission. "He was very protective of my not being involved with what-ever he was doing," McGuire recalled. "I sometimes wonder if I hadn't been so inno-cent if he would have loved me as much. Maybe that was one thing that attracted him to me, I don't know."

While in Miami to help organize the Castro assassination attempt, Sam talked constantly on the phone with Phyllis, who was in Las Vegas. He became increasingly jealous and possessive. The McGuire Sisters were appearing with comedian Dan Rowan. Sam sensed Phyllis might be attracted to the handsome and suave comedian (later a co-star of TV's *Laugh-In*). Impulsively, Giancana wanted to jump on a plane to Vegas right away and confront Rowan.

Maheu panicked when Giancana announced his plans to depart Miami. The CIA cutout pleaded for him to stay. With the agency's assassination plans in midstream in October 1960, "we didn't want him to leave," recalls Maheu. "We were right in the thick of things."

Giancana's power and influence were vital, especially in convincing fellow Mafioso Trafficante to work with the Spanish-speaking Cuban exiles. Sam's sudden departure would only aggravate delays. The Agency's lab was taking longer than expected to prepare improved poison pills for "Macho" Gener to hand off to Juan Orta. The agency officials wanted lethal pills *guaranteed* to contaminate Castro's food, not melt or dissolve as Marita Lorenz claimed hers did in a cold cream jar.

Friends like Johnny Roselli knew it wasn't healthy when Sam became jealous. They didn't want the comedian Rowan to wind up like poor Angelo Fasel. This twenty-eight-year-old Chicago bank robber was secretly courting another Giancana girlfriend who announced her intention to marry Fasel. Sam warned Fasel in July 1960 to stop seeing her, according to FBI records. Soon Fasel "disappeared," never to be seen again. The same FBI memo, recounting this unsolved apparent murder, also warned Giancana had "a vicious temperament" and reportedly carried a gun.

Unsure what to do, Maheu contacted his CIA handler Jim O'Connell about Giancana's disruptive demands for help in spying on his girlfriend's suspected lover. "I got a call from Bob Maheu and he said that Giancana was quite upset because he heard that his girl friend—at the time Phyllis McGuire of the McGuire sisters—was having an affair with Dan Rowan," recalled O'Connell. "[Maheu said] if I don't do it, he is going to take off and he is going to go back and straighten this whole thing out himself in Las Vegas."

O'Connell then went up the chain of command, asking the agency's head of security, Sheffield Edwards, what they should do.

"Well, can Bob [Maheu] get somebody to do it?" Edwards asked. He indicated the CIA was for any black bag job necessary to keep the Mafia boss happy and their assassination juggernaut on track.

After much ado, Maheu convinced the mob boss to remain in Miami by making an outlandish promise. He agreed the CIA would hire private detectives to go to Las Vegas, where they'd install electronic listening devices in Rowan's hotel room and check whether the Phyllis McGuire rumor was even true. "Giancana felt that he was being cuckolded by Rowan and took advantage, in his jealousy, of his new and novel relationship with the CIA," a government investigator later surmised.

Johnny Roselli helped broker the deal. In a slight twist, he suggested the secret move was necessary to make sure McGuire hadn't mentioned the top-secret Castro plot to the comedian. Of course, everyone knew the real reason. They needed to assure Sam that his princess-like "Wonderful" hadn't been unfaithful (even though Sam suffered no such moral constraints himself).

"He (Maheu) was doing it to see if any loose conversation was going on," Roselli later explained about the reason for the CIA approval. "The other was to do him (Giancana) a favor."

Using the CIA's money, Maheu first hired a friendly Miami private detective, Ed DuBois, to follow Rowan and keep an eye out for Phyllis. Instead DuBois farmed out the job to another private eye named Arthur J. Balletti. What should have been an easy no-brainer spy operation soon became a mindless one. As O'Connell ruefully recalled, "It became like a Keystone [Kops] comedy from there on in."

At the Riviera in Las Vegas, Balletti waited for comedian Rowan to leave his hotel room before entering with an unidentified accomplice. The funnyman was blissfully unaware of his mortal danger from Giancana, the Mafia brute. Somehow, though, Balletti misunderstood his marching orders. The freelance private eye was supposed to place a hidden microphone inside Rowan's suite to hear what was going on. Instead he and his accomplice added a tap to the comedian's phone that could record telephone conversation but no sounds of passion in the bedroom.

"That was the first mistake," Maheu recalled. "Guys don't make phone calls when they're making love."

Impulsively, Balletti abandoned his eavesdropping work midway to go hear a performer at the hotel's club. He left his equipment in Rowan's room. A maid soon discovered the wiretapping tools and alerted hotel security. They called the Las Vegas County sheriff's office, which confiscated the transmitters, receivers, Minox cameras, and several professional lockpicks. Balletti was charged with a felony but his accomplice, identified only as "J. W. Harrison," managed to escape arrest.

Returning to his room, Rowan was stunned to learn about the break-in and of the many secrets surrounding McGuire, the woman he hoped to marry. "I was in love with her—and had absolutely no inkling she was also involved with Sam Giancana," Rowan recalled. "Our relationship ended after I found my hotel room ransacked."

No fool, Rowan decided not to press charges against Balletti and informed McGuire he could no longer see her.

"Phyllis, if someone that powerful is after you, I don't stand a chance," the comedian told her. "I'll be in the bottom of Lake Mead if I don't cool this."

When he heard this comical outcome to the Rowan escapade, Sam broke out in laughter with Roselli.

"I remember his expression, smoking a cigar," Johnny recalled. "He almost swallowed [his cigar] laughing about it."

Some observers later viewed Giancana's reaction as pure cynicism, that he cared only about CIA favors he could squeeze from this government folly. But the laughter also may have stemmed from Sam's macho sense of scaring away Rowan and amusement that "J. W. Harrison," the accomplice in this botched wiretapping, got away.

It was never clear who "Harrison" might be. Congressional investigators later suggested the accomplice may have been Richard Cain, Giancana's slippery associate so well-versed in wiretaps, polygraphs, and other hi-tech listening devices. FBI records showed Cain was in Miami when the Rowan scheme was hatched. As a Congressional report later stated, Sam's jealousy toward Phyllis McGuire "could have prompted Giancana to direct Maheu to use a person of Giancana's choice: Cain fit that role perfectly."

The wiretap fiasco threatened to draw attention to the CIA's secret assassination plot at a crucial moment. Hoping to contain the damage, Roselli arranged for a Las Vegas gambler friend to pay for Balletti's bail. The private eye quickly skipped town. But Roselli sensed the trouble wouldn't go away as fast.

Johnny was annoyed with the cavalier attitude of both his pal Giancana and Maheu who bungled the simple standard detective's task of checking on a cheating lover.

"I just blew my top, because had I known it [the wiretapping] ahead of time, I think I would have stopped them from doing it," explained Roselli. "It was a silly thing and I think maybe it would blow our cover—which it did, no question about it. Blowing every kind of cover I had tried to arrange to keep quiet."

As friends, Roselli knew the Chicago mob boss wasn't about to be lectured to, especially on a matter that involved his love life. But Johnny, usually so affable, made his annoyance known. "When I confronted him with that, and why this thing happened, he [Giancana] just smiles and walked away, and I was just mad enough to walk away from him," Roselli recalled. "The same with Bob Maheu."

The CIA's spymasters also were upset with Balletti's arrest but didn't do anything about it. All the way up the agency's hierarchy—from O'Connell and Shef Edwards to Richard Bissell and Allen Dulles—they weren't inclined to alert law-enforcement authorities or pursue the matter any further. As a rule, spooks never called the local cops, especially since the CIA's charter prohibited domestic spying.

However, the county sheriff's office in Las Vegas did care enough about the wiretap incident to refer it to the FBI. At first, Hoover's investigators had no idea what this strange wiretap break-in was all about, where it might lead.

But over the next several weeks, the FBI would launch an extensive probe, both in Las Vegas and Chicago, exposing some of the deepest secrets of this CIA-Mafia plan.

Johnny's hunch about lasting trouble was right.

CHAPTER 15:

A THOUSAND SPIES

"Above all, do not get into any trouble; for I suppose you know that, if anything happened to you, it would be of no use to talk of your mission. We should be obliged to know nothing about you, for ambassadors are the only avowed spies."

—INSTRUCTIONS TO FICTIONAL SPY AND FAMED LOVER
JACQUES CASANOVA, QUOTED IN ALLEN DULLES'S BOOK,
GREAT TRUE SPY STORIES

After several months, "Little Al" proved more valuable than a thousand spies. The hidden microphone, planted illegally in the downtown Chicago headquarters of Sam Giancana's Outfit, yielded a wealth of information for the FBI.

More than any snitch, "Little Al" opened the eyes of FBI chieftain J. Edgar Hoover to the Mafia's widespread criminality around the country.

One recorded conversation between Giancana and his senior consigliere Tony Accardo seemed like an encyclopedia of *La Cosa Nostra*. Sam explained what happened at a recent national commission meeting, identifying all the regional dons and their brewing vice.

"It is difficult to understand just how excited we were when we taped this conversation and then played it back, word for word, many times in order to gain the full impact of what was discussed," recalled William Roemer, a top Chicago agent on the FBI's aptly-named Top Hoodlum Squad.

"Little Al" was so successful that the FBI finally decided to go ahead and install a second bug in Giancana's suburban hangout called the Armory Lounge, a local bar and grill with a giant neon flashing sign in front.

The federal government's initial constitutional worries about illegal eavesdropping now gave way to more practical concerns. Chicago FBI agents fretted over how to place a hidden microphone in the Armory without getting caught. Most patrons were Giancana's gangland associates. They knew the awful penalty for talking to the feds.

With fellow hoodlums, Sam insisted on *omerta*, the Mafia's code of silence, and the grave importance of keeping their eyes open and lips sealed. "You see that fucking fish?" Giancana once barked at a nosy associate, calling attention to a swordfish trophy hanging from the wall. "If he'd kept his mouth shut he wouldn't have got caught."

Giancana's mob hideaway, not far from his home in Oak Park, was more isolated and protected than the Outfit's downtown headquarters. Though miles from the South Side slaughterhouses—and pungent odors that gave Chicago its title "hog butcher for the world"—this "command post" had a gritty industrial park appearance that compounded the grayness of winters and made sunny places like Vegas, Miami, and Havana so appealing.

While the Armory Lounge was used to greet visiting hoodlums and friendly entertainers like Sinatra, it also could be a fortress of paranoia. Through a window, Sam sometimes peered with binoculars at the empty parking across the street owned by the US Navy. He kept staring ahead, hoping to catch some spy watching him from the shadows. FBI records show Giancana "apparently feels this lot is being used continually for surveillance purposes of his activities."

Eventually, federal agents came up with a masterstroke of deception. They confronted the Lounge's night janitor with an FBI "wanted" poster of a suspect that looked vaguely like him. The G-men asked the janitor to come down to headquarters to clear up the matter. The janitor reluctantly agreed.

Arriving downtown, the agents asked the janitor to empty out his pockets before going off to another room to be fingerprinted. Over the next several minutes, while the janitor was rolling each inky finger onto a print card, an expert locksmith secretly made a copy of the Armory Lounge keys.

Soon after, in the wee hours before dawn, the FBI entered the Armory Lounge. They placed a large pineapple-shaped microphone behind a wall where Giancana kept an office. Then the agents strung a connecting wire down a wall to the basement and eventually outside, where a signal would be transmitted to the FBI.

The new listening device, nicknamed "Mo" for the Lounge's most prominent habitué, helped Roemer and the FBI sleuths learn of another startling and previously unknown mystery.

Along with conversations about the Mafia's national commission and deals with corrupt local politicians, the FBI heard Giancana discussing plans to kill Fidel Castro.

Hoover and his G-men had no idea of the CIA's top-secret assassination plan featuring the two Mafia hoodlums, Sam and Johnny, in prominent roles. Details from the listening devices, however, connected the dots to this puzzle for the FBI agents. As Roemer recalled, "Very soon we learned why Sam had been so knowledgeable about Cuba."

On October 18, 1960, Hoover alerted the CIA. His memo claimed Giancana knew all about a murder plan against a foreign leader, Fidel Castro. On its face, the claim seemed outlandish and, if successful, sure to cause an international incident. The FBI director based his report on "a source close to Giancana." Hoover didn't reveal to the CIA whether his source was a hidden microphone like "Little Al" or some secret informant.

But FBI records, released publicly decades later, show the first tip about the Castro murder plot apparently came from John W. Teeter, a businessman then married to Phyllis McGuire's sister, Christine. Privately, Teeter approached the bureau in July 1960 about the family's deep concerns that Phyllis had fallen under the sway of a gangster and couldn't be talked out of the troubling relationship.

"He [Teeter] remarked that Phyllis McGuire is a headstrong know-it-all type who is unable to be controlled in situations such as this" and is receptive to Sam's money and very expensive gifts, an FBI memo described. Apparently, Phyllis had no idea of her brother-in-law's cry for help to the feds.

Two months later, the stakes intensified. Teeter alerted the FBI that Giancana had shared details about a Castro assassination plot during dinner together in New York City. The McGuire Sisters were in town on business. The two couples—Sam and Phyllis, sister Christine and her husband John Teeter—gathered at an Italian restaurant. When the leisurely conversation turned to Cuba, Sam declared he had some inside information. At first, Phyllis and Christine expressed doubts, especially when Sam confidently claimed Castro would "be done away with very shortly."

Giancana wasn't deterred. As waiters and other customers swirled around them, he spelled out the killing scheme being launched in Florida. Stunningly to Teeter's ears, Sam used the specific term "assassin."

According to Giancana, he met with the would-be assassin on three separate occasions. The last visit took place on a boat docked outside the Fontainebleau Hotel in Miami Beach. Sam boasted that "everything had been perfected for the killing." Under the plan, the unknown assassin had arranged with a mystery "girl"—also not identified—to drop a poison pill into Castro's food or drink.

Acting on this tip, Hoover's warning to the CIA appeared urgent because Giancana "assured those present" that the Castro killing would take place in November 1960— only a few weeks away.

The bureau took swift action. Records show Hoover directed FBI agents to report immediately if Giancana flew to Miami, to monitor his long-distance telephone calls, and see whether he met with any "anti-Castro elements." Hoover also instructed agents in Florida to find out the "identity of the person who allegedly met with Giancana at a boat docked at Fontainebleau Hotel."

To protect Teeter's identity, the FBI instructed undercover agents to be "discreet so as not to jeopardize New York source." When conducting surveillance, Teeter warned, agents should remember that all three McGuire Sisters could "read lips from any distance" and were "expert" at it.

Who did Giancana have in mind in referring to Castro's "assassin"? Congressional investigators later suggested Richard Cain, the corrupt former Chicago cop under Sam's control, was working at that time with "a mistress of Castro to accomplish the deed." The unsuccessful Cain assassination plan was an independent Mafia enterprise, the investigators concluded, not the CIA's pending conspiracy.

That other poison plan brewing against Castro—the CIA's efforts with Juan Orta, orchestrated by the agency's cutout Maheu with the mob—was still months away, not launched until early 1961, because of delays in developing foolproof pills.

Unaware of the CIA's involvement with the Mafia, Hoover dispatched his October 1960 memo to America's intelligence agency and awaited a response. He repeated Giancana's boast that Castro was "to be done away with very shortly."

However, Hoover's missive landed with a proverbial thud on the desk of Richard Bissell, the second in command at CIA to director Allen Dulles. The overseer of the agency's anti-Castro campaign had no intention of stopping, regardless of the FBI director's warning.

"Hoover's rivalry with the CIA was one of long standing," observed CIA historian Thomas Powers. "This [memo] should have given Bissell pause, but he went ahead with the plan anyway, a fact which ought to be taken as tacit confirmation of the pressure Bissell felt to 'get rid of Castro.'"

Years later, Bissell's recollection was murky. But Bissell admitted he did share Hoover's warning memo with Shef Edward, the CIA's head of security. "I am sure I referred it to Mr. Edwards who was the individual in the Agency directly in charge of that liaison with Giancana," Bissell testified, "and I probably asked Mr. Edwards whether this represented a threat to the security of the whole relationship."

Little exists in declassified documents about the CIA's reaction to Hoover's warning. Apparently there was never a formal response to the FBI chief. In reality, the agency didn't want to draw attention to its ongoing use of the Mafia against Castro.

"If mobsters were bragging about knocking off Castro, Bissell could forget about his hopes of maintaining 'plausible deniability,'" wrote historian Evan Thomas. "Bissell had to try to plug the leak, but his agents blundered and drew the CIA in deeper."

To protect himself, Director of Security Edwards created a secret file about Roselli that he kept in his personal safe. This dossier was kept in a manner different than normal procedures for even the most secretive of US spies. According to a CIA memo released in 2017, Roselli's file was marked under "Project Johnny." Other documents referred to this "Johnny file" with Edwards's handwritten notation. It was given a number "667-270" but couldn't be found years later by other CIA officials looking for it. Clearly, Edwards and his CIA bosses were determined to keep "Project Johnny" under wraps as much as possible.

By November 1960, the FBI's investigation into Giancana's activities had turned into a double-headed monster. Gradually, investigators realized the bureau's probe into Castro assassination threats was somehow connected to its investigation of the Dan Rowan bugging in Las Vegas. And eventually, both inquiries led to Johnny Roselli, a major character in these schemes as well.

While the two gangsters practiced strict silence, their associates talked freely when pressed by the feds.

Weeks after the private eye Arthur Balletti was caught in Rowan's room, FBI agents in Miami interviewed Edward DuBois Jr., the detective who had subcontracted the Vegas job to him. A worried DuBois quickly pointed to Robert Maheu as his patron. "He [DuBois] said Maheu's operations often smack of the 'cloak and dagger' type of affair and that Maheu is very closed mouthed," FBI officials noted.

As a dutiful cutout, Maheu alerted his CIA handlers and, as a former FBI special agent, he also tried to get the bureau to stop sniffing around this very sensitive national security matter. Undeterred, the FBI traced Maheu's activities in Miami to the Kenilworth Hotel where he stayed and also paid the room fees for another individual who signed in as "J. A. Rollins." Maheu initially refused to identify Rollins—a name that FBI agents believed was an alias.

Hotel workers remembered "Rollins" as a handsome, middle-aged man who very much resembled Johnny Roselli. Eventually, the FBI checked the Kenilworth telephone records and found out that "Rollins" had made long-distance calls to Chicago and the Desert Inn in Las Vegas. At one point, FBI investigators thought "J. A. Rollins"—Maheu's comrade in Miami—might be the same person as "J. W. Harrison," the accomplice with Balletti in Las Vegas. But the timing and physical descriptions didn't match. Eventually, the FBI confirmed "Rollins" was Roselli in disguise.

Maheu's hopes of closing down the FBI probe as a professional courtesy—by hinting about the CIA's involvement—didn't go very far. As the investigative heat intensified, Maheu worried about getting in legal trouble. "It was obvious a criminal investigation had begun, and the potential for my arrest, along with Giancana's and Roselli's, certainly existed," Maheu recalled. So to his previous employer, the former G-man revealed much of the CIA's assassination scheme. He admitted being recruited in summer 1960 by the CIA for this highly sensitive mission. He explained the Rowan bugging grew out of concern that their top-secret work had been leaked accidentally to the comedian.

Then Maheu coughed up the names of Johnny and Sam. He said Shef Edwards asked him to recruit the Chicago mob boss because of his past gambling interests in Havana and that "the CIA believed that Giancana would still have sources and contacts in Cuba which could possibly be used by the CIA." Maheu also revealed Roselli's alias as "Rollins" at the Kenilworth and admitted the West Coast mobster was working with him for the CIA. When the FBI contacted the CIA's Edwards, he confirmed Maheu's account without much explanation.

For Giancana, the matter became personal when the FBI chased after his girlfriend Phyllis McGuire looking for answers. She dodged the agency for a while but finally agreed to be interviewed in New York. Phyllis said she had no idea about the plan to bug Rowan before it happened. Sam blew up when he learned of McGuire's inquisition by the feds.

At the same time, the FBI's investigative pressure on Sam and Johnny never let up. Agents closely followed Giancana's every step in Chicago and wherever he might land in other cities. The FBI also monitored Roselli's activities in Las Vegas and at his home in Los Angeles, where telephone records revealed many tantalizing clues about the two mobsters' circle of friends and associates.

Maheu tried to keep the Castro assassination plan moving ahead, without scaring away the two gangsters. One night while having dinner with Roselli, he noticed FBI agents were tailing them, but he didn't tell Johnny.

"The big problem was keeping the [FBI] surveillance a secret from Roselli and Giancana," Maheu recalled. "I was in a horrible position. Let's face it, they weren't neophytes. I presumed both could spot a tail a mile away. My credibility was on the line. As it turned out, I was lucky. Neither man suspected anything."

But that wouldn't last for long.

The FBI's desire to find out more—and the CIA's determination to keep much of it hidden from view—was part of an interagency squabble with no easy resolution. As Eisenhower prepared to leave the White House in November 1960, it wasn't clear if either Hoover or Dulles would remain in their jobs.

What to do with this highly sensitive information—especially the impending CIA plot to assassinate Fidel Castro—would have to wait for the next president to decide.

CHAPTER 16:

WHAT WOULD
JAMES BOND DO?

In America's 1960 presidential campaign, Cuba and its Communist leader Fidel Castro loomed as one of the crucial issues. Rumors of a pending invasion were rampant. But only a few knew of the CIA's top-secret plan for assassination by two mobsters—apparently not even the candidates themselves.

This disquieting fact left director Allen Dulles and others in the agency feeling quite vulnerable.

"Everyone had to face the reality of a possible change in political direction," recalled Richard Bissell, second-in-command to Dulles. "Eisenhower was leaving office after two terms, and depending on which of the candidates, Richard M. Nixon or John F. Kennedy, succeeded him, an entire modification of the Cuban operation and other covert activities might conceivably take place in the near future."

Bissell first briefed Nixon in March 1960 about the agency's covert Cuba operations—including use of "goon squads" paid to undermine Castro's supporters—but with no mention of impending assassination attempts. As Vice-President, Nixon was aware of the CIA's support and training of Cuban exiles for a future invasion. Dutifully, Nixon didn't mention this secret plan on the campaign trail.

In July 1960, after Kennedy became the Democratic nominee, Eisenhower directed the CIA to brief JFK on Cuba and other agency activities abroad. Dulles met personally with the candidate at the Kennedy summer home in Hyannis Port, Massachusetts. Both men remained cryptic about their discussion.

"It is not my practice to give interviews," Dulles told the press, as the two posed for photographs. He later minimized its significance: "I just told Kennedy what he could've read in the morning *Times*."

The *New York Times*, like others in the media, portrayed the meeting as cordial and introductory, as "this tour of Mr. Dulles's carefully concealed world." But in fact, the Hyannis Port meeting was part of Dulles's campaign to keep his job at the CIA. His behind-the-scenes courting of the Kennedys began years earlier and was far more extensive than most anyone knew, including Nixon.

Dulles focused his attention on Joseph P. Kennedy, the family patriarch. Years earlier, the two men had socialized at the Kennedys' winter home in Palm Beach Florida, where they shared several wealthy friends. In 1956, Old Joe served briefly on a US foreign intelligence advisory panel but came away unimpressed with the CIA. "I know this outfit and I wouldn't pay them a hundred bucks a week," he groused.

Aware of the FBI's bureaucratic rivalry with the CIA, Joe Kennedy suggested to J. Edgar Hoover in 1957 that the venerable spymaster Dulles wasn't as up-to-date as he ought to be. "Allen Dulles came down to visit Palm Beach and asked me to lunch with him yesterday," Kennedy wrote. "I asked him what he thought of [Hollywood actresses] Marilyn Monroe, Jayne Mansfield and Anita Ekberg. He said that he had never heard of the last two and then I asked him how he liked [popular singer] Perry Como and he asked me what he did."

The following year, Dulles met privately with the senior Kennedy at the family's Palm Beach estate and underlined his keen interest in remaining America's espionage chief. "He (Dulles) is very aware of the fact that Jack may be the next President," Joe wrote to a close confidant at the Vatican after the 1958 Dulles meeting, "and while he had always been very friendly to me, I think that he is more than ever anxious to please."

During several Florida sojourns in the mid-1950s—often to visit a mutual friend, oil millionaire Charles Wrightman—Dulles chatted at get-togethers with Joe Kennedy's son, the ambitious Senator from Massachusetts.

"I remember at the time that Jack Kennedy was working on his *Profiles in Courage*," Dulles later recalled, referring to JFK's Pulitzer Prize-winning book. "The contact was fairly continuous because my trips to Palm Beach were quite frequent. He was very often there. And whenever he was there, we always got together. I respected his views. I thought he had a very keen appreciation of foreign problems, and being in the intelligence business, I pumped him as much as I could to get his views on things and his reaction to things."

By 1960, Dulles's eagerness to please Kennedy extended to developing a fondness for the imaginative killing methods of James Bond, the British fictional spy code-named "007," created by novelist Ian Fleming. JFK loved Bond's bravura style and so did his wife, Jacqueline, who gave Dulles a copy of Fleming's 1957 novel, *From Russia, With Love*.

In March 1960, Kennedy invited Fleming to be guest of honor for a private dinner at the Senator's Georgetown home in Washington, DC. Kennedy also invited Dulles. At the last minute, however, the director couldn't attend, so he sent along a surrogate.

During dinner, the talk turned to Castro's Cuba. Kennedy asked the James Bond author how best to topple the fiery Communist tyrant.

"Ridicule, chiefly," Fleming replied.

Fleming then reeled off a fanciful list of methods to eradicate Castro and any memory of him. As one scare tactic, he proposed the CIA fly a huge cross across the Cuban night sky as sort of a Second Coming, a fake divine warning to Catholics about their atheist leader. Fleming also suggested showering Havana with pamphlets claiming that nuclear testing by Fidel's pals in the Soviet Union would bring about radiation poisoning, enough to cause impotence and for bearded men to have their hair fall out.

Kennedy was amused by Fleming's comments. Apparently, Fleming didn't need to mention "honeytrap" sexual seduction techniques by an attractive double agent because this played out in *From Russia, With Love*. Kennedy told *Life* magazine it was one of his personal top ten favorite books. Defending his old boss, former aide Arthur M. Schlesinger Jr. later dismissed JFK's fondness for Fleming's spy thrillers as nothing more than "a publicity gag."

But the next day, when informed about the dinner talk, Dulles contacted the novelist, serious about the agency adopting his James Bond-like ideas.

"Allen admitted that the flamboyant Bond bore 'very little resemblance' to a real spy, yet to a certain degree both he and Kennedy conflated reality with the Bond novels," observed Stephen Kinzer, a Dulles biographer. "It was a case of life imitating art imitating life, as when gangsters watch gangster movies for tips on how they should behave."

Dulles liked the heroic impression of the CIA fostered by the Bond novels. He kept a full set of Fleming's books, such as *Casino Royale* and *For Your Eyes Only*, in his home library. "Some of the professionals working for me in the CIA never could understand this weakness of the Boss," Dulles admitted about his James Bond fixation.

Perhaps most inexplicable was Dulles' directive to the CIA's technicians to duplicate as many of Bond's cinematic spy devices as possible in real life. In conversations with Dulles, Fleming wasn't impressed with the CIA's super-secret U-2 spy plane and other aerial reconnaissance. Instead he suggested "special devices" for undercover agents on the ground. One successful example was a spring-loaded shoe from which a poisoned knife jolted out of the toe. But CIA scientists found it too difficult to recreate a homing-beacon device inside a car to track its location as seen in *Goldfinger*, the famous Bond flick.

"When a new Bond movie was released, we always got calls asking, 'Do you have one of those?'" recalled Robert Wallace, former director of the CIA's Office of Technical Service. "If I answered 'no,' the next question was, 'How long will it take you to make it?'"

Imitating the world of James Bond, regardless of its practicality, was undoubtedly a good political move for Dulles in seeking re-appointment by Kennedy. However, JFK was even more impressed by Dulles's lieutenant, Richard Bissell, whom he met at a subsequent dinner party given by journalist friend, Joseph Alsop. The private discussion was set up for JFK to learn more about the CIA's operations. Bissell later said he told Dulles about the encounter but declined to serve as a political double agent for the Kennedy campaign.

"I found Kennedy to be bright, and he raised a number of topics on which I had something to say," Bissell recalled. "I made it clear to him, however, that I was still working for Eisenhower and therefore could not do anything of an active nature for him. I also told him truthfully (although perhaps inappropriately since I was part of the current administration) that I agree with most of his philosophy." In a letter to a friend, Bissell said he believed JFK's aides understood "the extreme crisis that we are living in" with the Cold War and that "the Democrats will be far less inhibited in trying to do something about it."

Kennedy liked Bissell's Ivy League background but also his rambunctious style. Bissell was notorious for speeding through one-way streets in Washington whenever urgent duty called. Later asked by aides whom he might trust in the intelligence community, Kennedy gave one name: Richard Bissell.

However, Bissell never disclosed to Kennedy—and apparently Nixon either—that he was overseeing a Castro assassination plan involving mobsters Sam Giancana and Johnny Roselli.

How much Dulles and the CIA shared with candidate Kennedy became a bitter controversy for Nixon. In the final weeks of the 1960 campaign, JFK lambasted the Eisenhower-Nixon administration for being weak against communism. The Democrat proposed helping Cuban exiles in Florida to overthrow Castro's government. In fact, the CIA was already training the exiles for exactly such a pending invasion.

Nixon later claimed in his 1962 memoir called *Six Crises* that Dulles disclosed the secret invasion plans to Kennedy before the election, giving him an unfair political advantage. Nixon said his Democratic opponent knew he'd have to keep quiet about the plans—and actually discount their existence to the public—in order to preserve the CIA's top-secret mission.

"I was in the ironic position of appearing to be 'softer' on Castro than Kennedy—which was exactly the opposite of the truth, if only the whole record could be disclosed," Nixon complained.

After Kennedy's victory in November 1960, the new President-elect promptly called both Dulles and Hoover and, at his father's insistence, asked them to stay in their highly sensitive positions. (Some historians suggest Old Joe had gleaned the top-secret information about the Cuban invasion plan from Dulles and shared it with his son's campaign.)

Later that November, Dulles flew with Bissell to the Kennedy winter home in Palm Beach, Florida, to further brief the soon-to-be president on the CIA's covert operations around the world, especially in Cuba. But again, neither Dulles nor Bissell told Kennedy about the two mobsters and their Castro assassination plan, by then in full motion. Nor did Robert Maheu, who was invited to Kennedy's January 1961 inauguration as Howard Hughes's special emissary.

"Luckily, the CIA gave me time off from my delicate mission," recalled Maheu, who left Roselli and Giancana back in Florida to attend the Kennedy celebration. "It wasn't my idea of fun, but it actually turned out to be quite enjoyable."

Through Maheu, Hughes gave a sizeable contribution to Kennedy's inauguration. The mega-millionaire hoped to curry favor with the new administration and that they'd forget his previous generous support for Nixon. With Hughes's money, Maheu paid for hotel suites and limousines for inaugural guests. At the request of Frank Sinatra, the gala's entertainment organizer, Hughes also made a payment to the Democratic Party that funded a jetliner to carry showbiz performers back and forth between Los Angeles and the nation's capital.

Maheu glad-handed and escorted everyone on the plane, including Sinatra's musical arranger Nelson Riddle. The Sinatra band serenaded the in-flight passengers with Frank's favorite love songs.

This light moment was in stark contrast to the violence that lay ahead. As Maheu recalled, "The fact that all this hoopla could be plotted in the shadow of the planned assassination of Fidel Castro illustrated the bizarre world in which I found myself operating at the time."

CHAPTER 17:

THE HEALTH
ALTERATION COMMITTEE

Johnny Roselli hated the first weapon he received from the CIA's secret lab. And he made sure his handlers knew it.

At the Fontainebleau in Miami, CIA agent James P. O'Connell conferred with Roselli in November 1960—during the early stages of their covert scheme against Castro—and suddenly pulled out a cigar.

"What's this?" Roselli said. His face was contorted in skepticism, as if he'd smelled something foul.

"When Castro smokes this, it will make his beard fall off," the CIA agent explained.

O'Connell was accustomed to getting orders from higher-ups at Quarters Eye, the agency's operational center in Washington, and following them without question.

"How soon does he die?" Roselli asked pointedly.

Big Jim's confidence appeared undiminished.

"This doesn't kill him," the CIA man declared.

O'Connell explained the CIA lab's cigar contained a depilatory, designed to make Castro's beard fall out, rather than drop dead. "It makes him a laughingstock. He'll be afraid to go outside."

Roselli wasn't pleased. He and Giancana had signed on to whack Castro, not to poke fun at him.

"I thought we were here for a legitimate hit," Johnny said incredulously. "You want us to a play a . . . *joke?*"

Roselli had survived in the Mafia by being careful, especially when planning a murder. A botched attempt could land you in jail forever or worse. In Chicago and Las Vegas, legendary stories were told of hitmen who failed—a gun that didn't go off or not enough bullets pumped into the intended victim—and were never seen again themselves.

Both Roselli and Giancana had little tolerance for ineptitude, especially with such a high-risk target as Castro. Unhappy conversations with these two mobsters, relayed by O'Connell to his CIA bosses, resulted in the promise of lethal pills sure to do the job. They had been waiting since the initial plans were drawn up at an October 1960 meeting with Tony Varona and Jose Aleman in the little Havana section of Miami. O'Connell and Maheu assured them that the deadly capsules from the CIA's lab would arrive soon.

At the Fontainebleau, Giancana's frustration quickly erupted. He made it clear he didn't like waiting around, even though their top-floor suite had a big kitchen and dining room. When Maheu tried to keep things light by bragging about his cooking, Sam's impatience boiled over.

"Okay, smart-ass," Giancana proclaimed. "You've been bragging about your cooking. This is going to be an opportunity for you to either satisfy my taste . . . or I'm going to throw your butt out of the goddamned window."

Trying not to let his nervousness show, Maheu acted like it was all a joke. But the aura of random violence and Giancana's hair-trigger temper reminded Maheu that he could become its target at any moment.

For several weeks, the plan to slip poison into Castro's food or drink remained on hold, while agency technicians dilly-dallied with different types of pills and lethal liquids. Ultimately, the search for the right poison was placed in the hands of the agency's top expert, Dr. Sidney Gottlieb, a man known as the "Borgia of the CIA."

Allen Dulles, appreciative of life's ironies, was amused by the euphemism given to Gottlieb's task force within the CIA's Technical Service division. This gruesome effort, devoted to homicide and venom, was called "the Health Alteration Committee."

Within the CIA, Gottlieb reigned as a sort of mad scientist, a chemist sanctioned by the agency to come up with new ways of killing. Emboldened by Dulles and Bissell, Gottlieb became the agency's "Dr. Strangelove," as he later admitted, with a fondness for inventive methods that rivaled the fictional scientific wizard "Q" in James Bond movies.

In particular, Bissell pushed the CIA lab chief to come up with numerous gadgets and deadly potions to use against America's perceived enemies. Bissell wondered about a "death ray" projected from a long distance or using animals like cats as living bombs. "He fancied himself a technological promoter and entrepreneur," Gottlieb recalled of Bissell. "He wanted to know, could you assassinate someone without anyone ever finding out about it?"

Gottlieb's background didn't suggest a future as an all-American assassin. Born in New York City to Hungarian immigrant parents, Gottlieb grew up with a slight stutter and clubfoot that prevented him from fighting in World War II. He studied biochemistry at Cal Tech and was a socialist before joining the CIA in 1951. His devotion to espionage was such he even consulted a master magician to learn sleight-of-hand and misdirection techniques he could teach to other spies.

Through a program called "MK ULTRA," Gottlieb gained renown within the agency for his bold and ultimately controversial mind-control experiments. He distributed the drug LSD to numerous unsuspecting patients—including mental patients, prisoners, drug addicts, and prostitutes—who served as human guinea pigs. One recipient, suffering from LSD's effect, jumped out a window, a death that the CIA covered up for years afterwards.

Viewed from a Cold War perspective, Gottlieb was "unquestionably a patriot, a man of great ingenuity," said historian John Marks. "Gottlieb never did what he did for inhumane reasons. He thought he was doing exactly what was needed. And in the context of the time, who would argue? But with his experiments on unwitting subjects, he clearly violated the Nuremburg standards—the standards under which, after World War II, we executed Nazi doctors for crimes against humanity."

However, these condemnations and moral niceties by critics came later. In the early 1960s Cold War against Communism, Gottlieb's superiors treated him as a great asset. He was part of the agency's push to rely more on high-tech spying devices rather than human sources. Instead of messages left at "dead drops" or exchanged in a "brush pass" between two agents on the street, his office helped install "audio dead drops" where spies could relay their information into a hidden one-way microphone dug into a tree or the side of a building.

Eventually, Gottlieb collaborated with other CIA colleagues, including Cornelius Roosevelt, a grandson of President Theodore Roosevelt, to devise new and more effective methods. Instead of the nuclear weapons of mass destruction found in other arms of government, his lab specialized in pinprick killings by miniatures laden with toxins. In the secret war against Castro, Gottlieb kept fine-tuning the cigar trick until he eventually got it right.

"The cigars were so heavily contaminated that merely putting one in the mouth would do the job; the intended victim would not actually have to smoke it," the CIA's Inspector General later reported.

With deadly access to the Cuban leader promised by Roselli, Giancana and their co-conspirators, the CIA ordered Gottlieb to come up with the perfect assassination pill. Early efforts had failed or didn't travel well, like the pills found dissolved in Marita Lorenz's cold cream jars. While the two mobsters waited in Miami, Gottlieb's trial-and-error with the pills in the CIA's lab continued. An initial batch of pills was dropped into a glass of water—simulating Castro's cup of tea or coffee—but never disintegrated as expected.

Gottlieb decided to focus on pills containing a botulism toxin. Once consumed, this bacterial poison would take several hours to be fatally absorbed in the body. The time elapsed would allow an assassin ample time for escape. In CIA lingo, the agency believed this "natural" method would prevent political ramifications—making Castro's murder untraceable to the agency and thus avoiding any confrontation with his Soviet backers.

But Gottlieb's testing on guinea pigs proved unsuccessful. The furry creatures had a hearty immunity to the toxin. For a time, the botulism approach seemed in doubt. If the pills didn't harm these little mammals, how could they be expected to kill the bearded Cuban leader?

Gottlieb returned to the drawing board. Eventually, he tried new and improved poison pills on lab monkeys. The results were different this time. All the monkeys dropped dead, just as Gottlieb hoped.

After nearly six months of waiting, the pills were finally ready in March 1961. They were shipped south to the Fontainebleau Hotel in Miami Beach, Florida, for delivery to Johnny and Sam who would get them into the hands of Juan Orta, their designated assassin in Cuba.

———

Throughout Miami Beach, as CIA spies prepared to meet with the two mobsters, an undercurrent of violence filled the air. That weekend at Convention Hall, Roselli watched as Floyd Patterson beat up Ingemar Johansson of Sweden in a brutal heavyweight title fight. Later at the Fontainebleau, Santo Trafficante accompanied Johnny and Sam as the three watched Sinatra perform on stage in his scintillating tough guy way.

Soon Maheu joined them at the hotel, bringing along the deadly pills and a brief-case full with ten thousand dollars in cash. Maheu also brought along his own associate, Joe Shimon, a shady Washington police detective. In an odd form of street logic, Shimon was so crooked as a cop that both Sam and Johnny knew and trusted him.

As he did whenever staying at the Fontainebleau, Giancana ordered expensive champagne and gray beluga caviar flown in every day from New York. Sinatra called Sam at his room and they chatted amicably. But Giancana was nervous about draw-ing any FBI attention to the assassination plans about to be discussed.

"I was with Sam at the Fontainebleau when Sinatra was appearing, and Frank must have called our suite twenty times trying to get together with Sam—he wouldn't leave Sam alone," Shimon recalled.

Finally, Sam told Johnny and the others to join him in meeting Sinatra downstairs for a drink. Giancana warned them not to discuss any of their plans with the famous singer. He recalled how a New York mob boss, Lucky Luciano, got into trouble when someone overheard Sinatra bragging about his Mafia pals.

"We're going to have to see him sometime," Sam said wearily of Sinatra. "Might as well get it over now, but watch what you say because the guy's got a big mouth."

Downstairs at the bar, Sinatra came over to Giancana's table, sounding like a lost puppy.

"I can't even keep up with you," Sinatra whined. "Where you been keeping yourself?"

"Look, I'm busy," Sam replied. "You know I got to keep moving around."

Sinatra didn't seem to grasp Giancana's reason for nervousness. Instead, he noted that Sam was wearing the Mafia friendship ring he'd given him, just like the one Roselli had shared with Columbia's Harry Cohn.

"I heard you hadn't been wearing the ring," Frank complained. "I hear you never wore it."

Giancana insisted the ring never left his finger. Frank acted hurt. Finally Shimon, the rough-hewn gumshoe, burst out, "What is this? Are you two bastards queer for each other or what?"

Sam laughed uproariously. Frank ignored the comment. The singer seemed mor-tified and soon slinked away.

Inside the hotel's nightclub called the Boom-Boom Room, the two mobsters tried to relax with the CIA middleman Maheu. They complained to each other about the unwanted government visitors they spotted in the lobby, tracking their moves.

"I do recall something about Maheu saying that he thought there were some FBI agents around," Roselli later said. "I know that we've had drinks in the Boom-Boom Room, cocktails prior to one or two dinners that we had."

In fact, the undercover G-men took photos of Giancana from a distance. They used restaurant menus as camouflage to avoid being seen with their cameras. However, the FBI agents were unaware that they were witnessing an assassination plot by the CIA.

Eventually, Sam got up from his seat and left. Johnny and the others soon followed. They were mindful that the feds were still investigating the Dan Rowan wiretap matter and Giancana's other organized crime activities. Maheu assumed his room was being bugged.

Finally, the big hand-off occurred. The conspirators met inside a Fontainebleau suite with the Cuban exiles, Tony Varona and Rafael "Macho" Gener, who accepted the cash and poison pills. Local mobster Santo Trafficante Jr. acted as both Spanish translator and facilitator of this deal. The CIA agent O'Connell helped Maheu handle the package of poison pills, which he personally delivered from the lab in Washington. "I gave it to Roselli—I don't know who he gave them to, I think he may have given them to Giancana," recalled O'Connell. "I met 'Joe,' who turned out to be Trafficante. He was identified as the man who was going to be the courier."

Always one for a dramatic gesture, Maheu "opened up his briefcase and dumped a whole lot of money on his lap," Roselli later recalled. Maheu "also came up with the capsules and he explained how they were going to be used."

The huge amount of cash convinced the Cuban exiles that they could collect even more CIA largesse if they finished off Castro. Varona, ever the politician, said he wanted some money to buy weapons for his exile army training in Miami rather than as a personal payoff. The red-headed Gener took the six poison pills and promised he'd get them to Havana, where Orta would drop them into Castro's drink at a favorite restaurant.

Maheu carefully explained to the Cubans how the pills were to be deployed. "As far as I can remember, they couldn't be used in boiling soups and things like that," recalled Roselli, "but they could be used in water. Otherwise they couldn't last forever." Maheu reiterated the instructions from Gottlieb's CIA lab that the botulism pills would slowly react in Castro's body, allowing Orta plenty of time to get away without being caught.

To the Cubans, the CIA's presence underlined that the American government was fully backing this venture. Yet when asked who was in charge, Maheu again deferred.

"Johnny's going to handle everything," Maheu said. "This is Johnny's contract."

Shortly after the Fontainebleau exchange, Roselli received good news. He informed the CIA's O'Connell, through his go-between Maheu, that the pills had reached Orta in Havana. Within a short time, rumors arrived from Havana, claiming Castro had fallen ill with the flu.

Maheu was delighted. Surely the "flu" was the deadly toxin taking effect. Maheu called his pal Shimon.

"Did you see the paper?" the CIA's buffer asked his friend. "Castro's ill. He's going to be sick two or three days. Wow, we got him."

Days went by, however, with Castro still alive. There were no funereal announcements on Havana radio of the Cuban leader's sudden demise. No black crepe hanging or Cuban flags at half-mast for Castro. *El Máximo* was still as healthy as his other nickname *El Caballo* (the Horse) suggested. The CIA and their gang of co-conspirators wondered what happened. Eventually, they learned the truth.

Orta never really got close to killing Castro. The dictator never ingested any poison pills slipped to him by Orta, as Sam and Johnny urged, nor was he targeted by any gangland-style shooting spree, as the CIA brass originally requested.

"After several weeks of reported attempts, Orta apparently got cold feet," a CIA memo summarized in a sheepish tone.

That head-shaking excuse just hung out at the end of an incredible sentence—*"cold feet"*! It's not apparent from available CIA records how close Orta got to his intended victim with his "reported attempts." Or if he actually tried at all.

But clearly after months of waiting, Orta's failure of will or opportunity disappointed the CIA and his Mafia endorsers in their first assassination attempt at Castro.

Part of the fault seemed to be bureaucratic delay. When the plan was first concocted in mid-1960, Orta worked in a ministerial role in Castro's government office, presumably close enough to launch an assault of some sort. Orta had come highly touted as a double agent by Giancana and Roselli and their mob pal Santo Trafficante, who once employed Orta in their now defunct San Souci casino. The mobsters said Orta "received kickbacks from the gambling interests but had since lost that source of income and needed the money."

However, the deadly plan with Orta likely soured because it took several months for the CIA to finally send their poison pills to him, making everything more risky.

By that point in March 1961, Orta had developed "cold feet" when he realized the extent of G-2's security precautions surrounding the Cuban dictator. The CIA's delay in preparing the poison pills had only compounded his spying problem. It allowed the G-2 enough time to identify Orta as a suspected "counter-revolutionary."

Worried that he was about to be exposed as a double agent and shot by Fidel's firing squads, Orta asked for asylum in the Venezuelan embassy. Safely inside, he'd stay there for the next three years. Somehow Orta, the once touted CIA assassin, also managed to return the poison pills dutifully to the US spy agency like some overdue library book.

Meanwhile in Miami, the frustrated Castro co-conspirators went back to the proverbial drawing board. Trafficante and Roselli beseeched Tony Varona to come up with another Cuban assassin. Trafficante knew Varona well, as both malleable and corrupt. In recent years, the two had formed a corporation in South Florida to buy up property cheaply, sometimes through extortion.

But the CIA ordered another delay. Any further assassinations attempts against Castro would have to be coordinated with the agency's plans for an upcoming invasion by a Cuban exile army with more than one thousand men.

This directive meant Johnny and Sam, along with their Mafioso pal Trafficante, would have to wait for the CIA's green light, passed along by Maheu like some traffic cop. In effect, the assassination plan against Castro appeared dead, a victim of bureaucratic ineptitude and plain old bad luck.

Roselli would stay in Miami. But a disgusted Giancana returned to Chicago, increasingly convinced that doing business with the government was a fool's errand.

CHAPTER 18:

ENFORCING ONE'S WILL

"This world is the will to power—and nothing besides!"

—FRIEDRICH NIETZSCHE

As the semi-retired consigliere of Chicago's crime family, Tony Accardo wasn't happy with Sam Giancana. He worried about the Outfit's future.

Decades earlier, this multi-million-dollar criminal enterprise had been nearly wrecked by boss Al Capone's extravagant ways. Capone attracted the government's wrath and they sent "Scarface" to jail.

Accardo had warned Sam not to let history repeat itself.

But the headstrong Giancana ignored the senior padrone's advice to stay out of the limelight. Through his own provocative actions, Sam became a lightning rod of unwanted attention from law-enforcement. Watching from undercover locations and listening through hidden microphones, federal authorities noted the contrasting styles between Accardo and his outspoken devil-may-care successor.

"Accardo always tries to maintain a low profile," observed FBI agent John Roberts. "He never loses his cool when confronted by police or other law-enforcement agents like some others, such as Giancana. He merely says nothing or responds in the briefest manner if forced to talk."

Accardo's own lifestyle was hardly Spartan. He lived in a huge mansion with gold-plated bathroom fixtures in the tony suburb of River Forest. Every Fourth of July, Accardo shot off a spectacular fireworks display into the air to please his neighbors. He even tolerated his loud-mouthed wife Clarice who expressed open contempt for those who displeased her.

"She's the toughest one in that family—outwardly, anyway," observed Jerry Gladden, later chief investigator of the Chicago Crime Commission. "She will give you the finger, swear at you. But he won't say a word, because he's got guys who would kill you."

Accardo's extravagances, though, were modest and homegrown compared to Giancana's seemingly reckless and far-flung adventures.

Sam's highly-publicized romance with singer Phyllis McGuire seemed like the mid-life crisis of a man whose saintly wife had died and left him unmoored. His friendship with Frank Sinatra also drew attention, like the time a Customs agent doing a pat down search of Giancana found Sinatra's private telephone number in his pocket. Overall, Sam tried to make up for his sloppy indiscretions by arranging a private "command performance" by Sinatra and Dean Martin at Accardo's home.

Still, Accardo and senior mobsters like Murray Humphreys weren't satisfied. In a sense, Giancana was the day-to-day CEO of the Outfit but they comprised its board of directors. Humphreys complained Sam was "neglecting" their local illicit businesses in Chicago. They frowned upon Giancana's gallivanting with Sinatra's Rat Pack, his headline-grabbing romance with McGuire, and his participation in Florida with Johnny Roselli in the secret CIA plot to kill Castro.

"They were starting to call Mooney and Johnny 'star struck,'" recalled Humphrey's wife Jeanne. "The fear was that they were getting off on hanging out with Sinatra and CIA guys."

Unlike Sam with his fancy tailored clothes, Accardo looked and dressed like an undertaker. He adhered to old school rules that mob bosses should shun publicity. And the elder don witnessed Sam's most flagrant violation of that principle.

Accardo was an honored guest at the wedding of Sam's daughter Antoinette, when Giancana blew up in a frenzy of emotion. Sam felt increasing FBI pressure in his daily life and was appalled when undercover agents staked out his daughter's big day.

The Giancana family wedding was a classic Mafia celebration, with eight hundred guests in two ballrooms at the La Salle Hotel in Chicago. "The scene smacked of a grade B movie, with a slew of scar-faced, sinister-looking men dressed to kill, and a flock of flashy femmes in gorgeous gowns and jangling jewelry," described the *Chicago American* newspaper.

At first, Giancana, dressed in a tuxedo, refused to acknowledge the uninvited FBI observers. When he caught them writing down the names on place cards—an assortment of Mafia dons from around the country—Sam became upset.

"Why bother us this way?" he asked in a loud, mournful voice.

The G-men kept scribbling notes.

"Sure, some of us are ex-convicts, but are we supposed to suffer forever for a few mistakes we made in our youth?" pleaded Giancana, who'd been a suspect in three murders during his teens.

In reaction, Sam gave an impromptu interview to the press—a brazen, headline-grabbing spectacle that no mob boss in Chicago had dared since Capone. "Gang Boss Speaks His Mind," the *Chicago Tribune's* headline blared. "Irate Mobster Can No Longer Keep Silent."

Prodded by *Tribune* reporter Sandy Smith, Giancana defended the Outfit and its motives as nothing more than an expression of American capitalism.

"What's wrong with the syndicate?" he argued in an impromptu interview. "Two or three of us get together on some deal and everybody says it's a bad thing. But those businessmen do it all the time and nobody squawks."

Giancana's final act of bad judgment was in confirming that the World War II Army draft board had rejected him because he was in a "constitutional psychopathic state." Typically, Sam thought he was just being smart by pretending to be nuts. "When they called me to the board they asked me what kind of work I did," he recalled. "I told them I steal for a living."

This wiseguy repartee made Giancana laugh for a minute. "They thought I was crazy but I wasn't," he explained, amused at his own twisted humor. "I was telling them the truth."

But the joke was on Sam. As Giancana left his daughter's wedding, federal agents served him a subpoena to appear before a federal grand jury investigating organized crime. His comments to the *Trib's* reporter wound up trumpeted on the front page.

Such unfortunate public displays didn't engender confidence in Sam's judgment or his stewardship of Chicago's Outfit. Perhaps sensing Accardo's unhappiness—and its dire potential outcome—Giancana took steps to reassert his authority as boss. He did so by the most effective means he knew. He used violence.

When word came that William "Action" Jackson had been seen talking to Chicago FBI agent Bill Roemer, Giancana swiftly retaliated. Sam hated the FBI's overeager, sanctimonious Roemer who was constantly on his tail. He needed to make sure that anyone in the Outfit seen talking with Roemer wouldn't be tolerated.

Mounting FBI pressure made Giancana particularly nervous about snitches—the possibility that soldiers in his battalion of hit men, extortionists, and loan sharks might flip their allegiance under the threat of going to jail. Sam was well aware Johnny Roselli had spent three years in federal prison because fellow gangster Willie Bioff turned into a government informer in the Hollywood racketeering case. He didn't want to take any chances with Jackson.

For many years in Giancana's West Side neighborhood, "Action" Jackson had been a very productive loan shark for the Outfit. Jackson was friends with many of Giancana's top hoodlums in Chicago's "Little Italy"—the section of town where Jane Addams once ran Hull House for newly-arrived immigrants a half century earlier. One of Jackson's pals, Richard Cain, remembered how the balding, rotund loan shark, nearly three hundred pounds in girth, portrayed Santa Claus at Christmas time to the delight of children.

But Jackson's good fortune ran out when Roemer approached him on the corner of Roosevelt and Ashland. The FBI agent, as was his habit with hoodlums, offered to take him to lunch. Jackson refused. The mob juice collector knew the rules and quickly departed.

Yet somehow rumors soon spread that Jackson was becoming a snitch. "Had Jackson been our source, we would have been very careful to use his information judiciously so as not to compromise him," Roemer later explained. "However, since he refused our advances, we were not in that position. I guess some of his activity was handled in such a way that the mob got the idea that he was a stool pigeon for the FBI."

To dole out his punishment, Giancana called upon his favorite killer, Sam "Mad Sam" DeStefano and a group of other mobsters. They whisked Jackson off the streets and imprisoned him in a meat-processing plant.

During the next three days, Jackson was hung from a meat hook stuck into his rectum. With an electric cattle prod, a baseball bat, and knives, Jackson's assailants tortured him savagely, almost gleefully.

"You shoulda seen the guy," explained one of the attackers, Fiore "Fifi" Buccieri, who often acted as Giancana's bodyguard in town. "Like an elephant, he was, and when Jimmy hit him with that electric prod . . ."

Jimmy "Turk" Torello chimed in. "He was floppin' around on that hook," Torello boasted in conversations picked up by FBI listening devices. "We tossed water on him to give the prod a better charge, and he's screamin' . . ."

With his wild scalp of sweaty, greasy hair and a deranged look in his eyes, "Mad Sam" DeStefano was a sociopath who enjoyed the bloodbath. Jackson was only his latest assault in a long line of victims.

At Giancana's bidding, DeStefano would eliminate anyone. He proved that grisly fact when ordered previously to murder his own brother. Michael DeStefano suffered as a heroin addict and Giancana worried he'd become an informer. So Giancana ordered Michael killed by Sam DeStefano and his other brother Mario. They dumped Michael's body in the trunk of a car. When police questioned Sam DeStefano, all he could do was laugh without remorse.

DeStefano's sadistic love for cruelty and violence seemed boundless. Married with three children, "Mad Sam" kept a torture chamber in the basement of his brick bungalow house. The agony he inflicted on others seemed to bring him pleasure rather than remorse.

One victim, local restaurateur Arthur Adler, was skewered with an ice pick after falling behind on a "juice" loan. Adler's punctured body was found months later in a sewer. Another victim, a bail bondsman delinquent on his loan, was chained to a radiator naked, beaten, and then urinated on while the victim's wife was forced to watch.

When taken prisoner by DeStefano and his crew, "Action" Jackson pleaded for mercy. He claimed, quite accurately, that he wasn't a snitch.

Sobbing in pain from repeated blows, Jackson insisted he didn't say anything to the FBI's Roemer and would never reveal mob secrets. By that time, however, Giancana's violent campaign to exert his will over the Chicago Outfit was in full gear. Before Jackson's abduction in August 1961, there had already been ten gangland murders in nine months, all low-level hoodlums in Giancana's world who somehow ran afoul.

Even for a city accustomed to tales of St. Valentine's Day massacres and other shootouts, the reality of Jackson's murder was shocking.

DeStefano and the other executioners repeatedly slammed Jackson's kneecaps with hammers. They shot him in the torso and hit him, again and again, with a baseball bat. They pierced his body with ice picks and cut off his limbs. With a blowtorch, they scorched his skin and flesh and, as the coroner's report noted, incinerated his penis.

Jolted by increasing electric shocks from the cattle prod, Jackson eventually fell unconscious. His limp body remaining hoisted on the hook, slowly dripping into a pool of chopped flesh and bodily fluids, until he finally died.

A few days later, Jackson's nearly naked remains were found stuffed in the trunk of a green Cadillac. Police found the unlocked car, with its keys in the ignition, parked in a darkened corner of the underground highway running beneath Chicago's Loop district. It was registered to a "William Kearney," the alias used by Jackson.

Headlines of his brutal murder appeared the next day, spread across the front pages of all Chicago newspapers. It became a permanent part of the legacy of fear surrounding Giancana and his henchmen such as "Mad Sam" DeStefano.

If he feared losing supremacy in the Outfit, Giancana's succession of violent outbursts and intimidating murders—topped by the awful butchery toward Jackson—proved he was still in control. For now, Accardo would remain in semi-retirement and so would Paul Ricca, the other former boss in Chicago, without a challenge to Giancana's rule.

However, the constant surveillance by Roemer and the FBI remained undaunted.

At Chicago's O'Hare Airport that summer, Roemer, the bold and sometimes impertinent agent, confronted his prey for the first time. Giancana brushed him off.

"I got nothin' to say to you guys," Sam snarled, as he got off an American Airlines plane from Phoenix accompanied by Phyllis McGuire.

For months, the FBI had been tailing him and McGuire. "Sam was like a wild man over the FBI's public intrusion on his romance with Phyllis," recalled his daughter Antoinette.

Roemer and another agent, Ralph Hill, followed the couple through the airport terminal. A FBI memo later described Giancana as "alternately obscene, abusive and sarcastic," adding that he didn't cooperate with the agents' questioning about whether he knew entertainer Dan Rowan or private eye Robert Maheu.

"Why aren't you investigating the Communists?" Giancana demanded, according to the FBI report. Flippantly, Sam joked that he was "going to get the hell out of here and go to Cuba."

Then Giancana quickly reversed himself. He underlined his own patriotism with a veiled allusion to his participation in the CIA assassination plot against Castro.

"I love this country and I would sacrifice my life for it," Sam insisted. "I proved this not long ago."

Roemer didn't know what he was talking about. The top-secret CIA plot was still largely unknown to Hoover's FBI, even though vague references were heard on the hidden microphone installed in Giancana's headquarters. Roemer had no idea of Sam and Johnny Roselli's clandestine meetings in Miami with the CIA men and Cuban exiles.

The Chicago mob boss provided no more clues at the airport. As Roemer noted in the FBI report, Giancana "was asked to clarify the last remark and he refused to comment."

Walking through the O'Hare terminal, Giancana told the agents to stop pestering him. Roemer, with his own bravado, took note of the notorious Mafia boss carrying Phyllis McGuire's bags, including her purse.

"I heard about you being a fairy but now we know, don't we?" said the agent, who later admitted the unprofessional comment was "beyond the policy of the FBI." Frustrated by Giancana's recalcitrance, Roemer eventually lost his temper.

"Take a look at this piece of garbage!" the FBI man shouted to a crowd of passengers surrounding them. "This is Sam Giancana, the boss of the underworld here. Take a good look at this jerk!"

Sam seethed at the comment but didn't retaliate. Instead Giancana urged Roemer to report his comments to the FBI's boss, J. Edgar Hoover, and to the "super superbosses."

When asked whom he meant, Giancana blurted out, "You know who I mean—I mean the Kennedys."

As with the Cuban assassination plot, local agent Roemer had no idea of Sam's connection to Judy Campbell, her involvement with the president, or JFK's swinging times with Sam's pal, Frank Sinatra.

"I know all about the Kennedys, and Phyllis knows a lot more about the Kennedys, and one of these days we are going to tell all," Giancana threatened.

This ultimatum was far from the expectations that Sam and Johnny once held for their dangerous work with the CIA and for their social and political connections to Sinatra with the new president. If Giancana thought he'd earn a special dispensation for his work with US intelligence, this confrontation with Roemer was a rude awakening.

To Giancana's frustration, the FBI seemed clueless about the government plot to assassinate Cuba's Communist leader, nor to honor Sam and Johnny's self-described patriotism in these plans with a special kind of immunity.

"I thought we were all on the same side," Giancana said exasperatedly to the federal agents.

The FBI had no idea what he meant. As Roemer acknowledged years later, Sam's telling comment about the Kennedys "passed over our heads at the time."

CHAPTER 19:

HOODLUM COMPLEX

Johnny Roselli's remarkable success in Las Vegas meant he could devote countless hours in Florida to the government's covert operation against Castro, becoming an unknown assassin in a ghost war.

Roselli was gone inexplicably for days with his CIA mission. He left his telephone number with Desert Inn casino manager Ruby Kolod, just in case a problem came up. But he felt confident his place on the Strip was secure.

By 1961, the triumph of Las Vegas—a brightly-lit oasis in the desert devoted to legal gambling and licentiousness—was testament to Roselli's business acumen as the Mafia's top negotiator.

In Sin City, Johnny seemed to have a piece of everything—even the ice-making concessions and a hotel gift shop. On his watch, more than two hundred million dollars in reported profits came annually from the Strip's casinos, not to mention money skimmed off the top by Roselli's mob friends and from an assortment of other illegal activities, including drug selling, loan sharking, and prostitution.

"There's money pouring in like there's no tomorrow," Johnny enthused about Las Vegas at that time. "I've never seen so much money."

With his friendly, dashing manner, Roselli knew how to get along with fellow gangsters from several competing mob families around the country. He fixed deals and made things work. In a masterpiece of understatement, his blank-white business card listed only one occupation: "STRATEGIST."

Even the feds recognized Johnny's unique ability to keep the peace among killers and thieves. "It is his purpose to settle minor difficulties and he is to see that things run smoothly," said a FBI report summarizing Roselli's "overall control" of Vegas for *La Cosa Nostra*.

As Sam Giancana's right-hand man in Vegas, Roselli had built a powerhouse of entertainment, politics, and the mob. Just like the song title Sinatra adapted for JFK's

1960 campaign, Johnny and Sam had "High Hopes" that this arrangement might last for years.

Not everyone was enamored with Roselli, however. Chicago's senior Mafioso felt he was a bad influence on Giancana, distracting the boss from his duties in the Windy City in order to chase starlets, party with entertainers, and engage in unnecessary risks out of town. Murray Humphreys disparagingly called him "the Hollywood Kid."

Accardo never trusted Johnny. Though he couldn't prove it, Accardo suspected Roselli of cheating, holding back some of Chicago's winnings from the booming casinos in the Outfit's control.

At one point, Accardo ordered Johnny to Chicago for a rancorous meeting with Giancana and himself. An FBI informant later said Roselli was "admonished" at this face-to-face for his "indiscreet actions" in Las Vegas.

Roselli felt Accardo had long held a grudge against him. Johnny later explained to a friend that Accardo "never liked me . . . He was jealous of my position with [Al] Capone. Ain't that incredible? Something that happened a million fucking years ago, and he's still got a hard-on."

During this meeting, Giancana's comments seemed designed only to placate Accardo, not disrupt Roselli's actions. Undoubtedly, Sam sided privately with Johnny. After all, they were having too much fun together in the afterhours of Vegas.

Although Roselli didn't own any buildings or have his name on one, Vegas was very much his town. One source of power along the Strip derived from his control of the Monte Proser Agency. Virtually every singer, comedian, dancer, and animal act appearing in town had to go through the Proser firm, a way of making sure they were in favor with Roselli and the Mafia.

Publicly, no one knew of Roselli's involvement. There was no mention of him when the *Hollywood Reporter* heralded "the biggest deal in club entertainment history" between the Proser firm and Hilton Hotels to produce all the shows in its global hotel chain. But privately for years, the Proser firm provided important connections for Roselli, an entrée to the rich and famous.

Roselli's previous encounters in America's entertainment world would include two powerful figures—Frank Sinatra and the Kennedys. Like foreshadowing in a play, it would help explain some of the deep personal complications surrounding the 1960s Mafia spy plot and why it would remain a secret for so long.

Decades earlier, Roselli first met Joseph P. Kennedy, the father of the future president, when the Wall Street multi-millionaire became a Hollywood studio producer adding to his overall fortune. The two played golf occasionally, Roselli later testified.

On the greens, they could relax in a leisurely game, with discussions that a gangster like Johnny could enjoy as much as any business exec. "Well, yes, I knew him as Joe Kennedy," recalled Roselli. "He just knew me being around the motion picture business."

Roselli's tangential involvement in Kennedy's world became more complex in 1946 when Tom Cassara—Kennedy's liquor company representative in Chicago—was shot in the head outside a nightclub. (That same year, Kennedy abruptly sold his New York-based liquor firm, Somerset Importers, out of publicity concerns for his son, John F. Kennedy, a newcomer running for Congress.)

Despite his near fatal wound, Cassara recovered enough to leave Chicago and seek solace with Johnny's friends in Hollywood. Cassara found work with the Monte Proser talent agency, then controlled by Roselli's mob associates. FBI records later showed Roselli listed as a Proser vice-president, authorized to write checks for large sums of money from the firm's account. Over the next several years, Cassara helped the Proser theatrical firm run the Copacabana nightclub in New York and set up nightclubs in Los Angeles and Miami.

Sinatra's involvement with the Proser firm dated back to 1947, when he asked that a friend's orchestra be booked into a Hollywood club as a favor. Monte Proser, the unassuming front man for the booking agency that bore his name, refused to tell the press who were his firm's backers. By 1956, Sinatra talked about buying into Hollywood's then favorite nightclub—Mocambo—with Proser and singer Eddie Fisher. Sinatra also became involved with another booking agency controlled by Giancana's Chicago organization. Sam "was very close to Frank Sinatra," observed one FBI memo, "and that anything that Sinatra does, Giancana is a part of it."

Sinatra's bad-boy fascination with Sam and Johnny's criminal world was always a source of curiousity and alarm for showbiz friends like Fisher. "I'd rather be a don of the Mafia than president of the United States," Sinatra told him. Fisher was aware Sinatra had traded pinky rings with Giancana. Frank's onstage persona, once soft and tender with the "bobbysoxers" a decade earlier, now adopted a hardened worldly demeanor. Together with Dean Martin by his side, the two "Rat Pack" entertainers seemed like wise guy reflections of buddies Giancana and "Handsome Johnny" Roselli. At the end of their shows, Frank would gustily sing, "My Kind of Town (Chicago Is)," as if in tribute to his gangster pals.

The FBI documented Sinatra's repeated social contacts with Giancana and Roselli in Las Vegas, Los Angeles, and at Miami's Fontainebleau Hotel. The feds offered an explanation for Frank's attraction to the dark side that sounded a bit like Freudian psychology. The blue-eyed singer suffered from a "hoodlum complex," agents theorized in a report. One informant told Hoover's investigators that "Sinatra enjoys surrounding himself with hoodlums and believes that Sinatra would give up his show business prominence to be a hoodlum himself if he had the courage to do so."

The FBI's thick dossier on Sinatra was full of his thuggish acquaintances, beyond just Giancana and Roselli. It dated back to the singer's late 1940s trips to mob-run Havana casinos in pre-Castro Cuba, where he was seen in Lucky Luciano's company at racetracks and parties. Despite his affinity for Mafia chieftains, however, Sinatra once volunteered to become a government informant. In 1950, at a low point in his career, he offered a "proposition" to Hoover's bureau, then enmeshed in the McCarthy era's anti-Communist scare.

"Sinatra feels he can do some good for his country" by snitching on "subversive elements" and "by going anywhere the Bureau desires," an agent reported. But the FBI rejected Frank's offer. "We want nothing to do with him," Hoover and his top aide agreed.

Like extras in his movies, Sinatra's real-life hoodlums came in many shapes and sizes. Joe "Stingy" Fischetti, a bald chubby man with thick lips and bushy eyebrows, was one such mob confrere. His notorious family pedigree included cousin Al Capone, to whom he bore a striking resemblance, and two brothers, Rocco and Charles "Trigger Happy" Fischetti, also Outfit members. According to FBI files, Joe often accompanied Sinatra at the Fontainebleau, where the hotel gave him a job briefly as "talent agent."

Just for laughs, Sinatra, Fischetti, and Giancana notoriously threw cherry bombs down from the Miami hotel's balcony. No one dared take a swing at Frank so long as his pal Sam was around.

Judith Campbell also noticed Sinatra's sycophant tendencies. She recalled watching Frank kowtow to a Mafia hoodlum, ex-con John Forman aka "Johnny Formosa," while preparing music for the *Ocean's 11* movie. She was sitting in Sinatra's

California desert home, where Frank tinkered at the piano with songwriter Jimmy Van Heusen and actor Peter Lawford. Both entertainers fawned over Sinatra. But Frank deferred to this gargoyle-looking gangster—with a rap sheet as a pimp and narcotics kingpin—who answered to Roselli and ultimately Giancana in Chicago.

"Frank was particularly pleased that Formosa was there," Judy recalled. "He liked being with him, having him around. Frank always seemed partial to underworld types. You could tell when he was around someone like that. He enjoyed them more than anyone else. Sometimes I think he was just a frustrated hoodlum. It was an element that he thrived in."

Giancana recognized the utility of having friends in show business. Ever since Sinatra's days performing in Havana, the FBI had suspected him of carrying cash and messages for the mob. "They make great bagmen," Sam explained. "Everybody's too busy being dazzled by a star and asking for their autograph to ask what's in the briefcase."

Sinatra's chief interest with Giancana was business too. The pop singer viewed Sam as "a wizard, a business mastermind who understood big money better than anyone else in the world," recalled Sinatra's personal assistant, George Jacobs. While Sinatra had been friendly with several other mobsters, Giancana was special, a loyal friend. In the early 1950s, Jacobs said, Giancana kept Sinatra "afloat when he was drowning," helping him land gigs after Frank's marriage to actress Ava Gardner fell apart and his famous baritone suffered a breakdown.

With abiding confidence in the artistry of Sinatra's singing, Giancana ordered fellow Mafioso Paul "Skinny" D'Amato and "other gang-related club owners around the country to book Sinatra and to keep booking him, despite his voice problems, despite his dwindling allure," said Jacobs. "Sam Giancana's confidence that Sinatra would come back became a self-fulfilling prophecy."

This strange affinity between the gangster and the famous singer eventually found another stage—politics.

During the 1960 presidential campaign, Sinatra drew upon his friendship with Giancana to request a particular political favor. According to Sinatra's daughters (and suggested by FBI memos), Joe Kennedy asked the singer to enlist Giancana's help in securing support for JFK, both in Chicago and during the crucial West Virginia primary. Many wondered whether the predominantly Protestant state would vote for Kennedy, a Roman Catholic.

"Since anti-Catholic sentiment ran high among voters there, the senior Kennedy suggested that my father ask Sam Giancana for help in swinging the election; if JFK won West Virginia, he would be considered an electable candidate despite his religion," wrote Nancy Sinatra. "My father approached Giancana, an old acquaintance, making it clear that this was a personal favor to him and not a quid pro quo with the Kennedys."

Eventually, "Skinny" D'Amato, the nightclub owner friendly with both Sinatra and Giancana, was dispatched to West Virginia, spreading money from the Mafia to local politicians and union leaders to help JFK win this decisive primary battle.

Other historical accounts claim Roselli organized a meeting in February 1960 at a fancy Manhattan restaurant between the senior Kennedy and top members of Chicago's Outfit, including Accardo, fixer Murray Humphreys, Giancana, and Roselli. Some Outfit members doubted the wisdom of helping the Kennedys in any way. In particular, Humphreys recalled Robert Kennedy's prosecutorial zeal in questioning Giancana during the Senate Rackets Committee hearings. Privately, Humphreys warned "Joe Kennedy could be trusted as far as he [Murray] could throw a piano." But Joe Kennedy assured them that his son Jack was the candidate, not Bobby, and that his request for their support was "business, not politics."

Eventually, Sam and Johnny were convinced by Sinatra to assist the Kennedys in their time of need. Perhaps the two mobsters expected a future reward for their assistance, using the same logic inherent in their top-secret CIA assassination plan against Castro. Perhaps an administration run by Jack Kennedy, with his compromising sexual behavior and friendship with Sinatra, would go easy on them.

Historian Evan Thomas later quoted FBI assistant director Cartha DeLoach, a top Hoover aide, saying the agency's hidden microphones in the Outfit headquarters picked up Giancana's boast that the Outfit contributed twenty-five thousand dollars to JFK's campaign, most likely at Joe Kennedy's request.

Both Giancana and Roselli trusted Joe Kennedy's non-aggression promise. "He was a guy on the inside and he owed us big," Sam explained. "We didn't care if he wanted to play high-and-mighty . . . as long as we could work with the guy . . . because if there ever was a crook, it's Joe Kennedy."

———————

Back in Chicago, Tony Accardo's worries about Giancana and Roselli persisted. The semi-retired mob boss doubted their assurances of a favorable payoff, either for the

Kennedy political aid or their scheming as homicidal spies for the CIA. Too much was at stake. In particular, Accardo didn't want the cash cow of Las Vegas to suffer in any way because of Johnny's absences.

For several weeks in 1960, Roselli spent time away in Miami with Cuban exiles hell-bent on eliminating Castro. Without calling for Johnny's dismissal in Vegas, Accardo suggested to Sam that "another strong hand" was needed overseeing Sin City.

Johnny wasn't pleased. Confiding in another Mafia friend, Roselli complained that the Outfit had "no vision, no imagination"—except for the ambitious plans devised by Giancana and himself. Too often in Chicago, Las Vegas, and Los Angeles, Roselli said, the Mafia was ruled by "the greed and jealousy of little men."

Sam and Johnny were a different kind of mobster than old-school Accardo, more dynamic, more . . . *entrepreneurial*. Their strategies were reaping extra millions for the Mafia, including establishing new territories and casinos in the Caribbean and Middle East.

Yet most homegrown wiseguys were poor businessmen and didn't appreciate those with talent. When LA mob boss Jack Dragna died, no one asked Johnny to become his replacement despite his accomplishments. "I could see everybody jockeying for position," he complained. "Nobody asked me if I wanted to be boss."

Nevertheless, Giancana adopted Accardo's suggestion for a "stronger hand" and used it to solve another of his problems. Sam certainly had no intention of replacing his longtime friend Johnny in Vegas. But he did add another Chicago gangster to the Vegas management team—the hot-headed hit man named Marshall Caifano. The reasons had nothing to do with good business.

Caifano wasn't afraid of violence, considered a gangland virtue among his peers. He had murdered plenty of opposing wise guys. He avenged those like Willie Bioff who turned into government informants against the mob. Perhaps his most gruesome crime was tying up, beating, and setting ablaze a mobster's girlfriend suspected of cooperating with federal authorities.

This cold-blooded approach was different than Roselli's cool demeanor. Over the years, Johnny had shown a preference in Vegas for calm negotiations rather than butchery. Even when an assassination was necessary, Johnny made sure it didn't happen near the Strip, so none of the tourists would be scared away.

Given the best spin, the selection of Caifano would provide a little more muscle in

Las Vegas, ensuring competing mob families wouldn't take advantage of Johnny's gentlemanly style. But the real underlying reason for Caifano's move had to do with Giancana's desire to see him leave Chicago so Sam could continue his affair with Caifano's beautiful blonde-haired wife, Darlene. The FBI learned of Sam's affair with Caifano's spouse thanks to their constant undercover surveillance (and Darlene's propensity for speaking loudly about her love life after a few drinks).

One Friday evening, FBI agent Bill Roemer followed Giancana and Darlene to the Thunderbolt Motel, where Sam had a hidden financial interest. The Thunderbolt, a roadside palace of quick assignations, wasn't far from the Armory Lounge, Sam's suburban headquarters. Watching from afar, the FBI snoops eventually realized Sam met with Caifano's wife every Friday evening.

A FBI memo recounting this illicit romance described Darlene as "a crude hillbilly" from the mountains of Kentucky until she married Marshall Caifano "who polished and dressed her to the point" where she became "a very attractive woman." Darlene's raw natural beauty appealed to Giancana. After collecting enough evidence of the affair, Roemer tried to convert these Friday night rendezvous into fodder for making Caifano jealous—perhaps enough to turn him into a government informant against Giancana.

Within the moral codes of the Mafia—such as they were—an underling like Caifano could be excused, if not forgiven, for seeking revenge on another made man who dallied with his wife.

"We thought we were causing trouble for Giancana, that his man in Vegas might come over to our side ('flip' in FBI lingo) and inform on Giancana and his other mob associates, especially about their interests in Las Vegas," Roemer recalled.

But by then, Caifano's transfer to Vegas was well under way. When the FBI confronted Caifano with their potentially explosive discovery, the ferocious hitman didn't erupt. He wasn't mad at all.

Caifano was "actually very pleased that Darlene interested his boss," Roemer remembered. "That was fine as long as the trade off was a big step up for him in the Outfit. Period. He obviously had made his own deal, giving Giancana Darlene in exchange for Las Vegas."

Before Caifano left for Vegas, Accardo lectured him about keeping his temper, not upsetting the lucrative world Roselli had established so well in the casinos. Caifano gave his word. He even changed his identity to an alias "John Marshall"—ironically the same name as America's famous chief justice—to make it harder for the authorities to recognize him.

But whether Caifano, the savage tiger looking to change his stripes, would follow Accardo's advice in Vegas remained to be seen.

In early 1961, the Mafia's move with Caifano allowed Roselli to spend more time in southern Florida with anti-Castro forces. Working with Maheu, Trafficante, and the Cuban exiles in Miami, Johnny hoped the CIA's plans to assassinate Castro would coincide smoothly with even bigger plans by the agency for a military invasion.

The two pals, Sam and Johnny, were ready for the biggest deal of their lifetimes, backed by the military plans of the United States government. With their own business foresight, they hoped to restore the mob's casinos in Havana, just as they built them up in Las Vegas. It seemed a sure bet that Castro's days would be numbered, especially when US-trained Cuban exiles finally landed along Cuba's coastline—at a swampy remote place known as the Bay of Pigs.

CHAPTER 20:

BLOOD IN THE BAY

*"Dulles gave them a foreign policy with one hand, Kennedy takes it
away with the other. They're getting waspish."*

—JOHN LE CARRÉ, THE SPY WHO CAME IN FROM THE COLD

Being a middleman for the CIA and the Mafia wasn't easy for Robert Maheu. For more than a year, he had dealt gingerly with Giancana and Roselli. Like a lion tamer among the meat-eaters, he remained wary of any sudden unexpected moves from these two would-be assassins and their gangland associates.

Yet working with the CIA—the spy agency that paid him a monthly retainer— could be even more vexing. Often CIA higher-ups in Washington kept him in the dark about their overall plans, none more so than the imminent invasion of Cuba at the Bay of Pigs.

In March and early April 1961, Mahue picked up hints that a military assault by an army of Cuban exiles was near. All of *Calle Ocho*—Southwest 8th Street in Miami's Little Havana neighborhood—buzzed with rumors that Castro's days were numbered. But the clearest indicator for Maheu came in a roundabout way: with a random set of auto keys left by a stranger in a scene right out of a Hitchcock film.

"I knew we were getting close to action when the CIA told me that a car would pull up in front of the Fontainebleau and the driver would get out, leaving the keys for me in an envelope at the front desk," Maheu recalled. No other clues were offered—just show up at the Fontainebleau.

From that grand hotel along Miami Beach, home to Johnny and Sam when they were in town, the CIA's cutout followed the agency's cryptic instructions. He grabbed the car keys from the envelope and drove the car about ten miles north to Hollywood, Florida. When he arrived, Maheu parked the car in a proscribed location and left it.

Then, another car suddenly appeared. Maheu got in. The driver travelled south again, where Maheu was dropped off in front of the Fontainebleau once more. He later learned the parked car contained a high-powered radio transmitter, intended for use by the invading Cuban exiles when they arrived in their homeland. But at the time no one in the CIA gave him a reason or explanation for all the subterfuge.

Everything about the government's plans in South Florida seemed shrouded in mystery and delay. As it turned out, CIA officials wanted their Castro assassination attempt to coincide with a massive takeover of the island by an army of Cuban exiles trained by the agency. This government-sponsored assault against Castro would be massive, no simple "bang-bang" Mafia clip job once envisioned against the Cuban leader.

For several weeks, Maheu had waited patiently for a signal from the agency that Juan Orta—their hidden assassin in Cuba—should go ahead and poison Castro. But the fatal order never happened. Though frustrated himself, Maheu advised Roselli and Giancana to be patient. When they traded cash and poison pills in mid-March, Maheu instructed the mobsters to wait and follow the agency's commands. Unhappily, the two acquiesced but blamed Mahue for a seeming runaround. Sam later grumbled to a friend that Maheu was "conning the hell out of the CIA."

By early April 1961, Maheu was still in the dark about the US government's plans against Castro. He had yet to learn that Orta had gotten "cold feet" about killing the Communist leader. Indeed, on April 17, when the CIA-sponsored invasion began at the Bay of Pigs, Maheu was still waiting in vain for the assassination go-ahead with Orta. As he later recalled, "The go signal never came."

––––––––––––

The confusion with Orta was minor compared to the monumental fiasco quickly unraveling on the southern coast of Cuba. The Bay of Pigs invasion proved a political disaster for the CIA and for the new president John F. Kennedy. But it was a particularly deadly and fateful moment for the brave army of more than 1,400 Cuban exiles who confronted Castro's awaiting troops on a desolate beach called *Playa Giron*.

Known as Brigade 2506, the CIA-funded band of counter-revolutionaries left from their Guatemala training ground in a flotilla of boats. Under the cover of night, their attack was meant to be a surprise. Instead, when they reached the Bay of Pigs shoreline, a swarm of heavy armed fire greeted them. It was clear Fidel had been tipped off.

All of El Comandante's forces were put into place to resist the invasion by *Yanqui imperialismo.*

After a bloody day of fighting, most of the exile soldiers surrendered or fled. The final tally was 114 killed and more than 1,100 taken prisoner. In Washington, cocksure officials seemed stunned how their can't-miss plans had gone so awry. As the CIA-sponsored attack by the Cuban exiles faltered, both Dulles and Bissell expected Kennedy would order US air forces to fly in and save the day. Instead the new president refused, claiming such a move would provoke a war with Cuba's ally, the Soviet Union.

During the Bay of Pigs fighting, the CIA-trained commandos looked in vain for US air support. Defeat for Brigade 2506 would bring a sense of betrayal.

"Do you people realize how desperate the situation is?" radioed an exile commander Pepe San Roman to the Americans. "Do you back us or quit? All we want is low jet air cover . . . need it badly or cannot survive."

With bullets whirling past, San Roman realized their battle was lost. He spotted a good friend lying in a jeep "bleeding all over, as if he had exploded inside. He was lying there as a person that is going to die very soon . . . and he had the courage to tell me, 'I may not see it but I am sure we will win.' And then he shouted, and I will never forget it, 'Beat them! Beat them!'"

Both San Roman and the exile group's gung-ho leader Manuel Artime—called the CIA's "Golden Boy" by *Time* magazine—escaped into the wooded swamps with other exile fighters but were later captured. They would remain bitter about what happened at the Bay of Pigs for the rest of their lives.

Meanwhile in Florida, the team of Castro assassination conspirators remained on the sidelines. Angrily, Maheu watched from afar, along with Roselli and their growing band of Cuban friends, as the invading exiles were slaughtered or captured at the Bay of Pigs. They too wouldn't forget.

"If we weren't going through with all aspects of the invasion, we had a responsibility as a nation to intercept those boats and bring those men home," Maheu later said. "Instead, the government let those young men land on the beach and be destroyed. I call that murder."

Within the US government, much of the blame for the Bay of Pigs was leveled at Bissell, the mastermind of the anti-Castro effort. For months, Bissell's power within the CIA had grown because of President Kennedy's support for covert actions over traditional intelligence-gathering and because he liked the young, hard-driving Ivy Leaguer's "can do" attitude. "You can't beat brains," Kennedy said of Bissell.

Most expected Bissell would soon replace Dulles, who had managed to hang on for a new administration but seemed increasingly distant. The old spymaster had lost his influence in Washington. "I've always felt that intelligence ought to be kept out of politics," Dulles insisted, a maxim he knew from experience wasn't so.

Prior to the ill-fated invasion, Bissell had ignored several troubling signs. Some advisers warned the paramilitary force of Cuban exiles was way too small for their mission. How could they conquer Castro's armed force of up to four hundred thousand men? Nor did anti-Castro dissent forces within Cuba ever rise up in rebellion against the Communist dictator as Bissell expected.

Indeed, Castro's G-2 security force went on high alert after several CIA spy missions on the island were discovered and thwarted. The large amount of arms and supplies, dropped from CIA planes and recovered, clearly were meant for a military action. Maheu may have not known much about the pending invasion, but the Communists surely did. In the days before the Bay of Pigs, Castro's secret security agents rounded up at least ten thousand Cuban dissidents and either shot them or sent them to prison.

When all else failed, Bissell placed his faith in the Castro assassination plans by Roselli, Giancana, and their Mafia friends. In the name of "plausible deniability," Bissell kept his distance from these hitmen and Maheu. He didn't want to be blamed for any bloody outcomes. But as the Bay of Pigs attack neared, Bissell felt Castro's demise was essential to his strategy.

"As I moved forward with plans for the brigade, I hoped the Mafia would achieve success," Bissell later explained.

In the wake of the Bay of Pigs disaster, so many contributing factors to failure became clear. Bissell and Dulles had oversold the whole plan to Kennedy, which he inherited from Eisenhower, as a quick solution and certain winner. The young chief executive's inexperience and willingness to believe the agency's bold expectations— as if they were in a James Bond movie—cost him dearly.

Admitting defeat in this undeclared war, Kennedy went on national television to accept personal responsibility. Privately, he feared the fiasco had crippled his presidency.

"I've got to do something about those CIA bastards," Kennedy fumed. "How could I have been so stupid?" He wished he could "splinter the CIA into a thousand pieces and scatter it into the winds."

How much Kennedy may have known about the CIA's scheme to eliminate Castro is lost to history. Even the Administration's severest doubters of the Bay of Pigs plan, such as Arthur Schlesinger Jr., claimed neither JFK nor anyone else in the White House knew of the murder plot.

"Though the assassination plan was confided to Robert Maheu, though it became a staple of Sam Giancana's table talk and a joke among the mob, there is no evidence that any Agency official ever mentioned it to any President," Schlesinger insisted, absolving Eisenhower with the same broad brush.

But a Senate committee, reviewing the Castro conspiracy a decade after the Bay of Pigs, came to a somewhat different conclusion. "Although Bissell testified that Allen Dulles never told him that Dulles had informed President Kennedy of the underworld plot, Bissell told the committee that he believed Dulles had so informed President Kennedy and that the plot had accordingly been approved by the highest authority."

Years later, perhaps feeling the sting of history's judgment about the Castro assassination plot, Bissell was more pointed about the Kennedys. "Allen Dulles had reason to believe that JFK knew, and there is no doubt that it was fully known to the Attorney General," Bissell told historian Richard Reeves. "It is inconceivable to me that the President didn't know, particularly considering their relationship. Inconceivable."

Kennedy broached the top-secret subject during a November 1961 conversation with a *New York Times* reporter. Discussing his post-Bay of Pigs options in Cuba, Kennedy suddenly asked, "What do you think if I ordered Castro to be assassinated?"

The journalist, Tad Szulc, immediately called it "a terrible idea" that would lead to worldwide condemnation.

"I'm glad you feel the same way," Kennedy told the Timesman who kept his secret.

Like a man with a constant headache, the new president conceded he felt under constant pressure from his advisers to carry out such a homicidal plan.

In Miami, the Cuban exile community was shocked, hurt, and angered by the igno-minious Bay of Pigs defeat. Suddenly this nation within a nation realized there would be no easy way home.

Just before the invasion, Tony Varona, the roguish leader of the exile movement and Trafficante's pal, was humiliated to find himself rounded up by CIA officials and sent to the agency's facility at Miami's remote Opa-Locka airport.

US officials claimed Varona and other top exile leaders were kept there for safe-keeping. They were expected to form the new Cuban government once the invasion was declared successful. They would emerge from the wings and enter the world stage in glory.

Instead, at this time of urgency, Varona and the others felt impotent and stuck in Florida as they learned of the Bay of Pigs disaster in their homeland. "We don't know if we are your allies or your prisoners," Varona told the Americans bitterly.

Under the earlier CIA plans, Varona was supposed to relay the "go" signal to Orta or whatever potential Castro assassins lay in wait in Cuba. But that possibility remained holed up with Varona in an aircraft hangar at Opa-Locka.

Johnny Roselli learned of the invasion about the same time as Maheu, who was appalled that Kennedy was not backing up the invading exiles army with air power. "One of my CIA contacts alerted me to the fact that the precision bombing and ade-quate air cover were being pulled out of the plan the day before the invasion," Maheu recalled. "I couldn't believe it."

Desperately, Maheu called a friend, the president of the steelworkers union with strong Kennedy contacts, and pleaded that "it was imperative I talk with the president concerning a matter of great national security." Only a few months earlier, Maheu had been a major contributor to JFK's inaugural gala, using his client Howard Hughes's largesse. But no one in the White House responded to Maheu's desperate call.

Politically, Dulles realized this disaster would end his illustrious career. Soon after the Bay of Pigs, he visited former ally Richard Nixon at his Washington home. Dulles ruefully told him what had occurred. He blamed himself for not pressing Kennedy enough about US support.

"This is the worst day of my life," Dulles moaned, as Nixon gave him a drink. "I should have told him [JFK] that we must not fail. And I came very close to doing so, but I didn't. It was the greatest mistake of my life."

JFK informed Bissell—the man he envisioned as the future CIA director, the embodiment of the smart, sophisticated spy agency he imagined—that both Dulles and he would have to leave once the Bay of Pigs furor dissipated. Both were gone within a few months.

Bissell later recalled Kennedy's memorable farewell. "He said, 'If this were a parliamentary government, I would have to resign and you, as a Civil Servant, would stay on; but being the present government that it is, a Presidential Government, I cannot resign and you and Allen . . . will have to resign." The Kennedys offered another face-saving administration position to Bissell, which he turned down.

Dulles got his wish to stay on long enough to preside over the November 1961 opening of the CIA's new building in Langley, Virginia—a project he'd championed for years. In true James Bond style, one of the two roads leading to this fortress was unmarked; the other mislabeled as the "Bureau of Public Roads."

With hundreds of staffers in attendance, the president warmly praised Dulles and pinned him with the National Security Medal. The amiable ceremony made it appear as if all had been forgiven, if not forgotten. But as a CIA history later noted, "Dulles never worked in the building he created."

Despite rancor over the Bay of Pigs invasion, the secret Castro assassination plan never leaked out. Johnny and Sam's role would remain hidden, known to only a few.

With his usual bluster, Maheu claimed Giancana thanked him for keeping his mouth shut. Walking through the Desert Inn in Vegas, he said, one of Sam's mob associates approached the CIA's middleman.

"Our friend Sam asked me to tell you how grateful he was about your silence after the affair," said the mobster to Maheu. "He'll never forget it."

Sam's loyal appreciation was misplaced. Unbeknownst to Giancana, during that same time in early 1961, Maheu was blabbing to the FBI about the Dan Rowan wiretapping incident and the CIA's plans against Castro. Hoover and his suspicious agents wouldn't let the matter go.

What Maheu told the FBI would eventually lead investigators to an ever greater secret, and what Giancana and Roselli had been up to with the CIA's backing.

CHAPTER 21:

CLOSE BUT NO CIGAR

"I confess, it is my nature's plague
To spy into abuses, and oft my jealousy
Shapes faults that are not."

—WILLIAM SHAKESPEARE, OTHELLO

As the CIA's Director of Security in 1961, Col. Sheffield Edwards never dreamed keeping Cold War secrets would be a problem for his two recruited assassins, Sam Giancana and Johnny Roselli.

"We never paid Johnny or 'Sam Gold' a cent," Edwards recalled, referring to Giancana's alias. "We never paid them because . . . they were more anxious to get Castro than anybody else was."

After the Bay of Pigs disaster, however, the CIA's wall of secrecy loosened considerably.

The Kennedy administration, realizing how they'd been duped, demanded answers from the agency about its ill-fated plans in Cuba. With his two CIA bosses, Dulles and Bissell, on their way out the door, Edwards tried to keep the lid on the top-secret killing scheme against Castro. He wanted to shield his Mafia assassins from any scrutiny, especially from another arm of the government—the Federal Bureau of Investigation.

Three days after the Bay of Pigs, Edwards sent an urgent message to the FBI. He asked J. Edgar Hoover's law-enforcement agency to drop its Las Vegas wiretap investigation, involving Robert Maheu and the two mobsters, because it "might reveal information relating to the abortive Bay of Pigs."

Since the October 1960 incident in Las Vegas, FBI agents had pieced together the circumstances surrounding the bugging of comedian Dan Rowan's hotel room. It was no longer a laughing matter for Giancana, the jealous boyfriend of singer Phyllis McGuire.

After FBI agents approached McGuire about the hotel break-in, they interviewed Giancana's other girlfriend, Judy Campbell, still unaware of her relationship to the president. Campbell told the inquiring FBI agents she knew a "Sam Flood," another alias used by Giancana, but refused to say more.

"I wouldn't have told him anything about Sam if my life depended upon it," Judy recalled. "Sam was my friend, and regardless of what anybody said about him, he had my loyalty."

The weakest link was Maheu. Initially, he gave obfuscating answers to the FBI, hoping the matter would die on the vine. The federal probe endangered his status as a private investigator and future business. His firm, King and Maheu Associates, represented not only Howard Hughes but received CIA referrals for publicity work with such figures as South Vietnam's president Ngo Dinh Diem, looking to improve his image in America.

Eventually, Maheu realized the six-month-old FBI investigation wouldn't go away. At first, CIA officials took Maheu's betrayal—revealing the Castro murder plot to the FBI—in stride. They seemed convinced Hoover's agents would end their wiretap probe in the name of national security.

But the two mobsters were unaware of Maheu's disloyalty. Perhaps Sam and Johnny couldn't imagine their middleman spy, obsessed with concealment, flipping so quickly on them. With his smooth delivery and confident voice, Maheu always seemed a steadfast pal during their time together in places like the Fontainebleau and Las Vegas.

Giancana remained ignorant of Maheu's double-cross, luckily for this cutout. Usually, suspected squealers about Giancana's activities—such as William "Action" Jackson who was cut up and tortured on a meat hook—suffered a far crueler fate. Only over time did Roselli realize the extent of Maheu's betrayal.

"I knew that Bob Maheu had given the FBI some information [during the Rowan wiretap probe] . . . when his men got arrested in Las Vegas, and that then is when he gave my name out," Roselli conceded years later. "And of course, they [the FBI] had my phones tapped and things like that." Perhaps Johnny also thought the CIA would prevail in making the matter disappear.

But FBI Director Hoover, ever competitive in Washington's corridors of power, resented how his criminal probe of Mafia figures had been undercut by the spy agency. True to his bulldog appearance, Hoover refused to let go of this investigation. He demanded the CIA spell out its reasons for using known criminals.

In a May 12, 1961, reply memo, Edwards explained why the spy agency wanted the two mobsters' cooperation. Because "the underworld" once controlled gambling in Cuba, Edwards said, the CIA assumed the Mafia still had "sources and contacts in Cuba which perhaps could be utilized successfully in connection with CIA's clandestine efforts against the Castro government."

Edwards didn't detail how the two mobsters planned to kill Castro, only describing it as "dirty business." The Rowan wiretap misadventure was meant to ensure the Chicago gangster's ongoing help. "Giancana gave every indication of cooperating through Maheu in attempting to accomplish several clandestine efforts in Cuba," Edwards explained, according to FBI files.

Long-simmering tensions between the two powerful agencies were evident in this exchange. Despite the FBI's own illegal devices in the Chicago mob headquarters, Hoover "expressed great astonishment" at the CIA's involvement in the wiretap of Rowan's hotel phone, particularly "in view of the bad reputation of Maheu and the horrible judgment in using a man of Giancana's background for such a project."

But Edwards kept waving the flag. He replied that national security trumped any possible criminal concerns. Eliminating America's number one international boogie-man, Fidel Castro, was more important than arresting another face on the FBI's most wanted list. All else would have to be ignored or made secondary if a chance remained of doing away with Cuba's cigar-smoking leader exporting Communism around Latin America.

While none of the Mafia efforts had "materialized to date," the CIA's security chief acknowledged, several plans "still are working and may eventually 'pay off.'"

Eventually, Hoover brought the Rowan matter to the attention of Attorney General Robert F. Kennedy. In these early months of his Justice Department tenure, Kennedy didn't realize how much the Mafia-CIA scheme would threaten his brother's administration. What was quite clear, however, was the still reverberating political disaster of the Bay of Pigs and how Castro's presence in Cuba continued to mock the Kennedy brothers. Both Kennedys were more determined than ever to do something about it.

The attorney general sent Hoover's note to a top aide, Courtney Evans, with the directive—"I hope this will be followed up vigorously." This Kennedy handoff meant that the CIA had prevailed and the two Mafia spies were in luck. By August 1961, the

US Attorney in Las Vegas, Howard W. Babcock, informed the FBI that he was "somewhat reluctant" to pursue any prosecution revealing Maheu's work for the CIA and his contact with Giancana.

"Mr. Babcock stated that it could conceivably cause embarrassment to the CIA and of course the US Government," the FBI's Las Vegas office reported back to Hoover.

Thus, the Rowan wiretap case died out—overshadowed by the government's animus toward Castro.

———

For a while, Giancana and Roselli's status as government assassins seemed to be working in their favor. The special treatment they had hoped for—with a top CIA official going out of his way to shield them from prosecution—provided a kind of "Get Out of Jail Free" card in the Rowan case. It was the kind of insurance policy the two mobsters expected for their services, even if they said they'd never accept the government's $150,000 bounty on Castro's head.

But while Hoover may have lost on the Rowan case, he would soon prevail on bigger matters involving the two mobsters and the Kennedys.

At RFK's urging, Hoover's agency stepped up its investigative efforts against organized crime. Kennedy's 1960 book, *The Enemy Within*—about his time on the Senate Rackets panel—would vilify Giancana as "chief gunman for the group that succeeded the Capone mob" and an enemy worthy of government pursuit.

Despite his father's warning about challenging the Mafia, Robert Kennedy vowed an unprecedented fight by his Justice Department against criminals like Giancana and Roselli. The FBI installed more telephone wiretaps and concealed listening devices than ever before against America's organized crime families, at times regardless of their legality.

In one case, a Hoover loyalist arranged for the attorney general to listen to one of the tapes of Chicago wiretap conversations. Over the speakers, Kennedy cringed as he heard a Giancana henchman brag how their gang had tortured and dismembered William "Action" Jackson, suspected of cooperating with the FBI's Bill Roemer. (Kennedy apparently didn't realize he'd been set up by Hoover, by listening to a conversation recorded without court approval. From then on, RFK was unlikely to complain about the FBI's illegal surveillance).

As if currying favor with the White House, Hoover also jumped into the race to kill Castro. The FBI chief later informed RFK that he too had an informant willing to arrange Castro's assassination. Aware of the CIA's failings, Hoover told Kennedy that this assassination attempt must be made without the spy agency's intervention.

"Our relationship with [the informant] has been most carefully guarded and we would feel obligated to handle any recontact of him concerning this matter if such is desired," Hoover instructed.

It's not clear if Robert Kennedy took up the FBI director on his offer. But by then, the Kennedy administration was well under way with preparations and even more money and military resources devoted to a "second wave" effort, designed finally to rid Cuba of Fidel Castro.

CHAPTER 22:

AGENTS IN THE SHADOWS

Throughout 1961, the FBI's surveillance of Giancana and Roselli filled up endless memos to Hoover, detailing their criminal world and those in it—including hoodlums, entertainment figures such as Frank Sinatra, and various girlfriends, particularly Judy Campbell.

"A review of telephone calls of Judith E. Campbell, an associate of Roselli, revealed four calls in December 1961 to the Palm Spring California residence of Frank Sinatra," reported one understated FBI memo that rippled with consequences throughout the bureau.

Perhaps feeling invulnerable because of the Rowan case, Sam and Johnny carried on undaunted together, free-wheeling in their criminal deeds and free-swinging in nightclubs across the country. FBI agents in Chicago, Los Angeles, Las Vegas, New York, and Miami followed their constant movements. Often Campbell was in their company. Eventually, she became an FBI target of inquiry as well.

Despite many tantalizing details, Hoover and his investigators were slow to piece together all these loose ends and realize their full meaning. Not until months later did Hoover—a purveyor of secret files on politicians' sex lives and personal peccadilloes—finally grasp the big picture.

In Hollywood lingo, there emerged a "love triangle"—with America's president and top mobster sharing at the same time the affections of Campbell, a beautiful mixed-up young woman. Through their friend Sinatra, Roselli and Giancana had helped arrange Campbell's secret liaison with Jack Kennedy, assuming their intimate knowledge of the president's affair would be another insurance policy against possible government prosecution. But Sam's courting of Judy—more gentlemanly and courtly at first than passionate or carnal—added another complicating factor.

This three-way relationship was so improbable, so loaded with obvious danger, that perhaps Hoover could be forgiven for failing to conceive of such a reckless White House situation.

At first, Judith Campbell seemed nothing more than a plaything for the two mobsters. She was one of several friendly women, starlets, and showgirls whose affections they traded or offered as a dazzling incentive to Vegas high-rollers to stay another night in town. With low-cut blouses and a girlish come-hither look in her eyes, Judy proved irresistible to men.

Over time, though, Campbell transformed from an object of manipulation into an endearing friend for Johnny and especially Sam. She laughed at their tough guy patter while downing cocktails, and always appeared buoyant and fresh late into the night. They enjoyed Judy's sweet-hearted, almost naïve, company and included her in their mix of social acquaintances, like Johnny's girlfriend Betsy Duncan, a singer at the Desert Inn.

Campbell also followed them to Florida. In Miami, Sam and Judy had dinner with his pal Skinny D'Amato, an Atlantic City mobster who got his start with gangster Enoch "Nucky" Johnson (inspiration for the television series *Boardwalk Empire*). Johnny later joined them for a nightcap with a local girlfriend.

Over drinks, Roselli shared a story of how he first met Campbell at a Hollywood party. Johnny recalled that Judy was "prettier than Elizabeth Taylor."

Giancana acted jealous. "What are you trying to do—turn her head?" he complained.

Roselli knew the game. He responded with humor, just like the fast-quipping Rat Pack members would among themselves.

"A fact's a fact," he explained to his buddy. "Listen, I think I know something about beauty. I know Liz and I'm telling you this gal has it all over her."

Judy smiled at the comparison. With a blasé voice, Sam snapped, "What else is new?" and gave a teasing wink to Campbell.

It was clear Sam and Johnny were longtime friends who trusted each other. They'd shared so many times like these at the Fontainebleau and along the Vegas Strip. Their confidences extended far beyond the women they knew. They exchanged many incriminating business secrets that could get them killed or arrested, arguably the least of which was the Castro conspiracy with the CIA.

In Las Vegas, the two mob pals used Judy as an intermediary for messages between them. "He [Johnny Roselli] began calling me quite regularly to inquire about my health and state of mind," Campbell recalled. "I noticed that his calls were more frequent when I was not in contact with Sam, who would occasionally disappear for

periods of time. Other times he would call and asked me to relay a message to Sam—
'When you talk to Sam would you have him call me at such and such a place, at such
and such a time.' Then Sam would do the same thing."

On another occasion in Los Angeles, Johnny escorted Campbell and his own date,
Diane Gussman, to Romanoff's, the famous restaurant on Rodeo Drive in Beverly
Hills. Above the din, a familiar voice called out Judy's name.

"Hey Campbell, what the hell are you doing here?" yelled Frank Sinatra.

Sitting on a stool at the bar, Campbell seemed unimpressed. She told the famous
singer he looked "in a good mood." She still resented Frank's cavalier treatment when
they dated briefly—asking her to be part of a sexual threesome—and appreciated how
Sam instead treated her with respect.

"What do you mean by that crack, Campbell?" Sinatra asked, with a frown. "Are
you implying something nasty?"

Roselli jumped up. "You better watch it, fella," he warned Sinatra with a smile. "I
don't think you know who you're hustlin' here."

Though Giancana wasn't around, Johnny's actions seemed to remind Sinatra of
Judy's relationship with the Chicago mob boss. Unlike other barroom encounters, the
entertainer didn't fling a glass or start arguing with Roselli. Instead, Frank shrugged
and raised his arms, with a reverential bow.

They all laughed and shook hands. They finished the night with a drink at Frank's
place.

Giancana wanted Judy to move to Chicago. But she insisted on maintaining her
own independence in Southern California. She had enough alimony and family
money to do so. In Los Angeles, Judy would later move to an apartment building on
Fountain Avenue, where Johnny also eventually relocated. By that point, FBI agents
in the shadows were following both of them on a consistent basis. Records show the
feds in LA had placed a hidden microphone into the "wall of Roselli's apartment,"
just as they'd done previously at his Vegas place.

"Christ, with the both of us living here, this has got to be the safest place in town!"
quipped Johnny, referring to the bureau's surveillance.

On her way for lunch with Roselli one day at the Brown Derby in Beverly Hills,
Campbell realized she had forgotten some jewelry. She drove back quickly to her
apartment. As she walked in, two intruders startled Judy in her living room. Just as she
was about to scream, the two FBI agents flashed their identification papers. This

invasion of her privacy by government investigators angered Judy even more than if they had been thieves. She shrieked until both male agents scampered away.

Later at the Brown Derby, Judy arrived upset and frazzled. She recounted over lunch what had happened with the FBI men searching through her darkened apartment. Johnny asked if she recognized the faces of the agents. She didn't. It wasn't Roemer, the Chicago FBI agent with the husky farm-boy appearance, who had once questioned her at O'Hare airport.

In the restaurant booth, Johnny paused to consider their next move, in the cautious way other businessmen sitting around the Brown Derby might do.

"He advised me not do to anything about it until he had a chance to talk it over with someone," Judy recalled. Roselli had previously introduced her to criminal defense lawyer, James P. Cantillon, whom Johnny entrusted with all such legal matters.

When Judy talked to Sam that night over the phone, they shared complaints about the FBI surveillance ruining their lives.

"Coming to my front door, stopping me in parking lots, things like that," Judy recounted about her confrontations with the FBI.

To make things right between them, Sam sent her yellow roses or sweet little gifts.

"I adored getting flowers and he could tell that I was getting a big kick out of it," she recalled. "He was winning me over right where I lived."

Before they hung up, Sam agreed with her decision earlier that day at the Brown Derby to use Roselli's lawyer. "His advice was to let Johnny handle it," she recalled.

The steady persistence of FBI investigators, urged on by Hoover's darkest suspicions, yielded very telling clues about Sam and Johnny's world.

The tracing of four phone calls made by Judy from Roselli's place to Sinatra's Palm Springs home in December 1961 was only part of a pattern, which extended from Sam Giancana—in wherever city he happened to be—to Campbell's other admirer in the White House.

"Judy was pushy and reckless," recalled one of her friends. "She'd go to Johnny's place and call everyone she knew from his phone, or she'd call Sam at his home and at the Armory Lounge in Chicago, where he hung out. So the Feds picked up her tracks."

Eventually investigators discovered approximately seventy telephone calls dialed between Campbell and the President's secretary, Evelyn Lincoln. Judy seemed unaware how easily her steps could be traced to the two Mafia pals and especially Jack Kennedy.

"To be perfectly honest about it, I think I was caught up a little with the intrigue of it," she recalled years later. "The sneaking around, a mild form of cloak and dagger, the anticipation, and 'Boy, we didn't get caught!'"

Roselli, perhaps emboldened by his CIA credentials, seemed confident Hoover's FBI would only collect information but be too intimidated to do anything legally with it.

When FBI agents approached Judy's Hollywood friend, Betsy Duncan—one of Johnny's many girlfriends—she too gave a confident and galling reply.

"If you want to know anything about Judy Campbell, I know she just came back from the White House," Duncan said in a mocking tone. "Why don't you go ask the president?"

Johnny later repeated the story to Judy, proud of his girlfriend's sassiness. "Good for her," he beamed.

Gradually, the FBI began to piece together Johnny's deepest secrets. In assembling a voluminous in-depth background file on him, agents began to wonder about Roselli's claim of growing up in Chicago. More so, they began to believe his name "Johnny Roselli" was an alias, hiding a more nefarious past than he'd ever admit.

But what worried Roselli most was the possibility that somehow his status as an illegal immigrant would be discovered. If the feds found out his true identity, he feared being deported, forced to leave the only life he'd ever known.

For years, authorities had used deportation to get rid of troublesome Mafioso, especially those who came to the United States as youngsters without the requisite papers. Charles "Lucky" Luciano, New York's top mobster, was pushed out shortly after World War II. At his zenith, Luciano formed the national commission of organized crime families and helped oversee the mob's development of Havana's casinos. Born "Salvatore Lucianno" in Sicily, he reinvented himself in America by adopting a new name. After deportation, however, Lucky never recovered his powers.

More recently, in April 1961, Roselli and other gangsters were stunned by Attorney General Robert F. Kennedy's decision to suddenly deport Carlos Marcello, the Mafia don in New Orleans and a close ally of Santo Trafficante Jr. (Carlo claimed he was just a tomato salesman). Marcello wound up in Guatemala for two weeks until he could return to the United States, where he fought a protracted legal battle over his immigration status.

The deportation cases of both Luciano and Marcello were well known, and Johnny feared it might be his fate as well. If the feds found out his real name of Filippo Sacco, he might soon be on a one-way boat ride back to Italy.

Johnny tried not to let his worry show. Characteristically that summer, he turned his contempt for federal investigators into a joke he shared with Sam and Judy. Campbell had flown into Chicago for an extended visit, staying at the Ambassador East, one of the city's finest hotels. She agreed to meet up with Sam and Johnny at the Armory Lounge, where they shared several drinks in the afternoon.

"Come on, let's get some fresh air," Sam suddenly declared.

The three friends squeezed into Giancana's black sedan and went for a joy ride. They suddenly stopped at Queen of Heaven Cemetery in Chicago's suburbs, a Roman Catholic facility filled with white stoned crypts, mausoleums, and tombstones. It was the final resting place for several departed Chicago mobsters.

Sam and Johnny started laughing uproariously. A bit drunk, they began searching through the cemetery grounds, looking for a tombstone with the name "Roselli" on it. Each time they found a familiar name in the ground, they guffawed.

"Ah, I remember him well," Johnny boasted, with Sam and Judy in tow. The two pals seemed amused by an inside joke, as if they knew something more about Roselli's origins than Campbell did. She laughed along like a good egg.

Over the grassy terrain, past the marble statues and stained glass, Sam and Johnny kept examining the names of the dead.

"Ah, poor Uncle Giuseppe," Johnny said, grinning over a large tombstone. "Died of *lead poisoning!* What a prince among men he was, my Uncle Giuseppe!"

Sam was in stitches, as if he was watching the Rat Pack gang doing their act in Vegas or in a movie. Johnny didn't let up with the gallows humor.

"Very rich . . ." Roselli said, gesturing over the grave. "Big man in olive oil and machine guns, wanted to put me through college—*embalming* college. But I preferred the other end of the business!"

By that point, both men were hysterical with laughter in the cemetery. After cheating death so much in real life, here they were dancing on graves and contemplating mortality through their wisecracks.

Humor accented Roselli's charm and attractiveness. As he smiled, his glimmering teeth, leathery tanned face, and silvery locks made him appear more a matinee idol than a monster. And rather than the rage that always seemed just below the surface, Giancana's face glowed with a warmth he rarely exhibited. This shared laugh for Sam and Johnny was the kind of private moment that underlined their friendship and deep knowledge of each other's background.

Judy didn't know about Johnny's fake identity but still enjoyed the merriment. Years later, when she found out about his hidden past, she wondered if Johnny was looking that day for 'Roselli' tombstones so he could connect himself to some phony relative.

Just in case a FBI agent should ask.

PHASE III:
THE PATRIOTIC ASSASSIN

"Marked for the knife of the patriotic assassin."
—NICCOLO MACHIAVELLI, *THE DISCOURSES*

"In a wilderness of mirrors/ What will the spider do."
—T.S. ELIOT, "GERONTION," A FAVORED POEM OF
CIA COUNTERINTELLIGENCE CHIEF JAMES JESUS ANGELTON

CHAPTER 23:

THE SECOND WAVE

In the sleepy, swampy outback of southern Florida, several miles from Miami Beach, America's undeclared war against Fidel Castro was supervised from a hidden headquarters on secluded land near the local zoo.

Everything about this spy center was built on deception.

An outside sign, marked *"Zenith Technical Enterprises,"* suggested a private firm rather than the government entity known among insiders as "the Company." Barbed-wire fences, armed guards, and attack dogs warded off curious passersby. Even dons of the University of Miami, who leased this 1,500-acre portion of their south campus, were blind to what was going on.

Zenith was "a front," the phony name for a dummy corporation set up by the Central Intelligence Agency in an old plantation-like building. To mislead visitors, make-believe sales charts and state licenses hung from the walls of its main office. Even an award for donating to charity was a fake. Other nearby CIA "fronts" included boat stores, real estate firms, travel agencies, and gun shops.

Behind its forbidding walls and phony trappings, Zenith contained one overriding truth—the United States government's renewed effort, bigger than ever, to overthrow Cuba's Communist government. Millions of government dollars were poured into espionage, sabotage, and commando raids against Castro.

Most Americans believed the April 1961 Bay of Pigs debacle had dulled the Kennedy administration's desire for any more Castro confrontations. Publicly, the president seemed unaware of any private warfare conducted in his name.

"We cannot, as a free nation, compete with our adversaries in tactics of terror, assassination, false promises, counterfeit mobs, and crises," JFK said in a November 1961 address at the University of Washington.

But at his brother's urging, Attorney General Robert Kennedy spearheaded a renewed covert war based in Florida. This secret ragtag army would include hundreds of CIA agents and employees, Cuban exiles such as Tony Varona, and soldiers of fortune with questionable backgrounds. A January 1961 memo from the FBI's Hoover warned the attorney general that "gambling elements" had offered up two million dollars to finance Varona's organization in the hopes of reviving the mob's Havana casinos. But the prospect of organized crime involvement didn't deter RFK from an even larger perceived threat—Castro and the spread of Communism.

"Bobby felt even more strongly about it than Jack," recalled Gen. Edward Lansdale, an organizer of "Operation Mongoose" within the Defense Department. "He felt his brother had been insulted at the Bay of Pigs. He felt the insult needed to be redressed rather quickly."

Six months after the Bay of Pigs, the CIA's "wave station"—shorthand for Operation Mongoose's home in South Florida codenamed JMWAVE—was in high gear, despite the agency's charter forbidding spying within the United States. "It was run as if it were a foreign country, yet most of our agents were in the state of Florida," recalled Ray S. Cline, a top CIA analyst. "People just overlooked the fact that it was a domestic operation."

Paramilitary weapons, including automatic guns, high-powered rifles, and explosives, filled several "Zenith" warehouses and bunkers. A powerful radio antenna beamed messages around the Caribbean. Dozens of military vehicles were fueled and serviced by the camp's own gas station. Spy planes flew from the secret Opa-Locka military airbase nearby and clandestine naval attacks were launched repeatedly from the Florida Keys. This multi-headed colossus would become the largest CIA installation in the world outside of Langley, Virginia.

In South Florida, the massive influx of money and workers at "Zenith" was an open secret, creating a boomtown atmosphere amid the mangroves and alligators. Though the national press seemed unaware of its presence, this second wave against Castro became, as author Joan Didion later described, "a kind of action about which everybody in Miami and nobody in Washington seemed to know."

Prior to the Bay of Pigs, attempts to learn about the CIA's spy encampment in Florida failed miserably. A group of curious neighborhood teenagers nearly got killed when they discovered the agency's hidden training facility in the thick brushlands. Mischievously, the kids tossed some firecrackers over its fence. Mistaking the crackling sounds for enemy gunfire, the Cuban exiles grabbed their weapons, including a .30-caliber machine gun. They started shooting, hitting one of the youngsters in the head, almost fatally.

Both local police and FBI opened a criminal probe of the shooting, but the State Department convinced them to shut down their investigations. FBI chief J. Edgar Hoover was particularly incensed that the Cuban exiles and CIA were violating the Neutrality Act. It prohibited precisely the wild freelance military assaults on another country that were being launched from southern Florida. (Eventually a different training camp for the Cuban exiles was set up in Guatemala, which became a staging ground for the Bay of Pigs invasion).

When the *Miami Herald* heard about the Florida shooting, they investigated the clandestine circumstances. But CIA director Allen Dulles convinced the newspaper not to run anything.

"If you publish that kind of information, you'll seriously damage national security," warned Dulles. Even after the Bay of Pigs fiasco, the CIA operation in Florida kept running along merrily, with the Kennedys more determined than ever to force a change in Cuba with its "second wave."

Overseeing this resurgent anti-Castro effort was William King Harvey—a hard-drinking, potbellied CIA agent who seemed far different from the reserved Ivy League types found in the higher reaches of the agency.

Harvey possessed a deep booming voice and a cocksure attitude reinforced by two pistols always kept by his side. At first glance, he appeared almost comical, described by one historian as "a red-faced, pop-eyed, bullet-headed, pear-shaped man with a duck-like strut that was part waddle and part swagger." Yet as a sharp, intuitive investigator, Bill Harvey became a Cold War legend, a man who understood the game of espionage as well as anyone. In Washington, he kept secret papers in three combination safes inside his Quarters Eye office wall as well as a one-ton safe he imported privately at home.

Educated as a lawyer from Indiana, Harvey first joined the FBI in the 1940s. But he resigned in a huff rather than face demotion for sleeping off heavy drinking from a party the night before. Signing on with the CIA, he quickly displayed his audacious talents as a spy. In the early 1950s, he helped sniff out British intelligence official Kim Philby, the notorious Soviet double agent. As a clandestine operator in West Berlin, he brazenly drilled a five hundred-yard tunnel into the east side of the divided city, allowing him to eavesdrop on hundreds of Soviet telephone lines reporting back to Moscow.

As if to add to his macho mystique, Harvey bragged of bedding dozens of women and was quick to fight any man who crossed him. With a few drinks under his belt, Harvey was inclined to tell you exactly what he thought—bluntly, like a punch in the nose.

Upon returning to America in 1960, Harvey was assigned by Bissell to come up with "executive action" plans. This highly sensitive project had the codename, ZR/Rifle. It would include the possible assassination of foreign leaders, most notably Castro. But it would be a separate operation from the active killing plan already in place with Giancana and Roselli.

From the very start of the Kennedy Administration, there was talk within the CIA of state-sponsored murder. "One of the first things that John Kennedy—John, not Robert—asked Dick Bissell for in January 1961 after he had gotten inaugurated, one of the first things was an assassination capability," recalled Sam Halpern, a CIA official who worked with both Bissell and Harvey. "Create one please," said the president about this foreign assassination plan, without naming a particular target, according to Halpern's secret account disclosed in 2017 under the JFK Assassination Records Act.

Despite Halpern's claim, no document has been discovered with such an alleged directive by JFK. However, CIA officials from that era, like Richard Bissell, had a similar recollection about the Kennedy White House. Though claiming his memory was fuzzy, Bissell later acknowledged discussing the ZR/Rifle plan with two top JFK aides (deputy National Security advisor Walt Rostow and his boss McGeorge Bundy) and indicated the president approved of the project.

"My belief is that he [JFK] knew of it," Bissell testified in 1975. "What they meant by an Executive Action capability, of course, embraced a great deal more than assassination. It embraced means of discrediting a political leader, possibly means of physically incapacitating him but without permanent injury, possibly assassination as last resort." (Rostow denied any such conversation but Bundy did recall the plan "in a general way.") Notes kept by Harvey quote Bissell as telling him: "The White House has twice urged me to create such a capacity."

One of Harvey's CIA officers, Charles Ford, was assigned "to establish contacts with the underworld to look for possible assets for use against Castro," according to Halpern and Harvey's superior, Richard Helms. Using the alias "Rocky Fiscalini," Ford reported to the Attorney General. Although he dealt with some "shady characters" with this assignment, Ford said he never met Giancana or Roselli and denied he was ever directed by any government official to seek out underworld figures or kill Castro directly.

Mostly, Ford said, Robert Kennedy wanted him to enlist certain Cuban exiles intent on sabotage and overthrowing Castro. As Ford later explained in a confidential memo, "I had never engaged in plotting with Cubans regarding assassination but that I had many conversations with Cubans regarding their desire to conduct paramilitary activities which, as a by-product, might well result in Castro's death."

Defenders of RFK, including friends and family, later said CIA men like Halpern and Helms smeared Kennedy's reputation to hide their own wrongdoing. Nevertheless, documents show Bobby remained the biggest cheerleader in the Kennedy adminstration's "get Castro" campaign. "Time, effort, manpower, dollars are not to be spared," he instructed those gathered in his office in January 1962, according to a confidential memo released in 2017. "The President has indicated that Castro cannot be tolerated and the final chapter to this has not been written."

Recruiting Mafia hitmen appealed to Harvey's bold tastes, though initially he was not directly involved with Roselli and Giancana, deferring to others at the CIA like Shef Edwards. After the Bay of Pigs fiasco in 1961, however, Harvey was put in charge of Castro's demise.

With his characteristic panache, Harvey referred to government-sanctioned assassination not by name but by euphemism. He called it "the Magic Button," or the "last resort beyond last resort." Suitably impressed and eager to please the Kennedy White House, Gen. Edward Lansdale of the "Mongoose" group touted Harvey as "America's James Bond."

JFK seemed bemused by the difference between this movie hype and Harvey's actual appearance. When he first met him, Kennedy stared for a moment at the overweight, middle-aged agent, hardly reminiscent of actor Sean Connery.

"So you're our James Bond?" teased the president.

Unlike the cinema, though, real-life spying didn't always go so smoothly. Harvey soon realized the Mafia killing plan, loosely run by the CIA's Shef Edwards and "Big Jim" O'Connell, had gotten out of hand without results.

The wiretapping fiasco involving Dan Rowan's Vegas hotel room was a major internal embarrassment for the agency. It also convinced Harvey that Sam Giancana couldn't be trusted. He was appalled how the CIA had been bamboozled by the Chicago mobster's whims.

Yet Harvey remained impressed by Roselli. Johnny kept his own counsel. He seemed genuinely dedicated to the government's cause of rubbing out Castro. Most CIA agents were ill-equipped or unwilling to be a part of the newly sanctioned "executive action" plan to kill Castro. So Johnny's stock as a volunteer hitman never waivered.

Records suggest Roselli's zeal extended to more than one Caribbean trouble spot for the CIA. As a prelude to Cuba, Roselli was linked to another "executive action" against Dominican Republic dictator Rafael Trujillo, assassinated gangland-style in May 1961. While riding in his blue Chevy Bel-Air, the military ruler was ambushed by gunmen waiting in the bushes.

The Trujillo attack appeared to have been planned two months earlier, when Roselli and CIA agent E. Howard Hunt, later of Watergate infamy, visited the Dominican Republic. The pair apparently met with Trujillo's homegrown assassins. The agency later admitted supplying weapons but escaped direct blame for the killing.

Roselli's handiwork as a spy was impressive to Harvey. He wanted to keep Johnny on, especially when CIA deputy director Bissell, in one of his last actions in November 1961, instructed that a second Castro assassination plan "had been fully approved" by the White House. But in going forward with Roselli, Harvey would insist on a new set of ground rules.

––––––––––

Back at CIA headquarters, "Big Jim" O'Connell awaited his pending transfer from the anti-Castro operation in Miami to a faraway post in Okinawa, Japan. He would no longer be the agency's overseer of the two hitmen.

In April 1962, O'Connell's immediate boss, security chief Sheffield Edwards, called him into his Langley office to tell him the news.

"Bill Harvey is going to take over Roselli," Edwards said bluntly, "so we will have to arrange to get them together."

O'Connell, a pliant government servant, didn't seem to mind. But Edwards couldn't have been too pleased. The futile Castro murder plots were so far blamed on him.

Following the Bay of Pigs debacle, venerable CIA men like Edwards lost much of their credibility. The young Turks in the Kennedy administration viewed the colonel, who parted his slick dark hair down the middle in 1920s style, as ineffective and out of touch. He'd been part of the discredited Dulles old guard. Though Edwards would later say he was happy to rid himself of Sam and Johnny, the longtime CIA bureaucrat realized that he was being stripped of sizeable authority—and the chance for future in-house glory—by handing over the Mafia assassins still intent on killing Castro.

As instructed, O'Connell called Roselli. They agreed to meet with Bill Harvey on a Sunday night at a fancy hotel in New York City. Maheu joined them for nostalgia's sake rather than any real purpose. A few months earlier, O'Connell had called Johnny at Edwards's direction to say "the operation was off." But now, O'Connell said a second Castro attempt was back on, with Harvey in charge.

That night, the four men shared a late dinner at the Elk Room inside a nearby hotel. Maheu picked up the tab, no doubt part of his expense account charged to Howard Hughes.

Roselli insisted on a nightcap. The comrades in conspiracy wandered around midtown Manhattan until they came to the Copacabana, the nightclub once run by Roselli's frontman, Monte Proser. Rather than seats at the bar, they were given a table near the floorshow, to watch the opening night of singer Rosemary Clooney. To their surprise, at another table in the audience was Sam Giancana's girlfriend, Phyllis McGuire, seated next to Liberace and columnist Dorothy Kilgallen.

Johnny suddenly appeared ill at ease. He asked the CIA men to switch their seats, so his back would be to McGuire. He didn't want Giancana's girlfriend to spot him and think he was spying again on her for Sam, just like the Rowan fiasco.

The night ended without incident, though from what was said, Johnny wasn't sure he'd ever see Maheu again. The "cutout" had been cut out of future operations. As Johnny later testified, "After the Bay of Pigs, Bob Maheu was not around anymore on that particular mission."

A few days later, Roselli came to Washington to meet again with Harvey and O'Connell at Langley. Johnny wasn't sure he liked or trusted Harvey. Their first encounter had not gone well. Harvey seemed tougher and more demanding than the avuncular, glad-handing Maheu or the docile civil servant O'Connell. At Johnny's request, O'Connell stayed on three more weeks to smooth their transition.

"I am not saying this in any denigrating way, but he [Harvey] has sort of a very unusual gait, he sort of stalks," O'Connell later explained. "And I remember Roselli started to call him 'The Panther' because of the way he stalked."

At their second Langley encounter, Harvey got down to business. He underlined his new rules.

"I do not want *anything* to do with these two men—Maheu and Giancana," Harvey demanded. He waited to see Roselli's response. Harvey had been debriefed enough by Edwards and O'Connell—recalling good times in Las Vegas and at the Fontainebleau in Miami Beach—to know Johnny and Sam were close friends.

But keeping Giancana in the dark was less of a problem than Harvey feared. Sam believed the Castro plot, dormant for months, had become too risky. He warned Johnny that he might get shot or even captured by Castro's security forces during one of the clandestine boat raids run by the "Zenith" task force.

Though Sam respected Johnny's "patriotism," the two gangsters no longer talked greedily about restoring Cuba's casinos as they once did.

"You don't have to worry about that," Johnny replied to Harvey, his new CIA boss. "As far as Giancana is concerned, he will not hear anything from me because I hardly ever talk to him about it anyway, and he probably would care less."

Harvey added one more name to his blacklist. He ordered Santo Trafficante Jr., the Florida Mafia boss, also frozen out. He said Trafficante must not be told about their new plan to kill Castro. Roselli agreed he wouldn't discuss it with either Giancana or Trafficante.

It's doubtful Johnny kept his promise. Under the Mafia's own ground rules, Roselli's activities in Florida had to be sanctioned by the top bosses affected, namely Giancana and Trafficante. Johnny was a dead man if the Mafia bosses ever believed he was going behind their back.

Besides, Trafficante provided an important link to Tony Varona, who remained one of the top Cuban exile leaders, more determined than ever to seek Castro's removal. Varona was not only an underhanded figure with his own personal agenda, but also a well-publicized anti-Communist figure in Miami. During the Bay of Pigs crisis, Varona and other Cuban exile leaders had visited with President Kennedy at the White House. He'd been featured in the *New York Times* as a heroic figure and "not a radical." The CIA couldn't afford to lose Varona as an asset.

The Langley meeting ended with an uneasy agreement: Roselli would go down to Miami and reach out to Tony Varona on his own, without Trafficante. Harvey planned to meet Roselli later in South Florida, to start this new phase in the plot to kill Castro.

Only one thing was certain: neither man trusted the other.

Before he left for Florida, Harvey picked up a new batch of poison pills (one capsule and three tablets) from the CIA's Office of Medical Services.

The new Castro assassination plan sounded eerily like the old one involving poison. Roselli told him that Varona had developed another potential assassin known as "Maceo" who worked at a Havana restaurant favored by Castro. Varona said his homicidal friend would drop the lethal pills into Fidel's food if the CIA agreed to another request. Varona wanted more guns and explosives for his exile group's covert war against Castro.

Harvey never hesitated. He approved the arrangement immediately. After all, he wasn't installed by the Kennedys to dawdle.

Roselli, as a private citizen, couldn't be listed as a buyer of certain military weapons. As a result, Harvey and Ted Shackley, whom he appointed as chief of the "wave" station outside Miami, rented a U-Haul cargo carrier. They filled it to the brim with arms and equipment. The U-Haul eventually contained five thousand dollars worth of explosives, detonators, twenty .30 caliber rifles, twenty .45 handguns, two radios, and one boat radar. As instructed by Roselli, they left the bright orange U-Haul vehicle and its volatile contents parked at a drive-in restaurant in Miami.

Eventually, Roselli showed up. In the parking lot, Harvey gave the U-Haul keys to Johnny, who promised he'd pass along the weapons to Varona's group.

But Harvey still didn't trust him. After leaving with Shackley, Harvey kept a surveillance eye on the parking lot, to see who would show up. He still wasn't sure whether Roselli was hoodwinking him.

Johnny had a similar fear. He left the keys inside the U-Haul in the parking lot and drove away. Like Harvey, Roselli also kept up surveillance on the big orange vehicle from a distance. Johnny sat in a nearby car with his old CIA handler, "Big Jim" O'Connell, who was on his last mission in Miami.

Neither Harvey nor Roselli realized the other spy was keeping a watchful eye on the parking lot, to see what happened next.

Finally, another car pulled into the parking lot. It stopped beside the U-Haul. The driver and a passenger exited and looked around warily to see if they were being watched.

"We were going to see who picked it up," O'Connell recalled. "They were a couple of Cubans. We saw those two men—they looked like Cubans—get out, and they hooked it to" their car. Then they drove away.

Later that day, the Cubans dropped off the empty U-Haul at the drive-in parking lot. They left the keys too, hidden away, just as arranged. Harvey brought the U-Haul back to the rental agency. Roselli had lived up to his end of the bargain. But Harvey never found out what happened to the guns and explosives.

Despite such a distrustful beginning, Harvey and Roselli learned to work together, developing a slow respect for one another.

Two months later, on his way to his new CIA posting in Okinawa, O'Connell stopped in Los Angeles to visit Maheu at his home and then had lunch with Roselli. "At that point he [Roselli] told me, 'Harvey isn't all that bad a guy,'" O'Connell recalled. "They were apparently developing a rapport."

To Harvey, the much-vaunted spy known as "the American James Bond," Johnny had proven himself as a man who knew how to keep a secret. Eventually Roselli confided an apocryphal tale to Harvey, claiming his Mafia pal Sam Giancana had asked him if any more murderous plans by the CIA were in the works against Castro.

"Nothing's happening," Roselli assured him.

Sam seemed disappointed. "Too bad," he said.

CHAPTER 24:

THAT'S ENTERTAINMENT

"The Mafia, some protestors said, was only a small part of organized crime, while other protestors said there was no Mafia at all –it was merely a creation of the media and the FBI."

—GAY TALESE, HONOR THY FATHER

R obert Maheu faced a life-and-death choice. But unlike "The Lady or the Tiger," unlike "Truth or Dare," the pick between angering the CIA or the Mafia was an easy one.

The criminal empire of mobsters Sam Giancana and Johnny Roselli was a verboten topic for Maheu. When the FBI debriefed him, he easily gave away the CIA's top-secret Castro murder plot involving the two mobsters.

But when FBI chief J. Edgar Hoover asked what he "might have learned concerning Johnny and Sam's 'business ventures,'" Maheu recalled, "I turned him down flat."

Undoubtedly, Maheu understood the penalty for squealers about the Mafia. In his disingenuous way, the savvy investigator deflected the Bureau's inquiry by citing CIA "confidentiality." He spoke like some priest granted access to the inner sanctum, doomed to hell if he revealed secrets from the confessional.

"Needless to say, my position did not please Hoover," Maheu explained in his memoir thirty years later. "In fact, he became extremely annoyed."

While Maheu had moved to Los Angeles, retained full-time by Howard Hughes, he still didn't want to offend either mobster. By late 1961, the entertainment business was booming for Sam and Johnny in Las Vegas and Hollywood, the two cash-rich territories ripe for plundering by the Chicago Outfit. Through their Rat Pack friends, the two mobsters wanted to get into the motion picture industry—a great place to launder cash from their other businesses.

Despite Maheu's reticence, the FBI found others willing to talk. According to one bureau memo, an informant said Giancana flew out to Los Angeles in July 1961 to meet with Roselli to discuss various entertainment business options. For years, the two friends had talked about get-rich schemes the excited way other men shared golf scores or boasted over a beer at the local tavern.

At first, they chatted about investing in a Los Angeles location where they could install slot machines. Eventually their talk turned to movies. One conversation focused on a 5 percent stake for Sam and Johnny with an unidentified film already being made. The foreign version would feature nude scenes but, in the American version, actresses would be covered to conform with the industry's existing moral codes. If it was a hit, Johnny expected a "reshuffle" with future sequels.

Eventually, Roselli sought to produce a major film starring the Rat Pack, meant for a wide audience and a big payday. In Culver City, down the street from Columbia Pictures, Roselli was behind a company called Showcase Enterprises. The firm was trying to raise money for a motion picture, originally called "Las Vegas at Night," according to an FBI informant.

In Hollywood, Johnny had learned many tricks from moguls like Harry Cohn and felt confident he could succeed as a producer. He gained "oral commitments" from Frank Sinatra, Dean Martin, and Sammy Davis Jr. to appear in this new Vegas film. Johnny wanted Lewis Milestone—who directed the previous year's Rat Pack hit movie *Ocean's 11*—to repeat his magic.

Johnny "obtained contracts from all major hotels to shoot scenes in the casinos," said a March 1962 FBI memo. "Investigation indicates Roselli may be handling various matters in Las Vegas for Sam Giancana, Chicago gambling figure." Roselli's other partners in this film project were Hal Roach Jr. and Joseph I. Breen Jr., the sons of well-known Hollywood figures.

The documentary-style Vegas film was scheduled to begin shooting in early July 1962. Shortly beforehand, Roselli talked secretly to Sinatra in Lake Tahoe. The singer was a partial owner there of the Cal-Neva Lodge & Casino, a beautiful rustic resort straddling the Nevada and California border. Dean Martin also had a small interest. "I'm the only entertainer who has ten percent of four gangsters," Martin joked.

Cal-Neva featured a helicopter landing pad and private bungalows connected by carpeted tunnels to the main showroom—an ideal getaway for visiting celebrities. Through his mob pal Paul "Skinny" D'Amato, Giancana became the resort's silent half-owner with little upfront investment, according to FBI records. "I'm gonna get my money out of there," Sam bragged, "and I'm gonna wind up with half of the joint with no money."

While Sam focused on Sinatra's live entertainment in casinos, Johnny tried to eke out Hollywood profits from the Las Vegas film project. On the weekend before July 4, Roselli visited the Cal-Neva to attend Sinatra's opening show. Privately, Frank convinced Johnny to "foul up" the filming plans, by threatening a union strike, so they might make the movie themselves at a later date on more favorable terms.

Johnny returned to Las Vegas and "made such demands that the start of the filming did not take place," the FBI recorded. Eventually, the project was filmed in 1963 at the Dunes and Tropicana hotels. One musical number featured Juliet Prowse, a Sinatra girlfriend. Yet neither Frank nor any other Rat Pack members appeared on screen. When the movie finally opened in 1967, now renamed *Spree*, there was no mention of Roselli or Sinatra in the credits.

Like some B-movie auteur, Johnny pursued Hollywood projects close to his heart. Through his Monte Proser Productions firm, Johnny helped sign up a Jesuit to prepare a screen treatment about a hero priest from the American Civil War. It was a curious choice for a mobster. Despite his own life full of sin and violence, Johnny seemed intent on finding redemption in film, where the church's teachings could inspire even if he was ignoring them. That movie was never made, however. Roselli recoiled from other Hollywood deals when he learned the FBI was investigating the Proser firm's finances. He didn't want to leave a paper trail that might get him indicted for tax evasion.

Roselli and Giancana could be severe Hollywood critics. They wanted to kill entertainer Desi Arnaz, producer of *The Untouchables*, because they found the hit TV show's depiction of Chicago mob characters offensive to Italian-Americans. They complained the FBI acronym was short for "Forever Bothering Italians." But the murder plans against the Cuban-American entertainer Arnaz—famous for his own TV comedy show with wife Lucille Ball and singing "Babalu"—went further than anyone watching *I Love Lucy* could ever imagine.

From his hangout at the Friars Club in Beverly Hills, Johnny made a phone call to hitman Jimmy Fratianno and arranged for a friendly meeting with Sam Giancana in Los Angeles. Later in a car with Jimmy, driving along a Pacific Coast roadway, Roselli waxed at length about his friendship with Giancana. "Sam and I go back a long way.

We know how it was in Chicago in the old days," explained Roselli, recalling his start with Capone.

Eventually, Johnny explained the murderous assignment: they wanted a rubout of Lucy's husband because of *The Untouchables.*

"Millions of people all over the world see this show every fucking week," Roselli complained. "And what they see is a bunch of Italian lunatics running around with machine guns, talking out of the corner of their mouths, slopping up spaghetti like a bunch of pigs."

Fratianno didn't think a silly TV show should get under the skin of two tough-minded gangsters, but they were quite serious about revenge.

"Jimmy, what I'm about to tell you has been decided by our family," Roselli said solemnly. "The top guys have voted a hit . . . We're going to clip Desi Arnaz, the producer of this show."

Roselli and Fratianno agreed a high-profile assassination of Arnaz would require a lot of preparation to avoid detection. Johnny promised to get back to him soon. Thankfully, the plan was dropped over time.

Aware of Sam's anger, however, Frank Sinatra adopted the cause as his own.

"I'm going to kill that Cuban prick," Sinatra declared, as Arnaz walked into a Palm Spring Country Club with two large bodyguards. Frank complained to Desi about the TV show's portrayal of Italians.

Arnaz gave him a flip answer: "What do you want me to do—make them all Jews?"

Frank admitted he hadn't actually seen the show. Arnaz refused to back down.

"Stop getting your nose in where it doesn't belong, you and your so-called friends," Arnaz said, before walking away unharmed.

Frank, feeling outmanned, seemed embarrassed that he hadn't made good on his threat. There were no fisticuffs. "I just couldn't hit him," he muttered. "We've been pals for too long."

Nevertheless, Sinatra pulled his own production company out of the giant Desilu Studio facility.

Sam's personal interest in the entertainment business concentrated mostly on his girlfriend, Phyllis McGuire.

Like a starstruck fan, Giancana followed Phyllis and her singing sisters to performances around the country. In London, an astute paparazzi photographer snapped a quick photo of the couple, smiling and raising a toast glass. The much-publicized photo made fellow Mafia leaders, loath for attention, further question Sam's judgment. It also helped ruin Phyllis's popular reputation as an American princess.

FBI agents who closely tracked Giancana couldn't understand his appeal with beautiful women such as McGuire and Judy Campbell. "He was a runty, bald and big-nosed gentleman who talked in street-bully accents ('dese', 'dem' and 'dose')," observed his nemesis, Chicago agent Bill Roemer. "But in the eye of Phyllis and dozens of other women, he seemed to have a special charm."

Maheu had no problem chatting with the G-men about Sam's romance with McGuire. According to a FBI memo, Maheu said Sam was "very much in love" with Phyllis and that the mob boss had asked her to marry him. In the same FBI memo, Maheu added it was "his understanding that Miss McGuire had rejected Giancana's offer but was still considered a close personal friend of Giancana."

They were close enough that the couple, when Phyllis and her sisters performed at the Desert Inn in Las Vegas, stayed together at the nearby Green Gables Ranch, leased in her name. Instead of his usual fedora and sharkskin suit, the Mafia don dressed like a cowboy with a ten-gallon hat. "McGuire was observed sunbathing in the nude while a person resembling Giancana sprayed her with garden hose to keep cool," FBI agents, presumably with binoculars, reported to Hoover.

When in Manhattan to appear with her sisters on the Ed Sullivan television show, Phyllis joined Sam with Frank Sinatra and his ex-wife Ava Gardner for a private dinner. Sinatra eventually gave Phyllis a supporting role in his film *Come Blow Your Horn*, based on the Neil Simon play. During its 1962 filming, Giancana could be seen watching silently on the movie set, as the cast and crew buzzed about their strange visitor.

"If Sam said something, Sinatra was on his feet, saying, 'I'll get it for you, I'll get it for you,'" recalled the McGuires' road manager, Victor LaCroix Collins.

Giancana acted like an old-time movie magnate. "Frank was in awe of Sam," Phyllis remembered. "He adored him. They were the best of friends."

The Giancana and Sinatra friendship became particularly complicated with their business partnership in Cal-Neva, the rustic Nevada entertainment resort.

While the two shared partial ownership, Bert "Wingy" Grober, a casino manager who ran Cal-Neva for years, controlled another smaller portion. Wingy's nickname jocularly referred to his withered arm deformed since birth. Wingy was a longtime friend of Joseph P. Kennedy, the president's father, and the Kennedys were occasional guests at Cal-Neva in the late 1950s.

Many of Grober's alleged business ties with the elder Kennedy emanated from rumors in FBI files. One 1944 memo noted Grober operated a Miami restaurant with Charlie Boch, the southern representative for Kennedy's liquor company at the time, Somerset Importers. Some Kennedy biographers speculated about a 1964 FBI summary memo mentioning that "gangsters" had visited the elder Kennedy during the 1960 presidential campaign and that he played a role in a "deal" for the Cal-Neva ownership. Still others suggested that Peter Lawford, the president's actor brother-in-law and part of Sinatra's Rat Pack of Hollywood sidekicks, was also involved with the Cal-Neva's ownership as the elder Kennedy's surrogate. None of these rumors were ever proven. Yet there was no doubt of Sinatra's friendliness with the Kennedys or that Peter Lawford knew of Sinatra's close ties to the Mafia leader.

"You better believe that when the word got around town [Hollywood] that Frank was a pal of Sam Giancana, nobody but nobody messed around with Frank Sinatra," Lawford later said. "They were too scared. Concrete boots were no joke with this guy. He was a killer."

———————

By November 1961, Sam and Johnny were looking for their favors to be returned. They prevailed on Sinatra to get the Kennedy administration to curtail its aggressive investigation of their underworld business empire. They hoped to convince Attorney General Robert Kennedy to halt the ongoing FBI probe, just as they pressured the CIA to help them out because of their efforts to kill Castro.

"Here I am, helping the government, helping the country, and that little son of a bitch is breaking my balls," Roselli complained about Robert Kennedy.

To Santo Trafficante and other mob associates, Giancana sang a similar song. He implied his Chicago Outfit had helped get JFK elected in 1960. "That rat bastard, sonofabitch," Sam cursed. "We broke our balls for him and gave him the election and he gets his brother to hound us to death."

In Sam's name, Johnny asked the singer to make a direct appeal to Bobby Kennedy. It was a tall order, but not impossible. "Bobby liked Frank," Peter Lawford recalled. "He [Sinatra] worked very hard in Jack's campaign and Bobby appreciated it."

Some in the Justice Department thought Bobby was already going easy on Sinatra. "Bobby would always tell us, 'Peel the banana'— attack the respectable associates of the Mafia," one former official later told the *New York Times*. "But when we tried to go after Sinatra, rigorous new standards went up. It was Catch-22 time. To get authority for a thorough investigation, we had to have an airtight case against him, but we couldn't make the case until we got authority to investigate."

Eventually, the two mobsters decided Roselli would visit Sinatra surreptitiously at his California home to find out if he had any luck with the attorney general. By then, FBI agents were following Johnny constantly. He often tried to shake them. Various FBI reports from 1961 detail how agents monitored Roselli as he left his Los Angeles apartment on numerous occasions, driving his brand-new Cadillac into Beverly Hills, accompanied by one beautiful woman after another. Sometimes Johnny darted into Romanoff's restaurant or stopped at the Friars Club to play cards.

In December 1961, Johnny managed to reach Sinatra's desert home without anyone's detection. For two days, he stayed at the singer's place called "The Compound" with its airy, sunny accommodations, a movie theatre, huge kitchen with orange-colored furnishings, and a giant built-in pool and bungalows out back. Orange was clearly Frank's favorite color.

Like old pals, Roselli talked freely to Sinatra about their entertainment business affairs. They gossiped about friends, including Sam's relationship with Phyllis McGuire. Frank's estate looked out at the mountains in the distance. Johnny apparently believed he had evaded the watchful eye of the FBI, that their private conversation was safe. And he was right. No listening devices were installed in Sinatra's home.

After he left Sinatra's desert mansion, Roselli flew to Chicago to debrief Giancana. Listening through a hidden microphone at the Outfit's headquarters, the FBI heard the two mobsters discuss the Sinatra visit.

Johnny mentioned how he and Sinatra talked about the Cal-Neva resort and how to replace Paul "Skinny" D'Amato. The application by D'Amato to operate Cal-Neva, owned in joint partnership with Grober and others, was rejected by Nevada gaming authorities because of Skinny's previous prostitution conviction under the federal White Slave Traffic Act.

Eventually, Roselli said, Sinatra recounted how he attempted to influence the nation's top law-enforcement official. With a piece of paper in his hand, the singer approached the Attorney General outside of public view. He pointed to a name written on the paper.

Bobby stared at it. The name was Sam Giancana.

"This is my buddy—this is what I want you to know, Bob," Sinatra emphasized to the president's brother.

Sinatra expressed concerns that the FBI had approached Giancana's girlfriend, Phyllis McGuire. Somehow, it seemed terribly unfair to enmesh this beloved angelic-looking female singer in a federal probe of the Mafia. Surely, the Kennedys could understand, man-to-man, that girlfriends were out of bounds.

But ultimately, Sinatra admitted, he had failed with the attorney general. Frank told Roselli he had visited three times with the Kennedy patriarch, Joseph P. Kennedy, and talked about his concerns. As an FBI memo summarized, "Sinatra apparently feels that the Kennedy sons would not be faithful to Joe Kennedy and perhaps would not listen to any request made by Sinatra."

Sinatra seemed uneasy about disappointing the Chicago don. He shared his worry with Johnny.

"He's got an idea that you're mad at him," Roselli later explained to Giancana, ever smoothly. "I says: 'That I wouldn't know.'"

"He must have a guilty conscience," Sam muttered. "I never said nothing."

He didn't have to. They both knew Giancana had invested in Cal-Neva at Sinatra's urging in 1960 and that Sam convinced others in the mob to support Jack Kennedy's presidential bid, including Skinny D'Amato, who doled out cash like Christmas gifts to help swing the West Virginia primary. "If he [JFK] had lost this state here," Giancana declared, "he would have lost the election, but I figured with this guy [Sinatra] maybe we will be alright."

Sam grew angrier, recalling how he was duped by Sinatra's requests to help the Kennedys.

"After all, if I'm taking somebody's money, I'm gonna make sure that this money is gonna do something, like, 'do you want it or don't you want it?'" Sam said to Johnny. "If the money is accepted, maybe one of these days the guy will do me a favor."

At the Fontainebleau, when he last spoke with Sinatra, the singer promised results, Giancana said.

"Don't worry about it," Frank told Sam. "If I can't talk to the old man [Joseph Kennedy], I'm gonna talk to the man [President Kennedy]."

Now, Sinatra was telling Johnny that his overtures to old man Kennedy had failed too. Sam no longer believed any lame explanation coming out of Sinatra's mouth.

"One minute he says he's talked to Robert, and the next minute he says he hasn't talked to him," Giancana complained. "So, he never did talk to him. It's a lot of shit . . . Why lie to me? I haven't got that coming."

Johnny mirrored Giancana's feelings. He expressed irritation as to why Sinatra couldn't be upfront during his two-day visit. "If he can't deliver, I want him to tell me, 'John, the load's too heavy,'" Roselli exclaimed.

Always quick to gauge the temperature in the room, Roselli began to dump criticism on Sinatra, seconding Giancana's outrage. "He's got big ideas, Frank does, about being ambassador or something," Johnny explained.

Roselli then mocked the Kennedys for expecting the singer's loyalty over them.

"You got the right idea, Mo, go the other way—fuck everybody," Johnny said, using the shortened version of "Mooney," Giancana's nickname. "We'll use them every fucking way we can. They [the Kennedys] only know one way. Now let them see the other side of you."

That other side was Sam's world of violence. With any other *cafone*, the Chicago mob boss would have been merciless. Despite his frustration, however, Giancana couldn't bring himself to order a contract hit on Sinatra. Sam still admired Sinatra's artistry, the beautiful baritone and lush songs that made him remember his lost wife Angeline and had Phyllis melting in his arms.

"I'm fucking Phyllis, playing Sinatra songs in the background and the whole time I'm thinking to myself—'Christ, how can I silence that voice?'" he once confided to an associate. "It's the most beautiful sound in the world."

Deep down, this appreciation of Sinatra's voice, as a tough guy with a tender heart, seemed somehow to mitigate the extreme anger Sam felt at his betrayal. It kept him from responding the violent way to which he was accustomed. Luck was with Frank Sinatra once again.

"Too fucking bad," Sam finally uttered. "Tell him the Kennedys will keep him company."

Johnny suggested the Chicago mob boss approach Sinatra directly. "Why don't you talk to him?" Roselli asked.

There was no reasoning with Sam, not at this moment. "When he says he's gonna do a guy a little favor, I don't give a shit how long it takes," Giancana said, as if acting on principle. "He's got to give you a little favor."

Giancana's instincts seemed correct. Rather than end the matter, Sinatra's encounter with the attorney general on behalf of his two mobster friends only accelerated events.

The conversation between Sam and Johnny, captured by FBI listening devices, elated agents like Bill Roemer, the way a hound smells blood in the hunt. A telex summarizing everything was quickly sent to FBI Director J. Edgar Hoover in Washington. Ever calculating, Hoover realized the political ramifications for the Kennedys and himself.

The overture to Sinatra would bring more scrutiny by the feds, not less, in early 1962. Investigators took an even harder look at Giancana's holdings in Las Vegas, at Roselli's activities in Hollywood and Florida, and at the Cal-Neva resort in Lake Tahoe, where Sam was losing money rather than making it as Frank once promised.

For those investigating the extraordinarily complex world of Giancana and Roselli—the CIA spies and underworld entrepreneurs—a bigger and better understanding soon emerged from the wiretaps, hidden microphones, and the reams of FBI reports. The trail would lead to places few imagined.

When one of Sam's Chicago wise guys heard of Sinatra's failings, he volunteered for the simplest of solutions—exterminate the Rat Pack.

"Let's show 'em," growled John Formosa, Ginacana's gargoyle-like associate. "Let's show those asshole Hollywood fruitcakes that they can't get away with it as if nothing's happened. Let's hit Sinatra. Or I could whack out a couple of those other guys. [Peter] Lawford and that [Dean] Martin, and I could take the n——r [Sammy Davis Jr.] and put his other eye out."

Uncharacteristically, Giancana demurred. He would bide his time and hopefully still avoid the traps set by government.

"No . . ." Sam replied cryptically. "I've got other plans for them."

CHAPTER 25:

A SECRET IS SELDOM SAFE

"A secret is seldom safe in more than one breast."

—JONATHAN SWIFT

As a successful CIA spy, William Harvey trusted few people. To make a point, he might slam his pistol on a table or swear in his gravel-throated voice at an agency dullard. But he was loath to let anyone, beyond a certain operational circle, know his secrets.

"If you ever know as many secrets as I do," he said, "then you'll know why I carry a gun."

Gradually, the man touted as America's James Bond trusted Johnny Roselli as a compatriot. At first, it was a matter of necessity in the wake of the Bay of Pigs debacle. But by early 1962, his trust flowed out of admiration for Johnny's courage and can-do competency in covert actions against Cuba. Roselli had proven his resolve to kill Castro.

"Not knowing him from Adam at that point, I had to assess an unknown individual, as to not his past background or how he may have made his living, but as to whether or not I personally could trust his integrity," Harvey recalled of Roselli. As head of the CIA's Cuban operation, Harvey gave Johnny "very high marks for his personal integrity with me, for his loyalty. I believe that he was honestly motivated without any question of patriotism and not by self-seeking motives."

Unofficially given the title of "Colonel," Roselli oversaw late-night missions to Cuba by exile commandos. They were trained as snipers and munitions specialists for "boom and bang" sabotage assaults.

Roselli's marauders were based at Port Mary, an enclave carved out of beach and shrubs north of Key Largo, Florida. Today part of an out-of-the-way crocodile wildlife refuge, it was even more backwater then. Few knew about Roselli's role in this secret operation, not even Ted Shackley, Harvey's top assistant.

"Harvey was having periodic meetings with someone in Miami because he would go off for lunches or dinner by himself while on an inspection trip, but that he never told me whom he was seeing," recalled Shackley about the Harvey-Roselli get-togethers, which involved more than a few drinks. "If I didn't need to know about something, I wasn't told."

This deception about Roselli followed up the new chain of command within the CIA. Although Harvey was responsible for the huge Cuban project in Florida, he reported directly to Richard Helms in Washington. Helms had replaced Richard Bissell as Deputy Director for Plans. In turn, Helms answered to John A. McCone, the successor to Allen Dulles as Director of Central Intelligence—part of the CIA overhaul ordered by President Kennedy.

A lifelong spy, Richard Helms was trained in espionage and counterintelligence. In the past, he'd been privy to numerous CIA top-secret programs, including mind-control experiments with LSD. His biographer Thomas Powers memorably called Helms, "The Man Who Kept The Secrets." Wary of covert operations over traditional espionage, Helms initially frowned upon recruiting Mafia assassins and cutout handlers to kill foreign leaders.

But in 1962, as the new number two at the CIA, Helms went along with the existing program. He kept Harvey's details about Roselli and the Castro assassination plan to himself. Both Helms and Harvey decided not to tell their boss. They felt McCone, a Republican businessman and politician with no prior history in the CIA, couldn't be trusted. For nearly two years, CIA chief McCone didn't know about the active assassination plan within his own agency.

"I saw no reason at that time to charge him with knowledge of this, at least until we reached the point where it (the Castro killing) appeared it might come to fruition," Harvey later explained. At that time, there was "a very real possibility of this government being blackmailed, either by Cubans for political purposes or by figures in organized crime for their own self-protection or aggrandizement, which, as it turned out, did not happen, but at that time was a very pregnant possibility."

What little McCone knew about state-sponsored assassination, he didn't like. After an August 1962 White House security meeting about Castro and Cuba, McCone heard enough talk about possible "liquidation" that he later made a telephone call to Defense Secretary Robert McNamara. McCone didn't need a thesaurus to understand what McNamara meant at that meeting.

"I think it is highly improper," McCone told McNamara. "I do not think it should be discussed. It is not an action that should ever be condoned." A recent convert to Catholicism, McCone declared, "I could get *excommunicated* for something like this."

McCone's ethical objections were placated but ignored, including by his own subordinates, Helms and Harvey. Helms later said there was a clear directive from Robert Kennedy and other White House officials "to get rid of Castro."

Helms and Harvey made sure to paper over Roselli's reinvigorated plans for a Castro assassination scheme, so they could be still denied by higher-ups. Johnny didn't need any official sanction. Counting on the loyalty of Harvey, his new pal, "Colonel" Roselli, proceeded full-speed ahead with his Cuban commandos in Florida.

In Washington, the old guard of America's security apparatus seemed to be giving way to the new. Along with CIA's Allen Dulles, the Kennedy administration considered replacing longtime FBI Director J. Edgar Hoover in January 1962. Newspaper columnist Drew Pearson even floated the name of State Department security director William Boswell as a considered choice.

Soon after the 1960 presidential race, both Dulles and Hoover had been reappointed as favorites of family patriarch, Joseph P. Kennedy. But with their father's debilitating stroke in December 1961, the Kennedy brothers finally felt free to get rid of Hoover and all his extracurricular snooping.

"He's sending me stuff on my family and friends and even me, too—just so I'll know they are into all this information," Attorney General Robert F. Kennedy complained privately about Hoover and his voluminous files on the personal lives of public figures.

But unlike Dulles, the move against Hoover proved impossible. In the past few months, as part of the FBI's accelerating probe into Giancana and Roselli and their Mafia empire, the wily old bureaucrat had collected far more damaging information than the Kennedys realized. He unloaded it slowly, drip by drip, until the full picture was clear.

Hoover's first salvo arrived in early 1962, when his agency alerted Robert Kennedy's Justice Department about the involvement of Giancana and Roselli in the CIA's Rowan wiretap caper. Wrapped in a blanket of national security, a memo suggested CIA cutout Robert Maheu not be prosecuted because it would "embarrass" the government. The FBI also repeated CIA Security Director Shef Edwards's specious claim that the two mobsters were consultants rather than undercover assassins. Edwards said they were helping "efforts to obtain intelligence information in Cuba through the hoodlum element," rather than admit the CIA wanted them to kill Castro.

From this farcical start, Hoover soon raised the stakes. On February 27, 1962, he sent a confidential note to the attorney general and JFK's closest White House aide, Kenneth O'Donnell. Given its salacious contents, this memo could have been entitled, *"Cherchez la femme."*

"I thought you would be interested in learning of the following information which was developed in connection with the investigation of John Rosselli, a West Coast hoodlum," Hoover began. The memo detailed how the FBI's electronic devices had traced Roselli's contacts with Judith Campbell, and how she also made several telephone calls to Giancana, Frank Sinatra and, most damagingly, to Evelyn Lincoln, the president's White House secretary.

This FBI memo was a shocker for JFK's inner circle, especially his brother Bobby, even if they were aware of Jack's philandering. Hoover and his team of FBI agents—criticized only a few years earlier by the Kennedys for being too slow and dim-witted against the Mafia and obsessed with Communists under the bed—had come up with an investigative gem. They had pieced together the messy entanglement of the mobster Giancana, the adulterous president, and their mutual *goomar*, Judy Campbell.

The blackmail potential from this White House sex scandal was immense. If Giancana's intent in wooing Campbell with gifts and attention was meant as a "honeytrap"—rather than an act of affection or love—his Mephistophelian design worked brilliantly. After all, if the feds weren't going after Maheu for fear of being embarrassed about the Rowan wiretap, they surely wouldn't pursue criminal cases against Giancana and Roselli for their Mafia activities and run the risk of grave political damage to the president.

On March 22, 1962, Hoover's leverage was fully on display. Through the back door of the White House, he arrived for a private lunch with the President.

In his hand, Hoover presented a memo detailing the phone calls made by Campbell and her personal contacts with "prominent underworld figures Sam Giancana of Chicago and John Roselli of Los Angeles." Ominously, the memo ended by quoting an FBI informant who said that Sinatra "referred to Campbell as the girl who was 'shacking up with John Kennedy in the East.'"

Hoover couldn't have been more pleased. With this explosive checkmate, if the Kennedys intended to get rid of him, the FBI director had blocked their move thoroughly.

The lunchtime conversation between President Kennedy and his FBI director was never revealed to the press. But later that day, one last telephone call was made between the Oval Office and Judy Campbell, the final among dozens recorded in White House logs.

"Jack never mentioned any of this [Hoover meeting] to me," recalled Campbell, who claimed her secret two-year affair with this celebrated married man was dying of its own accord. "They [phone calls] stopped, not because of any outside force, but because of natural attrition. The spectre of the White House killed the romance. Not J. Edgar Hoover."

For Robert Kennedy, the disclosure of Sam Giancana's involvement with the same woman dallying with his satyr-like older brother must have been appalling. The highly compartmentalized life of JFK, with its extremes in behavior and judgment, had broached one of its lowest, most potentially damaging moments. Bobby left it to a trusted Justice aide, Joe Dolan, to inform the president about the FBI file mentioning Campbell's calls to the White House.

"He didn't have the guts to tell his brother," Dolan remembered. "He wanted me to do it."

But Bobby did clean up the bureaucratic mess. On May 7, the Attorney General met privately with two CIA officials—security chief Sheffield Edwards and general counsel Lawrence Houston—about Roselli and Giancana's role in the Castro murder plot. Nearly a year earlier, Justice had been alerted to "the dirty business" involving the two mobsters. Now Kennedy acted as though he was hearing it for the first time.

"If you could have seen Mr. Kennedy's eyes get steely and his jaw set and his voice get low and precise, you get a definite feeling of unhappiness," Houston recalled.

To RFK's surprise, the CIA did defend its Mafia spies on an important point. Col. Edwards described Johnny as more a patriot than a mercenary. "The Attorney General had thought that Roselli was doing the job (the attempt at assassination of Castro) for the money," a CIA Inspector General's report later found. "[Shef] Edwards corrected that impression; he was not."

Following the meeting, Robert Kennedy ordered a summary memo to be drawn up, including his directive that no Mafia figures be enlisted in future CIA efforts without his approval. This internal protect-your-ass memo composed by Edwards was thick with lies and cover-up. The CIA security chief's memo "was not true," Harvey later attested, "and Colonel Edwards knew it was not true."

In fact, the CIA had just revived its assassination program with Harvey and "Colonel" Roselli in the Florida Keys. And much of the get-Castro fever was at the urging of Bobby Kennedy himself.

Each player in this small CIA circle was more deceptive than the next. In Washington, Edwards and Houston never informed their CIA superiors, Helms and McCone, about their Kennedy meeting. Edwards acted as though the assassination attempts were in the past, shut down after the Bay of Pigs. Harvey had assured Edwards that "he was dropping any plans for the use of [Roselli] for the future." But on his own in Florida, Harvey used the Mafia hitman in a new "vest pocket operation" against Castro, which he kept private.

When Harvey finally informed Helms about the meeting with the attorney general, Helms instructed that McCone not be told about the Castro plot and its Mafia connection. For months afterward, the CIA's top spy, McCone, would remain clueless about his agency's biggest secret.

CHAPTER 26:

INTO THE DARKNESS

"We penetrated deeper and deeper into the heart of darkness."

—JOSEPH CONRAD, *HEART OF DARKNESS*

As night began to fall on the Florida Keys, Johnny Roselli and his crewmates prepared for a midnight run to Cuba. Looking out from Port Mary, the encroaching darkness was a reminder of the ninety-mile expanse to Castro's world and all the dangers in between. They had no idea what awaited them, except it would be full of risk.

Loaded with weapons, their vessel floated past a string of little islands. These mounds of earth were covered in brackish vegetation and shaded by mangrove trees tilting toward the tropical waters. Low-lying clouds drifted by, stretched out far and wide on the horizon. Evening ended in a blaze of colorful glory.

Cruising along this coral archipelago, Roselli's crew finally reached Key West—called America's "Southernmost Point"—but didn't slow down. Crossing the Straits of Florida, their boat picked up speed. They kept proceeding into the blackness of the ocean.

"Colonel" Roselli and his band of exile marauders were on their way, heading toward the Cuban shoreline, intent on executing their secret mission. They travelled aboard the *Texana III*, a converted Navy sub chaser owned by Miami millionaire Alberto Fernandez, a former Cuban sugar magnate and avowed Castro hater. The *Texana* had carried many death squads to Cuba in the past but this was the first time Johnny joined them.

At age fifty-seven, Roselli's grey wavy hair was turning white, his pompadour a little higher on his forehead than before. Yet Johnny's sun-bronzed appearance and taut musculature belied his age. He looked younger by more than a decade. He still possessed the physical grace of an active man who could handle himself well in any situation.

Johnny's presence demanded respect from both the Spanish-speaking exiles and the Americans assigned to the Cuban project. Roselli was "the dapper American agent in charge of the continuing attempts to assassinate Fidel Castro," recalled Bradley Earl Ayres, an Army officer assigned by the CIA to train anti-Castro guerilla fighters. He had no idea of Johnny's Mafia ties.

Though Roselli was close to William Harvey, the tough-minded CIA boss, he got along just as well with other CIA personnel with whom he shared more than a few drinks afterhours. At the Key Largo bar called Les Deux Violins, one operative recalled, Johnny "knew all the help by their first name, tipped hugely, and would tell farcical stories about his days with Al Capone."

Throughout 1961 and 1962, Roselli routinely traveled back and forth to Florida, and yet managed to tend to other business matters in Los Angeles, Las Vegas, and elsewhere. On one occasion, Roselli made a telephone call from the Friars Club in Beverly Hills to tell Harvey that another batch of poison pills had landed in Cuba, ready for use against Castro.

While serving as a dedicated CIA spy, Roselli constantly eluded FBI undercover agents, watching his every step. As he complained to Harvey: "I said that every time I had to meet anyone connected with these [Castro assassination] operations that I would have to first get rid of the tails of the FBI and then come again to wherever I had to do."

Eventually, Roselli told Harvey that he felt like a pawn in an interagency rivalry. "At that time, I was beginning to feel that this was a pressure on the FBI's part to gather me in for some nefarious scheme of their own—that they wanted to find out about the CIA," he recalled. "I was always under that impression and it proved to be that later."

While in the Keys, Johnny remained deadly serious about their mission. He knew Harvey faced White House pressure for better results against Castro. In particular, Bobby Kennedy couldn't understand why the CIA hadn't infiltrated spies successfully into Cuba.

From his front row seat, Johnny recognized the tactical difficulties for Harvey. He didn't doubt the agency's efforts to pierce Castro's defenses. He appreciated Harvey's skill and instincts as a master spy. For all of Harvey's rough edges, Johnny considered him "more of a pro" than the private detective Robert Maheu or "Big Jim" O'Connell, his previous CIA handler.

Increasingly, Johnny admired the heroism shown by Cuban exile fighters, more brave than skilled as soldiers. Many were former teachers, businessmen, or lawyers who lost everything in the revolution. All were dedicated to eradicating Cuba of its Communist dictator.

In his role as advisor, Roselli had prepared one team who nearly assassinated Castro at a Havana intersection in September 1961. Johnny never found out exactly what happened. But Castro's government later announced they'd captured the four exiles with bazookas, grenade launchers, and machine guns. All were executed. Johnny knew of other anti-Castro guerilla fighters—delivered at night by the *Texana* to Cuba's northern shores—who shared a similar fate before Castro's firing squads.

Things were different now than when Sam and Johnny first listened at the Fontainebleau to the CIA's assassination scheme. In this second wave, a post-Bay of Pigs covert war against Castro, Roselli became more of an active participant than a remote adviser. He identified with the Cuban exile cause more than ever. Johnny felt "sorry for the poor bastards left on the beach" at the Bay of Pigs, said a government memo, describing the gangsters' actions. "Roselli felt indirectly responsible for their deaths since he had encouraged many of them to participate in the invasion."

From a safe distance in Chicago, Giancana warned Johnny about getting hurt. Sam himself wasn't inclined toward a risky venture without a big payoff. But Giancana called his friend a patriot, worthy of the government's acclaim rather than scorn. Johnny was "the biggest flag-waving SOB in the country," Sam bragged.

Johnny's risky decision to partake in a mission to Cuba was at the heart of his growing friendship with Harvey. For all of his tailor-made clothing and careful Hollywood-style grooming, Johnny had guts, pure and simple. "It's not hard to imagine Harvey admiring Johnny for having put his life where his mouth was," observed Bayard Stockton, Harvey's biographer.

On this night, Roselli and the crew aboard the *Texana* stopped a few miles from Cuba's northeastern shore, near the Windward Passage, and readied their assault. Their mission aimed to create chaos in Cuba and help Castro's opposition by providing guns, poisons, explosives, and virtually anything else needed.

The CIA re-equipped the *Texana* with a virtual arsenal of weapons. There were concealed deck armaments, fifty-calibre machine guns, two fifty-seven-millimeter recoilless rifles and, most importantly, two small speedboats with muffled interceptor engines. It was part of an impromptu fleet of Cuban exile boats subsidized by the agency, from a five-hundred-foot mother ship to Boston Whalers, rubber boats, and numerous leisure craft painted over.

"They looked like they wouldn't even float but they had the fastest engines in them," recalled William Sturbitts, a CIA Latin American specialist. "They could outrun anything. They were extremely well armed."

Johnny climbed into one of the small boats and followed along with the other toward their designated Cuban site.

As they got closer to the beach, the muted roar of the speedboats could be heard in the dark. These two V-20 speedboats, though not as well-armed as the *Texana*, had gun mounts ready for action. Each were propelled by twin 100-horsepower motors, the kind that might pull water-skiers along in Florida but were also ideal for quick getaways during the CIA spy missions. A fishing net camouflaged the engines to avoid searchlight detection.

On this night, however, the Cuban security agents were waiting.

Whether they had been alerted by counterintelligence, or discovered Roselli's team by sheer good luck, would never be known.

Suddenly, a Cuban patrol boat chased after Roselli's speedboat in the blackish waters until close enough to start firing its machine guns. The spray of bullets ripped across Roselli's boat, tearing away at its bottom. Water rushed in. Johnny realized his boat was sinking rapidly.

Roselli understood the penalty if he were caught by the Cuban G-2 security agents. He was a Mafia mercenary, whom the CIA could easily deny had any connection to the US government. From the very beginning of his tenure as a spy—back at the Brown Derby when first approached by Bob Maheu—Johnny knew his espionage activities would be strictly off the books.

In this cat-and-mouse chase off Cuba's shore, there was no time for Johnny to consider any option but one. He jumped from his sinking speedboat and managed to swim to the other speedboat approaching him. He quickly climbed in. The second speedboat opened up its motors and raced back to the *Texana*.

What happened to the Cuban patrol boat was lost in the night, though it likely returned to shore.

Once Roselli and his crew of Cuban exiles were aboard the *Texana*, they headed back to Florida. Drenched and exhausted, Johnny was one of the lucky ones. Not everyone he had trained made it back in one piece.

During these lengthy CIA excursions, Johnny remained "underground" and out of sight. Giancana and other friends in the States had no idea if Roselli was still alive or dead. Several times, the Chicago mob boss called their mutual pal, Joe Shimon, the crooked former Washington police officer with a lot of Capitol contacts, wondering about Roselli's whereabouts.

"What do you hear from Johnny?" asked Giancana, with apprehension in his voice. He was powerless in getting any answers about his friend.

Shimon was no help. "I hadn't heard anything from Johnny and neither had he," Shimon recalled. A few months later, Shimon returned a call to Giancana with the same concern—what's happened to Johnny? "You know, you figure somebody might have killed him," Shimon later explained. "And he [Giancana] said, 'I don't know. I can't find out.'"

Safely back at Port Mary, Johnny recounted his misadventures in Cuba's midnight waters to Harvey and the other CIA officials, according to Harvey's biographer and other written accounts. With gnawing suspicion, they theorized Castro's patrol boats had been waiting for them, that somehow they'd been notified in advance.

But there was no doubt Johnny would try again.

CHAPTER 27:

BIRDS OF PREY

"You never know when a worm goes into someone's head."
—JAMES JESUS ANGLETON, CIA CHIEF OF COUNTERINTELLIGENCE

Fidel Castro was no easy prey. The Cuban dictator proved far more elusive than the US government expected. After three years, the CIA had spent millions for numerous assassination attempts that turned out botched or disappointing. These failures of nerve or planning were buried bureaucratically and kept unknown to the American public.

One haunting trend emerged. Too many times, Castro's G-2 security forces seemed to anticipate the CIA's moves in a deadly game of hide-and-seek. The failed powerboat landing at night by Roselli—which nearly cost him his life—was only one of many examples.

"*Castro Agent in US Informing on Sabotage Raids Against Cuba*," warned one top-secret Defense Intelligence memo. It described how a "security leak in the US" tipped off Castro's forces in advance. As a result, "all saboteurs that are apprehended upon arriving in Cuba are arrested because individual in US alerts GOC [Government of Cuba] regarding number of saboteurs, how, when and where they will arrive in Cuba."

Bill Harvey was determined to plug these security leaks. He too suspected double agents within the Cuban exile community, some placed in the Miami area deliberately to relay warnings and critical information to Castro's spies.

Much of his hunch was based on the kind of investigative instinct that Harvey used to expose Soviet spy Kim Philby in the 1950s. In fall 1961, he'd discussed the problem of Cuba with his friend James Jesus Angleton, the legendary counterintelligence chief. Angleton was far more focused then on sophisticated Soviet spies and "moles" in his own agency than whatever security threat Castro's infant G-2 posed.

At lunch with a British MI5 spy friend, Angleton and Harvey discussed how best to get rid of the pesky bearded Communist leader.

"What would the Brits do in Cuba?" the MI5 agent was asked. "Would you hit [Castro]?" During the 1956 Suez crisis, the British had discussed murdering Egyptian president Gamal Abdel Nasser, a troublesome figure, but never executed the plan.

Without mentioning Roselli, Harvey indicated the CIA was now in the same kind of killing game. "We're developing a new capacity in the Company to handle these kinds of problems," he explained. "And we're in the market for the requisite expertise."

By April 1962, when Harvey shared drinks with Roselli at the Miami Airport, he expressed his conviction that the earlier plots to kill Castro "had been penetrated." It was CIA lingo for learning that a double agent was in their midst, feeding important operational details to the enemy.

Inside the cocktail lounge, Roselli and Harvey made an improbable pair. Bald, sweaty, and overweight, the intense CIA agent seemed an odd contrast to Johnny, who favored snappy clothes, alligator shoes, and a two thousand dollar watch. Yet as they worked together as partners on the plan to kill Castro, they learned that they shared many similar views and judgments of people. Both lived by their instincts.

As he sipped a double martini, Harvey explained to Roselli why he didn't trust Santo Trafficante Jr., the Florida-based Mafia leader who had acted as a Spanish-speaking go-between with Sam and Johnny, the CIA, and the Cuban exiles. He spoke of Trafficante in suspicious tones. But Johnny wasn't ready to agree.

In Roselli's estimate, Trafficante was merely doing a favor for his "good friend" Sam Giancana and his Hollywood mob associate. Along with his thick glasses, the Florida don usually wore a bow tie and seersucker suit in public, making him appear more like a pleasant bookkeeper than a cunning assassin.

Privately, Trafficante remained skeptical of the CIA's plans. "I looked at Johnny and I thought he must be some kind of idiot to believe that somebody could just go down there and kill Castro," Trafficante later told his mob attorney Frank Ragano. "Sam told me to play along to help Johnny and I introduced the CIA guys to some of my Cuban friends."

Trafficante made it sound like he'd stumbled upon some government boondoggle. He didn't seem like a turncoat trading secrets with a foreign nation. "The CIA had all this foolish talk about poisoning Castro—those crazy people," he said to Ragano.

"They gave me some pills to kill Castro. I just flushed them down the toilet. They paid us a lot of money and nobody intended to do a damn thing. It was a real killing."

But Harvey smelled a rat. Too many "favors" offered by Trafficante didn't add up. Perhaps the previous CIA team of Maheu and O'Connell were too naïve or lazy to detect how Trafficante had misled them. Certainly the Florida mobster put his own interests first. As his lawyer Ragano later admitted in his own confessional book: "Santo was no patriot and had no reservations about swindling the government."

Rather than motivated by anti-Communist ideology, Trafficante's contacts were often related to his Mafia drug business. For example, Trafficante introduced the CIA's Maheu and O'Connell to Raul Gonzalez Jerez. Years earlier, Gonzalez had worked with Trafficante at the Mafia-run Sans Souci casino in Havana, and also owned the 21 Club restaurant in Southern Florida's "Little Havana" section. As an exile in Florida, Gonzalez remained in Trafficante's underworld organization and was "deeply involved in narcotics trafficking," a later FBI memo said.

Drug money was vital to Trafficante's empire. The international flow of cocaine, heroin, and marijuana from the Caribbean into Florida depended in part on Castro's cooperation. For years, Santo had been considered a major financier of the narcotics trade though he always managed to evade authorities. Similarly, Trafficante's duplicity as a spy led other US investigators by 1962 to develop the same suspicions as Harvey. "The implication was that he [Trafficante] had sabotaged the CIA's first assassination attempt on Castro, and had probably betrayed the CIA in other ways as well," recalled Charles Siragusa, a federal narcotics investigator who specialized in mob probes.

Harvey also doubted Tony Varona, the Cuban exile leader involved in the Castro poison plot, who had a number of corrupt business deals in Miami with Trafficante.

Too much trust had been placed in the hands of Varona and his Havana insider, Juan Orta, who supposedly got "cold feet" with the initial attempts. When he inherited the Cuban Project, Harvey signed off on a similar poison pill scheme against Castro that also went nowhere. Feeling duped, Harvey directed Roselli to forget about such plans. Instead, at Port Mary, Roselli concentrated on readying snipers for death squads secreted into Cuba at night.

Orta turned out to be an odd choice to entrust with a Castro assassination plot. In checking out his background, US intelligence officials needed only to go to a local library and find Orta's name in the *New York Times* annual index. A front-page March

1960 story identified Orta as Castro's "personal secretary" who had rigged an illegal plane flight over Cuba to make the incident look like US aggression. Both Orta and Ramiro Valdes (later head of Cuba's G-2 spy agency) were linked to the plane's pilots, the story said. Given his past history, Orta was more likely a double agent for the Cuban spy agency than, as Trafficante claimed earlier, a friendly volunteer agreeable to killing Castro.

Sharing the same doubts, Kennedy historian Arthur M. Schlesinger Jr. later recalled how Trafficante managed in 1959 to spend time in a Castro prison without facing the firing squad like so many others. Schlesinger quoted a 1961 Federal Narcotics Bureau document saying Castro had "kept Santo Trafficante Jr. in jail to make it appear that he had a personal dislike for Trafficante, when in fact Trafficante is an agent of Castro. Trafficante is allegedly Castro's outlet for illegal contraband in the country."

Castro wanted the millions in Mafia narcotics revenue to prop up his own revolutionary government, Schlesinger suggested. But in the early 1960s, Schlesinger's White House colleagues, as well as top CIA officials above Harvey, were far more concerned about the spread of Communism than drug addiction.

Cuba's network of spies and double agents grew exponentially after the Bay of Pigs. The CIA-sponsored invasion heightened Castro's awareness of assassination plots against him. He urged Cubans to inform against their fellow citizens as a "patriotic duty." Castro's constant suspicions and need for protection made the lethal task for Harvey and his hitman Roselli infinitely more difficult.

Castro asked the Soviets to train hundreds of G-2 agents within its *Dirección General de Inteligencia*." The Russians had a long history of espionage and the Cubans learned quickly. Castro relied on Ramiro Valdes, an old comrade who fought with him in the 1950s, to keep a tight fist on his spy agency and those who would betray them. His double agents were nefarious. Some were able to pass polygraph tests with undetected lies. More than four dozen Cubans working as CIA spies were actually double agents for the Cuban government.

Security became the Castro regime's constant concern. Along with Valdes, the dictator's brother, Raul Castro, was important to security as well as Ernesto "Che" Guevara, the charismatic Marxist. They mercilessly imposed firing squads and imprisonment against dissidents.

Overseeing all spying, however, was Fidel. Like a puppet master, he allowed his double agents to leak sensitive Cuban information just so that the CIA would be thrown off or to avoid scrutiny. "The Cubans' skill at keeping their own double-cross system secure for so long was an unparalleled accomplishment," observed historian and former US intelligence officer Brian Latell.

Inside Cuba, the Americans tried to maintain their own top-secret set of spies and double agents. One was known by his cryptonym AMFOX-1. He would remain undetected by Castro for more than a decade. Secret writing (SW) techniques allowed double agents to communicate with the CIA's station in Florida. Once relying on lemon juice, milk, or urine as undetectable ink, the United States developed special chemicals and papers so agents would not be caught by Cuban security.

Several CIA spies had transmitters inside Cuba. To avoid radio detectors, some agents would signal coded messages at a prescribed time and frequency. Another "burst" method sent numerically coded messages quickly through a high-speed transmitter.

One of those informers with a radio transmitter was Castro's sister, Juanita. Using the codename "Donna," she helped opponents of her brother's government avoid detection, capture, and possible execution. To signal whether she had a message or not, Juanita would play a waltz or a song from the opera Madame Butterfly to alert the CIA.

Juanita Castro later said she became a spy in mid-1961 against her brother's government because of all the bloodshed it caused. She refused any money from the CIA or to participate in anything violent. "Did I feel remorse about betraying Fidel by agreeing to meet with his enemies?" she wrote. "No, for one simple reason: I didn't betray him. He betrayed me."

Juanita's painful stance reflected how much Fidel himself had changed. This once idealistic Jesuit-trained young man had turned to Communism and its embrace of atheism, all for political gain. Fidel became an apostate for power, rejecting their family traditions. Her brother's revolutionary government grabbed and nationalized their dead father's large sugarcane plantation, where much of their family still lived. Fidel condemned the Catholic Church in which they were raised by their devout mother. And he expelled the Jesuits from Cuba, including his former teachers, with the same coldness he treated his political opponents.

In Juanita's eyes, her brother was nothing more than a pawn in the struggle between two superpowers. "Fidel's radical conversion to communism was not made from political conviction but simply because he needed power, which is the only thing that he has ever cared about," she later wrote. "Without the Russians he would not have been able to carry on."

In the gamesmanship of Cold War espionage, Harvey knew what a prize turning Castro's sister into a double agent would be to his bosses back in Washington. She had only one condition. As Harvey relayed in a memo, the CIA had "obtained Juanita's agreement to provide intelligence on the Cuban political leadership and to work against the Cuban communist regime, short of engaging in activity which might result in direct personal harm to her brothers Raul and Fidel."

Apparently, Juanita didn't have a clue, not an inkling, what murderous plans the CIA already had in store for her brother Fidel.

The attempts on Castro became more violent in nature under Harvey. He no longer agreed with the CIA's previous approach of using poison or some lethal sedative. Harvey wanted the Bearded One to exit this world with a bang.

A death squad of three CIA operatives managed to land at night and locate themselves in an apartment overlooking the presidential palace. They waited for Castro to appear at a ceremony for visiting Soviet cosmonauts. They aimed to blow apart his podium with bazookas which they had carried in their small speedboat.

However, when Harvey's spies tried to fire the bazookas, they didn't work. They were still too wet from their journey. G-2 security agents soon arrested these operatives and found explosives and submachine guns hidden in a false wall of their apartment.

With numerous plots against him, Castro kept an array of bodyguards. He went to great lengths to protect his own safety. Roselli tried to break through his wall of protection by using a three-man team of exiles to infiltrate Cuba and take another long-distance shot at Castro during a public event. That attempt failed as well. Plans in September 1962 to send another three-man death squad never got off the ground.

Ironically, it wasn't until March 1963 that Castro came closest to death—from a poison capsule still lingering in Cuba. It was from the second batch that Harvey approved and Roselli sent to Cuba through Tony Varona's contacts.

One of the CIA conspirators, Santos de la Caridad Perez Nunez, once worked for the Mafia in their Havana casinos. He longed for the old Batista days instead of

Cuba's socialist regime, mired in poverty and memories of yesteryear. If Castro was eliminated, Caridad hoped the American gangsters would return and reopen Sans Souci and the other opulent casinos.

One evening, opportunity for murder presented itself. Caridad was serving as a waiter at the Hotel Havana Libre, a Castro favorite, when the dictator suddenly showed up in his café. Fidel asked for a chocolate shake.

Inside the kitchen, Caridad reached into a refrigerator, where a smuggled capsule was hidden along a back panel. Unfortunately, the capsule froze against its metal siding. He tried to free it, but the capsule burst.

Unaware of this drama, Fidel blithely drank his shake. He then thanked his would-be assassin and returned to his normal routine.

After so much failure, Harvey relayed his doubts about this elaborate game of assassination to his CIA boss Richard Helms. Too much of the CIA's efforts relied on characters like Tony Varona and other Cubans mixed up with Trafficante. Roselli's courageous actions were one of the few bright spots he could offer.

Helms urged Harvey not to give up. "If you needed somebody to carry out murder, I guess you had a man who might be prepared to carry it out," Helms later remarked about Roselli. Harvey's superiors, all deskmen, made the job of killing Castro sound easy, like swinging at a spinning piñata. All that was needed was one good hit to knock the stuffing out of everything.

However, lacking the kind of bloody results that Kennedy officials in Washington were demanding, Harvey and his Florida station chief Ted Shackley blamed the Cuban exiles for this failure rather than themselves. Assassinating the Communist dictator would be much harder than they imagined.

"While brave and dedicated to the cause of defeating Castro, Cubans did not see themselves as being prepared to pay the ultimate price—their own lives—in order to kill Castro," Shackley complained. "Built into all of their assassination outlines was action at a distance, an element that inevitably reduced any prospects of success."

The Americans liked to think of themselves as cowboys rather than cowards. Yet these same CIA higher-ups also kept their distance. They displayed the same aversion to cloak-and-dagger danger as the Cuban exiles did. Both didn't want their hands stained by this "dirty business."

CHAPTER 28:

SING FOR YOUR SUPPER

Villa Venice was a hit. The newly renovated supper club outside Chicago, secretly owned by Sam Giancana, opened to rave reviews and a sold-out holiday audience.

"It's been like old times to see the crowds and the familiar faces at the Villa Venice, where Frank Sinatra, Dean Martin, and Sammy Davis Jr. are winding up their one-week stand tonight," the *Chicago Tribune* observed in December 1962. "The chairs are pushed so closely together you can't shove your way between them."

Packing them in was the penance Giancana demanded from Sinatra, his star attraction. He blamed the singer for "disloyalty" with the Kennedys and being unable to dissuade them from the government's relentless Mafia investigations. Instead of killing Sinatra in retribution—as some grisly suggested—Sam demanded the crooner and his Rat Pack buddies perform for free.

Top mobsters and high-rollers flew in from around the country. Seated courtside were home-grown hoodlums like Joe Fishetti, Sinatra's pal at the Fontainebleau in Miami, and Marshall Caifano, the Outfit's man in Las Vegas when Roselli wasn't around. "Practically all of Chicago's top hoodlums, with the exception of Giancana, were present," reported one FBI memo.

Regardless of whose name appeared on the Villa Venice deed, everyone seemed to know whose house it was—Sam Giancana's. He used an alias, "Mr. Flood," but made his presence felt. A week earlier, when Sinatra arranged for singer Eddie Fisher to appear, Sam was more conspicuous. He sat in the front row with girlfriend Judy Campbell.

Insisting that the Rat Pack, then America's most celebrated entertainers, appear *gratis* was a clear sign of Giancana's clout.

Dressed up in tuxedo, Martin made light of the tension. "Hold the noise down," he instructed, pointing to a penthouse apartment overlooking the stage. "There's a gangster sleeping up there."

Sinatra arranged for a stream of entertainers to play the Villa Venice, which garnered big crowds. Patrons floated to their seats in Venetian boats manned by gondoliers, who steered them across a man-made canal to an 800-seat auditorium. Between shows, the big spenders shuttled back and forth to a nearby Quonset hut, where casino-like gambling tables were set up.

The roulette wheels, craps, and blackjack games, all crooked, were the main enticements where Sam made his big money. Giancana and the Outfit collected an estimated three million dollars from the illegal gambling and gala entertainment at the Villa Venice, before it soon closed down like a traveling circus.

Sinatra and his Rat Pack friends appeared under "what can only be termed a command performance," the FBI reported. Agents quizzed Sammy Davis Jr., like the other reluctant performers, about his knowledge of Giancana's Outfit.

"Baby, let me say this," explained Davis, who lost his left eye years earlier in a car accident. "I got one eye, and that one eye sees a lot of things that my brain tells me I shouldn't talk about. Because my brain says that, if I do, my one eye might not be seeing anything after a while."

During a rendition of "The Lady Is A Tramp," Martin worked a sly joke into the song about their situation: *"I love Chicago, it's carefree and gay; I'd even work here without any pay."*

Missing from the Chicago festivities was Peter Lawford, the president's brother-in-law. A few months earlier, Sinatra had dumped him from the Rat Pack.

Lawford's banishment was a jarring reversal. In the late 1950s, the actor introduced Jack Kennedy to Sinatra and his swinging entertainment world in Las Vegas and Los Angeles, a friendly alliance full of women and good times that carried through the 1960 election.

But as the Justice Department compiled an increasingly thick dossier on Giancana and Roselli, Attorney General Robert Kennedy warned his brother to steer clear of Sinatra because of his devotion to his Mafia friends. Lawford tried to intervene to stop Bobby's anti-Mafia campaign, just as Sinatra did, but was firmly rebuffed.

"You know, as much as I like Frank, I can't go there, not while Bobby is handling this [the Giancana] investigation," the president explained to Lawford.

The rift became deeply personal in March 1962, when the White House asked Lawford to inform Frank that the president, during a West Coast visit, wouldn't be staying at Sinatra's California home as planned but rather a nearby place owned by singer Bing Crosby. Sinatra was stunned by the rebuff. He adored JFK and had built a helicopter pad for his arrival. He devoted a room in his Palm Springs house to their friendship. On a wall, there hung a framed note signed by the president: *"Frank— How much can I count on the boys in Vegas? JFK."*

Lawford blamed "security" concerns for the last-minute cancellation. But the real reason was Sinatra's connections to Giancana and their mutual affair with Judy Campbell. In fact, the day before Kennedy arrived at Bing Crosby's home, the president had met with the FBI's J. Edgar Hoover at a private White House lunch about the very compromising matter.

After Lawford's call, Sinatra reached Bobby Kennedy himself.

"What is this shit?" Frank was heard saying. Bobby refused to budge. Sinatra listened for a moment, furious at the betrayal. Then he flung the phone against a wall. The singer peered out a window, unable to say anything.

"There was an endless silence," recalled his assistant, George Jacobs. "He stood there staring out at the desert, as if someone had told him his folks had died. It took him about five minutes before he could tell me."

After hearing of the reaction, the president called Sinatra to emphasize the decision was made by the Secret Service. He urged him not to blame Lawford. "Frank didn't buy that for a minute," Lawford recalled, "and with a few exceptions, he never spoke to me again."

While he still admired the president, Frank aimed his rage at Lawford. He cut him out of all future Rat Pack activities.

To the mob, their man Sinatra had been played for a fool. "They [the Kennedys] used him [Sinatra] to help them raise money, then they turn around and say they're great fighters against corruption," complained mobster Vincent "Fat Vinnie" Teresa, in a howl picked up by FBI microphones. "They criticize other people for being with mob guys. They're hypocrites."

The accumulation of FBI evidence—based on telephone traces, listening devices, and constant surveillance—documented numerous contacts between Sinatra and Giancana. It also cast a spotlight on Jack Kennedy's libertine lifestyle, both before and after he became president, which appeared reckless and open to blackmail.

One FBI memo dated August 1962 claimed President Kennedy personally telephoned Sinatra while he was appearing with Dean Martin at an Atlantic City nightclub where Giancana was a special guest. Another memo said Giancana stayed at Sinatra's home the following month.

Testimony released decades later suggested still another reason why the Kennedys dropped Sinatra—FBI listening devices picked up conversations between Giancana and the singer about Frank's alleged affair with Pat Lawford, the president's sister, as a possible way of compromising her brothers. "These tapes were played back to Bobby [Kennedy] and Bobby went, wow, and overnight you saw Sinatra out," recalled Joe Shimon, the crooked Washington cop who befriended Sam and Johnny.

. Overall, these FBI files reflect both Hoover's obsession with the Kennedys as well as the poor judgment of Jack Kennedy, whose private behavior and philandering would later disappoint his Camelot admirers.

The pressure mounted for Giancana and Roselli. On the street, they felt the constant presence of FBI agents always following them. Typically, Johnny made light of it. As he entered one Los Angeles building, Roselli held open the door for the agents chasing him.

"I know, I know, you're just doing your job," he said with a smirk.

Unlike Sam's defiant confrontations, Roselli believed he could somehow beguile the agents into liking him. Part of the Bureau's fascination was with Johnny's playboy lifestyle. One prying FBI agent noted pruriently how Roselli "stopped and picked up a blonde woman" in Beverly Hills and then they drove off together into a nighttime of delights.

The bureau's waiting game, with its prying and snooping, continued as it had for years. Johnny resented the hounding by Robert Kennedy's Justice Department. He had a feeling that every private conversation was being listened to. Staying at the Diplomat Apartments in Los Angeles, Johnny warned the manager that he would sue if he found his residence had been bugged.

Roselli suspected the purpose was to keep him quiet about JFK's affair with Judy Campbell and her links to Sam. "He was just trying to discredit me," Johnny later said of RFK. "That's all I can think . . . . I think he was trying to save the image—we will discredit this guy if he does open up or if he does talk about it."

For Roselli, it was hard to figure out the federal government's puzzling view toward him. The FBI's harassing approach was directly contrary to the steady flow of compliments the CIA bestowed in their fight against Castro.

By mid-1962, Sam Giancana was no longer a good soldier in America's spy wars. "Operation Lockstep"—the Justice Department campaign to track Giancana's every move—had taken its toll.

"He trusted no one, not Phyllis [McGuire], not his daughters, not those he worked with," recalled his eldest daughter Antoinette. "He was paranoid about being watched, about there being a government agent behind every door, and with some justification."

For a short time, Sam didn't trust even his good friend Roselli. He ordered another mobster, Charlie "Babe" Barron, to keep an eye on Johnny, in case he might be short-changing him in Las Vegas.

FBI agents followed Sam everywhere. They could be seen watching in restaurants, driving behind him in Chicago neighborhoods. "Here I am!" he taunted one cop who lost him on a tail.

While relaxing at the Fontainebleau Hotel, Giancana discovered an agent hiding in a palm tree. The G-man slipped and tumbled in front of him. Sam wasn't amused.

Both Sam and Johnny, who golfed together whenever possible, spotted FBI agents tailing them on the links. Some agents played right behind them.

"As far as I know, this is the first PGA-sponsored golf tournament in which victory is shared by the Cosa Nostra," joked Chicago columnist Mike Royko, describing a local country club event featuring Giancana's pals.

In his zeal, Chicago FBI agent William Roemer perversely enjoyed upsetting Sam. "At the golf course, I'd follow him to the men's room and stand next to him," Roemer explained. His confrontation at the urinal mortified Sam. "He had shy kidneys so when I was there he couldn't go."

Roemer's aggression seemed sanctioned by Attorney General Kennedy. Early in his tenure, Kennedy visited the FBI's Chicago office, where the number of agents climbed from five to seventy. "He was most knowledgeable about the Chicago mob," said Roemer about Kennedy. "I was surprised he knew so much about one guy in particular: Sam Giancana."

Eventually, Giancana became fed up with the constant heat, the pervasive government surveillance. "This is like Nazi Germany and I'm the biggest Jew in the country," he complained crudely.

Giancana decided his entire Mafia empire, generating millions of dollars every month, should be shut down immediately rather than run the risk of a long-term jail sentence. "Tell everyone that everything is off," he ordered associates after a round of coercive tactics by FBI agents like Roemer. "This is it, because of the G. we ain't spending another nickel. Everyone is on their own. They got to make it any way they can."

Stopping the open spigot of money flowing into the Outfit's coffers was an unacceptable option, however. Sam's impulsive command didn't sit well with senior consigliere Tony Accardo, who again urged caution to Giancana. "You can't go giving these [FBI] guys abuse," Accardo advised. "You got to talk to them."

Instead Sam proposed killing Roemer. "I've had enough of that guy," Sam urged. "I'm putting up a fund of $100,000 to figure out how to get that guy!"

Accardo shook his head. "That would be counterproductive," Accardo advised. "The whole FBI would come down on us from all over the country if we hit one of them. Call it off. Now."

Sam took another route, though hardly a compromise solution.

Giancana decided to file a federal lawsuit against the FBI, claiming the agents were violating his civil rights with their surveillance. He cited the alleged harassment on the golf course by Roemer and others. To nearly everyone's surprise, a federal judge agreed and ordered Hoover's agents to remain a certain distance as Giancana putted on the green. Only one FBI car could follow him through the neighborhoods as well.

Later, an appeals court overturned the decision. Regardless, Accardo and the other senior Mafioso in Chicago, Paul Ricca, weren't thrilled with Giancana's impudence. His rash, bullheaded decision-making drew many blaring headlines and unwanted attention from the government. As Antoinette recalled, "I know that it was Paul (Ricca) who guided Sam along, who sponsored his elevation to boss of Chicago, and it was he who was most disappointed and hurt when my father deviated from the ways of the Old Country, became involved with women in the entertainment world, and focused attention on himself and the Chicago mob."

Like his friend Sinatra, Sam stood his ground and remained doggedly independent. The US government—which had once considered Giancana good enough to fight Cuban tyranny—wasn't going to tell him what to do or take away his liberties.

"When you talk about heat, you're talking to a man who's been through the mill," Giancana explained about the FBI intrusion. "I took the feds to court and won the fucking case but the appeals courts stayed it. Still, you know, you've got to fight back. Or they'll suck your blood until you're nothing but a fucking corpse."

CHAPTER 29:

THE DOUBLE AGENT

*"And they tell me you are crooked and I answer: Yes, it is true I have
seen the gunman kill and go free to kill again."*

—CARL SANDBURG, "CHICAGO"

Writhing in pain, hoodlum Billy McCarthy refused to tell his tormentors
what they wanted to hear. He remained defiant even while his head was
being squeezed in a metal vise.

In May 1962, McCarthy and another burglar, Jimmy Miraglia, faced the ire of
Sam Giancana's Outfit for murdering two fellow hoodlums in Elmwood Park. The
outrage didn't stem so much from their double homicide, but rather that such savagery took place in the suburban Chicago neighborhood where many top gangsters
lived nearby.

McCarthy was the first to be caught and tortured. The most sadistic of Giancana's
enforcers, Sam "Mad Sam" DeStefano and his apprentice Tony Spilotro, demanded
McCarthy reveal the whereabouts of his accomplice.

When McCarthy refused, they beat him severely and pierced his scrotum with an
ice pick.

"We finally got so pissed off we put his head in a vise and turned it," Spilotro
recalled of McCarthy's ordeal. "The kid's eyeball popped right out of his fuckin' head.
Billy begged me to kill him. He gave up Jimmy's name just before he died."

Eventually the two enforcers caught up with Miraglia, the second burglar, and
strangled him. They stuffed his bloody body and McCarthy's corpse into a car trunk.
Both were left to rot until a passerby discovered their putrid remains.

Gruesome death scenes were a notorious specialty for DeStefano. He was a veteran
executioner, known for splaying victims inside his home's soundproof cellar.

Spilotro, a relative novice, saw this dual torture death as a career opportunity to earn his "spurs" as a made man in the Mafia. Eager to impress, Spilotro kept hacking and whacking away with greater bloodlust than Mad Sam.

"Find Torture Angle in Auto Trunk Deaths—Two Beaten Beyond Recognition," thundered the *Chicago Tribune* headline, with no clue of who had instigated the murders.

Along with unwanted publicity like this, Sam Giancana's reign as gangland general in Chicago was marked by a disturbing lack of discipline among his troops. Senior gangsters like Tony Accardo and Paul Ricca, both of River Forest, were appalled that two young punks would violate their unwritten codes by committing a murder adjacent to their hometown. Even the FBI knew better.

"Every thief in Chicago knew that Elmwood Park and River Forest were off-limits in those days because so many of the top leaders of the Outfit lived there," recalled Chicago agent William Roemer Jr. "The mob ordered that those two bedroom communities of Chicago were to be kept clean so that the police could not swoop down on the mobsters in their homes and embarrass them in front of the neighbors and the kids. So when M&M [McCarthy and Miraglia] did their thing in Elmwood Park, they were in big trouble."

Despite the community outrage, nothing seemed to come of "the M&M killings," as the newspapers called it. During this time, Giancana and his crew perpetrated some of Chicago's most heinous crimes, yet they appeared immune from any prosecution. Giancana's bulletproof status re-enforced his reputation as a mob potentate.

This aura of invincibility, however, depended on Giancana's own system of spies. In particular, the public didn't realize how much Giancana relied on Richard Cain—the defrocked Chicago cop—as a double agent in the Cook County Sheriff's Office to provide him with inside information.

Like a true spy, Cain constantly played one alliance against the other. He informed and betrayed, over and over again—between law-enforcement and the Mafia, between the CIA and the FBI, between angry Cuban exiles and those leftists who favored Castro. He covered up crimes, selectively investigated others, and committed some himself.

In the center of this maelstrom was thirty-one-year-old Cain, a made member of Giancana's crime family, hoping he wouldn't get caught or get killed.

After leaving the Chicago police department under a cloud in 1960, Cain went to work ostensibly for a detective agency in Florida, but secretly collaborated with Sam Giancana and Johnny Roselli in the CIA's assassination plans against Castro.

In the Miami area, Sam relied on Cain to keep an eye on the anti-Castro Cuban exiles, just as he had done within the Chicago police department. He shared their hope of returning to Havana someday. "He [Dick Cain] knew that if he was able to get in tight with the Cubans and participate in their recovery of Cuba, then he would be a big man indeed in the eyes of Sam Giancana and the rest of the organized crime bosses," observed his half-brother, Michael J. Cain.

But the loyalties of Richard Cain were never clear. In Chicago, he once visited the CIA's local office, offering to squeal on anti-Castro Cuban exiles in the city. Yet later, while in Mexico City, he reported to CIA agents about pro-Castro Cuban Communist clandestine operations going on locally.

For his own purposes, Giancana relied on Cain—who spoke Spanish fluently—as his international man of mystery. On one mission, Cain worked with two other Giancana aides, Carmen Peter Bastone and Leslie "Killer Kane" Kruse, looking to establish casinos in Latin American locales like the Dominican Republic.

Flush with fast money from the Villa Venice success, Giancana had visions of an international Mafia gambling empire dancing in his head. His longtime compadre Roselli had urged this ambitious idea for years. International casinos and their countless riches seem like diamonds sparkling from afar. Johnny already had provided such get-rich advice to another casino owner in Guatemala.

Doubters of these foreign plans, like Tony Accardo, had to be impressed with Giancana's bundles of domestic cash from the Villa Venice, Sinatra's Rat Pack show and the Quonset hut gambling in November 1962. Villa Venice was merely the "modest beginnings for a grandiose scheme by my father and the Outfit to establish the power of the Chicago Mafia in casinos all over the world," recalled his daughter, Antoinette.

Sam and Johnny were looking for action globally because the shutdown in Cuba had changed everything. The Chicago mob pursued gambling possibilities in Puerto Rico, Jamaica, Freeport, and the Grand Bahamas after the failed Bay of Pigs invasion made it clear Havana's mob-run casinos wouldn't be revived anytime soon. Judy

Campbell recalled the two pals discussing gambling plans for South America, though she didn't give it much mind. "It was just conversation that meant nothing to me," Campbell later testified vaguely. "Maybe gambling casinos and things like that."

Cain became the Chicago mob's main agitator abroad. "Cain is believed to have been Giancana's contribution to the CIA attempt to overthrow Castro," the *Chicago Tribune* later reported, before Roselli's involvement became widely known. "Cain already made a survey of gambling casino possibilities in Lima, Peru and the Caribbean during the 1960s."

During this time, Cain never lost his loose CIA connections. Cain worked with Tony Varona, the Cuban exile leader with agency connections, as well as Roselli and Santo Trafficante Jr. in various shady deals. His trips to Florida and Cuba seemed more than coincidental, suggesting Cain might be a would-be assassin as well. "The suspicion is that Cain was being sent by Giancana to supervise the poisoning attempt on Fidel Castro," investigators later concluded.

In April 1962, Cain showed up at the US Embassy in Mexico City, telling CIA officers that he was operating an investigative agency and "looking into communism in Central America." However, two months later, Mexican authorities ousted Cain for violating his work permit to train others in using lie detectors and other high-tech surveillance devices. Perhaps more tellingly, authorities also deported Cain for carrying a loaded revolver and brass knuckles. It was hardly the calling card of a diplomat.

––––––

Cain's greatest duplicity, however, occurred when he got back to Chicago. He spent his first day having lunch with Sam Giancana. Then he shared dinner with Dick Ogilvie, the soon-to-be elected Sheriff of Cook County, who promised to be an anti-corruption reformer with a squeaky-clean reputation. Cain's amazing personal reach across the criminal spectrum—from Chicago's top hoodlum to a top lawman—was part of his paradox.

Ogilvie always seemed to trust Cain. He became impressed with Cain in the late 1950s as a federal prosecutor investigating Tony Accardo for tax fraud. Cain was then a Chicago police officer assigned to Ogilvie's special unit in the US Attorney's office with access to many sensitive cases.

Privately, though, Cain acted as a mole for Giancana. Ogilvie had no idea about this great betrayal. Another investigator in that unit, FBI agent William Roemer, admired Cain's dexterity with listening devices and wiretaps. But unlike Ogilvie, Roemer's admiration for Cain's detective skills gradually turned to doubts about his honesty.

During Accardo's November 1960 trial, Cain secretly provided inside information to Giancana. Sam sought to help his consigliere avoid going to jail for a tax crime as Al Capone once did. A jury convicted Accardo but his case was later overturned on appeal, thanks to flaws in the case pointed out by Cain. Before it could be retried, three key witnesses were murdered. Yet Ogilvie never suspected Cain, whom he considered upright and hard working.

Two years later, when Ogilvie was elected sheriff, Roemer warned him not to hire Cain as his top investigator. But Ogilvie, a respected Republican later elected Illinois governor, didn't believe rumors that his faithful Cain was a spy for Giancana. So Cain got the job.

As chief of the Sheriff's Special Investigations Unit, Cain pursued a quisling course of selective law enforcement. Giancana and Accardo paid him under the table to ignore Mafia wrongdoing. That included recent homicides such as William "Action" Jackson, tortured on a meat hook, and the killing of the M&M hoodlums. Cain heeded the desire of mob-controlled politicians in Chicago to go easy on their corruption. Yet to fanfare in the media, Cain cracked down on bookmakers and drug sellers who weren't protected by the Outfit. Reporters relied on him as a good source.

In fudging the truth, Cain proved an ace with manipulating a polygraph machine. At Giancana's request, Cain gave lie-detector tests to five bank robbery suspects, not to solve crime but rather to find out who was an FBI informant. Unfortunately, Guy Mendola, a tipster known as "Lover Boy," flunked the polygraph test. He was soon shot five times in a gangland-style ambush outside his home.

"Who would kill my son?" Mendola's father cried as his son's body was taken from his bloodied late model Cadillac and rolled away on a stretcher. "Why would they do it?"

In the *Tribune* and other newspapers, lawman Cain's reaction was quoted. He assured the public his office was taking every step to solve the murder.

Cain's ruse, a Mafia made man playing a good guy, carried on for nearly two years in Chicagoland. It allowed his mentor Giancana unbridled freedom in building up his criminal empire without legal repercussions. Giancana's henchmen, such as

"Mad Sam" DeStefano and Tony Spilotro, obviously believed they'd have an easier time getting away with murder too.

One victim was Leo Foreman. When DeStefano insisted on getting paid by Foreman, one of his juice loan collectors, Mad Sam found himself surprisingly tossed out of Foreman's insurance office instead. This indignity wasn't something that a psychopath like Mad Sam could ignore.

Despite his momentary victory, Foreman had a premonition about his fate. "If you find me in a trunk, DeStefano is the man who put me there," he confided to a friend.

Furious about Foreman's disrespect, DeStefano enlisted Tony Spilotro and another hoodlum, Chuckie Crimaldi, to help teach him a final lesson.

The threesome lured Foreman to the house of Sam's brother Mario. Down into the basement they dragged Foreman and tied him to a chair. With a hammer, they slammed his knees, then head, ribs, and crotch. Foreman pleaded for his life.

"I told you I would get you," Mad Sam swore, pulling out his favorite torture device—an ice pick—and stabbing Foreman twenty times.

Dementedly, Mad Sam prolonged his victim's agony by shooting him in the buttocks. Then he sliced up Foreman with a butcher's knife. Giancana's favorite crew of killers took turns cutting chunks of flesh from their victim's arms.

Six months later, a garbage truck driver found Foreman's decomposed body nearly naked in the trunk of a rented car. Witnesses claimed DeStefano was the last one to see Foreman alive.

But thanks to Richard Cain, the perennial double agent in the sheriff's office, this murder, like others linked to the Outfit, would go unsolved. It remained a mystery, just like Cain's shadowy involvement with the CIA.

It was Chicago justice, Giancana-style.

CHAPTER 30:

THE BLACK BOOK

Back in Las Vegas, Johnny Roselli wanted to relax before returning to his adventures as an undercover CIA spy.

Most mornings, Roselli played a round of golf at the Desert Inn Country Club, followed by a steam bath, perhaps a haircut and trim, and a meal at a table overlooking the eighteenth hole. Evenings were spent sharing a few drinks and charming words with beautiful women such as entertainer Betsy Duncan.

"I never saw a dark side of him," recalled Duncan, a singer who dated the suave but older Mafioso in 1962. "I always saw him as generous and very nice and polite."

Not even the hot-headed exploits of Marshall Caifano—chosen by Giancana to oversee Vegas in Roselli's absence—seemed to upset Johnny's unruffled demeanor.

One evening in the lounge where she appeared on the bill, Duncan was horrified as FBI agents barreled in and grabbed Caifano for an arrest. It caused an extended commotion that distracted the audience. Caifano was charged with extorting a rich oil millionaire, Ray Ryan, and trying to kill him. Eventually he went to prison.

But that night, Duncan was surprised by Johnny's nonchalant reaction as Caifano—who used his alias "John Marshall"—was hauled away by federal agents. Caifano, a short muscular man with a boxer's mug, screamed he would get Ryan someday.

"I was singing at the Desert Inn and the FBI came in and carried him out of the casino by his legs," Duncan recalled of Caifano's arrest. "I even asked Johnny Rosselli about that. He said, 'Ah, he's all right.' I said, 'Well, he's not all right when he puts out that he's going to kill somebody.' [Johnny] said nothing."

Roselli's philosophic response deferred to his friend Sam Giancana's judgment. The Chicago chieftain had relocated Caifano to Las Vegas, partly as unique payback for being such a good sport. When Caifano found Giancana was having an affair with his good-looking wife Darlene, he acted flattered by the boss's interest rather than upset.

But Caifano wasn't a pushover in financial matters. As Sam expected, Caifano did take a tougher line with Vegas deadbeats than Roselli, who generally abhorred violence along the Strip as bad for business.

In Chicago, Giancana wasn't averse to extreme acts of violence with those who owed him money. He wanted to let everyone know who was *capo di tutti capi* (boss of all bosses). His power needed to be constantly refreshed by acts of violence. "Some guys are squeamish like little girls," Giancana explained. "They look big and tough and the minute they see a drop of blood they faint dead away."

Caifano, a former Chicago hitman, came from the same school of hard knocks, though his moody acts of violent retribution weren't well received in sunny Vegas. Since his arrival, Caifano had shown remarkably poor judgment. He made outlandish threats and invited retaliation. Yet Caifano's biggest blunder was publicly challenging Nevada's gaming authorities. He quickly alienated those who issued the all-important licenses for casinos where the Chicago Outfit made millions every year.

The Nevada Gaming Control Board, in an effort ostensibly to keep organized crime out, put together a prohibition list of known gangsters—the so-called "Black Book." It banned eleven Mafia figures from any activity in a Nevada gambling establishment. As a result, Roselli had to get rid of his Tropicana Hotel concessions—where he was listed as the owner along with frontman Monte Proser—though he managed to hold on to other business surreptitiously.

The "Black Book" also banned Caifano, Giancana, and Tony Accardo. While none of the mobsters were joyful about being declared *persona non grata*, Caifano decided to file a civil rights lawsuit in federal court, alleging state investigators had treated him unfairly. In testimony justifying their ban, the board chairman, Edward A. Olsen, claimed Caifano had been a suspect in half a dozen murders though never convicted.

Publicity surrounding Caifano's Black Book lawsuit put an unnecessary national spotlight on the Chicago Outfit's control of Las Vegas. Accardo didn't want Caifano stirring up more trouble from the feds. Tony recently had beaten his own tax case. He boasted that he had never spent a night in jail. But Caifano's action threatened more government scrutiny for the Outfit.

"Now Accardo decided enough was enough" and wanted Caifano replaced, the FBI's Roemer recalled. "But as long as Giancana was the boss he chose not to cross him. He talked to Sam but Giancana was adamant. He had promised Caifano this spot and he was a man of his word."

That promise came at great cost. The "Black Book" ban particularly caused difficulty for Giancana at the Cal-Neva Lodge in Lake Tahoe, where he had a secret
interest since 1960. Frank Sinatra was among those named publicly as co-owners.
Under the Black Book rules, Giancana couldn't be seen at this beautiful casino
where, FBI records showed, he was reportedly an owner. Over time, the Cal-Neva
proved a magnet for trouble for both Giancana and his front man Sinatra.

One controversy involved actress Marilyn Monroe. The thirty-six-year-old Hollywood star visited Cal-Neva in July 1962. She stayed in one of its hideaway bungalows
as a guest of Sinatra. That same weekend, Sam and Johnny were also guests, careful
to remain out of view under the "Black Book" ban.

Sinatra and Roselli had known Monroe in Hollywood during the 1950s, both as a
friendly party-goer and a convivial companion in bed. "I met Roselli with Marilyn a
couple of times," recalled actress Jeanne Carmen, a Monroe pal who also dated
Roselli. "We had lunch together. They were being charming." Carmen, who shared
the era's "buxom blonde" look with Monroe, first met Johnny inside Marilyn's
apartment.

But it was Sinatra and fellow Rat Pack pal Peter Lawford who first introduced Jack
Kennedy to Marilyn. There were some parallels to their treatment of Monroe and the
lesser-known Hollywood beauty, Judy Campbell. According to Sinatra's personal
assistant, George Jacobs, the singer passed around attractive women to his powerful
friends like hors d'oeuvres. Sinatra "could bestow a Judy Campbell, or, if he was feeling magnanimous, he could bestow a Marilyn Monroe, such was his beneficence,"
wrote Jacobs. "Marilyn was actually Mr. S's celebrity version of Judy. He had brokered
assignations not only between her and JFK, but also Giancana and Johnny Rosselli."

Famously in May 1962, Monroe sang and cooed "Happy Birthday Mr. President"
to JFK at a huge Madison Square Garden celebration. Various chroniclers have contended Monroe had an affair with both JFK and his brother, Robert, though family
and friends strongly deny it.

What happened at Cal-Neva during that July 1962 weekend is even less clear.
Several published accounts claim Monroe abused pills that weekend and somehow
Giancana had sex with her in an intoxicated condition.

Shortly afterwards, in murky conversations heard through "Mo"—the FBI's listening device in Giancana's Chicago headquarters—agents picked up Johnny Roselli
speaking to Giancana about the Cal-Neva trip.

"You sure get your rocks off fucking the same broad as the brothers, don't you," said Johnny.

This coarse joke between two friends, with a hint of Rat Pack sass, resembled their audacious laughter in a cemetery about Roselli's phony name. Presumably only Johnny could say such provocative things to Giancana without winding up dead.

FBI agent Roemer later claimed the listening devices indicated Monroe "engaged in an orgy. From the conversation I overheard, it appeared she may have had sex with both Sinatra and Giancana on the same trip."

A week later, Monroe died of a barbiturate overdose in Los Angeles. Her dead body was found in August 1962 sprawled across a bed inside her home. Investigators said the movie star had been depressed and suggested she either accidentally overdosed or deliberately took her own life with pills.

The following day, Monroe's friend, Jeanne Carmen, learned of her death from Roselli. Marilyn had earlier bought Jeanne a trio of golf clubs as a gift. The two friends planned to try them out at a place in Monterey.

Instead that morning, Carmen received Johnny's harrowing message. "I heard the phone ring and I thought it was Marilyn," Carmen remembered, "and it turned out that I was getting the bad news."

Authorities ruled the actress's death a "probable suicide," without inquiring much about her earlier stay at Cal-Neva. Reports of Monroe's encounter with Giancana at the casino resort didn't emerge until years later. Despite numerous theories floated in the press (including that Marilyn somehow had learned of the Castro plot), prosecutors found no evidence to suggest foul play.

Neither Sam nor Johnny were ever questioned by police about Monroe's 1962 death. But a year later at Cal-Neva, the two gangsters faced much greater scrutiny on another matter with Sinatra, in a way that suggested their overall luck was beginning to turn.

———————

In summer 1963, Sam Giancana seemed at the height of his powers. He'd won a surprise victory in Chicago, with a federal judge ordering the FBI to desist from its "lockstep" surveillance of the gangster. At least for now, Sam had managed to get agents like Bill Roemer off his back. Sam's successes dispelled the doubts of Accardo and other Mafiosi uneasy with his flashy methods.

"Tony Accardo at this time had let Giancana have his head," recalled Roemer, the FBI agent who later chronicled the Outfit in his true-detective books. "What was there to lose? I don't believe he thought Giancana had a prayer of winning—none of us did—but when he did, Giancana became cocky as hell. He had, after all, done something no other mobster anywhere at any time had done. He'd taken on the FBI and won. Now he became . . . his own man. To hell, he thought, with Tony Accardo."

Sam decided to get away and celebrate. Eluding local police and federal agents curious of his whereabouts, he flew off to Cal-Neva for a long vacation with Phyllis McGuire.

Reflective of his new confidence, Giancana's on-and-off relationship with McGuire appeared on the upswing at Cal-Neva. He apparently had no idea that her brother-in-law had been an FBI informant about his Castro assassination plans. He also didn't seem deterred by her steady refusal to marry him. Despite the couple's past difficulties, Sam tried to ingratiate himself through more gifts and by advancing McGuire's solo career through Sinatra. Undoubtedly, he felt the showbiz connection to Sinatra would help her.

McGuire performed with her sisters at Cal-Neva's Celebrity Room, the theater built by Sinatra. For a flight from Los Angeles, Sam and Phyllis had used an airport limousine registered to Sinatra's production company, FBI records show. (Frank still very much wanted to please his gangster pal. When "Come Blow Your Horn" finally debuted in 1963—the film featuring Sinatra and co-starring McGuire—Frank arranged a Chicago "private showing" for the benefit of friends in Giancana's city.)

During their Cal-Neva stay together, Sam and Phyllis huddled inside Chalet 50, a cottage perched above the sparkling blue lake. To avoid detection by authorities, Sam ate his meals alone in the chalet. He steered away from the lodge's big inviting pool. But the couple could be seen sunning themselves on the porch of Chalet 50, with Frank stopping by to chat with them.

Giancana's rendezvous with McGuire became known because, in the bushes surrounding Chalet 50, investigators for the Nevada Gaming Control Board were watching their every move. In Chicago, Roemer and other local investigators realized Sam had left for Lake Tahoe and alerted Nevada gaming authorities. Investigators snapped several photos of Sam and Frank together at Cal-Neva. Giancana's presence was a clear violation of the "Black Book," what one writer called "The Unsocial Register" of Nevada's gaming world.

Eventually, Sinatra learned of the gaming board's secret surveillance of his guests. Angrily, the singer sought out the gaming board chairman, Ed Olsen, and complained over the telephone.

"Frank called me every name in the book," recalled Olsen, whose aides listened to the conversation on an extension telephone. "I had never heard some of the things he called me."

Though he recognized the voice, Olsen asked officiously to whom he was speaking.

"This is Frank Sinatra! You fucking asshole! F-R-A-N-K, Sinatra," the singer screamed into the receiver. "Now, you listen Ed! I don't have to take this kind of shit from anybody in the country and I'm not going to take it from you people . . . I'm *Frank Sinatra!*"

Cal-Neva employees, both loyal and afraid of its owners, resisted Olsen's follow-up investigation. They claimed they never saw Giancana at its crowded betting tables. "This place was so busy," explained one hireling, "that if Abe Lincoln himself were playing blackjack he wouldn't have been noticed."

Olsen was particularly upset when Paul "Skinny" D'Amato, the mobbed-up pal of Frank and Sam who managed the Cal-Neva, offered bribes to two gaming agents to call off their investigation.

Instead, the Gaming Board took steps to take away Sinatra's license for the Cal-Neva. Sinatra bitterly called the board's actions unfair. He readied for battle at a hearing.

Then at the last minute, Frank blinked. Sinatra sold out his half interest in Cal-Neva and also his 9 percent interest in the Sands Hotel in Las Vegas, which cost him plenty of money because of his questionable friendship with Giancana.

However, Sinatra wouldn't dump his friend Sam, not as the Kennedys had done to him. "This is a way of life and a man has to lead his own life," Sinatra later said about Giancana, the only explanation he ever offered.

One powerful friend tried to help Sinatra with the Cal-Neva dilemma. During this dispute, President Kennedy flew into Las Vegas for a fundraiser and broached the subject with Governor Grant Sawyer while riding together in a motorcade. He asked the Democratic governor if there was anything he could do to help Sinatra's predicament.

"Aren't you people being a little hard on Frank out here?" asked JFK.

Sawyer later told Olsen how dumbfounded he was by Kennedy's comment.

"Well Mr. President, I'll try to take care of things here in Nevada, and I wish you luck on the national level," Sawyer said he replied.

Besides the legal confrontation, Giancana's stay at Cal-Neva was upset by a violent fight—arguably the build-up of tension from his relationship with Phyllis McGuire.

After the McGuire Sisters' opening night, Phyllis invited all their friends back to Chalet 50 for a little party. Phyllis's magnificent blonde beauty, a constant source of pride to middle-aged Gianana, lit up the room. As drinks were passed around, the simmering resentment between the McGuire entourage toward Sam came to the fore.

Too often, the hoodlum's presence seemed to compromise Phyllis's judgment. The bad publicity had taken its toll on their once highly-successful sisters act. Critical comments were made of Phyllis at the party. She kept poking the arm of their skeptical road manager, Victor LaCroix Collins, until, not so playfully, he pushed her back. Phyllis slipped and landed on her rear.

Giancana ignited into a fury. He lunged at Collins, pummeling him with his fists. Sam's diamond ring cut him above the eye. A melee erupted. Witnesses said Collins, a young former bronco rider, was getting the best of the older Mafia don as they wrestled on the ground. Blood spilled on Sam's pearl-gray suit.

Alarmed by the commotion, the hotel staff and Sinatra soon entered the fray. "When Victor made a move, Sinatra jumped on him and held him as tight as he could, while Sam the tough guy punched Victor's lights out," said Roemer, who later talked to Collins about it after he was put in hiding by the FBI.

Sam quickly exited Chalet 50. Sinatra warned Collins that Giancana's henchmen would be out for vengeance. With the mob leader's presence now exposed, Sinatra moaned he'd lose all his money in Nevada casinos.

"What do you mean, your money," Collins replied indignantly. "You don't have a dime in the place. It's all Mafia money and you know it."

An account of the messy encounter—including Sinatra's ties to Giancana and the mob—later appeared as an exposé in *Life* magazine and many other media outlets around the nation. It was more bad publicity for Giancana's detractors to read back in Chicago.

Following the Cal-Neva fiasco, Giancana flew in Sinatra's private plane to Palm Springs, California, where he spent some time at the singer's desert estate before going home to Chicago. He regretted Sinatra's angry provocative call to the gaming board.

"Sam couldn't get over the fact that Frank had done that," McGuire recalled about the profane Olsen telephone exchange. "Sam said, 'If he'd only shut his damned mouth.'"

After seeming invincible, the national glare of publicity for Giancana—and the loss of Cal-Neva, a highly expensive gamble for the Outfit—once again put Sam's authority in doubt. Accardo and Ricca, the senior dons, were definitely not smiling. As FBI Chicago agents said in a prescient August 1963 memo to their Washington superiors: *"Advise that Giancana in extremely tenuous situation because of publicity and consideration seems to be that Giancana may be replaced . . ."*

The end of Sam's reign was nearing, even if he didn't recognize it.

In the past, Giancana had survived threats and challenges with swift retribution and streetwise cunning. But events over the next several months would escalate his precipitous fall in ways Sam and Johnny couldn't have ever imagined.

CHAPTER 31:

THE WAR AT HOME

The "medicine" was still in place.

After months of lethal training in Florida and cultivating spies in Cuba, Johnny Roselli offered some good news in a September 1962 message to his CIA overseer William Harvey. Cryptically, Roselli referred to the "medicine"—a new batch of poison pills recently smuggled into Cuba to kill Castro—and to a second death squad, which would soon be on its way.

These assurances for "Phase Two," as Harvey called it, sounded similar to an initial poison plot called "Phase One" a year earlier.

This time, a three-man team of assassins, who sneaked into Cuba in June 1962, were still alive and safe with the pills, Roselli reported. And a second team of assassins, he said, would feature "militia men whose assignment was to penetrate Castro's bodyguard."

Perhaps if they were fortunate, Castro would be dead and the Cuban crisis over before the mid-term elections that fall.

Despite the Kennedy White House clamoring for results, Roselli had ample reason to believe US officials were satisfied with his assassination planning.

That summer, in a rare moment at home in Los Angeles, Johnny met for lunch with the CIA's Director of Security Sheffield Edwards and their friend, Robert Maheu. The three men chatted about attempts to assassinate Castro. Maheu had been scrapped already from the top-secret operation at Harvey's insistence. But Johnny, without authorization, wanted his old friend Maheu at their table. Presumably, no one, not even Shef Edwards, ever told Harvey about this informal California meeting.

Over lunch, the CIA security chief Edwards assured Johnny that the Kennedy administration liked his courageous actions with Cuban exile groups against the dreaded Communist leader. Later recalling that luncheon to the CIA's inspector general, Edwards "said he took the occasion to express his personal appreciation to

Roselli, and told Roselli that he, Edwards, had personally told Attorney General [Robert] Kennedy of what Roselli had tried to do in the national interest. We know that Kennedy was merely briefed on the operation—and only on Phase One at that—but Roselli may have inferred that Kennedy had an active role in the operation."

Indeed, Robert Kennedy was extremely active with Operation Mongoose, the CIA's plan to encourage the overthrow of Castro. Both the attorney general and his brother were determined to free thousands of exiled attackers imprisoned after the failed 1961 Bay of Pigs raid, including its much admired leader, Manuel Artime.

Ousting Castro was "the top priority of the United States government," Bobby told the new CIA director John McCone. "No time, money, effort, or manpower is to be spared." Harvey was instructed by other CIA superiors to keep working with Roselli "because no matter how, when, why or through what means, the President wants to get rid of Castro."

How much the Kennedys knew about the Mafia's involvement in the CIA plans to kill Castro remains a matter of historical debate.

In his meeting with Edwards and CIA legal counsel Lawrence Houston, the attorney general had acted surprised when told about Giancana and Roselli's collusion with the CIA. "I trust that if you ever try and do business with organized crime again—with gangsters—you will let the Attorney General know," RFK growled in May 1962.

Despite his rebuke about the Mafia, Robert Kennedy—who arguably had become the nation's top spy with the Cuba mission as well as its top law-enforcement official—didn't seem to care what it took to get rid of Castro. Several in Bobby's inner circle had already entertained such an idea.

A December 1961 memo, sent from the Defense Department's Brig. General Ed Lansdale to CIA top advisers of Operation Mongoose, suggested "exploiting the potential of the underworld in Cuban cities to harass and bleed the Communist control apparatus. This effort may, on a very sensitive basis, enlist the assistance of American links to the Cuban underworld. While this would be a CIA project, close cooperation of the FBI is imperative."

In the clamor to get Castro, the US clandestine world unleashed other dangerous proposals, including assassination-like shootings of Cuban émigrés within America's borders. One top secret memo from the military's Joint Chiefs of Staff suggested a phony "Communist Cuban terror campaign in the Miami area, in other Florida cities and even in Washington, "designed to rile up American public support for a Cuban invasion.

"We could foster attempts on lives of Cuban refugees in the United States even to the extent of wounding in instances to be widely publicized," said the March 1962 report, made public decades later. "Exploding a few plastic bombs in carefully chosen spots, the arrest of Cuban agents and the release of prepared documents substantiating Cuban involvement also would be helpful in projecting the idea of an irresponsible government."

A focal point of Roselli's CIA activity involved the Cuban exile leader Tony Varona, who was first introduced to him by Santo Trafficante in 1960. Johnny's optimism about "the medicine" and two deaths squads was largely based on arrangements set up by Varona.

"He [Varona] was running his own little army," recalled CIA handler "Big Jim" O'Connell, before leaving on another assignment. "I saw two boats that allegedly belonged to him. Roselli drove me down one day to a marina, and he said, 'These two boats belong to Varona.'"

Varona was positioned to benefit no matter who prevailed in Havana. The boisterous, barrel-chested former Cuban prime minister under President Carlos Prior always seemed to have his hand out, looking for a piece of the CIA's fifty million dollar largesse in Florida with its covert war against Castro. If Roselli and his Mafia friends revived their casino empire in Havana, they expected Varona would be the new Batista, a proven government friend of the mob.

"DeVarona [sic] was understandably pleased to permit both the U.S. Government and criminal syndicate to offer him support and asked no questions as to the sources of the funds or the motive of his benefactors," said a later CIA summary. The report mentioned top Miami gangster Meyer Lansky as one of Varona's anti-Castro benefactors in 1960 before Lansky deferred to Giancana with the CIA.

Within the American government, Varona also found a friend with the Kennedys. Varona came to the administration's defense when other Cuban exiles, upset by the failure of the CIA-sponsored Bay of Pigs attack, criticized JFK for not aggressively planning a second invasion of Cuba. "I am not in favor of Cubans breaking with Washington," Varona told the *New York Times*. "Our biggest and best ally is the United States."

Despite doubts he shared with Roselli, CIA handler William Harvey went along with the new push for Varona's handpicked death squads. "I was very, very dubious

A, that there was anything here of real substance; B, that we could even depend on the statements that came from the Cubans that they had actually gone into Cuba or gotten anything into Cuba," Harvey later explained. "With the hazy character of this, we did the best we could." He later learned the first group of Varona's assassins had failed and the second death squad didn't even get to Cuba.

Not a shrinking violet himself, Harvey faced intense pressure from Robert Kennedy.

"Why can't you get things cooking like 007?" RFK demanded of Harvey, referring to his legendary reputation.

The hard-boiled CIA spy could barely contain his contempt for the boyish attorney general and his amateurish expectations.

At one top strategy meeting in Washington, Kennedy floated the idea of training some Cuban exiles at his Hickory Hills estate in Virginia, where his wife Ethel and seven children lived. Harvey burst out: 'What would you teach them, sir—*babysitting?*'

Between Washington and Florida, about four hundred staffers worked on Harvey's special task force that was part of Operation Mongoose. Harvey "came down to Miami every four to six weeks, mostly to see Johnny Roselli," recalled Ted Shackley, manager of the Operation Mongoose station in South Florida. After a few drinks, Harvey called Kennedy "the fucker" and choice epithets while conferring with Roselli and other intimates.

When Robert Kennedy visited the CIA encampment, he wandered around impulsively. At one point, the attorney general ripped a newly-written message from a telex machine and began reading it. Harvey grabbed the paper out of his hand. Regardless of his Justice Department position, Kennedy was unauthorized to read CIA messages, Harvey reprimanded.

The two men remained at odds. While Kennedy said the CIA wasn't being imaginative enough in Castro coup attempts, Harvey complained the White House was tying his hands, preferring high-risk sabotage attempts rather than a full-fledged invasion as the Cuban exiles urged.

Harvey believed trying to infiltrate CIA-trained exiles into Cuba was difficult enough—often deadly business—without sophomoric meddling from politicians. Shackley particularly recalled his worry when one anti-Castro counterspy, who had met Robert Kennedy earlier in Washington, was captured by Cuban security while attending church. If the spy mentioned his direct contact with the president's brother, it could turn into a publicity coup for Castro, who was constantly accusing the United States of trying to overthrow his government.

Cuban G-2 interrogators grilled the exile spy about what he knew, before torturing and eventually executing him. To Shackley's relief, however, this martyr to their cause never mentioned the president's brother.

———

Along the Florida Keys, a battalion of Cuban exiles, tutored by the CIA, prepared again to attack their homeland. Americans slowly learned of this covert war operation, because local police and newspapers were cautioned not to report what was going on.

There was a Wild West character throughout the Keys and Southern Florida, while a growing population of Cuban exiles and burgeoning street signs in Spanish gave it the flavor of Havana. Large hangars with military planes, herds of jeeps and soldiers in armored vehicles were hidden among palm trees and Everglade alligators. Gun shops throughout Miami hawked military equipment to a variety of "resistance groups." Prostitution flourished with young women hired by many men with loads of money in their pockets.

"I ran across a lot of soldiers of fortune looking for a fast buck," recalled CIA agent Justin F. Gleichauf, who collected information from inside Cuba. "I did like one tall Texan who flew small planes. He 'specialized' in setting Cuban sugar cane fields on fire. He did not heed my warning to stop, and he was shot down and killed."

Roselli was among the CIA's most talented freelancers. In ways that earned Harvey's respect, middle-aged Roselli ventured out again on nighttime CIA sabotage missions to the Cuban coastline. In Harvey's estimation, a wise guy in it just for the money wouldn't take such risks.

For a second time, Roselli's group of exiles encountered Cuban patrols that fired on their lead boat and sank it. Johnny climbed into a small dinghy. He reportedly floated alone for more than a day until an American cruiser rescued him. While doubts later arose about these accounts, Harvey was convinced of Johnny's bravery.

Inside Cuba, the risk of capture and execution always remained clear. Roselli's gung-ho pal, William "Rip" Robertson, a CIA operative known as a "cowboy," urged his exile counteragents to be as merciless as Castro's G-2 agents would be with them if caught.

"He [Robertson] was always trying to crank us up for the missions," recalled Ramon Orozco Crespo, an exile commando who carried out twenty-five infiltrations within Cuba. "Once he told me, 'I'll give you $50 if you bring me back an ear.' I brought him two, and he laughed and said, 'You're crazy,' but he paid me $100, and he took us to his house for a turkey dinner."

In fall 1962, Robertson trained an exile group for its biggest mission—an attack on the Matahambre copper mine complex. Matahambre was a major industrial site for Castro considered vital to his economy. After a firefight at the valuable site, Cuban security forces caught six of Robertson's eight saboteurs, without any of their intended explosives going off.

Once more, this 'black ops' failure seemed caused by Castro's spies being apprised in advance. Back in Washington, Robert Kennedy complained relentlessly about the CIA's lack of success. A subsequent attack at Matahambre killed some four hundred workers.

But the CIA undercover campaign soon found its most important victory in Florida. At the Opa-Locka airport near Miami, where newly arrived exiles were debriefed, the CIA heard rumors that Russian missiles were being assembled within Cuba. Another CIA spy inside Cuba provided the exact location of the Soviet missile launch facilities. High-flying U-2 reconnaissance planes confirmed it.

Meanwhile on the ground, Bill Harvey contacted Roselli by telephone while Johnny was visiting Giancana's Chicago. Under orders from his CIA handler, Roselli rushed to Washington, DC for further instruction. Then Johnny headed to South Florida where he'd been cultivating Cuban sources for many months. Roselli recognized the urgency of the moment. The mobster claimed he had successfully, "through his Cuban contacts, attempt to verify the location of the Russian missiles in Cuba," according to a CIA record of Roselli's actions released in 2017.

The surprise discovery of nuclear arms led to the Cuban Missile Crisis, an epic thirteen-day showdown in October 1962 between the Kennedy administration and Soviet leaders. After months of death squads and assassination attempts, the covert war against Castro had now emerged into the open, with the potential of creating World War III.

Soviet premier Nikita Khrushchev shared Castro's concern about an impending US invasion. He agreed to install medium- and intermediate-range ballistic missiles inside Cuba. Once fitted with a warhead, they could, at least theoretically, devastate much of the United States. The Russians made this bold strategic move in the Caribbean as a way of balancing out the power struggle created by US nuclear defenses maintained in Europe, not as prelude to a first strike.

But Castro seemed ready for an all-out conflagration. In what historians later called "the Armageddon letter," Castro urged a Soviet nuclear attack of the United States if there was an invasion of his island nation. To the older and more cautious Khrushchev, Fidel was "young and hot-headed." Though Castro later denied it, Khrushchev in his memoir said he chastised Castro for his recklessness.

"If the war had begun we would somehow have survived, but Cuba no doubt would have ceased to exist," Kruschchev said he told Castro. "It would have been crushed into powder. Yet you suggested a nuclear strike!"

Eventually, President Kennedy rejected calls for a US invasion by his military advisers. Instead, he opted for a naval blockade—a so-called "quarantine"—of incoming Soviet ships with warheads and carefully negotiated a face-saving deal with Khrushchev that ended the confrontation.

The Cuban Missile Crisis proved the finest moment of Kennedy's presidency, leading to a slow de-escalation of the Cold War arms race that once seemed frighteningly close to killing millions of innocents from nuclear bombs and leaving a world saturated by deadly radiation. But in effect, the agreement also would leave Castro in place.

———————

The conflict between the White House and William Harvey, the CIA's top spy in Florida, remained in full fury. During the height of Cuban Missile Crisis tensions, Robert Kennedy was furious to learn that Harvey had approved three exile sabotage teams to enter Cuba. RFK said Harvey had "gone off the reservation" and ignored stand-down orders during that doomsday emergency.

At a meeting in the Cabinet room, Harvey claimed that he'd never heard of any White House order to stop his task force's ongoing missions. Some teams were already deployed and couldn't be stopped, he added.

"You're dealing with people's lives in a half-assed operation," RFK said, disgustedly.

Harvey refused to back down. The simmering antagonism between them finally spilled over.

"If you fuckers hadn't fucked up the Bay of Pigs, we wouldn't be in this fucking mess!" Harvey yelled, as Kennedy left the room.

CIA director John McCone, who was friendly with Kennedy but still kept in the dark about the Castro assassination plans, was appalled by Harvey's behavior. "Harvey has destroyed himself today," McCone said. "His usefulness has ended."

Roselli remained loyal to his friend, Bill Harvey, and his version of events. "There was never a time a halt was called," Roselli later testified. Even after the Cuban missile crisis, the campaign to kill Castro continued on, he said.

Shortly after the October crisis, Harvey dispatched Johnny to Washington, DC, "to find out certain intelligence that was going on." While in the capital, the Mafia spy bumped into two top Cuban exile leaders who said they were going to meet with the attorney general. "They were assured of an audience with him" to chat about the overall Cuban situation, Roselli recalled. "They still had high hopes that they were going to get a lot of help from the government."

Exiles such as Tony Varona had friends and relatives still imprisoned by Castro from the failed Bay of Pigs invasion. Worried about firing squads and torture, they pushed the Kennedy administration to negotiate for their release after months of captivity. Eventually in December 1962, the Kennedy brothers negotiated a trade—fifty-three million dollars worth of baby food and medicine in exchange for the 1,100 surviving members of Brigade 2506.

A week later, President Kennedy and his wife Jacqueline welcomed home the ex-prisoners at an Orange Bowl celebration. In fluent Spanish to the crowd, Jackie hoped her son, John Jr., would grow up to be "a man at least half as brave as the members of Brigade 2506."

Standing next to the First Couple was Manuel Artime Buesa, the handsome leader of the Bay of Pigs brigade. Trained as a physician, Artime first met JFK along with Varona and other exile leaders at the Democratic Convention in summer 1960. He became a "golden boy" for the US effort against Castro and was paid more than fifty thousand dollars a month by the CIA to build a new anti-Castro resistance movement.

But Artime's other CIA connections remained a secret. Prior to being caught by Castro at the Bay of Pigs, Artime had worked with Roselli, Giancana, and their ilk in the assassination plan. *"Artime and his group were supported by the CIA. He also was used by the Mafia in the Castro operation. This information should not be released,"* the agency said in documents compiled in 1977 but released in 1993, twenty years after the Bay of Pigs.

The anti-Castro campaign's lack of success soon took its toll. Following his own Cuban missile fiasco, Harvey was summarily removed from Miami and shipped to a new CIA posting in Rome. The burly, outspoken CIA legend made no apologies for his bold, sometimes rash decisions. He refused to make excuses for those he recruited in Florida or what they did in Cuba. During this time of crisis in the Cold War, he certainly wasn't asking forgiveness for relying on his Mafia friend Johnny Roselli.

"Very frankly at that stage—and with the deep concern that we had at that point over what, rightly or wrongly, I think all of us then felt was a very vital matter of the security of this nation—I was not about to terminate any possible asset," Harvey explained.

Before Harvey left for Rome, Johnny went deep-sea fishing with his CIA buddy in Florida in April 1963. They shared dinner and drinks at the Eden Roc Hotel, next to the Fontainebleau. They stayed at the Plantation Yacht Marina in the Keys, where Roselli signed the register for his room with one of his aliases—John A. Wallston. It wasn't far from Port Mary where Johnny had launched nighttime missions to Cuba in boats filled with armed Cuban exiles.

During this Florida trip, Harvey told Roselli his services for the agency were no longer needed. He thanked him sincerely for all his patriotism and courage. The two had faced several life-threatening situations together and forged a lasting bond of admiration and loyalty.

As a sign of his respect, Harvey gave Roselli a check for one thousand dollars—a "termination fee" as a would-be Castro assassin. It was a mere pittance of what Johnny had spent out of his own pocket, flying back and forth to Miami. Harvey also gave him a first-class plane ticket to Chicago, so Roselli could explain what happened to his boss Sam Giancana.

As much as their circumstances would allow, the CIA man and the Mafia hitman parted as true friends.

Then in typical 007 style, Harvey put the whole adventure on his government expense account.

CHAPTER 32:

SPIES WITHOUT PORTFOLIO

As a marked man, Fidel Castro wanted revenge desperately. His intended bloody retribution against the United States—payback for all the CIA assassination attempts against him in Cuba—was launched in late 1962, with a plan to blow up New York City for the Christmas holiday season.

At the height of October's Cuban missile crisis, Castro sent Roberto Santiesteban Casanova, a well-trained terrorism expert, to its United Nations mission. The twenty-seven-year-old spy posed as a diplomatic "attaché" with a phony official passport.

Trained at Castro's G-2 spy school, run by the Russians near Havana, Santiesteban soon became the "ringleader" of an elaborate sabotage plot in New York and the focus of an intense manhunt.

Through its surveillance, the FBI learned of Santiesteban's plan—with more than a dozen other pro-Castro spies—to bomb Macy's, Bloomingdale's, and another big department store, Gimbel's. Relying on a large cache of weapons and explosives, including TNT and grenades, the Cuban saboteurs wanted to blow up the Statue of Liberty, Grand Central Station, the 42nd Street Port Authority Bus Terminal, as well as military bases and oil refineries in nearby New Jersey.

Santiesteban was chosen to mastermind Castro's bomb conspiracy, intended for Black Friday, the busy shopping day after Thanksgiving. Santiesteban's plan of attack had an eerie similarity to that of a future terrorist named Osama bin Laden, whose 9/11 terrorism brought so much death and destruction to New York City decades later. But in this case, the FBI managed to prevent disaster, not a moment too soon.

On the Upper West Side, Santiesteban was spotted walking along like any Manhattan commuter, wearing a dark raincoat and brightly striped tie. When federal agents—tipped off to the Cuban spy's whereabouts—confronted him on Riverside Drive, he started running. Armed with a loaded pistol, Santiesteban stuffed papers into his mouth, with secret formulas for explosives, including nitroglycerine, written on them.

After being chased and captured by six agents, US officials charged Santiesteban with "conspiracy to commit sabotage in this country." Other Cuban spies in New York were also rounded up.

But a few months later, in April 1963, Santiesteban boarded a plane in New York—the city he meant to bomb and terrorize with countless deaths—and headed back to Cuba.

Santiesteban's release from federal prison, along with other Cuban spies caught in the United States, was the finale in an exchange with the Castro government overseen by American lawyer James B. Donovan.

Trading one spy for another was Donovan's specialty. The Wall Street lawyer became famous negotiating the 1962 release of American U-2 pilot Francis Gary Powers for a Soviet spy caught in America (a 2015 movie of that exchange, *Bridge of Spies*, starred actor Tom Hanks as Donovan).

Later that year, at the Kennedy administration's secret request, Donovan went to Cuba as a "volunteer" to broker a deal leading to the release of all 1,100 Bay of Pigs prisoners.

Success would require nothing short of a miracle. "I've already done the loaves and fishes," Donovan joked to friends. "Now they want me to walk on water, too."

During negotiations, Castro mentioned his desire to see US officials release Santiesteban. The Cuban spy was awaiting trial when Donovan helped with his release in April 1963 as part of a swap for American spies caught in Cuba.

In dealing with Castro, Donovan was debriefed by the CIA, which had homicidal plans of its own. The "executive action" squad wanted Donovan to pass along a scuba-diving suit lined with poison, prepared by its secret lab. According to a declassified CIA history released decades later, the covert action squad "devised a plan to have Donovan be the unwitting purveyor of a diving suit and breathing apparatus, respectively contaminated with Madura foot fungus and tuberculosis bacteria, as a gift for Castro."

Fortunately for Castro, the scheme failed. Instead of giving out the CIA's scuba gear laden with toxins, Donovan decided, on his own, to present Castro with a clean new diving suit. Once more, this canny guerilla leader enjoyed a seemingly charmed existence.

"Castro is crazy like a fox," Donovan later told overconfident Americans expecting regime change at any minute. "Whether certain elements want to accept it or not, the island of Cuba belongs to Castro."

John McCone, the agency's top director, didn't know about the poisoned scuba suit. In fact, McCone remained unaware of the long series of Castro assassination attempts, dating back to Giancana and Roselli's recruitment in 1960. Of all the CIA's secrets, the one within Langley's executive suite was perhaps most mystifying.

As the replacement to Dulles, McCone expressed his moral objection to the idea of killing foreign leaders. Because of this perceived halo over McCone's head, his small circle of aides never informed him of their highly classified foul play. His top assistant, Richard Helms, deliberately didn't say anything. Nor did Desmond Fitz-Gerald, the Harvard-trained lawyer who replaced William Harvey as overseer of assassination attempts on Castro.

It wasn't until August 1963, nearly two years after he became the CIA's top spymaster, that McCone read an account in the *Chicago Sun-Times* detailing Sam Giancana's connections to the CIA. Sandy Smith penned it, the same reporter who once landed an exclusive interview with Sam at his daughter's wedding.

The *Sun-Times* article was a bit sketchy. It said Giancana was working with the CIA "in the hope that the Justice Department's drive to put him behind bars might be slowed—or at least affected—by his ruse of cooperation with another government agency." However, the *Sun-Times* article didn't mention any specific plan to kill Castro.

Embarrassed by the published account, McCone did some checking within Langley of its veracity. Calling Helms into his office, McCone finally learned about the elaborate assassination scheme with Johnny Roselli and Giancana. "This is the earliest date on which we have evidence of Mr. McCone's being aware of any aspect of the scheme to assassinate Castro using members of the gambling syndicate," the CIA's inspector general later confirmed.

McCone's reaction to this stunning news was purely bureaucratic. There was no moral outrage by the man who worried aloud about getting excommunicated from his church for any complicity in an assassination plot. McCone seemed relieved when Helms pulled out the May 1962 memorandum sent from Sheffield Edwards to Robert Kennedy, claiming that the assassination attempts by the two mobsters had stopped after the Bay of Pigs in April 1961.

"Well, this didn't happen on my tenure," McCone replied simply.

However, none of the claims about Roselli and Giancana stopping their murderous intent was true. In May 1962, Harvey assured his superiors he was no longer using

Roselli as a CIA operative, but it was a lie. Instead Harvey ramped up the murderous midnight excursions into Cuba with Johnny and his band of armed exiles based at Port Mary.

With the stakes so high, the secrecy around Roselli was never greater, more politically radioactive. The unofficial "PROJECT JOHNNY" file, created by the few CIA officials still doing business with the Mafia spy, was kept in the personal safe of Edwards, the CIA's director of security. It eventually received a file number—"667 270," according to a CIA document released in 2017.

Perhaps most significantly, a copy of Edwards's May 14, 1962, memo to the attorney general—the same day he met with RFK about the use of Roselli and Giancana—was also placed in Edwards safe. Presumably, Edwards, a cautious administrator, wanted a backup file about Roselli if Harvey's covert operation in Florida was exposed. Years later, Congressional investigators couldn't find this "Project Johnny" file—only references to it in other documents. The file, like its namesake, remained an enigma.

By early 1963, though Johnny had received a "termination fee" to end his CIA spy operation, plenty of private incentives still existed for Roselli and Giancana to continue their hunt for Castro. The CIA's $150,000 bounty was still kept in place, as Harvey made clear to Johnny during their booze-filled luncheon in Los Angeles before the erstwhile handler left for Rome. More importantly, Johnny's wishful thinking about Mafia-run casinos reappearing in Havana coincided very much with Giancana's strategy of spreading his control of gambling throughout the Caribbean.

Now on their own, without CIA backing, covert actions involving Roselli and Giancana became murkier and more difficult to trace. Johnny never told his band of Florida contacts that Harvey had ended their arrangement. As a result, Roselli's trained death squads of Cuban exiles, armed with US military equipment, kept fighting.

In March 1963, a band of five men—armed with "bazookas, mortars and machine guns"—was captured by Cuban security. They'd planned to shoot at Castro from a house near the University of Havana, until they were spotted. The team was tortured and confessed to be working for the US government. Roselli later "identified the team as his own."

Another hazy Giancana plot involved Eduardo Perez, nicknamed Eddie Bayo, affiliated with mobster Santo Trafficante Jr. Inside a Miami Beach hotel, Giancana reportedly offered thirty thousand dollars to Bayo for Castro's death, US government documents say. Bayo entered Cuba with another team but was never seen again.

Throughout 1963, word spread in Florida that assassination could be a high-paying task. The CIA heard rumors that Tony Varona, Roselli's best contact in the Cuba exile community, had received a huge sum of money from Johnny's mob associates. "Gangster elements in the Miami area were offering $150,000 for anyone who would kill Castro," an internal CIA document reported. "These bits of information, fitted together, could provide the basis for an explanation of why Varona was so readily available when approached by Roselli."

In Chicago, Richard Cain, Giancana's talkative double agent inside the sheriff's office, informed the FBI that Giancana and his mob financier Murray Humphreys had recently provided a huge sum for a private Castro assassination plan. It sounded just like the amount offered to Varona and his freelancers. "Johnny's involved," Cain added about Roselli.

During this international skullduggery, the FBI kept a keen eye on both Giancana and Roselli domestically. There was no letup from the Kennedy Justice Department's ceaseless campaign against organized crime. In June 1963, FBI agents following Roselli in Los Angeles realized he was going to take a plane bound for Washington, DC. They quickly alerted the bureau's agents there.

When Roselli landed, FBI agents intended to shadow him around the capital, to see whom he would meet. Johnny didn't make it easy. On his boarding pass, he used one of his favorite aliases—"J. Ralston."

Leaving Dulles Airport, Roselli quickly walked out with his bags. He jumped into a station wagon driven by a heavyset bald man with a middle-aged woman beside him and took off. The FBI swiftly pursued the car without revealing themselves.

As it turned out, Roselli wanted to meet once more with Bill Harvey, his friend and former CIA handler. They had said a formal goodbye in April, with Johnny receiving his "termination fee" as if it were a booby prize. Since then, Harvey had sold his home outside Washington, DC. and was about to leave for his new CIA assignment in Italy.

The FBI traced the station wagon's license plates and discovered the identity of its owner. On the face of it, this secret meeting appeared very disturbing. Hoover's agents wondered why one of the nation's top hoodlums had flown cross-country to meet with Harvey, a CIA agent and former FBI man. The feds decided to wait for the right moment to approach Harvey, without alerting Johnny.

During his stay, Roselli went out to eat with Harvey and his wife at a local restaurant. In the middle of the meal, the waiter alerted Harvey that he was wanted on the house telephone. When Harvey picked up the receiver, a voice asked him, "Do you know who your dinner guest is?"

Harvey recognized the voice as belonging to Sam Papich, the bureau's liaison with the CIA. Harvey said he indeed knew the real identity of the man who'd called himself "Mr. Ralston" on his airplane ticket. Papich expressed concern about this odd get-together with Roselli. But he tried not to sound too alarmed. Instead Papich asked Harvey to meet him for breakfast.

The next morning, talking face-to-face, Papich reminded Harvey that, under FBI regulations, Papich was required to report any meeting between former FBI personnel and known criminals. To Papich, the CIA's involvement with Giancana and Roselli seemed sheer madness.

"Very early I did make it clear that I couldn't understand why the Agency ever considered getting involved with Johnny and his tribe," Papich recalled years later. "One could say that because he was green in the OC [organized crime] field, Harvey would have been completely dominated by Johnny. However, I do not exclude that H[arvey], in his own way, established a relationship which benefitted the objectives of the Agency."

In a no-win position as FBI liaison, Papich had cultivated his own friendly relationship with the CIA. During World War II, Papich had worked undercover for the FBI and understood the needs of spies. Nevertheless, he would have to tell Hoover about Harvey's cross-country meeting with Roselli, a known gangster. Harvey said he respected the FBI's rules but asked for one favor.

As a professional courtesy, Harvey asked Papich to tell him if FBI chief Hoover felt it necessary to contact his boss, CIA director John McCone. (At that time, McCone still didn't know about his agency's assassination plotting against Castro. It was still two months away from when McCone learned of it in the *Chicago Sun-Times*.) Papich said he'd let him know in advance if the FBI planned to reach out to McCone.

Soon after, Harvey advised Helms of his FBI conversation. The two seasoned CIA agents discussed whether McCone, with no prior training in spying, should be told by them about the Castro assassination plans, rather than learning it from the FBI's Hoover. After much thought, the two men decided to keep their mouths shut. Harvey was leaving town, and this meeting was supposed to be his final closeout with Roselli.

Helms decided he would tell CIA director McCone about the Castro assassination plans—both past and present—only if it became absolutely necessary. Rather than his own boss, Helms took his directions from the White House, particularly Bobby Kennedy.

"If the Attorney General told me to jump through a hoop, I would have," Helms later explained.

Murder was in the air throughout 1963, in a way almost palpable to Robert Kennedy. If vindictive mobsters like Sam Giancana didn't kill him because of the Justice Department's war on organized crime, then perhaps some Cuban assassin loyal to Castro would. Homicidal concerns rippled into his personal life. After mobsters in New York blinded an investigative journalist by throwing acid into his eyes, Kennedy sought greater protections for his family.

"We were told they were going to do the same with our children," remembered his wife Ethel in 2012. Extra security became the norm. "We couldn't leave school with the other kids at the end of the day," explained his eldest daughter Kathleen Kennedy Townsend. "We had to wait in the principal's office to be picked up."

During summer 1962, the FBI had become aware of an assassination plan against the attorney general discussed by Teamster president Jimmy Hoffa. For months, the corrupt Teamsters chieftain had been a target of Kennedy's "Get Hoffa" squad at Justice, investigating the union's ties to organized crime. Hoffa was later indicted in June 1963 for defrauding the Teamsters pension fund, a piggybank for Mafia casino investments. One of Hoffa's associates informed the FBI about the threat on RFK's life and passed a lie-detector test given by the bureau.

This threat unnerved the Kennedys enough so that the president mentioned the murder plot to his friend, *Washington Post* editor Ben Bradlee. When Bradlee expressed his doubts, JFK cut him off. "The President was obviously serious" about it, Bradlee recorded in his private journal.

While FBI listening devices picked up angry rumblings about the Kennedys by Giancana and Roselli, nothing was more blunt than what Santo Trafficante and Carlos Marcello, the New Orleans mobster, discussed in 1963.

"That fucking Bobby Kennedy is making life miserable for me and my friends," said Marcello, who faced deportation proceedings for his illegal immigration status, just as Roselli feared for himself. "Someone ought to kill all those goddam Kennedys."

Unlike Giancana, these two mobsters, Trafficante and Marcello, had favored Nixon in the 1960s. They hadn't been fooled by the idea the Kennedys would go lightly on the mob. Getting rid of them was the equivalent of the old Sicilian phrase *"Livarsi na pietra di la scarpa!* (Take the stone out of my shoe!)"* which Marcello angrily invoked.

In private, Trafficante expressed similar sentiments to his lawyer Frank Ragano: "Bobby Kennedy is stepping on too many toes. You wait and see, somebody is going to kill those sons-of-bitches. It's just a matter of time."

This late-in-life admission by Ragano seemed to back up another claim about Trafficante's intent. In Florida in mid-1963, Trafficante singled out the ttorney general to a group of anti-Castro Cubans. They included Rafael "Macho" Gener, part of the 1961 assassination plot with Roselli and Giancana, and Jose Aleman Jr., a Cuban businessman who later testified about Trafficante's comments.

"Mark my words," Trafficante warned, "this man Kennedy is in trouble, and he will get what is coming to him."

The murderous tensions between Castro and the Kennedy administration again seemed to boil.

Under the cover of darkness on October 21, 1963, a former US Navy patrol boat called *The Rex* moved towards the western tip of Cuba. It carried an assortment of cannons and large-scale armaments as well as two twenty-foot speedboats, each with two large machine guns. A group of armed Cuban exiles entered the two speedboats and made their way to the shoreline.

As the exile warriors approached the beach, a spotlight suddenly illuminated them. Castro's security forces had been alerted somehow. Cuban soldiers immediately started firing at the two boats. They captured one crew while a second, terribly battered by gunfire, struggled back to *The Rex*. The survivors returned to home base in Florida with several fighters mortally wounded.

A few nights later, Castro gave a three-hour television address, accusing the CIA of orchestrating this attack from *The Rex* and "stepping up its activities against Cuba." He said the five exiles captured would face a firing squad as spies. Four of them later appeared on television in Cuba to confess plotting against Castro.

The nighttime attack, one of several during 1963, appeared to contradict back-channel efforts by the Kennedy administration. They wanted to approach Castro and see if some peaceful settlement between the two nations might be reached. The would-be assassination attempt also seemed a rebuke to Castro's much-publicized warning from a month earlier.

"We are prepared to fight them and answer in kind," Castro vowed. "United States leaders should think that if they are aiding terrorist plans to eliminate Cuban leaders, they themselves will not be safe."

More than ever, the Kennedys feared that Communism, the driving force of the Cold War, might spread from Castro's island to other Latin American nations. On November 1, 1963, the CIA's Richard Helms showed Bobby Kennedy one of many rifles confiscated from a secret Cuban hiding spot in Venezuela. The identifying codes on the rifles had been scratched off. But once again the CIA's ace lab technicians came through with an acid that allowed the original codes to be read and identified as coming from Cuba.

Bobby rushed to the White House with Helms—carrying the weapon in a canvas bag—to show the president proof of Castro's intent. After answering JFK's questions, Helms put the rifle back in the bag.

"I am sure glad the Secret Service didn't catch us bringing this gun in here," Helms laughed kiddingly.

JFK grinned and shook his head. "Yes, it gives me a feeling of confidence," he said, with the sardonic tone heard in James Bond thrillers.

Robert Kennedy wasn't about to let up on the Castro threat, certainly not with the 1964 presidential re-election on the horizon. "Bobby was as emotional as he could be [about Cuba], and he always talked like he was the President, and he really was in a way," recalled Ray S. Cline, the head of the CIA's analytical branch. "He was always bugging the Agency about the Cubans. I don't doubt that talk of assassinating Castro was part of Bobby's discussion with some Agency people."

In replacing William Harvey, Robert Kennedy wanted someone in charge of the secret task force whom he trusted, someone he could count on to get the job done.

The CIA had looked for months to find a would-be assassin close to Castro. They wanted someone who was a respected figure, who could rally his fellow Cubans in a coup against the tyrannical leader.

And by late 1963, the agency seemed confident they'd come upon a Castro insider who would take care of things once and for all.

PATRIOT ASSASSIN: Gangster Johnny Roselli (right) was recruited as a "patriot" by the CIA to kill Cuban leader Fidel Castro. This top-secret assassination plan included mob boss Sam Giancana and other Mafia figures, American spy agency officials, and various Cuban exile commandos in Florida. *(Library of Congress)*

AMERICA'S TOP MOB BOSS: Sam Giancana was the most powerful Mafia boss in America in 1960 when he joined his pal Johnny Roselli in the CIA's assassination plot against Fidel Castro. A mobster of extreme violence and great ambition, Giancana hoped his spy work for the government would keep the feds from investigating his criminal activities. *(Library of Congress)*

CIA MASTERMIND: Allen Dulles looked more like an Ivy League professor than America's top spy masterminding killing schemes. Not until 2007 did the CIA admit its former director had approved the assassination plot against Castro using the two Mafia hitmen, Roselli and Giancana.

ALL THE PRESIDENT'S SPIES: During the early 1960s, President John F. Kennedy's administration was obsessed with a secret "Get Castro" campaign run out of Florida and overseen by the CIA. Pictured (l-r) CIA director Allen Dulles, his CIA No. 2 Richard Bissell, JFK, and John McCone, who replaced Dulles as director. *(CIA photo)*

KILLING CASTRO: When Cuba's Fidel Castro died in 2016 at age 90, few remembered how the CIA and Mafia had once targeted the fiery Communist leader for assassination without success. Documents show the CIA was involved in about a dozen attempts, but Cuban historians say there were hundreds more.

BLOODY REVOLUTION: Fidel Castro violently seized power in Cuba by imprisoning political opponents, shooting dissidents, and closing most American businesses, including the Mafia-controlled casinos. In this photo, Castro's brother Raul (second from left) blindfolds a prisoner facing a firing squad.

THE CIA "CUT-OUT": Robert Maheu, a former FBI agent turned private investigator, served as the CIA's middleman—a "cut-out"—in putting together the Castro killing scheme with the two mobsters, Giancana and Roselli. Maheu said both gangsters were "patriots" who rebuffed the agency's $150,000 bounty for Castro's head and said they'd kill him for free. (*UNLV University Libraries Collection*)

SPYING ON SINATRA: Along with his CIA work, Robert Maheu was a paid fixer for multi-millionaire Howard Hughes who hired Maheu's detective firm to "spy" on actress Ava Gardner in Nevada as she awaited her finalized divorce from Sinatra. "My job was to find out if any men visited her and what her relationship with them might be," Maheu recalled, "especially if one of those men was Sinatra."

BANG-BANG AT THE BOOM-BOOM ROOM: The famous lounge at Miami's Fontainebleau Hotel hosted the CIA's first secret meeting with gangsters Sam Giancana and Johnny Roselli about the Castro assassination plot. Giancana didn't use his real name when he first met Maheu, the CIA's go-between. In the Boom-Boom room, Roselli introduced his pal to Maheu as "Sam Gold", one of Giancana's favorite aliases. (*Library of Congress*)

SANS SOUCI. HAVANA

TROPICAL GOLD: Before Fidel Castro seized power and threw them out, Mafia figures like Johnny Roselli and Sam Giancana made a mint from gambling and entertainment in Havana's clubs. The American gangsters hoped to return and reopen the Sans Souci (seen in this postcard) and other opulent casinos if Castro was eliminated through the CIA assassination scheme.

ANTI-CASTRO FIGHTERS: One of the conspirators in the CIA's murder plot was Manuel Antonio de Varona ("Tony Varona"), leader of a Cuban exile group in Florida. Publicly, Varona met with JFK and was touted as a possible Castro replacement. But privately, he worked with Johnny Roselli on ways to kill Castro. *(Library of Congress)*

HEROES OF BRIGADE 2506: Months after the disastrous Bay of Pigs invasion, the Kennedy administration negotiated the release of more than 1,000 Cuban exile commandos captured by Castro, including their leader Manuel Artime (third from left). JFK and his wife Jackie celebrated their freedom in Florida. The First Lady hoped her son, John Jr., would grow up to be "a man at least half as brave as the members of Brigade 2506." Artime stayed active in the campaign to kill Castro. *(JFK Library)*

CASTRO'S CUBA: Fidel's rise to power was fueled by stark differences between Havana's poor and the lush life of the gangsterismo running the nearby Mafia-controlled casinos. When Castro closed down their lucrative gambling palaces, gangsters like Roselli and Giancana vowed revenge.

COLD WAR CIRCLES OF HELL: In a great spy moment, the CIA secretly discovered how Castro allowed Russian-made nuclear missiles to be based in Cuba, prompting an October 1962 confrontation between the Kennedy administration and the Soviet Union that nearly wound up in atomic war. This CIA map illustrates how far these missiles could strike within the United States. (*JFK Library*)

THE FBI'S KEEPER OF SECRETS: In the early 1960s, FBI director J. Edgar Hoover slowly learned how two gangsters, Johnny Roselli and Sam Giancana, were recuited by the CIA to kill Castro as well as how President Kennedy was involved in an extramarital affair with a young woman also being courted by Giancana. Hoover used both secrets to his powerful advantage. (*Library of Congress*)

WEARING TWO HATS: After the Bay of Pigs embarrassment, Attorney General Robert Kennedy (seen on right with JFK and the FBI's Hoover) oversaw much of the CIA's covert war against Castro, based largely in Florida. "Time, effort, manpower, dollars are not to be spared," RFK instructed in January 1962, according to a confidential memo released in 2017. "The President has indicated that Castro cannot be tolerated and the final chapter to this has not been written." (*JFK Library*)

CUBA'S ULTIMATE SPYMASTER: With Russian help, Castro created a sophisicated Cuban spy agency that punished his internal critics and placed double agents in Florida that tipped him off to impending CIA-sponsored attacks by Cuban exile commandos. Castro also authorized a 9/11-like attack to blow up New York City by Cuban spies that was thwarted by the FBI. (*U.S. State Department*)

ACTING ON JAMES BOND NOVELS: When he found out the Kennedys enjoyed James Bond novels, CIA director Allen Dulles encouraged his secret lab to come up with 007-like killing devices for the covert war against Castro. "Some of the professionals working for me in the CIA never could understand this weakness of the Boss," Dulles admitted about his James Bond fixation. *(JFK Library)*

"HOODLUM COMPLEX": Once a boyish singer, Frank Sinatra toughened his public image by 1960 in a way that resembled his pal and business partner, Sam Giancana, with whom he shared a "friendship" ring and many other interests. FBI experts theorized Sinatra had a "hoodlum complex" that eventually caused the Kennedys to steer clear of him.

MASTER MANIPULATOR: Sam Giancana with his pal Johnny Roselli exploited their relationship with Sinatra, pressuring him to get the Kennedy Justice Department off their backs. At times, Giancana wanted the famous singer and his "Rat Pack" entertainers to perform in his mob-controlled events and proposed movies. Privately, Giancana had a disdain for Sinatra's fawning approach with him and considered killing the entertainer for not living up to his promises.

CASANOVA'S WIFE: As a suave Hollywood ladies' man, Johnny Roselli dated a number of famous actresses, including Donna Reed, Lana Turner, and Betty Hutton. But his marriage to actress June Lang ended quickly when he ordered her to quit her movie career and stay home.

FINDING AN ANGEL: After his beloved wife Angeline died of a stroke, Sam Giancana became a widower with three teenage daughters, looking for another "princess" he might marry. In Las Vegas, he thought he found his angel when he met Phyllis McGuire (seen in center), part of the famous McGuire Sisters singing trio.

NO LAUGHING MATTER: During the Castro murder scheme, the CIA and Johnny Roselli helped bug comedian Dan Rowan's Las Vegas hotel room as a way of placating jealous mobster Sam Giancana who suspected his girlfriend Phyllis McGuire might be having an affair with Rowan (left). The botched spy attempt in Rowan's hotel room resulted in an FBI criminal probe that eventually unravelled the top-secret CIA plan.

PRESIDENTIAL INDISCRETION: Rumors of President Kennedy's alleged extra-marital affairs with women, including actress Marilyn Monroe (second from left), were known by both the FBI and gangsters like Giancana and Roselli, who threatened to make it public. *(JFK Library)*

WOMAN IN THE MIDDLE:
Johnny Roselli introduced Campbell, a
beautiful California divorcee, to Frank
Sinatra before she began an affair with
JFK and eventually Sam Giancana. In
retrospect, she suspected that Giancana
used her to compromise the president.
"Now that I know of his involvement
with the Central Intelligence Agency, it
is possible that I was used almost from
the beginning," Judy later admitted. "It
never occurred to me that Sam's
interest in me was simply because of my
association with Jack Kennedy."

LESSONS OF CAPONE: In handing
over the reins of the Chicago mob,
Tony Accardo warned Sam Giancana
to keep a low profile and not draw the
wrath of federal authorities—
responsible for the demise of Chicago's
famous gangster Al Capone. When the
outspoken Giananca failed to do so,
Accardo took dramatic action.

THE POWER OF VIOLENCE: Long before his homicidal plans with the CIA, Sam Giancana learned that violent men like Sam "Mad Sam" DeStefan, a psychopathic killer, could help him enforce his own power on the gritty streets of Chicago.

THE DOUBLE AGENT: A secret ally to Giancana, Richard Cain, a Spanish-speaking former Chicago cop, became a shadowy figure in the worlds of the CIA, the Mafia, and the plot to kill Castro before he was murdered himself.

AMERICA'S JAMES BOND:
A talented CIA spy assigned to the
Castro assassination plot, William
King Harvey was compared to the
fictional 007 though he didn't look
like Sean Connery at all. Harvey
admired Johnny Roselli's
"patriotism" in working with the
Cuban exile commandos in
Florida. But Harvey clashed with
Attorney General Robert Kennedy
and soon lost his post.

DON'T TELL THE BOSS: A top CIA
official, Richard Helms decided with
William Harvey not to tell incoming
CIA boss John McCone about the
agency's plans to kill Castro for many
months. Helms eventually became the
CIA's director. *(National Archives and
Records Administration)*

THE ASSASSINATION PLOT NEVER CONSIDERED:
Robert Kennedy urged President Lyndon Johnson to put former
CIA director Allen Dulles (right) on the Warren Commission
investigating JFK's 1963 death. But members like Gerald Ford
(second from left) were later surprised that Dulles failed to
inform them of the Kennedy administration's top-secret plot to
kill Castro with the help of the two gangsters. *(LBJ Library)*

KEPT IN THE DARK: Lyndon B. Johnson didn't learn of the
secret CIA-Mafia plot to kill Castro until 1967, the fourth year of
his presidency. By enlisting Giancana and Roselli, the CIA "had
been operating a damned Murder Inc. in the Caribbean,"
complained LBJ, seen here in 1965 with FBI chief Hoover and
Attorney General Nicholas deB. Katzenbach. *(LBJ Library)*

THE LAST MAN STANDING: Florida mob boss Santo Trafficante Jr. (seen at the Sans Souci casino in Havana) helped Johnny Roselli and Sam Giancana in the CIA plot to kill Castro, though spies like William Harvey feared he was a double agent involved in narcotics trafficking and friendly to Castro's regime. FBI evidence suggests Trafficante had something to do with the still unsolved murders of Giancana and Roselli in the mid-1970s. Both Trafficante and Castro died of old age many years later. (*Library of Congress*)

CHAPTER 33:

DANGLE

Desmond FitzGerald, the CIA's replacement for Bill Harvey in January 1963, had infinite faith in the technology of espionage.

Unlike his predecessor who favored developing human "assets" such as Johnny Roselli, FitzGerald wondered if the agency's lab might concoct some innovative device to solve their Castro problem.

"Like many CIA people, in love with the subtle and the artful, FitzGerald was fascinated by gadgets, and resented skeptics who dourly suggested they would cost too much, or fail to work, or weren't even needed at all," observed Thomas Powers, biographer of Richard Helms, FitzGerald's boss at the CIA.

FitzGerald, a dashing, affluent Harvard lawyer with social ties to the Georgetown set, was a favorite of the Kennedys. He shared their action-oriented theories about ridding the world of Castro and his socialist kind. Taking events into one's own hand, cowboy-style, seemed part of the Kennedys' so-called "New Frontier."

One Monday morning, on his long ride into Langley from his country home in Virginia, FitzGerald ruminated about a daring and unprecedented idea: an exploding seashell. Something to take care of Castro in one fell swoop.

As soon as he arrived at work, FitzGerald asked the CIA's Technical Service division to come up with a bomb stuck inside a beautiful shell so it would attract Fidel Castro as he enjoyed his favored pastime of scuba diving.

"I thought he was crazy at the time and I told him so," remembered Sam Halpern, his CIA assistant. "There were a whole bunch of nutty ideas like that that kept floating around."

Despite its dubiousness, FitzGerald instructed Halpern to check with the CIA technicians working under Dr. Sidney Gottlieb about the feasibility of an exploding seashell. Halpern gave them a call.

"Sure, Sam, we can make anything blow up—it doesn't matter," explained a friendly technician. "But what are you going to do about how you're going to emplace this thing?"

The technician rattled off his concerns. "Emplacement" would require a midget submarine to sneak into the Cuban coastal water on a high-risk mission. While a waterproof explosive could be fitted into a pretty shell, what would keep another swimmer from accidentally picking it up? And how would the CIA plant such a device in the water without getting caught by Castro's security guards?

Halpern realized such an explosion would be an obvious assassination attempt, certain to be traced back to the United States. "So I went and told Des, 'They're saying that it doesn't make any sense,'" Halpern recalled. "And finally we just dropped it and nothing else happened."

Meanwhile, FitzGerald stepped up covert action rather than traditional spying. In 1963, twenty-five exiles sent by the CIA into Cuba as armed commandos were killed or captured by Fidel's security forces. Some presumably had trained with Roselli in Florida. Each month, FitzGerald wanted a new major act of sabotage, something he could point out to Robert Kennedy as a sign of progress in this guerilla conflict.

Mostly, FitzGerald wanted an apostate—a military officer close to Castro who had become disenchanted with the tyrannical Communist dictatorship. "The real payoff," FitzGerald wrote to his staff in March 1963, would be a defector "ready, willing and able to dispose of Castro and his immediate entourage."

Soon FitzGerald believed they'd found such a prize in Cuban Major Rolando Cubela Secades. His codename was AMLASH.

A longtime Cuban revolutionary, Cubela made his bones as an assassin by killing Batista's head of military intelligence in 1956. He shot him in the face while the official was reportedly smiling at him. Visions of that murder would reportedly haunt his dreams.

Cubela was a young man who resembled Castro with his dark flowing beard and military fatigues. During the Cuban revolution, he became a trusted member of Fidel's inner circle and was injured in battle. When Castro took power, Cubela rallied student groups to their cause and was rewarded with a high position.

However, as early as 1961, Cubela expressed to CIA spies his unhappiness with Cuba's Communist rule and his willingness to defect. Perhaps Cubela was sincere in his anti-Castro fervor, as FitzGerald wanted to believe, but his odd track record raised many doubts.

In traveling with a Cuban delegation around the world, Cubela met surreptitiously several times with CIA agents without any firm commitments to become a double agent. Instead of defecting, Cubela agreed he might be more useful staying in place in Havana.

Cubela proved a finicky asset with his own set of rules. He preferred to work alone rather than with a group of co-conspirators dedicated against Castro. He seemed offended when the word "assassinate" came up regarding Fidel.

"It was not the act that he objected to," his CIA case officer observed, "but merely the choice of words used to describe it. 'Eliminate' was acceptable."

Most tellingly in August 1962, when he met with a CIA case officer in Paris, Cubela "indignantly refused to be polygraphed," the report said. Without taking a lie-detector test—standard fare for spies under a cloud—how could the CIA be assured Cubela wasn't merely a plant by Castro?

By late 1963, Cubela appeared amenable to a plan to recruit disaffected Cuban military officers for a possible coup against Castro. But he told agents he wanted to first meet with Robert Kennedy, clearly the administration's top spymaster above McCone, "for assurances of U.S. moral support" for the proposed mission that would surely mean Castro's death if successful.

Top CIA officials, including Helms and FitzGerald, quickly rejected the idea of RFK meeting with Cubela as way too dangerous. In particular, the pros in CIA counterintelligence, trained at sniffing out double agents, strongly objected. They suspected Cubela was a "dangle"—a double agent sent out by Castro to verify that the United States wanted him dead. By definition, a friendly "dangle" was meant to prompt the other side into revealing its true intentions. Cubela, with his checkered past, certainly qualified.

Despite the CIA's protocol and methods—which relied on cutouts and other subterfuge to deal with uncertain spies like Cubela—FitzGerald decided to meet with him in Paris during October 1963. It was a bold action, either heroic or stupid, but the kind surely to Bobby Kennedy's liking when he finally learned of it.

At the time, neither McCone nor the president's brother knew about this trip. Nevertheless, FitzGerald told Cubela that he was sent as Robert Kennedy's "personal representative."

During their conversation, Cubela inquired about a high-powered rifle with a scope, a weapon he could fire from a long distance without getting caught.

"While Cubela was anxious to do away with Castro," CIA documents said, "Cubela was not willing to sacrifice his own life in exchange for Castro's."

FitzGerald later claimed he told Cubela that while the United States fully supported a coup, it would have no part in an attempt on Castro's life. It wasn't a very believable disclaimer. Records show FitzGerald approved a little gift bundle for Cubela—a "cache" hidden in Cuba with many weapons, including "high power rifles w/scopes" if he requested it. Cubela also asked for twenty hand grenades and twenty pounds of explosives in a cache to be dropped off at a Cuban farm run by one of his friends.

Soon another meeting was set up in Paris for late November 1963 between Cubela and a CIA case officer. Within a tight circle inside the CIA, there was much hope AMLASH would prove the silver bullet needed to kill off the Communist leader who nearly provoked World War III.

FitzGerald had one more bright idea. At his urging, the CIA Technical Service lab worked all day and much of the night on a new James Bond-like device—a Paper Mate pen fitted with a poisoned hypodermic syringe, capable of undoing Castro from close range. All Cubela had to do was fill it with poison when he got back to Cuba.

As if recommending a premium blend of gasoline, the agency suggested the pen be filled with Black Leaf 40, a lethal mix of nicotine and common pesticide, certainly fatal if ingested by humans. A CIA report later said the pen's "needle was so fine that the victim would hardly feel it when it was inserted—[like] the scratch from a shirt with too much starch." This deadly pen, just like the gadgets used by 007 in the cinema, would be more than capable of doing the job.

From CIA headquarters in Langley, the agency rushed the device to Paris, so it would be available to give out the next day. Dr. Edward Gunn, the top CIA technician, created this poison pen. Gunn later said FitzGerald discreetly monitored the birth of this monstrous device, "but didn't want to know" officially to keep his "plausible deniability" intact.

Assassination was once more in the wind. The agency's expectations were high, just like they'd been for many months with the two mobsters in Florida. Under this new scheme, Cubela, the suspected double agent, would receive the high-tech killing device from one of FitzGerald's case officers with the CIA's blessings. This exchange would be a sure sign of America's intent to eliminate Fidel Castro, taking place on what would prove to be a historic day—November 22, 1963.

CHAPTER 34:

NATURE OF THE BEAST

L onely and confused, Judy Campbell desperately needed help.

By fall 1963, Judy's clandestine affairs with two extremely powerful figures—Sam Giancana and John F. Kennedy—had been over for months, leaving her an emotional mess. Her existence had become, as she later described, "like I was in a giant maze . . . sick of the intrigue, of not knowing what was going on."

FBI agents became her constant stalkers. Knocking on doors, following her in the streets of Los Angeles, they asked what she knew, demanding her secrets. They particularly wanted to know about the cagey figure involved in the CIA's Cuban affair.

"Did you ever see John Roselli and so-and-so together?" she recalled the agents asking her, going through a litany of names, looking for connections. "Do you know where John Roselli was on such and such a date?"

In this high-wire drama, Roselli had been her initial friend, the one who'd introduced her to Frank Sinatra, which begat her relationship with Kennedy and then Giancana. Once again, she turned to Johnny in November 1963 for a place to hide and recover.

Roselli and his streetwise attorney Jimmy Cantillon first put up Campbell in the Airport Marina Hotel, a large place next to LAX, with planes roaring overhead. They "had me going from hotel to hotel so the FBI wouldn't subpoena me," she recalled. "I sensed I was in terrible danger."

Roselli later denied that he and Giancana deliberately tried to keep Campbell away from grand juries or federal investigators, where she might be pressured into testifying against them. Johnny claimed not to know what personal secrets Sam and Judy shared.

"You would have to know the nature of the beast," he'd explained about Giancana. "He did not waste too many words, or confide in too many people, including me . . . If he had pillow talk with any woman, I would not know."

Sexual compromise was always part of this game of secrets, with Campbell an increasingly valuable plaything. For months, the federal government had tried to secure her cooperation, promising protection. Each attempt unnerved Campbell— like the time two agents confronted the beautiful young woman walking alone to her car in the rear parking lot of a doctor's office. Just as Campbell had become a potential source of compromise for the gangsters against the president, she was now asked by the FBI to inform on Giancana and Roselli.

More than anyone, however, Judy relied on these two gangsters for emotional support.

"I would be loyal to Sam and Johnny because I had more feelings for them than I did for the FBI," she explained. "After what the FBI had done to me, I had no use for them. I wouldn't have talked to them even if Sam had been out to kill me."

At perhaps her lowest moment a few months earlier—when Judy suffered her most conflicted moment stemming from her affair with JFK—Giancana was there for her, in a way that she didn't expect.

In January 1963, Campbell found herself pregnant. She claimed it was the result of her last encounter with Jack Kennedy (a contention with enough substance for the *New York Times* to mention it in her 1999 obituary). Judy's affair with JFK apparently didn't end with the White House phone calls, but with a final trip to Washington in late summer 1962.

"I was 26 and in love," Campbell explained. "Was I supposed to have better sense and more judgment than the president of the United States?"

When Campbell later told JFK about her pregnancy, she said, she was weeping over the telephone. He wanted to know if she wanted to have the baby.

"You know I can't keep this child," Judy claimed to tell him. "The FBI is all over us, and has been since they first knocked on my door."

"I want you to know it's an option if you want to keep the baby," JFK replied, as she recalled. "We can arrange it."

"That's an absolute impossibility because of who you are," Judy said. "We'd never get away with it."

At his gentle urging, Campbell said she decided to terminate her pregnancy. With abortion then not legal in the United States, the only question was where. She said Kennedy then asked, "Do you think Sam would help us? Would you ask Sam?"

Though Giancana had courted her for months, Judy had never been intimate with him. There was no chance he could be the father. She didn't know what to expect if she told Sam of her pregnancy. She decided it was best to meet over dinner.

When Judy informed him at their table, Giancana blew up in anger at Kennedy's cavalier behavior, though he showed none toward her own. "Damn him!" Sam fumed. "Damn that Kennedy!"

Then Judy told him she needed an abortion.

Ironically, Campbell's dilemma wasn't the first time Giancana and Roselli dealt surreptitiously with the consequences of JFK's alleged extramarital affairs.

In spring 1961, Roselli met with friendly Los Angeles private detective, Fred Otash, at the Brown Derby. Otash was a highly skilled snoop with listening devices. A jealous husband had hired him to investigate his wife, a Hollywood actress. Otash supposedly came up with evidence she'd slept with several well-known figures including Frank Sinatra, Dean Martin, and Jack Kennedy.

At the Brown Derby, Roselli told Otash that he was acting "at the request of the Attorney General," and insisted JFK's name be dropped from any mention in a possible divorce lawsuit brought by the jealous husband. At a subsequent meeting, Giancana joined them, to emphasize the warning.

"Otash, you know, you're going to have some serious problems," Roselli warned about the mob's threatened repercussions. "If you persist in this, they're going to come down on you like a Mack Truck."

Although there's no evidence that Roselli's demand was sanctioned by the Kennedys, Otash had no doubt about the Mafia's seriousness. Soon the lawsuit went away.

This Otash skullduggery was apparently more successful than his earlier effort "looking for dirt" on Kennedy and his Rat Pack pals prior to Election Day 1960. According to an FBI memo, Otash tried to recruit "a high-priced Hollywood call girl" during the time of the Democratic National Convention in Los Angeles to approach Kennedy. Otash's plan called for her to wear "a recording device for taking down any 'indiscreet statements' the Senator might make," the memo said.

At that time, Otash was working with *Confidential Magazine*, a precursor to the *National Enquirer*. He wanted any information about "sex parties" she might have.

The Hollywood hooker refused to cooperate. Instead she reported the incident to the FBI.

Otash's obsession with the president's sex life didn't dim. Indeed, the private eye found a welcome home as an informant inside Hoover's Bureau. In this world, women like Judy Campbell were nothing more than roadkill in the pathway to power. One FBI memo in March 1962 underlined Campbell's connection to Kennedy by tallying up her telephone calls to the White House and described her as "associated with prominent underworld figures Sam Giancana and John Roselli." For good measure, the missive ended by quoting Otash. He "referred to Campbell as the girl who was 'shacking up with John Kennedy in the East.'"

Hearing once again about JFK's sexual duplicity incensed Giancana during his 1963 dinner with Campbell. Only as the meal progressed did his mood soften.

The vulnerability of Campbell seemed to touch him. She was a young woman—nearly the same age as his daughters—whom Sam had helped manipulate into an elaborate trap with the Kennedys. Now she found herself pregnant and looking for his help.

"I want to ask you something," Giancana said slowly. "Of course, I can arrange whatever you ask for, and I promise you'll be safe. But if you want to keep this baby, you can also do that."

His suggestion was not what Judy wanted to hear. In her mind, there was no way she could become an unmarried mother of a child.

"I can't," she replied.

Sam was undeterred. He leaned toward her and grasped her hands in his. For all of the viciousness in his world, there existed, for that single moment, an undeniable gentleness in Sam's eyes. The Mafia don offered a request.

"Then let me ask you this," Sam said, "Will you marry me?"

The sheer surprise of his proposal left her stunned, speechless at first. Judy then burst into tears.

At its heart, there seemed something so generous about Giancana's gesture, so fundamentally decent, as if the old padrone was gallantly placing his coat over a mud-died pathway. Despite the circumstances, he still treated her like a princess.

"I was so touched by Sam," she later remembered. "It broke me down. I was so emotional and needy. I never dreamed he'd say anything like that; I knew he was really in love with Phyllis McGuire."

Across the dinner table, with tears still streaming down her cheeks, Judy was temporarily the realistic one.

"Sam, you don't want to marry me," she murmured.

Giancana smiled at her honesty.

"Yes, maybe," he acknowledged, ". . . but you deserve to be asked."

His reply was so tender, so understanding. She later described that particular dinner exchange as "that moment when he tried to make it right." Judy never felt closer to this man, nearly double her age.

The mood of personal closeness extended into the night, as Judy went to bed with Giancana for what she said was the first and only time.

"We were intimate that night, although I certainly wasn't in love with him," she recalled. "I truly believe that not all intimacy is born of lust. A wide range of feelings was involved."

Shortly afterward, Giancana helped her with the necessary arrangements. Judy flew to Chicago and had an abortion at a local hospital in January 1963. Sam picked her up after two days in the hospital. Years afterward, Campbell would show the hospital records to interviewers to validate her story.

"He was helping me," Judy explained. "A lot of people can say, 'Oh boy, this is just something else he [Giancana] could hold over Jack's head.' I don't care what they say, I know what he did for me."

Throughout the rest of 1963, Campbell lived in Los Angeles, evading the FBI agents who were tracking her movements. Much of her time was spent at home, painting and thinking about her situation.

Some friends avoided her because of her Giancana connection; others because they'd been questioned by agents about her activities and didn't want any trouble. One set of agents even approached her about having an abortion. She denied everything.

"You people are insane!" she screamed. "How dare you walk in and accuse me of that."

"Well, we think you did," said one FBI man. "Take it easy, you're only helping yourself if you name the doctor who performed the abortion." She kept screaming until the two agents went away.

Campbell's evasive game with the FBI came to a temporary halt on November 19, 1963, when she and Cantillon visited the bureau's LA office. The lawyer she shared with Roselli complained about the surveillance and an alleged break-in at her apartment.

During this time, both Cantillon and Roselli kept "very close tabs" on Campbell, concerned what she might say if called to a grand jury. Her testimony could be disastrous, causing everything to unravel. There was not only the FBI's domestic criminal probe to consider, but also the two gangsters' still top-secret connection to the CIA plot to kill Castro.

Kept out of sight in various locales, Judy slowly realized the danger she was in. "I was sick to death of it all," she recalled, "all those lonely nights in hotel rooms, and it began to dawn on me that I could go to jail."

The following day, November 20, Judy moved again. This time, Roselli arranged for her to stay at the Beverly Crest Hotel. It was a place of self-described "charm and luxury," where she could sun herself beside the outdoor pool.

And maybe, for a moment, forget about Jack Kennedy and Sam Giancana.

CHAPTER 35:

DEATH IN THE AFTERNOON

At the Desert Inn, the heavy drapes in the upstairs suites kept everything dark. They muffled the outside blinking neon lights, muted the noises of the Strip, and prevented brilliant sunlight from pouring in. They were a nocturnal necessity for those in Las Vegas who lived for the nighttime, not the day.

Sometime early in the afternoon of November 22, 1963—the equivalent of morning by Vegas casino time—the telephone rang in Johnny Roselli's blackened hotel room. He'd been in bed for hours.

Roselli picked up the receiver and recognized the excited voice. It was Jonie Taps, an old friend of Harry Cohn's from Columbia Pictures. Roselli also knew him from the Friars Club in Beverly Hills. Taps was full of dreadful alarm. He said President Kennedy had been shot.

"I didn't believe it at first because I was in a sound sleep," Roselli recalled. "I got shocked because he mentioned the Governor [Texas Gov. John Connolly] was shot too, and I started to believe this man."

To the still-groggy Roselli, the Hollywood producer shouted over the phone, "Turn on your radio!"

As he listened to the mournful news reports from Dallas, Roselli came to a quick conclusion who might be responsible for Kennedy's assassination.

"Those damn Communists," Roselli told Taps before hanging up the phone.

After so much time in the Florida Keys, scheming with the CIA's exile militia to kill Castro, Johnny was well aware of the Cuban leader's threats to reciprocate.

"That was the first thing that came to my mind because a few months before that Castro had made a speech that was monitored in Florida, and I read it in the newspapers," Roselli explained, "It sounded just like him, that he was threatening the establishment here."

A few days before, the FBI had tracked Roselli flying from Los Angeles to Phoenix with his friend, Maurice Friedman, another mob-connected businessman and member of the Friars Club, who had helped finance the Frontier casino in Vegas. Johnny and Friedman travelled to a resort with two call girls named "Gina" and "Arlene," as the FBI discovered.

Agents kept following Roselli's trail with great suspicion. Unlike his usual method of flying—paying cash, grabbing a seat at the last minute and staying off the plane's manifest—Johnny booked the flight with his real name, not an alias. Eventually, the purpose of the trip became clear.

An "urgent" FBI memo—dated November 16, 1963 but not released until in 2017—contained political dynamite. It said Roselli, Friedman, and the two call girls stayed overnight in Phoenix before taking off again for the nation's capital. They were joined by a "high powered attorney" and "planned to meet unknown Congressman in Washington," said the memo. "Purpose of contact not known."

Finding out why a congressman might be meeting with such a mobster was clearly the urgency behind this memo. It had enough regard for Johnny's sartorial splendor to note he "dresses well in expensive clothes." The memo said one of the call girls, the blonde woman named "Gina," would "receive two thousand dollars for trip," while the other called "Arlene" would get a new car.

In Washington, FBI agents were dispatched to conduct "Fisur" (physical surveillance) at the House Office Building, spying on Roselli and company to see whom they might visit. In the memo's margin, a Bureau supervisor advised "extreme caution in light of proposed Congressional contact." But no other records exist on whether Roselli's group ever made it to the capital, hobnobbed with a Congressman, or whether Gina and Arlene ever got their rewards.

In fact, during the next week—from November 20 through 27, 1963—the FBI lost track of Roselli's whereabouts. It would lead to all sorts of theories, none ever proven, that Roselli was someplace other than the Desert Inn on November 22.

CIA director John McCone shared the same suspicion as Roselli about Communist involvement with JFK's assassination. At lunch inside Langley headquarters, an aide cried out news that President Kennedy had been shot. McCone telephoned his friend, Attorney General Robert Kennedy, and then rushed out the door.

"I'm going to Hickory Hill to be with Bobby," McCone told aides. After he reached RFK's home in Virginia, McCone watched as the president's brother took another call. It was the FBI's Hoover on the line. Bobby paused with a steely look and then exclaimed, "He's dead."

As friends and family slowly gathered, Bobby paced the lawn with a trusted aide, Ed Guthman. He confided his suspicions about the assassination. "There's so much bitterness," Bobby said. "I thought they'd get one of us, but Jack, after all he'd been through, never worried about it . . . I thought it would be me."

In the immediate aftermath, CIA officers around the world went into high alert. Some feared the Soviet KGB might be at play, particularly because the alleged assassin, Lee Harvey Oswald, had visited the Soviet and Cuban embassies in Mexico earlier that fall.

While the Russians were quickly ruled out, questions lingered about Castro. In private conversations years later, RFK asked McCone to assure him the CIA had no role in his brother's death. "I asked him in a way he couldn't lie to me, and [McCone said] they hadn't," Kennedy explained.

However, the CIA chief sensed something amiss. His friend Bobby seemed troubled by something he didn't want to disclose. McCone later said he felt "Kennedy may very well have thought there was some connection between the assassination plans against Castro and the assassination of President Kennedy." McCone was convinced Robert Kennedy had "personal feelings of guilt because he was directly or indirectly involved in the anti-Castro planning."

McCone didn't suffer similar pangs of conscience. For many months, his staff, including his chief deputy Helms, never told him of the Castro assassination plot. They assured him the conspiracy was over, even though the killing plans were still in place.

Robert Kennedy apparently wondered if the Mafia, especially Sam Giancana, might be to blame. He asked his Justice staff to investigate. Personally, he called Julius Draznin, a senior Labor Department investigator in Chicago and asked, "Do you have any angles on this?"

Draznin checked around but found none. "There's nothing," Draznin reported.

Among mobsters, the reaction to JFK's murder was one of muted joy. Santo Trafficante Jr., the Florida don so deeply involved with the Cuban exiles, toasted Kennedy's death, his lawyer later remembered. Trafficante still had visions of returning to Havana to reopen the mob's casinos.

"Now they'll get off my back, off Carlos' [Marcello] back," Trafficante crowed. "We'll make big money out of this and maybe go back to Cuba."

On November 25, shortly after JFK's death, a FBI microphone in Chicago heard Giancana remark about the assassin's accuracy with a rifle. When an associate called Oswald a "Marxist," Giancana commented, "He was a marksman who knew how to shoot."

On December 3, 1963, barely two weeks after the assassination, Giancana victoriously predicted the government's investigation of the Outfit would ebb, if not cease. He said the president's death would undoubtedly halt Robert Kennedy's Justice Department campaign against them. Perhaps Giancana also believed criticism of him by Accardo and others—that his brazen actions drew unwanted attention from the feds—might also go away.

"I will tell you something, in another two months from now, it will be like it was five years ago," Giancana predicted about the feds to one of his Chicago henchmen. "They won't be around anymore."

Jimmy Fratianno, Johnny's pal and preferred hitman on the West Coast, recalled how they discussed JFK's death.

"Maybe if you had clipped him [Castro], Kennedy would still be alive," Fratianno claimed to have said, according to a book about his life in crime.

Roselli replied, "Listen, Jimmy, in this business, you can't win them all."

No one answered the phone in Judy Campbell's room at the Beverly Crest Hotel. Roselli called repeatedly. The receiver just rang.

Finally, after five days of trying by telephone, Johnny went to the hotel. He feared the worst.

At the front desk, he convinced someone to let him into Campbell's room, alarmed about her safety. There seemed a nagging similarity to the circumstances of Marilyn Monroe's final hours.

Inside her suite, Judy was alive but a wreck. Johnny found her in a drunken stupor from Jack Daniel's whiskey, from lack of sleep and food, and from crying incessantly.

During the fateful moments of the president's assassination, Judy had been asleep at the Beverly Crest. She received a telephone call from her mother, telling her to turn on the television. The black-and-white screen was filled with photos and footage of JFK, the man she had loved.

"I couldn't believe it," Judy recalled. "I buried myself in that room for days, and all I could think of was 'My God, Jack is dead!'"

Roselli ignored her sad laments, her insistent demands to go away and forget about her. Johnny wouldn't let her die alone in that room.

Roselli had his reasons, both personal and strategic. He and Cantillon had put Judy in a series of hotels to keep her away from the FBI and being called before a grand jury. An emotionally distraught Campbell would be a ripe prize for FBI agents like William Roemer, intent on bringing down Giancana. If she was subpoenaed, the Outfit might make arrangements for her disposal, the way other witnesses had disappeared in the past.

As a friend and supplicant to Sam, Johnny felt a duty to alleviate any problems with Campbell, clean up any messes. But Roselli also had an empathetic side towards Judy. He'd known her as the beautiful fresh-faced wife of a young Hollywood actor in the 1950s living in his Los Angeles neighborhood, before she entered his fast-lane world of Vegas, Sinatra's Rat Pack, and the Kennedys. Johnny was one of the few human beings, outside of government, who knew of her affair with the president. In a sense, he was most responsible for initiating this deliberate "honeypot" trap.

Whatever his prior motivation, Roselli now took pity on this disheveled drunken woman, solitary in her dark confinement. He refused to leave.

"I didn't want to see him, but he patiently resisted me, until finally I agreed to have dinner," Judy remembered. "Except for what I nibbled on from room service, this was my first meal in all that time."

Gradually, Campbell recovered her strength, if not her spirits. The next day, Johnny convinced her to come along for the ninety-mile drive to Palm Springs, where they joined his girlfriend, Dorothy Towne, a blue-eyed, blonde actress. They all stayed for several days at the home of Paul Ross, a Hollywood publicist.

In Palm Springs, Roselli and the two women sat together at a table with another couple inside the new Canyon Country Club. It was a sprawling facility where Frank Sinatra held his annual golf invitation tournament, attended by many top golfers and celebrities. On rare off days, Sinatra would relax, with his golf hat on, at this club near his home.

That particular day, with Judy and Roselli already at their table, Sinatra and Dean Martin walked in. They sat nearby with a group of ten people. Judy noticed that Frank was careful not to make eye contact with her. "There was not one greeting from any of them," she recalled. "It gave me the weirdest feeling."

JFK's death hit Frank hard. Despite their difficulties over the president's 1962 stay at Bing Crosby's home, Sinatra still kept mementos from the 1960 campaign when he worked his heart out for his friend Jack.

"Frank was pretty broken up" when he called JFK's sister, Pat Lawford, to express his condolences, recalled Peter Lawford, still banished as a Rat Pack member. Sinatra "would have given anything to come back to Washington for Jack's funeral, but it just wasn't possible to invite him. He'd already been too much of an embarrassment to the family."

At the time of the assassination, Sinatra had been filming another Rat Pack musical, *Robin and the 7 Hoods*, in which art seemed to reflect real life. Frank played an ambitious mob boss in Chicago during the Roaring Twenties, not unlike Giancana at that moment. Strangely, during filming in a Burbank cemetery, Frank was unnerved while walking out for a cigarette smoke to find a grave marked *John F. Kennedy, 1873-1940*. After the news from Dallas reached their Hollywood set, Sinatra spent three days alone at his home in Palm Springs, virtually incommunicado.

Despite the chilly reception Campbell received at the Canyon Country Club, it probably had nothing to do with her, but rather with her companion Roselli. Sinatra had lost a fortune because of the scandal surrounding Sam Giancana's visit to the Cal-Neva resort. Ignoring Roselli—arguably Sam's best pal in Sinatra's mind—was undoubtedly better than suffering the consequences of being seen with a Mafioso.

Returning from Palm Springs a few days later, Judy didn't go back to a hotel. She went home to her empty Beverly Hills apartment. FBI agents waited in the shadows, once again checking on her like some Hitchcock thriller.

"They made me a prisoner in my own house," she said. Judy feared for her sanity. She slept with a gun under her pillow.

Once again, on New Year's Eve, Johnny came to her rescue. He invited Campbell to a big party at the Desert Inn.

"I jumped at the opportunity," she recalled. "I felt like a drowning woman being offered a life raft."

Campbell sat next to Johnny's beautiful blonde date for the evening and across from Moe Dalitz, introduced as president of the hotel. She danced with Dalitz, who was eager to know her better. At the end of the evening, Judy fell into a taunting conversation with the hotel chief, lubricated by drink.

"Come on, now, don't get so mad," Dalitz told her, after a slight peck on her cheek. Judy turned and belted Dalitz across the face. He walked away, disgusted.

Johnny was stunned. For a moment, no one said anything as Roselli stared right at her.

"You know something," Johnny finally said, as if he'd had a change of heart about Campbell. "You must be crazy."

———

Unlike Roselli, Sam Giancana had decided months earlier to keep his distance from Judy, lavishing attention instead on Phyllis McGuire. From Chicago, Sam wrote love notes under an alias to McGuire who was performing in Las Vegas: *"Your show is ending and you know how happy it makes me. Always remember how much I care for you and love you. Waiting to be with you. Always yours, Doctor Stein."*

During New Year's that year, Sam flew away with McGuire to Hawaii. In Honolulu, the FBI spotted him playing golf at a private club with baseball legend Joe DiMaggio. It was a chance meeting, Joltin' Joe later told the G-Men, though in fact he'd met Sam and Phyllis previously.

The FBI continued their surveillance of Judy Campbell for months after the assassination. In piecing together this investigative puzzle, she was the lynchpin between Sinatra, JFK, and Giancana. She could no longer rely on these three men for support, so she turned to Johnny for emotional comfort.

"Jack was dead and Sam was out of my life," she recalled. "My problem was that I didn't know what or where I wanted to be."

Eventually, Judy and Johnny slept together. Months later, in late 1964, she told Johnny that she was pregnant. The baby was his.

As gently as he could, Roselli made it clear he couldn't marry her. His life was too spread out among many different places, shared by too many women, for him to ever think of settling down. He and Sam had treated Judy as a lure in JFK's entrapment, enough to blackmail the federal government and keep it from taking any criminal action against them.

Now, Johnny was careful not to become entrapped himself. Judy let him know she planned to move in with her parents and give up the baby for adoption.

The FBI, perhaps aware of her pregnancy, still tried to flip Campbell, scaring her into cooperation. Two agents knocked on her parents' door when her father wasn't home. Her mother opened the door. One agent showed her mother a photo of Johnny Roselli while another held up a picture of Giancana.

"All we want to do is talk to you and your mother about these men," an agent explained to Judy.

Campbell immediately started screaming. "Get out of here!" she shouted. "And if you ever bother my mother again, I'll kill you."

Two months later, Campbell gave birth to a baby boy. It took her a while, but she finally decided after a year to give the child up for adoption. From all available accounts, Johnny Roselli never saw his son.

Despite the strife and turmoil in her life, Judy kept one promise to Giancana and Roselli. No one in the press or public would know about her involvement with the two mobsters and President Kennedy for at least another decade—not until the top-secret Castro assassination plan came to light.

CHAPTER 36:

THE STUFF OF LEGENDS

"Truth has a hard time once legends are established which appease our thirst for heroes and heroics."

—ALLEN DULLES

In the two years since leaving the CIA, Allen Dulles had worked hard to restore his tarnished image.

In October 1963, Dulles published a book called *The Craft of Intelligence*, a tribute to the art of spying. He gave speeches around the country, though he spoke little of the Bay of Pigs fiasco. And he remained proud of the fifty-million-dollar CIA headquarters in Langley, called "Allen's Folly" even by his friends.

On television, Dulles, with his tweedy clothes and professorial appearance, looked very much the part of a retired headmaster, contemplating all the world's secrets in his head as he puffed contently on his pipe.

Did Fidel Castro have a future? asked one television correspondent.

"I hope not," Dulles replied. "I rather think he might fade away."

On November 22, Dulles was resting inside his Long Island home, just returned from another speaking engagement, when he heard news of President Kennedy's assassination. A week later, the White House called. The new incumbent, Lyndon B. Johnson, asked Dulles to join a presidential panel investigating JFK's death. Supreme Court Chief Justice Earl Warren would head the commission, forever known by his name.

The nation had been horrified by the young president's shooting in Dallas and deeply disturbed by its aftermath. Following his arrest by police, Lee Harvey Oswald, JFK's suspected assassin, proclaimed his innocence, despite ample evidence pointing to his guilt. "I'm just a patsy," he insisted, creating a conspiratorial tone that would linger.

On November 24, while being transferred from one jail to another, Oswald was shot fatally by Dallas nightclub owner Jack Ruby. It was an execution caught by television cameras and watched repeatedly by millions.

The stunning turn of events prompted the FBI to investigate Oswald's activities prior to the assassination and whether Ruby's background might include organized crime connections. "We had thousands and thousands of hours of tape recordings of the top mobsters in Chicago, including Sam Giancana, and Ruby just didn't exist as far as they were concerned," recalled FBI agent William Roemer.

President Johnson was particularly concerned about a possible foreign motive behind Kennedy's death. The day after the assassination, McCone told him about Oswald's visits to the Cuban and Russian diplomatic outposts in Mexico earlier in the year. That day former President Dwight Eisenhower also warned Johnson about Robert Kennedy's outsized power over CIA covert activities. In putting together the Warren panel, some suggested a possible Cuban connection.

Still intimately familiar with CIA operations, Dulles seemed the perfect person to help decipher truth from fiction. He relished the chance to jump back into the Great Game, unravel whatever clandestine mysteries were behind Kennedy's murder.

"It was so tantalizing to go over that record, as we did, trying to find out every fact connected with the assassination," Dulles later recalled, "and then to say if any one of the chess pieces that were entered into the game had been moved differently, at any one time, the whole thing might have been different."

It was Robert Kennedy, more than anyone, who helped put Dulles on the commission investigating his brother's death.

As the new president formed his commission, White House aide Walter Jenkins sent a November 29 memo indicating both RFK and Deputy Attorney General Nicholas deB. Katzenbach had recommended Dulles for appointment. Katzenbach worked closely on Justice Department matters with Kennedy. But like President Johnson, he didn't know about the Mafia complicity in a CIA plot to kill Castro.

During this time, Katzenbach tried to ease Bobby's terrible burdens as much as he could, both as a colleague and friend. Dutifully, Kennedy returned to work the day after his brother's burial.

"He looked like the ghost of his former self, and his efforts to tell humorous stories about events at the funeral were brave but flat," Katzenbach recalled about Bobby.

In a memo, Katzenbach urged Jenkins and another LBJ aide, Bill Moyers, to focus on Oswald as the lone assassin. They agreed to curb any talk of conspiracy. Although the two didn't get along, Johnson deferred to the attorney general's wishes about the Warren panel.

"As for the makeup of the rest of the commission, I appointed the two men Bobby Kennedy asked me to put on it—Allen Dulles and John McCloy—immediately," Johnson later recalled in his memoir.

Though Dulles had been embarrassed by the Bay of Pigs, he didn't harbor any obvious animus toward the Kennedys, who had gently eased him out of the CIA. Robert Kennedy and the former spymaster felt no urgency to inform the new president—or anyone who didn't already know—about the Castro assassination conspiracy.

Dulles shared RFK's penchant for secrecy surrounding the Cuban project.

"Dear Bob," Dulles wrote to him on January 28, 1964, before giving an oral history to the Kennedy Library about his CIA stewardship. "I suggest that you and I might have a word together before I put anything on the tape with regard to Cuba, the Dominican Republic or like subjects." He even let Bobby pick his interviewer.

Neither Sam Giancana nor Johnny Roselli ever testified before the Warren Commission. The panel heard nothing about what they knew of the Mafia-CIA plans to kill Castro and whether it might be of any consequence in President Kennedy's death.

"I bet you any amount of money," Roselli allegedly told his confidant Jimmy Fratianno, "the CIA never tells the Warren Commission about their little deal with us."

In pushing toward a conclusion, the Warren Commission avoided any avenues of uncertainty. During its proceedings, Dulles steered fellow board members away from the CIA's long-running efforts against Castro and his own part in it.

Bobby Kennedy never voiced his doubts to the panel either. As early as December 9, 1963, Kennedy told historian Arthur M. Schlesinger Jr. that he believed Oswald was the shooter. But he added "there was still argument" about if Oswald acted alone or was "part of a larger plot, whether organized by Castro or by gangsters."

While a Congressional panel later found both Johnson and Robert Kennedy had "privately voiced suspicion about underworld complicity" in JFK's death, the Warren Commission in 1964 didn't investigate it to any significant degree.

The influence of Dulles had its desired effect. Commission staffer Burt Griffin, who checked out Jack Ruby's background, later said that "the possibility that someone

associated with the underworld would have wanted to assassinate the President . . .
[was] not seriously explored."

In the immediate aftermath of JFK's death, Johnson didn't want to provoke a war
of retribution by blaming the Soviet Union or its satellite Cuban government. But the
unexplored areas by the Warren Commission would create a lasting generation of
doubters and conspiracy mongers for years to come. Even supporters of the panel's
conclusions about Oswald as the lone crazed assassin seemed taken aback by its
incompleteness.

"That the CIA hid its operation to murder the Cuban leader from the Warren
Commission, as well as the details from its own President, raised questions about
what it might have withheld on Lee Oswald and the Kennedy assassination," wrote
Gerald Posner in his book *Case Closed,* a vigorous endorsement of its findings.

Forty years after JFK's death, an analysis by the CIA's chief historian David Robarge
found that then-CIA chieftain John McCone was part of a "benign cover-up" by not
telling the Warren Commission about the Castro plot. McCone's testimony was "neither frank nor accurate," concluded Robarge, and the agency "did not volunteer material even if potentially relevant—for example, about Agency plans to assassinate
Castro."

Ironically, several others at the CIA knew even more. Only a few months prior to
JFK's assassination, McCone was informed about the Castro killing plot. Yet even
then, the nation's top spymaster wasn't told by his underlings about the involvement
of Mafia figures like Roselli and Giancana, nor that the "executive action" against
Castro was still going on during his tenure.

CIA officials such as Richard Helms and Sheffield Edwards knew these bombshell
details. But they didn't tell McCone.

This deceit was painfully clear to "Big Jim" O'Connell when returning from
his Asian overseas assignment in 1965. Five years earlier, O'Connell had been the
agency's direct contact with Giancana, Roselli, and Bob Maheu in the plot against
Castro.

Upon arriving back in the United States, O'Connell caught up with his old friend
Shef Edwards. The Warren Commission had already issued its report by then with no
mention of the Castro killing conspiracy. O'Connell wondered aloud if McCone was
ever told about it.

Shef gave him half an answer. "He [Edwards] said something about, well, we never briefed McCone on this thing, because he didn't have anything to do with it, and it was just as well he didn't know anything about it," recalled O'Connell.

Dulles knew plenty, as the agency eventually conceded in 2007. But that didn't prevent Dulles from lying about it to a national audience in May 1965.

For an NBC television documentary *The Science of Spying*, anchorman John Chancellor interviewed the retired CIA director. At one point, Dulles mentioned the Soviet Union's successful spying operation within Castro's Cuba.

"Do we have an application of morality in our activities that they don't?" Chancellor asked.

"Oh, far more than they do, yes," Dulles quickly replied. "As far as I know, we don't knowingly engage in assassinations and kidnappings and things of that kind. As far as I know, we never have. As far as we know, they have and done it quite consistently."

Chancellor pursued the topic further.

"Did you apply, for example, moral standards to what you did when you were director of the CIA?" asked the newsman.

With smoking pipe in hand, Dulles sat up in his seat.

"Yes I did," he said. "Why? Because I don't think, given the calibre of the men and women I had working for me, I didn't want to ask them to do a thing that I wouldn't do. One or two said, even when I assigned them, that they would prefer not to do it and that was all right with me. I didn't ask them to do it."

Dulles didn't clarify what "it" was, but somehow all the implied nefariousness came through. With a far-off glance in his book-lined Long Island study, Dulles assured America that his intentions were always good in preventing acts of terror by the enemy.

"All I can say is that I am a parson's son, and I was brought up a Presbyterian. Maybe as a Calvinist, maybe as a fatalist—I don't know," he said, with his famously charming smile. "But I hope I have a reasonable moral standard."

CHAPTER 37:

GOVERNMENT IMMUNITY

U ndercover agents were waiting for Johnny Roselli in September 1964 as he landed in Chicago. The local FBI, accustomed to other familiar Outfit members, followed this mystery man from the West Coast as he visited Sam Giancana at his Oak Park home.

No ordinary visitor, Roselli was treated by Sam like an old friend. Both had been through so much together.

"Anytime I would go to Chicago, I'd have been at his [Giancana's] home," Roselli recalled. As agents tagged along incognito, Sam took his out-of-town pal to dinner, for a few drinks at downtown nightclubs, or to relax at the Armory Lounge.

When they got back to Oak Park, the two men went downstairs to Sam's furnished basement to talk about business without anyone listening. Giancana had built his modest three-story brick house in the Chicago suburbs into a fortress, the private domain of a powerful gangster more ambitious and personally complex than America had ever known.

Upstairs, a certain elegance pervaded his home, luxuriant with paintings, sculpture, gold carvings, silverware, and antique porcelains bearing names like Royal Doulton. This display of elegance and art—so far from Sam's crude everyday world of the streets—were lasting reminders of his beloved Angeline's tastes.

Roselli relaxed and enjoyed Giancana's hospitality. Family life was something he had never known, spending most of his evenings in nightclubs with an assortment of women. Sam's oldest daughter Antoinette—curious and somewhat resentful of this handsome visitor—caught snippets of their conversation downstairs.

"Sam didn't realize I could hear what he was saying or I'm sure he would have sent me upstairs or closed the conference room door," she remembered. "I heard portions of what he was telling Johnny Rosselli [sic], a Las Vegas flunkey of his, who sometimes angered Dad but was important to his scheme of things in the control of various Las Vegas casinos."

Giancana's daughter wasn't the only one kept in the dark. Neither the FBI—nor virtually anyone related to the Chicago Outfit—had a clear idea what Johnny and Sam were up to with the CIA. Perhaps it seemed inconceivable America's spy agency had a handshake deal with the two mobsters to murder Castro.

"In Chicago we were never able to establish definitively that there was in fact such an alliance," admitted FBI agent William Roemer.

Following JFK's death, the year 1964 started off full of promise for organized crime. With the Kennedy Justice Department finally off their backs, Giancana and Roselli anticipated a revival for the embattled Mafia, the way it was in the 1950s before Fidel Castro took over Cuba. From this outlook, the two mob pals, and their friend in Florida, Santo Trafficante Jr., could expect to be back in Havana with their lucrative casinos in no time.

By September 1964, Attorney General Robert Kennedy left to run for the US Senate in New York. No longer would he loom over their actions as the avenging prosecutor. On the day of his brother's assassination, RFK had been presiding over a meeting about expanding his vigorous assault against the Mafia. But after Dallas, Bobby's aggressive plans waned, like a sailboat suddenly without a breeze. "He never mentioned organized crime to me again," said Robert Morgenthau, then the US Attorney in New York.

The government's efforts suffered another blow when President Johnson ordered the FBI to remove all wiretap and listening devices placed illegally. Suddenly gone were "Little Al"—the hidden microphone in the Outfit's downtown headquarters—and also "Mo," the device in Giancana's Armory Lounge hangout in the suburbs. So were several other listening devices in Chicago and elsewhere, which had provided hours of raw invaluable intelligence about heinous crimes and widespread corruption.

Unlike John Kennedy's era, the Johnson Justice Department officials now seemed more concerned about civil liberties than putting bad guys in jail. Investigators like Roemer believed the federal eavesdropping ended because Johnson feared his own corrupt cronies might be caught. "When I received word of Johnson's executive order, I was flabbergasted," said Roemer. "How could anyone put such a roadblock in the way of our efforts to track the mob? I could hardly believe it."

Despite this windfall of good luck for the mob, Giancana's fortunes in Chicago's

Outfit appeared on the decline. Sam's high-profile personal life had led to greater FBI scrutiny at home and the loss of millions in Nevada and elsewhere.

In January 1964, the *Chicago Daily News* claimed Sam had been "booted" as acting boss and made an elder statesman. That April, an FBI memo said because of "the publicity Giancana got at the Cal-Neva Lodge earlier, there is a possibility that the 'bosses behind the scenes' may strip Giancana of his position in Chicago and replace him."

Even underlings didn't show the old respect. When Giancana advised his violent loan shark collector, Sam "Mad Sam" DeStefano, to stop his wild outbursts in public, DeStefano "used strong language in response," said the *Chicago Tribune*, which detailed the fractious power grabs in Giancana's onetime smooth-running "juice" operation around the city.

Old supporters, like Murray Humphreys, had enough with Giancana's carelessness. Before giving up their listening devices, the FBI had heard Humphreys become furious with Sam. At the Armory Lounge in 1963, Giancana instructed an aide to tell agent Bill Roemer, his constant bête noire, to stop harassing him and warned that "if Bobby Kennedy wants to talk to me, I'll be glad to talk to him and he knows who to go through." The message clearly pointed to Frank Sinatra as the go-between.

When Humphreys heard this story, he erupted. "The Hump" had spent his whole career as a political fixer for the Outfit. With the utmost discretion, he'd helped Johnny Roselli and Paul Ricca get out of prison in the so-called Hollywood Extortion case and arranged numerous deals under the table. In Humphreys's view, Sam's cavalier comment to the feds exposing Sinatra was incredibly reckless.

"For Chrissakes, that's a cardinal rule—you don't give up a legit guy," the Hump screamed. "He tells Roemer that Sinatra is our guy to Kennedy?" Humphreys swore to bring this matter to the attention of senior consigliere, Ricca and Tony Accardo.

But Humphreys soon got mired in Giancana's legal problems. The curly-haired fixer was arrested at his home for committing perjury before a grand jury investigating Giancana's activities. After he posted bail, the immaculately groomed Humphreys went home and dropped dead. Unlike other mobsters, Chicago scribe Mike Rokyo noted, Humphreys "died of *unnatural* causes –a heart attack."

Reluctantly, the old don Accardo realized he must replace Giancana. By late 1964, he decided to give up his semi-retired role and oversee the Outfit once again. The return of "Big Tuna"—and Giancana's loss of power—was a remarkable reversal for both men.

Though not as flashy, Accardo could be every bit as cruel and efficient as Giancana. As an example, two gunmen chased a key witness in Accardo's 1960 tax case, beer salesman Joseph Bronge, down a street. With their faces blackened, the assassins shot five times into Bronge's head. Another murder occurred when the contractor for Accardo's suburban mansion was also gunned down after he started talking to the Internal Revenue Service. Accardo was never charged in any of these homicides.

By the end of 1964, as Accardo's legal troubles seemed to lighten, Giancana was embroiled in a no-win confrontation. He became the target of a new federal probe into numerous Mafia activities, including finances surrounding the Cal-Neva night-club in Nevada.

At first, Giancana refused comment before the grand jury without legal consequence. But the FBI applied more pressure, making jail a distinct possibility for Sam. It also made Accardo's presence at the top of the Outfit's hierarchy even more necessary.

In December 1964, Giancana suffered further embarrassment. His secret ally, Richard Cain, was arrested for perjury in a drug store scam and eventually convicted. Cain's double life—both as a Mafia informant and government investigator—came to a sudden end. The Cook County Sheriff Richard Ogilvie fired his old friend when Cain's corruption was exposed, and he went off to prison.

In mid-May 1965, a federal grand jury insisted Giancana testify about what he knew under oath. After refusing twice, invoking his Fifth Amendment privilege against self-incrimination, Sam was called a third and final time.

Federal prosecutors decided Sam was too insulated from the lowly crimes of his Outfit associates and stood little chance of being convicted at the moment. So under an obscure part of the Federal Communications Commission Act, they granted Giancana immunity from any prosecution.

However, this immunity was hardly the special consideration Giancana thought he'd earned from the government for going after Castro. If there was a special arrangement with the CIA, these feds didn't want to know about it. With the Johnson Administration now in power, prosecutors didn't care what Giancana and his pals may have done in Cuba.

For Giancana, federal immunity was a double-edged sword. It meant one of two choices: he could either refuse to testify again before the grand jury and be sent to federal prison for contempt of court; or Giancana could testify and give vague, evasive answers. But that approach ran the strong risk of committing perjury, with even longer prison time. Giancana was in a jam.

"If he lied, we could get him for perjury," FBI agent Roemer later explained. "If he told the truth, his associates would get him."

Before Giancana's fate was decided in front of a grand jury, federal prosecutors called entertainer Phyllis McGuire. They expected her subpoena would infuriate Giancana. They were right.

For at least two years, Sam had hoped the internationally known singer might marry him. Inexplicably to her friends and family, Phyllis remained enamored by Giancana's earthy charms. He admired her beauty but seemed equally attracted to her fearless independence. She would stand up to him in a way that even hardened criminals wouldn't dare.

"I didn't need you to get where I am, and don't forget it," she teased, with undeniable firmness.

McGuire realized her "bad boy" fixation with Giancana had ruined her reputation. It made a mockery of the saccharine image of her showbiz act, so carefully cultivated with her sisters. Sam provided an excitement, a man so different from any she'd known. Like a self-destructive addiction, she couldn't bring herself to be free of him.

"I'm going to give him up," she swore to syndicated newspaper columnist, Dorothy Kilgallen. "It's terribly unfair, but I promise you it's true. Look at me and see if you can't tell by my eyes that I am not lying. I'm not going to see Sam again."

But again and again, she returned to Giancana. The bad publicity surrounding the Cal-Neva incident nearly destroyed her partnership with her sisters.

"You fellows have been writing bad stories about me and Sam," she complained to the press. "It makes me look terrible because I'm not a single—I'm part of the trio. If it was only me, maybe it wouldn't be so bad. But my sisters and my parents are heartbroken about this."

When in public with Phyllis, Sam wore his toupee and went out of his way to please her. He talked about marriage but somehow they never agreed on its terms. Giancana's daughters felt the memory of their mother, Angeline, somehow prevented Sam from any other union.

"Sam loved Phyllis in his own way," said daughter Antoinette. "He wanted to marry her at one point, but as close as they were, and they were almost inseparable for years, there was something missing, something Sam looked for but couldn't find."

Perhaps McGuire also sensed that Sam couldn't be faithful. He couldn't help having a girlfriend on the side, such as Bergit Clark, a dark-haired secretary for his brother-in-law's Chicago envelope company. As a way of provoking Sam, the feds decided to subpoena the little-known Clark as well as the high-profile McGuire.

"It was felt that Bergit might prove to be a psychological weapon on Ms. McGuire, who was known to be extremely jealous of Giancana's other feminine interests," recalled Vincent Inserra, part of the FBI's organized crime team. A ring that Clark said was given to her by Giancana was later reported stolen from a Los Angeles store.

On May 19, Phyllis McGuire showed up in a beige silk suit at the federal courthouse in Chicago with her Washington attorney Edward Bennett Williams. She testified for about an hour. Afterwards, she shunned the press by running away, until stopped in a dead-end corridor of the building.

Turning around to face reporters, McGuire wouldn't say if she took the Fifth before the grand jury. "I wish I could get out of here," she said. "I feel trapped."

An hour later, Sam arrived alone. He was very tanned, as if he'd been on a golf course the day before. To observers, he was snarly and very tense. Over the next week, Giancana was called again to appear before the grand jury. Each time, he refused to talk. Not even to give his telephone number.

Warned that he might go to jail, Giancana took solace at a local bar. He downed drinks and wildly cursed out the media's treatment of Phyllis and himself.

The government's strategy of granting immunity had worked. The next day, Giancana was ordered to prison until he agreed to testify before the grand jury.

"You have the key to your own cell," said the judge, William J. Campbell, no relation to Judy.

While McGuire went on with her showbiz career, Giancana's family visited him behind bars, proud of him as if he were there on a matter of principle.

"Sam chose the only course he could choose," explained daughter Antoinette. "He followed the Mafia rule of silence, refused to talk, and was cited for contempt."

There was no "Get Out of Jail Free" card, no special dispensation from the CIA. With Giancana now in jail for the foreseeable future, Tony Accardo became the acting boss of the Chicago Outfit—a position Sam intended to reclaim as soon as he got out.

CHAPTER 38:
"BOOM AND BANG" AND BUST

The brotherhood of war, albeit a covert one, formed a bond of lasting friendships for Johnny Roselli and his CIA combatants. These men shared a taste for blood and guts and, after hours, sipped more than a few Jack Daniel's. They harbored an abiding hatred for Castro and those who kept him in power.

In 1964, Johnny spent the Christmas holidays with Robert Maheu and his family, even though he hadn't worked with this CIA cutout for three years. Roselli also stayed in contact with Bill Harvey when "the Company" transferred Harvey to Europe. And that year, Johnny invited his last agency handler, David Sanchez Morales, to visit Los Angeles and vex over the political climate in Cuba.

Morales was the most recent CIA chief in Miami overseeing assassination plots. He helped Johnny train snipers. Though burly and short-fused, the man nicknamed "El Indio" got along well with Roselli. "Dave was very selective," said Bradley Ayers, another CIA operative, "but my observation led me to believe that he [Morales] and Roselli had a very close relationship."

A feeling of bitterness tormented all these men. They knew or personally trained dozens of brave exiles who wound up going to their deaths in Cuba. They believed the CIA's top-secret campaign would eliminate Castro and restore some form of democracy. Instead, nearly all these commandos wound up killed or imprisoned. Their valiant efforts seemed for naught.

By April 1964, President Johnson was backing away from the Cuban conflict, in favor of a bigger, far more overt war in Vietnam. Johnson told the CIA to "get out of the cloak and dagger business," according to a secret memo written by Director John McCone.

Johnson ordered no more "boom and bang operations" with midnight Cuba raids. The CIA closed its phony "Zenith Enterprises" and tore down its misleading signs.

The sprawling agency facilities in greater Miami, with its secluded airstrips and camouflaged launching docks, began to be dismantled.

For the first time since he took power, Fidel Castro seemed safe. "The bearded devil had won the war," Ted Shackley, another die-hard CIA official in Miami, concluded with resentment.

For many months, CIA men of action like Harvey had complained that Bobby Kennedy's campaign wasn't gung-ho enough, with rumors that a US invasion wouldn't happen until at least 1964. However, the death of John F. Kennedy didn't free up the government's restraints, as they hoped. Rather it left them feeling abandoned.

"The Kennedy administration had completed extensive top-secret plans for a second major invasion of Cuba in the spring of 1964 that were scratched by President Johnson after John F. Kennedy's assassination," observed writers Warren Hinckle and William W. Turner. "LBJ's objections to another Cuban invasion seem to have been prompted more by his well-known lack of love for Robert Kennedy—whose pet project it was—than an inordinate concern for the territorial integrity of Cuba."

The nagging question for the CIA was whether there had been "double agents" in their midst who alerted Castro to the American plans. And just who were these spies with more than one set of loyalties?

After Operation Mongoose formally ended, the CIA kept supporting individual Cuban exile leaders under the table. Roselli was essentially out of the picture. But his network of contacts remained active in South Florida, including Tony Varona, the wheeler-dealer involved in the first phase of Castro assassination plots, and Mafia leader Santo Trafficante. The allegiance of other exile leaders was equally murky.

Manuel Artime, who managed to survive the Bay of Pigs invasion, was a high-profile Cuban exile leader and Kennedy favorite. Artime's clean-cut good looks, personal bravery, and moderate politics appealed to his American benefactors. Over two years, his anti-Castro organization received seven million dollars from the CIA for "harassment, sabotage and psychological warfare" against Castro's government. His ties to Roselli and other mobsters were not well known.

As the CIA's "golden boy," Artime's group set up guerilla training camps in Costa Rica and Nicaragua for attacks on Cuba. They had a small armada—two large ships, eight small vessels, two speed boats, three airplanes, and more than two hundred tons of weapons and armaments. His ad hoc militia conducted four main missions but three failed, including an assassination attempt against Castro. As if a victim of bad luck and timing, Artime later said his effort fell apart "when Bobby Kennedy separated from the Johnson administration."

But all was not so simple with Artime. Investigators later found Artime had let his taxpayer-funded equipment be used for corrupt purposes. He ran a contraband whiskey operation from Costa Rica using his planes until shut down by local police. He also became a beef broker in business with Nicaraguan strongman Gen. Anastasio Somoza, who let him run anti-Castro missions off his coast.

Appalled by Somoza's Nicaraguan cooperation with the CIA, Cuban spies arranged years later for Somoza's own assassination—incinerated in his armored car by a bazooka-carrying commando.

Strangely, Artime's back-and-forth runs of military equipment intended for rebels inside Cuba had a way of constantly failing. From Florida, Dave Morales and Ted Shackley wondered why "it seemed something always went wrong during these sabotage operations . . . was our mechanism penetrated somewhere along the line?" The CIA-sponsored boats would arrive along the darkened Cuba shoreline loaded with armaments. But these crews would soon be met by Castro's soldiers, who killed or captured their invaders.

Castro later bragged that his own spy agency had infiltrated Artime's organization so he knew every step planned against him.

"No one knows how we know," Castro proclaimed in a speech, "but we know, and we know how we know."

Time was now short for Castro's would-be assassins. By December 1964, the Johnson administration, flush from its landslide November victory, moved to shutter its remaining anti-Castro operations. CIA officials knew they had to act quickly.

In one last desperate attempt, the agency decided to join Artime's guerilla campaign with a lone-gunman assassination attempt by Rolando Cubela, the double agent known as "AMLASH." CIA's Desmond FitzGerald had viewed Cubela as the ideal insider in Castro's world. He believed Cubela held out a better chance for success than his predecessor, Johnny Roselli, whose multiple attempts as an outsider had failed.

Plenty of concerns already surrounded Cubela. On the same fateful 1963 day when JFK was murdered, a CIA agent in Paris gave Cubela a "poison pen" with the intent of killing his boss Castro. That assassination plan fell apart in the aftermath of Kennedy's death.

Many wondered about the suspicious co-incidence of Cubela's meeting in Paris about Castro on the same day JFK was killed in Dallas. In particular, the CIA station in Mexico City, in tracing a visit there by Lee Harvey Oswald in September 1963, reported that another foreigner who had talked to Russian intelligence officers in that city was Rolando Cubela. As historian Tim Weiner later summarized: "The report from the Mexico City station raised a harrowing question: was Cubela a double agent for Fidel?"

However, the benefits of possibly slaying Castro—ending the Cuban crisis once and for all—overwhelmed American doubts about Cubela's loyalties. Cubela repeated his desire to defect to the United States. But his CIA case agents urged him to remain near Castro in Cuba, leaving them another chance for a clean shot.

More than a year after Paris, the CIA arranged for Cubela to meet in Madrid with Manuel Artime and a CIA case officer. The two Cuban men agreed to work together. Artime, known by his codename "B-1," would succeed Castro if they overthrew the government. Cubela "believed the only solution to the problems in Cuba would be to get rid of Fidel Castro," according to a CIA report of the early 1965 meeting. "He is able to either shoot him with a silencer or place a bomb in some place where Fidel will be."

The most developed murder plans called for Cubela to shoot Fidel with a long-distance rifle as he gave a speech during a 26th of July celebration. Artime and his commandos would infiltrate in advance, help Cubela escape after the shooting, and lead a revolution by Castro dissidents.

But this elaborate scheme fizzled when new doubts emerged about Cubela.

In a dramatic internal move, Desmond FitzGerald, the CIA's biggest proponent of Cubela, called off the assassination plan. He took the drastic measure when Eladio Del Valle, a former Cuban congressman, alerted the agency that Cubela was working for Santo Trafficante Jr., the Mafia leader in Florida.

Suddenly the trail of would-be Castro assassins had come full circle. Trafficante had been the Spanish-speaking intermediary for Johnny Roselli and Sam Giancana in the initial Castro assassination plots.

Over time, CIA officials realized Trafficante's interests weren't "patriotic," but rather pure greed. Trafficante lost not only a fortune when the Havana casinos were closed, but also his control of illegal narcotics flowing from Cuba into the United States. Trafficante was determined to maintain this drug trade even if he had to make secret accommodations with Castro and his spies, including Cubela.

Rumors of Trafficante's mixed loyalties had lingered for years. His special treatment in a Cuban jail in 1959 suggested that he had hidden connections within the Castro government. During the early 1960s, Artime "heard that Trafficante could have been a double agent, acting surreptitiously in the interests of Castro in spite of his anti-Castro stance," as Artime later told the FBI.

FitzGerald ordered the CIA to cut off contact with Cubela, who was still inside Cuba. Cubela was later arrested as a spy by Castro's security force. But Cubela's light penalty suggested that he'd been a friend of the Castro government all along.

After alerting Americans to the double agents in their midst, del Valle paid an awful price. His dismembered body was found by Florida police in a car, savagely ripped apart and shot in trademark Mafia style. His bald head was sliced open with a machete or an axe, as if it were a piñata. When asked, Artime said he believed del Valle "was killed at the direction of the Castro regime."

During this period, Roselli kept track of the covert war against Castro through his cutout friends and CIA handlers. Cuba seemed a fading memory as the nation focused on Vietnam and Johnny turned his attention again to Vegas.

The friendship and business alliance between Sam and Johnny was no longer as close, especially with Giancana in a Chicago jail for a year on contempt charges. But the Outfit still required Johnny's services on the Strip, especially with hotheaded Marshall Caifano sent off to prison for extortion.

The story of the CIA's secret plan to recruit two mobsters to kill Castro—along with its poison pills and code names, James Bond-like gadgets, double agents and dummy companies, and the gun-laden speedboats in the night—now seemed destined for a dusty government archive, where classified operations never see the light of day.

But the spy intrigue wasn't over for Roselli. In talking with Robert Maheu, Johnny would soon find his next undercover venture.

PHASE IV:
THE PRICE OF
EVERYTHING

"Once you've lived the inside-out world of espionage, you never shed it. It's a mentality, a double standard of existence."

—JOHN LE CARRE

CHAPTER 39:

A PLACE IN THE SUN

"I can buy any man in the world."

—HOWARD HUGHES

At Johnny's favorite watering hole in Beverly Hills, Bob Maheu shared drinks and stories with Roselli as they waited for lunch to be served. It was the kind of long leisurely afternoon at the Friars Club that only men with vaguely defined jobs could afford.

By 1966, Maheu had become rich as the front man for Howard Hughes. After several years together, the multi-millionaire Hughes still only conversed with him by telephone or written message.

Likewise, Roselli appeared as successful as any Friars Club patron with a beach-front mansion in Malibu. But he possessed neither a job nor any recorded property. Instead Johnny lived regally by his wits as a modern gangster.

Roselli was described in *The Green Felt Jungle*, a classic 1960s exposé about America's casino industry, as a respected racketeer "definitely of the new school—sharp silk suits, diamond accessories, swanky apartment, busty show girls in full-length minks, big Cadillac, gourmet taste, sportsman, golfer—the best of everything in the best of all possible worlds."

Those who wondered about Roselli's entry into the exclusive Friars Club—which included Milton Berle, Jack Benny, and Gary Cooper—eventually learned how other Hollywood bigwigs had sponsored his membership.

On this busy afternoon inside the club, a television set blared in the distance from Roselli and Maheu. A news flash caught the attention of both men.

"There was a flash on the TV that Castro was dead," Roselli later recalled.

As the moment lingered—*Fidel finally killed?*—Roselli and Maheu seemed transported from air-conditioned Beverly Hills back to the humid swamplands of southern Florida and the CIA's sprawling anti-Castro campaign in which they were once key players.

Maheu looked up at Johnny with a nod of familiarity.

"I guess it is still working," Maheu said. He clearly meant the CIA's clandestine murder operation had pulled off its long-awaited coup, a poisonous act of violence against the Communist tyrant. To these two friends, political assassination seemed neither shocking nor exceptional.

In the past, Maheu and Roselli had discreetly discussed murders, particularly their theories about President Kennedy's death. Over drinks together, they agreed Castro and his security squads somehow must be responsible for Dallas, certainly beyond the lone-gunman scenarios involving Lee Harvey Oswald.

But now faced with the prospect of Castro's death, Roselli wasn't so chatty. He remembered the orders of Bill Harvey and other CIA officials to remain silent about the agency's efforts in Cuba.

"Well, I wouldn't know," Johnny told Maheu. "I was told not to discuss anything."

Maheu wasn't offended by the stone-cold treatment from his former asset. Like virtually everything associated with Operation Mongoose, rumors of Castro's demise turned out to be wishful thinking. Fidel was still quite alive in Havana.

Between these two friends, however, another startling bit of news emerged— Howard Hughes wanted to move to Las Vegas. To smooth this transition among the competing mob families who controlled this "open" city, Maheu needed Roselli's help.

"Roselli was like a key to the city," explained Maheu, "the ultimate mob fixer in the desert. Hughes never knew Johnny—just knew of him. Both of us agreed he was a source that had to be used." Though Roselli wasn't a lawyer or business school grad, Maheu said, he had the unique ability "to accomplish things in Las Vegas."

Johnny was a virtuoso of manipulation in Vegas. He delicately arranged through mob friends for Hughes to stay at the Desert Inn, the resort and casino where Giancana and the Chicago Outfit owned a piece along with Moe Dalitz and a group of Cleveland gangsters.

Word spread that Hughes—flush from the recent $500 million sale of his Trans World Airlines company—might be interested in buying the Desert Inn. With Giancana in jail, some D.I. investors under indictment, and a lot of bad publicity about organized crime's control of Vegas, the timing looked ideal to sell if a ripe price could be negotiated.

Near dawn on Thanksgiving 1966, Howard Hughes arrived in Vegas by private railroad car.

The sixty-one-year-old recluse was then transported in an ambulance-like vehicle to the Desert Inn, where he rented out the entire penthouse suite and the floor below. Hughes liked what he saw from his mysterious vantage high atop the city. He soon decided to buy the Desert Inn, one of six casino/hotels he purchased during the next few years. According to Vegas legend, Hughes bought the Silver Slipper casino so its trademark blinking neon sign, in the form of a slipper, would stop shining into his bedroom window.

"We roped Hughes into buying the D.I.," Roselli said. "Now it looks like he wants to buy the whole town, if we let him. He's just what we need, especially with Maheu running the show."

Roselli's reputation was familiar to Hughes. Cryptically, Hughes said he'd known Johnny "for many years." Long before his encroaching madness became apparent, Hughes was a motion picture producer, back when Roselli was a mob enforcer in Hollywood prior to World War II. Hughes even dated June Lang, the blonde-haired actress who later met and married Roselli.

June remembered her introduction to Hughes on the Cocoanut Grove's dance floor in Los Angeles. "I found him sexless," said Lang, who ended their affair after a few dates. "He never even tried to kiss me."

To get the Vegas deal done, Hughes knew he had to negotiate with the Mafia without implicating himself in any improprieties. Hughes directed Maheu to use Roselli as a "facilitator" with the underworld—the same way Maheu acted as a buffer for the CIA.

Both men didn't want to get their hands dirty. As a former FBI agent with CIA connections, Maheu always managed a holier-than-thou style, keeping his own unctuous dealings seemingly beyond reproach. At one luncheon meeting with casino owners, the Holy Cross grad insisted on saying grace. Maheu played tennis with Nevada's governor and met with the local newspaper owner to gain enthusiastic support for Hughes as the new high roller in town.

Better for Las Vegas to be run by a corporate mogul than gangsters, Maheu suggested. Perhaps Hughes's millions would rid Vegas of organized crime, something the US Justice Department hadn't been able to do. Even if Hughes's business ethos wasn't much different, certainly there would be less criminal bloodshed in Vegas without the mob.

Publicly, Maheu kept an arm's length distance from Roselli when, in fact, they both had a hand in each other's pockets. In any hostile corporate take-over, there was always an insider who provided crucial information in advance of the buyout. Roselli was perfect for that role.

"I had found a person fitting the background that he [Hughes] had requested me to seek, to wit, a person who had connections with certain people of perhaps unsavory background as described to me by sources in the United States government agencies . . . the FBI and CIA," Maheu recalled.

Under the $13.6 million Desert Inn deal negotiated by lawyer Edward P. Morgan, who'd represented Maheu in the past, Johnny got paid a fifty-thousand-dollar "finder's fee" which came out of Morgan's reported legal retainer. But Roselli's real payday was apparently much more. "I just split four hundred big ones with Sam [Giancana]," Roselli rejoiced about the 1967 deal, completed just as Giancana finished serving time for contempt in Chicago.

Hughes planned to harness the cash-generating power of Sin City in the same way he made a fortune in movies and building airplanes. "Howard wanted every casino in town," Maheu recalled. "He wanted to become King of the Strip. He was acting like the Howard of old."

Unfortunately, cleaning up the notorious Las Vegas casino industry didn't go as well as expected for Hughes and his right-hand man.

For years, much of the money pouring out of the D.I. was from "the skim"—the Mafia's gleaning of revenues off the top from each day's revenues that no one ever paid taxes on. This illegal take was huge for Giancana and the Chicago Outfit at the D.I. and the Stardust, another casino it controlled, totaling a quarter of a million dollars a month.

Hughes might now own the casinos, but Roselli and his mobster friends didn't intend to give up their skim. All of the key personnel insisted upon by Johnny still reported to the mob.

"Now I want to tell you who the casino manager is going to be here, and who your entertainment director is going to be . . ." Roselli instructed Maheu.

For instance, the hotel kept its "official" greeter, former Chicago gangster Charles "Babe" Baron, who once worked for Santo Trafficante in Havana before he headed north. Moe Dalitz, the venerable mob front man, also stayed on as a manager. They made sure to keep the skim going like a constant leak, draining revenues meant to go to Hughes.

Despite his discomfort, Maheu eventually deferred to Johnny's orders, partly because of his own vulnerability. He knew what violence could befall people who crossed the mob. But Maheu was also in trouble financially. Although he received more than a half million in annual income from Hughes along with a hefty expense account, Maheu owed a large amount of back taxes to the IRS. Eventually, he was bailed out with the help of Johnny's friends.

Roselli traded one master for another, though it barely made a dent in his lifestyle. In overseeing the Desert Inn's sale from the Mafia to Howard Hughes, he still kept his suite at the hotel. He obtained a gift shop concession at another Hughes hotel in town, The Frontier. He helped Maheu buy the next prized casino in Hughes's growing empire—the Sands. And once again, Johnny got a "finder's fee" for the Sands that matched his D.I. bonanza.

"Welcome to Las Vegas—Howard Hughes' Monopoly set," Frank Sinatra joked to his audience. "You're wondering why I don't have a drink in my hand? Howard Hughes bought it."

In most minds, the Sands Hotel and Casino was Frank's place. The 1960 Rat Pack movie *Ocean's 11* had been shot there. Sinatra and his pals were photographed memorably in front of the Sands's large outdoor sign touting it as "A Place in the Sun." In January 1966, Frank recorded his first live album "Sinatra at the Sands" in its famous Copa Room, where Dean Martin and Sammy Davis Jr. also regularly performed.

The Rat Pack exerted an outsized influence on showbiz before the Beatles arrived. For a later generation, the Sands was "the Xanadu of Rat Pack lore," critic James Wolcott observed. "The fascination with the Rat Pack expresses a longing for an everyday masculine style that's cool and crisp, without being James Bond swanky . . . before the hippie insurgence feminized men, fluffing their hair and softening the sharp cut of their wardrobes into more flowing lines."

At the Sands, the constant flow of booze, "broads," and nonstop partying seemed to finally pull Sinatra out of the funk of his lovesick divorce from actress Ava Gardner. "Frank has gotten Ava completely out of his system, which now I'm sure of, after seeing how gay he is and apparently carefree," wrote gossip columnist Louella Parsons, after watching him one night at the Copa Room.

Behind the scenes, the Sands hosted many private Sinatra moments. His daughter Nancy married there in 1960. Six years later, Frank wed Mia Farrow, an actress half his age. The Sands also served as a halfway house for Sinatra's visiting underworld pals. Both Sam Giancana and Roselli had enjoyed themselves at the Sands with Judith Campbell and other shadowy friends of Frank.

But the two gangsters also played a significant role in Sinatra's departure from the Sands.

For years, Sinatra had owned nine percent of the Sands. He was the famous legitimate face on a consortium of hidden mob owners, which included the Chicago Outfit. When Sinatra's "red carpet" treatment of Giancana at the Cal-Neva resort prompted Nevada gaming authorities to ban him from running it, Frank decided to give up his Sands investment too.

Though he no longer owned the joint, Sinatra still considered the Sands as his Vegas home—until Howard Hughes came to town.

Perhaps Frank didn't know how much Hughes despised him. When the singer tried earlier to get Hughes to buy out his Cal-Neva interests, he was turned down flat, with no explanation.

The real reason was rooted in a case of jealousy dating back two decades, when Hughes dated a young Ava Gardner. If Frank still carried a torch for his ex-wife, Hughes held a huge grudge against Sinatra for stealing away Ava's affections in the first place.

To Hughes, part of the appeal of buying the Sands was throwing out Sinatra. He would do so with the unwitting but well-paid assistance of Johnny Roselli.

Maheu already knew of Hughes's obsession with Ava. In the late 1950s, Hughes hired Maheu's detective firm to "spy" on Gardner at Lake Tahoe as she awaited her finalized divorce from Sinatra. As a paid stalker for Hughes, Maheu recalled, "My job was to find out if any men visited her and what her relationship with them might be . . . especially if one of those men was Sinatra."

But Maheu decided to farm out the snooping to a local gumshoe—just as he did in the Phyllis McGuire-Dan Rowan eavesdropping case—which backfired in a similar way. The local private eye got caught by police following Sinatra in Lake Tahoe as he tried "to woo and coo, and talk Ava out of getting a divorce," Maheu recalled. The screw-up created "a huge stink" that landed in the press.

A decade later, Sinatra was mistaken if he thought anything with Hughes had been forgiven or forgotten.

During Labor Day weekend 1967, two months after Hughes bought the Sands for $14 million, Sinatra showed up for a regularly scheduled appearance. Frank was no longer treated like a king in his castle. At the Sands, it'd been commonplace for Sinatra, the biggest star attraction, to gamble extravagantly with the other high rollers. Usually, he pocketed his winning chips but fobbed off his losses on the house.

This time, however, Frank threw a fit when Hughes's managers refused him any more gambling chips on credit. (Ironically, the refusal at the window mirrored a similar scene in the earlier *Ocean's 11* film).

In a rage, Sinatra jumped up on a table. He screamed and threatened hotel employees.

"I built this hotel from a sandpile—and before I'm through that's what it will be again," he shouted.

Intoxicated, Sinatra tore his hotel room to shambles. He tried to set it aflame with a cigarette lighter. In the wee small hours of that morning, he then hopped on a golf cart and drove around wildly in front of the Sands hotel. Eventually, he smashed the golf cart into a plate glass window.

At 6 a.m., Carl Cohen, the Sands VP and a longtime friend of Frank's, was woken up by an urgent call and rushed to the casino floor. He tried to calm his star attraction.

"I'm gonna break your fuckin' legs!" screamed Sinatra. The singer pushed a table at Cohen, who ducked as a thrown chair nearly hit his head.

"Sinatra called Cohen every dirty name in the book, said he was going to kill him," Maheu later relayed to Hughes.

When Frank threw a punch at Cohen, the tall burly hotel manager reacted. His right fist landed on Frank's upper lip.

"You broke my teeth—I will *kill you*," vowed Sinatra, returning to his feet. He ordered two bodyguards to beat up Cohen. But even Frank's hired muscle understood Cohen, as the front man for several Mafia investors, had far deeper underworld connections than Sinatra.

"You make one move and they won't know which part of the desert to find you," Cohen growled, filled with visions of departed wise guys whose bodies were never found.

The next day, Sinatra agreed to a new contract to appear at Caesar's Palace, a rival hotel casino. After more than a decade, Frank had left his beloved Sands.

FBI documents say Roselli witnessed Sinatra's tantrum. They duly noted Johnny as "active in LCN [La Cosa Nostra] matters." One federal informant (most likely Maheu) suggested the Mafia might have staged Sinatra's uproar, allowing the Rat Pack leader to switch to one of their remaining Vegas hotel casinos, rather than toil for Hughes. But that scenario had its limits. As the FBI added, "Informant did not believe this was planned, however, to the extent that Sinatra would lose two teeth."

For all of his braggadocio and tough guy adoration, Sinatra endured some costly lessons from dealing with Sam and Johnny. Giancana's involvement with Sinatra at Cal-Neva in Lake Tahoe had cost a small fortune. And the Sands's sale to Hughes, engineered with the help of Roselli, cost Sinatra even more.

But the biggest loser in Vegas may have been the multi-millionaire Hughes.

Under Roselli's mob-connected management team at the Sands, Hughes lost millions of dollars from unbridled skimming. Instead of an expected 20 percent return on investment, Hughes's gambling properties garnered only 6 percent in 1968 and less than two percent the following year.

"Hughes made the nation think Las Vegas was now clean," a historian of Nevada's gambling industry observed, "but the IRS later would conclude that Hughes had been the victim of a vast mob skim, perhaps topping $50 million."

Skimming at the Desert Inn led to a fallout in the friendship between Roselli and Maheu, especially when Johnny tried to bring in Eddie Levinson, an ace gambling operator tied to gangster Meyer Lansky in Havana. At another Las Vegas casino, an FBI bug captured Levinson expounding on his theory of skimming: "You can't steal $100,000 a month and pay dividends. If you steal $50,000? Well, maybe . . ."

By 1970, after the Sands and his other casinos lost $10 million, Hughes decided to flee Las Vegas before his fortune was completely fleeced. He accused Maheu of creating this financial mess and fired him.

Privately to himself, Maheu blamed Roselli and his friends for robbing Hughes blind. But by then, Johnny had far more important things to worry about.

CHAPTER 40:

MESSAGES FROM HOME

*"Instead of the cross, the Albatross
About my neck was hung."*

—SAMUEL TAYLOR COLERIDGE,
"THE RIME OF THE ANCIENT MARINER"

The Giancana home in Oak Park stood dark and silent for Christmas. The owner was in jail.

"There were no colored lights or sparkling trees," described Sam Giancana's oldest daughter, Antoinette, who recalled the 1965 holidays as "the worst Yuletide I can remember." Even the undercover FBI agents, once hiding in the neighborhood, were gone.

During Sam's incarceration, however, Santa-like gifts appeared magically in his cell. Havana cigars, steaks, whiskey, and other delicacies were delivered to the don. At night, he watched TV in a separate room and sent messages by couriers to his crime family outside. All these amenities came courtesy of bribes handed out to jail guards like well-tipped elves.

By Memorial Day 1966, Giancana finished his yearlong sentence for contempt. He still refused to answer questions for the federal government. Yet he was allowed to return home amid cries of "fix" by the press and public.

A few days later, Giancana met with Tony Accardo at the Armory Lounge. With their listening devices ordered shut down, federal authorities didn't have an exact account of what transpired between the two top mobsters. But a FBI informant described a "vituperative" meeting between them.

"Giancana was as adamant as ever that he was coming back to run the Outfit," recalled agent William Roemer. "On the other hand, (Accardo) had already made his mind up . . . He was not going to be dissuaded by Giancana now. He told Sam he had to go."

Giancana considered defying Accardo, perhaps forcing a showdown. Not all of Sam's power had melted away in jail. But challenging Accardo would prove more daunting than he thought.

For more than three decades, Chicago's Outfit had avoided the kind of costly internecine bloodshed experienced routinely among New York's five competing crime families. With his stately home in the suburbs and fondness for deep-sea fishing in Florida, the semi-retired Accardo may have seemed old and soft to young hoodlums.

But during Giancana's stay behind bars, Accardo continued to use murder to enforce the Outfit's discipline. For instance, when hoodlum Angelo Boscarino failed to pay the sufficient "tax" for hijacking silver bullion, he wound up killed with an ice pick, his body thrown out on the street as a message. It was a reminder why "Big Tuna," Accardo's nickname with the press, was actually known by older gangsters as "Joe Batters"—a sick joke noting his preference for baseball bats in pummeling victims to death.

Eventually, Giancana realized most of the Outfit's *caporegimes*—including the retired boss Paul Ricca—preferred Accardo's quiet steady hand compared to Sam's erratic nature and much-publicized outbursts. Most blamed Giancana and his Hollywood pal Johnny Roselli for attracting way more trouble from the feds than they were worth. If Sam returned to his old job, the government pressure would only get worse.

Giancana's initial inclination to fight gave way to Accardo's peaceful accommodation—a unique arrangement that recognized Sam's many contacts and inherent genius for making money from gambling casinos around the world. For Sam, Accardo's deal held out the chance for a respectful "golden parachute" worth millions instead of a certain coffin. But it also meant Giancana would have to leave Chicago and keep a low profile.

Accardo's re-emergence was bad news for Johnny as well. They had clashed as young soldiers working for the Outfit and never forgot it. Accardo always suspected Roselli of getting more than his fair share of the "skim" at the Vegas casinos.

"My situation with 'Batters' is piss poor," Johnny admitted. "We never got along. There's a jealousy going back to Capone's days, and there's nothing I can do about it. The guy's got me on his shitlist, period."

Although Roselli engineered the casino sales to Howard Hughes with the mob's blessings, Accardo didn't back him when he tried to collect all of his outstanding fees from Moe Dalitz at the Desert Inn. Roselli wanted to beat the hell out of Dalitz until he paid up. "I talked it over with Sam (Giancana) first and he said shake him, but the little cocksucker runs to Chicago and I get called in and told to lay off," Johnny complained.

Roselli could only hope that Sam might become the top boss in Chicago once again.

Giancana's new home in Mexico was far more resplendent than his brick oversized bungalow in Oak Park. A 1967 *Life* magazine article, written by Sandy Smith, Sam's visiting observer from Chicago, briefly described his mansion as "a posh castle near Cuernavaca," a tropical enclave south of Mexico City favored by Americans.

Unlike the past, Sam kept his mouth shut with the press and the public. His profile had sunk so low he was practically non-existent in the newspapers. Giancana's gated estate, called "San Cristobal," wasn't listed in his name (mainly due to Mexican law prohibiting foreign ownership). He didn't use his real name in other matters, either.

Most of Sam's living arrangements were handled by his mob lieutenant, Richard Cain—an intense-looking man with tightly-woven dark hair, a jutting jaw, and eyes that stared cagily through black horn-rimmed glasses. He convinced Giancana that Mexico would be the perfect place to take his "extended vacation" from Chicago.

Cain served as Giancana's driver, Spanish translator, and fixer with equally corrupt local officials. He retained a politically connected Mexican lawyer to handle their financial matters. They laundered money from the States into various accounts abroad. Mexico would be their hub as Giancana extended the Mafia's reach throughout the Caribbean and into far-off lands.

Unlike Roselli's brotherly friendship, Cain acted like a son around Giancana. Some wondered (incorrectly) if he might be Sam's illegitimate offspring from a prior affair.

For years, Cain had provided crucial inside law-enforcement information to the Outfit until he was exposed while working for Sheriff Richard Ogilvie. Cain successfully appealed his 1964 conviction. Now he was determined to work once more as Giancana's right-hand man.

"Cain was not the average, old-neighborhood thug," observed Giancana biographer William Bashler. "The two men would either supremely complement each other, or chip away at each other. Those who knew them both in 1966 waited to see the results, knowing that with Giancana and Cain the wait would not be long."

By all measures, Giancana's plan for worldwide expansion turned out as schemed. For much of 1967, Sam moved around often, from hotel to villa, both internationally and within Mexico. He first invested in cruise ships with slot machines in the Mexican Caribbean. He eventually travelled to Rio de Janiero, Haiti, Caracas, and Panama City, promoting plans for swanky casinos like the Sans Souci he once controlled in Havana.

Early in Giancana's stay, Phyllis McGuire flew from New York to Mexico City, visiting Sam in an elegant hotel. At first, the FBI didn't realize Giancana had left Chicago but eventually sent agents to spy on him. They observed all was not well for Sam in paradise. After a brief blast of arguing, his tumultuous relationship with Phyllis had fallen apart once again.

Another showbiz friend—Frank Sinatra—met with Giancana at the Hotel Nacionale in Mexico City, inside Sam's fifteen-room penthouse featuring expensive paintings, a staff of servants, and a secret elevator. Regardless of their troubled past together, it made sense for Sam to stay in contact with performers like Sinatra who could draw American tourists to his future casinos. Documents show Giancana and the famous entertainer were still partners in at least one booking agency.

"Anything that Sinatra does, Giancana is a part of it," an informant told the bureau. That February 1967, Sinatra also dined with Santo Trafficante Jr. in Miami Beach, where the Mafia don took in Sinatra's performance at the Fontainebleau, just like old times when the CIA plot against Castro began.

Giancana's most far-flung businesses involved casino gambling in the Middle East. Sam moved into a Beirut hotel, overseeing gambling at the Casino of Lebanon. But his biggest deal came about in Iran, at the invitation of Louis J. Lederer, another Vegas gambling expert from Chicago. Sam showed up at a plush hotel in Tehran controlled by the Shah of Iran, intending to invest in the Ab-Ali Country Club & Casino. Giancana wound up bribing the Shah to allow Lederer to install slot machines at the casino and prohibit any non-Iranian operators other than themselves.

The FBI tracked Sam's trips around the globe as an ambassador of Mafia greed. In one 1967 memo in his file, a "close associate of Giancana" (sounding very much like Richard Cain) extolled Sam's business vision and how "the 'Jet Age' is completely revolutionizing organized crime in Chicago." While local gangsters relied on bookmaking from "two dollar punks and how much are you going to make from them?" the informant explained, Giancana was maximizing the huge profits from "high rollers" flying to casinos abroad.

Life south of the border, at least for a time, turned out to be lucrative and enjoyable for Giancana and Cain. During the day, Sam relaxed and smoked cigars at little cafes. At night, he might gaze through a rooftop telescope at the heavens above or listen below for the approach of unwanted visitors who might do him harm.

As Sam's deputy, Cain arranged for bundles of gambling money to pass over the Mexican border and find their way to Chicago. But his attempts to play double agent with US officials didn't work as before. While investigating Cain's "alleged Mafia connections," the FBI recommended that the CIA "terminate its association with Cain." Cain claimed to be a CIA operative, but agency files show clearance was never granted and he was never paid.

Occasionally, Cain returned to the Windy City on short jaunts to visit his family and friends. During a trip just before Christmas 1967, however, he wound up arrested by FBI agent Bill Roemer. He faced criminal charges for concealing details about a 1963 bank robbery from authorities.

Over the next several months, Cain prepared his own legal defense, arrogantly thinking that he could beat the conspiracy rap. At trial, he began his summation by quoting Sir Walter Scott: "Oh what tangled web we weave, when first we practice to deceive."

But the jury didn't believe Cain's claim of innocence. In October 1968, a judge sent him to jail for four years.

Meanwhile in Mexico, Sam Giancana would have to fend for himself.

———————

Along swanky Rodeo Drive, on his way to the Friars Club in Beverly Hills, Johnny Roselli remained discreet, aware that the FBI was still tailing him, keeping track of every move. Wise guys and other associates who wished to discuss business with Roselli usually received an advance preparatory phone call.

"Shamus, here," said the telephone voice, clearly Johnny's. "Call at one o'clock."

Later at that precise time, the business partner would reach Roselli on a special private telephone that Johnny had access to at the Friars Club.

Similarly, when Florida don Santo Trafficante Jr. came to town with his wife,

Johnny made sure their dinner together wasn't interrupted. He brought along a private eye to look out for any signs of snooping federal agents.

Given all his precautions, Roselli must have been shocked around noon on May 5, 1966, when two men abruptly approached him at the corner of Rodeo and Brighton Way. The two men identified themselves as FBI agents wanting to talk. The Beverly Hills confrontation took place near Cartier's jewelry store with its elegant window displays.

"See my attorney," Roselli growled, without breaking stride.

The agents kept walking with him along the sidewalk. In front of him, they waved a photograph of a small boy as well as an old birth certificate. If Johnny got a momentary glance at the two items from his past, he didn't let on.

"*Filippo Sacco,*" the FBI agents called out. They repeatedly mentioned his "true name" over and over.

The bureau's constant sleuthing had discovered Roselli's hidden identity, by far his biggest secret.

Like prizes they won at a scavenger hunt, the agents held aloft the photo of young Filippo Sacco and his mother, taken when he was in grade school in Boston. The birth certificate indicated Roselli wasn't born in Chicago or Boston, as he previously claimed, but came to America illegally as an immigrant from Italy. Investigators discovered a phony birth certificate, filed in 1936 for "Giovanni Roselli" in Chicago, that had a forged signature.

"We know where you were born and when you entered the United States," the agents informed him, as they later recounted in an FBI memo.

Roselli gave an unconvincing denial. "I don't know what you are talking about," he insisted.

But Johnny surely knew what this discovery meant. After years of fakery and covering his tracks—fraudulent testimony about his identity, and phony documents with incorrect dates and different spellings to his surname—Roselli came face to face with who he really was, his true identity.

The little boy in the photo had long ago left Boston as a young adult, under suspicion for murder or some other unknown deed. As if re-inventing himself under duress, he became "Johnny Roselli" to his fellow mobsters in Chicago and to all who met him in the bright lights of Hollywood and darkened casinos of Vegas and Havana. It wasn't clear if even those closest to him—such as pal Sam Giancana or his former wife June Lang or anyone else—fully knew his story.

The feds now had something on Roselli that he feared more than a criminal charge. They could deport him, just as the federal government had done to other Mafia figures such as Lucky Luciano and, more recently, Trafficante's good friend, Carlos Marcello, the don of New Orleans.

The two FBI men told Roselli the bureau wanted his cooperation, intending to flip him as an informer. They wanted to meet Johnny in three days at DuPar's Restaurant in Thousands Oaks and gave him a business card with its address.

Johnny first moved to take the card and then, instinctively, rejected it.

"Go see my attorney," he repeated.

The confrontation provided only a hint of the high stakes for the FBI as well as Roselli. Since the Kennedy administration, especially in the wake of JFK's death, Hoover's investigators had pursued why the CIA recruited Roselli and Sam Giancana.

In the complex political calculus of Washington, the FBI chieftain sensed an advantage over the rival spy agency if his agents could piece together the extraordinary story of how the two mobsters became government approved assassins against Castro.

By May 1966, the FBI had mostly figured it out. The CIA "compromised themselves by dealing with Roselli when they had him contact Sam Giancana, head of the Chicago 'family' of La Cosa Nostra, to get someone to assassinate Castro," explained the bureau's LA office in a May 23 memo to Hoover's deputy director, Cartha DeLoach. The memo stressed Roselli's potential as a "top echelon criminal informant," the highest ranking for a snitch.

Roselli clearly knew more about the Mafia's machinations in American business and politics than the celebrated gangster Joseph Valachi, who made headlines with his 1963 testimony as an FBI informer.

The childhood photo of young Sacco with his mother "apparently touched a sensitive spot" with Roselli, the memo said. It called for the bureau to "capitalize on his inner turmoil to develop" Roselli as a top informant.

Privately, Johnny vowed to kill whoever had betrayed him. Little did he know that the photo, birth certificate, and longtime secret about his origins—the FBI's biggest break in its long-running surveillance of Roselli—had been revealed purely by happenstance.

It began when the feds noticed Salvatore Piscopo, Johnny's fellow Los Angeles hoodlum, had failed to pay his taxes on bookmaking profits at various California horse racetracks. Like a small bug suddenly caught in a Venus flytrap, Piscopo (alias "Louie Merli") panicked at the thought of going to jail. Inadvertently, he would lead agents to Johnny's secret.

For nearly thirty years, Piscopo had performed a number of gangland tasks for Roselli. According to Vegas legend, Piscopo served as a getaway car driver for the 1947 mob hit on Ben "Bugsy" Siegel, the legendary casino owner. Bugsy was shot dead in the Beverly Hills home of his girlfriend, Virginia Hill, who would also have an affair with Roselli. Piscopo took note of Johnny's success with the ladies, enough to mention it later to the FBI. He said Roselli "is very good looking and all the girls go for him."

Presciently, Roselli worried about Piscopo's judgment. A possible slip of the tongue could land them both in trouble. He warned Piscopo that "a person's own telephone is the biggest stool pigeon in the world and never use it to talk to people."

As FBI surveillance followed Piscopo around town, they secretly photographed him meeting an unknown person at the airport. The stranger carried an overnight bag and gave Piscopo an affable hug, like a long-lost brother. Indeed, he was Johnny's brother—Albert Sacco.

Albert flew back to Boston with a satchel of cash, which would be given to his aged mother, Maria Sacco. For years, the money from Johnny in Hollywood had helped his family in Boston stay afloat financially, including his brother who worked as a janitor. The exchange usually took place once a year with Johnny's trusted bagman, Salvatore Piscopo, serving as his family's conduit.

The discovery of Johnny's brother was a boon for investigators. Under the veil of secrecy and great care, the FBI put together a complete dossier on Roselli's personal background. It took more than two years to find and piece together all the documents in various cities.

When the FBI finally approached Roselli in May 1966, the agents tried to appear warm and friendly. "This has nothing to do with you personally, John," said one of the agents, almost apologetic. "It's a matter of national security."

Though Johnny acted unperturbed, he immediately contacted his local defense attorney, Jimmy Cantillon, who put the FBI on notice not to speak with his client.

The next day, Roselli flew to Washington, where he spoke in confidence to Shef Edwards, the recently retired CIA chief of security. Through buffers and go-betweens,

Shef had overseen Johnny's covert work against Castro. Johnny explained the Sacco situation without seeking a deal. "I did not ask him to get the FBI off my back," Roselli later claimed.

Edwards, an old CIA hand, chalked off the immigration matter as an interagency rivalry within the government. As Johnny remembered, "they had a big feud going on between the FBI and the CIA."

But the family matter clearly haunted Roselli. He showed Shef a copy of the photograph—left anonymously outside his apartment—of the four-year-old boy and his mother. He acknowledged to Shef that "the child was himself at that age," records show.

The retired CIA man inquired about Roselli's mother, but Johnny remained "very touchy on this." Johnny angrily labeled this FBI attempt to turn him into an informant as pure "blackmail."

At first, Johnny had no idea who betrayed him. The FBI implied their discovery of Roselli's true identity—and the family he left behind in Boston—was the sole result of their sleuthing of documents rather than informant Sal Piscopo and his determination to stay out of jail. Smelling a rat, Johnny swore one day he'd find out the name of his double-crosser and get even.

In alerting the CIA, Roselli assured Shef Edwards that he'd honor his Cuban commitment. He'd keep his mouth shut about the top-secret assassination campaign against Castro. Any public disclosure of these previous plans would undoubtedly prompt all sorts of recriminations, including doubts about a possible Cuban angle to the JFK assassination.

As Shef suspected, Johnny had become a pawn between America's two premier investigative agencies. In a formal memo, CIA officials let Hoover's bureau know they didn't want Edwards questioned as a witness. They said Edwards's participation might "open the door" to exposing "an extremely sensitive intelligence operation." Most tellingly, the CIA admitted Roselli had the agency "in an unusually vulnerable position."

No one knew for sure what Johnny might do if he faced federal prosecution. And it came as a big surprise, especially to Roselli, when he was indicted for something far more serious than an immigration violation.

CHAPTER 41:

PRYING EYES

At the Friars Club, showbiz members boasted about "killing" their audience with rapid-fire jokes and punchlines that "knocked 'em dead." This pugnacious banter among Friars—traceable to the nightclubs of their youth—certainly reflected their competitive nature.

The only entertainment more hotly contested at the Beverly Hills club was the afternoon games of high-stakes poker and gin rummy. Those who lost often said goodbye to hundreds of dollars, if not thousands, in a sitting.

Comedian Phil Silvers, known as TV's "Sgt. Bilko," managed to make a joke out of his heavy losses. "Let's put it this way: Is that the freeway?" he quipped after one drubbing. "I'm hitchhiking home."

This merry group of Friars counted Johnny Roselli, a real killer, among its members.

Several years earlier, the club turned down Roselli for membership. After all, a mobster convicted of extorting movie studios has a way of lingering in Hollywood's memory. But on second try in 1962, Roselli prevailed with the endorsement of Rat Pack members Frank Sinatra and Dean Martin. If "my friend Johnny" was refused, Sinatra suggested, he wouldn't participate in the nonprofit club's fundraisers needed to keep the lights on.

Comedian Georgie Jessel, who founded the club, rubber-stamped Frank's endorsement. "There were other members who had served sentences," Jessel recalled about Roselli. "I said anyone who had paid his debt to society was O.K., so I made him a Friar."

Initially, Roselli spent afternoons either playing cards or wandering around the club. Then he stumbled upon the club's dirty little secret, ingeniously carried out with a precision that resembled *Ocean's 11*. Johnny realized some of the club's gamblers had rigged games of high-stakes poker and gin rummy by placing a secret peephole in the ceiling above the playing tables.

From above, a man named George Seach used a telescopic lens to spot every advantage. Seach alerted players in the conspiracy via transistor radio beneath their clothes. A buzz meant that an opposing player needed a certain card. The fixed card games went on for several years. Celebrity victims included Silvers, Zeppo Marx of the Marx Brothers, singer Tony Martin, and several wealthy businessmen, including one married to actress Debbie Reynolds.

From the hefty take, Roselli took 20 percent. His co-conspirators weren't delighted with Johnny's demands but were too afraid to face the alternative.

"Roselli's master coup was muscling in on and taking a big cut of one of the most daring and intricate card-cheating capers ever brought off," John Kobler later marveled in a *New York* magazine account. Johnny and his band of Friars Club cheaters bilked at least four hundred thousand dollars.

One day in early 1967, an FBI agent tracking Roselli spotted a man in overalls climbing out of the Friars Club's roof skylight. The curious exit prompted more investigation and the FBI's realization that Johnny was deeply involved in the scam. In July, a federal raid exposed the whole card-cheating scandal.

The FBI turned up the heat on George Seach, the peephole tipster, who became a key witness against Roselli. Seach was already in trouble on a burglary charge, so he quite willing cooperated with prosecutors. By year's end, Roselli would be indicted separately on both the immigration charge and the more serious Friars Club case.

Johnny's lawyers tried to figure out legal answers for his predicament, while he sought more homicidal solutions. Desperately, Roselli met with hitman Jimmy Fratianno in the confidentiality-protected office of his LA lawyer.

"The most important thing you could ever do for me is clip Seach—bury the motherfucker," Roselli told his longtime pal.

Fratianno placed his hands on Johnny's shoulder. "You can stop worrying," said Jimmy the Weasel. "I'll handle it personally. Just tell me where I can find him."

The two mobsters traced Seach to Las Vegas. Fratianno spotted him in the Stardust casino. That night, Jimmy asked a mob-connected hotel official to get Seach's home address so Fratianno's hitmen could kill him without any witnesses.

But the FBI, apparently learning of the danger facing Seach, moved their star witness into the federal witness projection program before any stray bullets or unexpected catastrophes could upset him.

Prior to the indictments, Roselli travelled with Jimmy Cantillon to Washington to see his politically connected lawyer Edward P. Morgan, who'd engineered the Howard Hughes casino deals. They met Morgan along with Johnny's friend Joseph

Shimon, the crooked Washington cop once involved with Roselli and Giancana in the anti-Castro campaign.

During a meeting inside his office, Morgan advised Roselli to become a government informant just as the FBI wished. The bureau knew all about Johnny's CIA involvement. Hoover was feuding too much with the spy agency to give its would-be assassin a break. The FBI was adamant with Roselli: Either cooperate or face deportation back to Italy.

But others in the room expressed strong doubts. Shimon dismissed cooperation as a bad deal for Roselli.

"Forget it—the first guy they want him to inform on is Sam [Giancana], his best friend," Shimon argued to Morgan. "There would be no end to it."

Cantillon also knew the penalty for betraying the Mafia. He warned Johnny that he wouldn't last twenty minutes on the street without being murdered.

Morgan pushed back, contending the FBI would keep Johnny safe in its federal witness program.

Roselli eventually interrupted.

"Look Ed, number one, I'm not going to snitch on nobody," Johnny said. Roselli insisted he wanted Morgan, a former top FBI official, to use his influence to get the bureau "off my back."

Most of all, Johnny wanted revenge on the snitch who revealed his deepest secret— about the Sacco family in Boston and his phony identity. He had spent his life as "Johnny Roselli" and now that very existence was being threatened.

"I want the name of the prick that turned me in," he told Morgan, still unaware that his Judas was old friend Salvatore Piscopo.

In Morgan's office, assured of lawyer-client confidentiality, Roselli revealed the whole story of his involvement with the CIA. He began with the 1960 meeting with Bob Maheu at the Brown Derby. He explained his recruitment of Giancana and Santo Trafficante Jr. into the CIA scheme at the Fontainebleau and described the various sabotage and killing attempts with Cuban exiles off the coast of Cuba.

Roselli wrapped up the whole tale of Operation Mongoose with a patriotic bow. He told Morgan he volunteered to fight Communism for the US government "because I owe it a lot." Roselli seemed to take stock. He told his lawyer-confessor that "it's the one thing in my life that I'm really proud of."

For several years, Roselli had honored the CIA's demands for absolute secrecy. He confided in Morgan only because he was looking for a way out of jail and deportation.

Along with the killing plans against Castro, however, Roselli dropped another assassination bombshell, one which the CIA didn't seem to know. It stemmed from the time in mid-1963 when Johnny was no longer formally working for the agency but was still in touch with the Cuban-exiles making swift boat runs to Cuba.

"One of our assassination teams was captured and tortured until they told all they knew about our operations which they said was ordered by the White House," explained Roselli. "In fact, one of our highly placed operatives actually heard Castro say that if that was the way President Kennedy wanted to play it, well, he too could play that game. I have it from a top source that the team was turned around—you know, *brainwashed*—and sent back into our country to kill Kennedy."

Morgan was astounded. As a friend and lawyer for Maheu, he knew about the CIA campaign against Castro but not in the vivid, firsthand detail that Roselli offered. How could this "blowback" assassination plot be verified? he asked. It sounded more like a fictional plot from *The Manchurian Candidate*—the Sinatra movie with its double agents and sleeper cells—than something provable that Morgan could use to keep Johnny out of jail.

When pressed, Roselli said he learned of this JFK killing scheme "in strictest confidence" from a source close to Castro and he would never violate that trust.

In the aftermath of the JFK assassination, most lawyers would have been inclined to dismiss such talk. But by 1967, the American media had begun to question some of the findings of the Warren Commission and whether the dead gunman Lee Harvey Oswald had acted alone.

Since the Lincoln assassination, there had always followed conspiracy theories about the shootings of presidents, as if the sheer awfulness of such a crime was beyond the capacity of just one single nut. Certainly in 1967, a Kennedy murder conspiracy was only beginning to boil in the minds of the American consciousness, something that would reach a fever pitch in the years to come. Like most Americans then, Morgan wondered why the Warren Commission hadn't found out about this Cuban connection.

"Listen Ed, as far as I know, all phases of this operation were approved by Allen Dulles and President Eisenhower," Roselli explained. "Well, as you know, Dulles was a member of the Warren Commission and I don't remember hearing him say anything about it. Did you?"

Morgan knew enough about the crusade against Castro to wonder why the ex-CIA chief had remained silent throughout the whole ordeal of the Warren investigation.

Roselli suggested maybe President Johnson "just wanted to keep the lid on" about the CIA's plot against Castro. "Maybe he thought it'd be bad for the country to know about this operation—you know, the government of the United States involved with the so-called Mafia to kill the leader of a foreign country and then it boomerangs."

Fanciful thinking wouldn't keep Johnny out of jail, but his supposition seemed to make sense to Morgan. There was so much more to find out.

The lawyer called the CIA's William Harvey to confirm some facts. The agent once known as "the American James Bond" called Johnny a "hero" for his unpaid service to the nation. His valor included getting boats shot out from under him by Castro's patrols, Harvey attested.

Morgan, a top negotiator, was armed with enough concrete facts—especially the very existence of a top secret plan to eliminate Castro—to convince the government to drop its case against Roselli before things went too far. First, he needed to get their attention.

Since Roselli didn't want his name revealed in public, Morgan figured the only way to get his story out there was as an anonymous source for the "Washington Merry-Go-Round," the famous syndicated newspaper column read by nearly every power-broker in the capital.

For years, the column had been written by Drew Pearson, a specialist in "scoops" provided by insider sources, including Washington's most powerful figures. A *Time* magazine poll listed Pearson as America's best-known columnist. He was joined by Jack Anderson, a junior staffer who would become a well-known investigative reporter too.

In early 1967, Morgan told Pearson about Roselli's claims. The columnist went directly to the top—Supreme Court Justice Earl Warren who headed the investigation into JFK's death. Warren considered the allegations "serious enough," according to Pearson, to pass them on to the Secret Service, which, in turn, gave them to the FBI. Soon, Hoover decided the bureau should drop its probe.

Nevertheless, Pearson had enough information to publish. He began his March 3, 1967, column with a blockbuster sentence: "President Johnson is sitting on a political H-bomb—an unconfirmed report that Sen. Robert Kennedy may have approved an assassination plot which then possibly backfired against his brother." The CIA "hatched a plan to knock off Castro," the column said. "Some insiders are convinced that Castro learned enough at least to believe that the CIA was seeking to kill him.

With characteristic fury, he is reported to have cooked up a counter-plot against President Kennedy."

Johnny's name didn't appear. There was no mention of the Mafia. But news of the CIA plot against Castro—and its possible link to JFK's death—galvanized President Johnson's attention. He ordered the FBI to interview Pearson's main source—Edward P. Morgan—and find out everything possible.

During his FBI debriefings, Morgan offered a mixed salad of fact and conjecture. He conflated two separate accounts: what his client Robert Maheu told him confidentially about the Castro assassination plot, along with Roselli's additional claims about a Cuban "blowback" plot against JFK.

FBI records detailed Morgan's startling claims. "He had clients (unnamed) who knew that Castro was aware of CIA's plot to assassinate him," summarized one memo. "According to Morgan, Castro responded by sending teams of assassins into the United States to kill former President Kennedy. Morgan, of course, suggested that these teams had assisted Oswald in the assassination." He said his clients "while not directly involved in the [JFK] assassination, had knowledge of the plot."

To bolster their credibility, Morgan described his one mystery client, presumably Maheu, as "a high type individual of the Catholic faith whose conscience bothered him."

As for Roselli, Morgan said, his other unnamed client got involved because "the project was so highly patriotically motivated that this overrode personal, ethical and moral considerations."

Morgan said he didn't believe these claims at first "but conducted enough inquiry to satisfy himself that his clients had some basis in fact for their position and he felt they were telling the truth."

Within a short time, Johnny's revelations had reverberated throughout Washington. They were suggestive of an underworld where matters of state could be decided by secret assassination and CIA-backed mobsters, rather than diplomats or Congressionally-declared war.

The FBI quickly identified Morgan's clients. In confidential memos, it described Roselli as a "hoodlum" tied to Chicago mob boss Sam Giancana and Maheu as Howard Hughes's "angel" in Las Vegas.

Perhaps the most surprising discovery, however, was how little President Johnson, a master of politics, actually knew of the CIA-Mafia machinations at this point in his presidency.

CHAPTER 42:

BLOWBACK

Shortly before Drew Pearson's column appeared, Lyndon Johnson asked his Attorney General Ramsey Clark about rumors of assassination plots involving the CIA, the Mafia, and Cuba's Fidel Castro.

A transcript of the taped February 1967 White House telephone conversation, released decades later, gives a sense of Johnson's obsessive desire to know more.

JOHNSON: You know [there's] this story going around about the CIA and their tryin' to get . . . sendin' in the folks to get Castro.

CLARK: To assassinate Castro.

JOHNSON: Have you got that full story laid out in front of you, and [do you] know what it is? Has anybody ever told you all the story?

CLARK: No.

Over the next several minutes, the president relayed to Clark a number of murderous details stemming from Johnny Roselli's account, including the toxic pills manufactured by the CIA to poison Castro. Supposedly, as the president explained, once Castro thwarted this plot in 1963, the Communist leader sent his own team of assassins, including Lee Harvey Oswald, into the United States to "get the job done" in retaliation against Kennedy.

Johnson said this fantastical tale came from "responsible people" like Drew Pearson and Edward P. Morgan. He suggested the Justice Department start an investigative file to cover itself, even if nothing came of the allegations.

"It sounded just so [wild] . . . just like you're tellin' me that Lady Bird was taking dope," the president joked to Clark, his fellow Texan.

Since that dark day in Dallas, Johnson had harbored many doubts about JFK's 1963 killing. This CIA-Mafia scheme to kill Castro—and the alleged "blowback" retribution it provoked—seemed as plausible as any theory.

"I'll tell you something [about John Kennedy's murder] that will rock you,"

Johnson said to ABC television anchor Howard K. Smith in October 1968. "Kennedy was trying to get to Castro, but Castro got to him first."

Smith pleaded for more details from Johnson, but the president begged off. "It will all come out one day," he assured. Johnson offered a similar version to CBS newsman Walter Cronkite. Both comments were not broadcast at that time.

While Pearson's 1967 article exposed how little the president knew about the Castro assassination plot, the columnist underlined that Robert Kennedy was privy to a great deal more information than he was telling. Or that RFK had shared with the Warren Commission.

Critics later pointed out that Robert Kennedy, upon learning of his brother's assassination, directed National Security Advisor McGeorge Bundy to protect the president's personal files in the Oval Office, with the locks changed immediately.

"Bobby Kennedy understood that public revelation of the materials in his brother's White House files would forever destroy Jack Kennedy's reputation as president, and his own as attorney general," concluded investigative writer Seymour Hersh. "He had spent nearly three years in a confounding situation—as guardian of the nation's laws, as his brother's secret operative in foreign crises, and as personal watchdog for an older brother who reveled in personal excess and recklessness."

Kennedy confidants, such as historian Arthur M. Schlesinger Jr., said Bobby's grief and concerns for his family's future overshadowed any desire to deeply investigate the circumstances of his brother's murder. "I do not know whether he suspected how much vital information both the FBI and the CIA deliberately denied the Warren Commission or whether he ever read its report," Schlesinger later wrote.

Privately, Bobby told Schlesinger in October 1966 that the Warren panelists did a poor job but that he was "unwilling to criticize it and thereby reopen the whole tragic business."

Undoubtedly, though, Robert Kennedy helped undermine the Warren probe by suggesting to President Johnson that former CIA director Allen Dulles be placed on the 1964 panel. As the commission investigated JFK's murder, Dulles carefully stage-managed inquiries with his old agency and steered staffers away from the CIA-Mafia collusion against Castro.

Johnson wasn't the only one kept in the dark.

Nicholas deB. Katzenbach, once RFK's trusted adviser at Justice, was appalled years later when he learned the Warren Commission was never told about the CIA's Castro plot. Katzenbach was the one who told Johnson's office of RFK's desire to see Dulles added to the Warren panel.

"I was unaware of the efforts by the CIA to assassinate Castro," Katzenbach wrote in a 2008 memoir. "Allen Dulles, the longtime head of the CIA and a member of the commission, never told his colleagues about the attempts on Castro's life, an inexcusable failure."

However, Katzenbach didn't address Bobby Kennedy's responsibility in this matter. If he knew the answer, Katzenbach didn't reveal why RFK never said anything to the Warren panel about the Castro plot.

To be sure, the 1967 Pearson column was political dynamite for Kennedy. It "badly frightened Bobby Kennedy," as CIA historian Tim Weiner later recounted.

The day after the column appeared, Kennedy had lunch with Richard Helms, by then director at the CIA, to find out what might be in their files. Meanwhile, as Weiner recounted, the FBI sent an update report to Johnson saying that "Robert Kennedy as attorney general knew about the CIA plot as it unfolded, and he knew the mob was involved."

Kennedy realized Johnson had been given a sword. The two men had been antagonists for years—ever since the 1960 campaign when Bobby, as campaign manager, pleaded with JFK and their influential father not to accept Johnson as the Democratic vice-presidential candidate. Now as US Senator from New York, Bobby had become a critic of the burgeoning Vietnam War and would eventually challenge Johnson in the 1968 presidential campaign. A public airing of the CIA-Mafia assassination plot could unravel everything for him.

Pearson's column claimed Robert Kennedy had personally managed the CIA's get-Castro campaign. Bobby assured his faithful aides that such claims were a lie. "I didn't start it. I stopped it," he insisted. "I found out that some people were going to try an attempt on Castro's life and I turned it off."

That same year, a CIA inspector general's review, ordered by Johnson, came up with mixed results. The agency IG said it wasn't clear if Dulles had approved the Castro assassination plan—something not acknowledged by the agency until 2007. But the report was sharply critical of the Kennedys.

"We cannot over emphasize the extent to which responsible agency officers felt themselves subject to the Kennedy administration severe pressures to do something about Castro," the report said. "We find people speaking vaguely of 'doing something about Castro' when it is clear that what they have specifically in mind is killing him."

Director Helms read the IG's large report about CIA assassination plans and briefed Johnson at the White House on its findings. It's not certain what the president instructed him to do. Helms locked away the only copy of the report—later nicknamed "The Family Jewels" by the agents who knew about it—and kept it in his private safe for many years to come.

Yet for the CIA, there still remained a vexing question: what to do with Johnny Roselli?

In October 1967, after his second beer at Hammel's, the German restaurant in downtown Washington, DC, William Harvey opened up, ready to talk about his friend Johnny. Sitting next to him was Howard Osborn—the CIA's new director of security who recently replaced the retired Shef Edwards.

They appeared to be alone, sharing a familiar lunch at this favorite haunt for old-time spooks and seasoned G-men. But in reality, the CIA and the FBI were monitoring this sensitive meeting. For different reasons, both agencies worried whether the Mafia involvement in the Castro plot would soon become known publicly.

Harvey considered Osborn a friend, though he likely knew Osborn would file a confidential memo about what was said between them. Indeed, Osborn's four-page memo later detailed virtually everything mentioned during their 1967 lunch.

Much of the discussion revolved around loyalty, betrayal and—without using the exact term—"plausible deniability."

Harvey emphasized he didn't intend to abandon Roselli now that he was in trouble.

"I don't give a damn—I don't turn my back on my friends," Harvey said. "And Johnny is my friend."

Several weeks earlier, Roselli had contacted Harvey—as he did others involved in the Castro operation—asking for some sort of government intervention to keep him from jail. Roselli and his former handler had not spoken since 1963, after Harvey angered Bobby Kennedy and was reassigned to Italy.

But in chatting together recently over the telephone, Harvey recalled once again why he liked Johnny so much. As Harvey later told the FBI: "If one left the criminal aspects of Roselli's activities out of the picture, he was a charming and personable man who could talk on a variety of subjects articulately and knowledgeably."

In memos, the FBI warned Harvey to stay away from Roselli, that no "Get out of Jail" card was possible, and to be mindful of Roselli's best friend, Sam Giancana, now in Mexico, who was a master manipulator. In this exchange, they also tried to figure out the personal dynamics and working relationship between these two gangsters.

Harvey said the two mobsters were more equal, more partners, than the traditional Mafia hierarchy of *caporegime* and soldiers. Johnny arguably had more vision, more ambition than Sam, if not the power.

"Harvey questioned [the] characterization of Roselli as a tool of Giancana and said that Roselli worked with Giancana but that he did not regard this as a boss/subordinate relationship," a FBI report summarized.

Undoubtedly Harvey's vantage was limited to the CIA's attempt to kill Castro rather than some psychological analysis. But he prided himself on being a good measure of men, as someone whose professional life and reputation depended upon it. Neither Harvey nor the FBI agents had ever witnessed such a thriving complicated partnership as the one between Giancana and Roselli.

After years of blood and mayhem, millions of dollars made and stolen, and countless women and men who had crossed their path, someone in their world had finally tried to define and reflect upon their unique Mafia friendship. Typically, it was not them.

After failing to stop the FBI directly, Harvey hoped for better success with Osborn and his own agency. The CIA didn't have any powers over domestic matters, at least according to its charter, but it could influence other investigative agencies if it invoked national security or potential "embarrassment" to the government.

At lunch together, Osborn first discussed Harvey's future. The world-weary agent, on his way to an early retirement, mentioned that he planned to re-start his own law practice in the nation's capital. Osborn underlined Harvey's friendship with a mobster like Roselli "could hardly be regarded favorably" by the legal bar.

Loyalty, as much as money, seemed to motivate Harvey's reply. He mentioned Roselli said he could "throw a lot of business his way"—at least a hundred thousand dollars a year in legal fees—but Harvey said he had "no intention" of taking on mobbed-up clients.

"The worse thing," Harvey insisted, would be for the CIA to forget about Roselli's patriotism in the Florida Keys and his heroism with the exiles in the darkened waters off the Cuban coast. This covert war against Castro now seemed replaced in 1967 by a new undeclared war against the Vietnamese Communists. But it wasn't right for the CIA to leave Johnny out in the cold, he argued.

More to the point, loyalty was a two-way street. Roselli could be counted upon to keep the CIA's deepest secrets. Johnny "would never 'pull the string' on us unless he was absolutely desperate," and felt deportation was certain, Harvey assured.

As a bitter critic of Robert Kennedy, Harvey felt the agency shouldn't be influenced by politics, certainly not by someone who was not the president. He said Roselli told him that Kennedy "knew all about the operation" in Cuba. He added Kennedy's attorney general office had been the source for an August 1963 *Chicago Sun-Times* story revealing Giancana's recruitment by the CIA. After years of secrecy, Harvey didn't want to "blow the operation" in Cuba purely for political expedience or to protect some politico's hide.

A hint of danger overshadowed their entire conversation. Harvey emphasized it "would be his neck" if the CIA failed to clamp down and let Roselli be exposed as a government spy. Repeatedly, Harvey made clear "his full realization of the hazard to him personally of his continuing his relationship with 'Johnny,'" Osborn's memo stated.

Surely the agency didn't want its controversial "James Bond" figure killed by an angry mobster.

———

However, Johnny Roselli's strongest sense of betrayal was aimed at Bob Maheu, who introduced him to the whole Cuban affair.

In recent months, Maheu and Roselli had worked together hand-in-glove on Howard Hughes's purchase of the Desert Inn and other Vegas hotels. But by late 1967, the two were at odds. The complex reasons included the mob's continued "skimming" at the casinos, which Maheu was helpless to stop, and the Pearson column's public mention of the Castro assassination plot, which upset Maheu profoundly.

Still living in California as Hughes's right-hand man, Maheu immediately sought out Ed Morgan's legal counsel. His sense of dread increased when Maheu received a visit from "Big Jim" O'Connell, the original CIA handler for the mission, who wanted to know what Maheu might have leaked to reporters or other sources. Maheu admitted he told his lawyer Morgan about the Castro plot.

"Damn it, you guys were sitting on your asses doing nothing," Maheu told O'Connell, his CIA handler, "and I have to protect myself."

Unlike the Company man Harvey, freelancer Maheu wasn't willing to help out Roselli now that he was in trouble.

Despite all their Fontainebleau drinks and Brown Derby meals together, Maheu never wanted it known publicly about his involvement with a mobster. As a former FBI agent and CIA go-between, Maheu expected better treatment by the government than what was offered to Roselli, but he told Johnny that he didn't have the clout to do anything about his dilemma. As a Hughes executive now involved in the casino business, Maheu couldn't afford to be associated with a man like Roselli.

After a bitter hour-long telephone conversation, Johnny realized Maheu was worthless to him. He underlined that point to Harvey.

"Sell anyone down the river to protect his own neck," Johnny growled about Maheu, with complete disgust.

Maheu's disloyalty was on full display when Roselli went to trial in the Friars Club cheating case. Under oath, his once solicitous CIA cutout would feign ignorance about all they had done together against Castro. The Friars Club court proceedings began in June 1968 and dragged on for six months. But Johnny could no longer avoid jail.

A jury convicted Roselli and his other pals of conspiracy in the rigged card games. In February 1969, Roselli received a five-year jail term and a fifty-five thousand dollar fine. That punishment would run concurrently with his earlier conviction in May 1968 on the illegal immigration charge, which had exacted its own emotional toll.

The judge in the immigration case chastised Roselli for "a very selfish life" at the expense of his family. In its zeal to prove him an "alien," the government dug up all sorts of secrets—including that Johnny's mother, after the death of his father, briefly wed another married man just to legitimize his step-sister born out of wedlock.

As a condition for Roselli's release while appealing, the judge required him to visit his dying mother, Maria Sacco, in Boston. In his robes assessing the record, the judge appeared like St. Peter with his ledger at the pearly gates of heaven, like a scene of eternal judgment once painted by Cosimo Rosselli at the Sistine Chapel. The jurist didn't seem to understand that Johnny, on the lam his whole life with an alias, still managed to send money home to support his mother and siblings. Indeed, that's how the FBI learned his deepest secret.

Before Roselli received sentencing in the Friars case, defense lawyers tried to lighten his penalty by revealing for the first time all of his patriotic actions in the top-secret Castro assassination plot.

At a key moment, Roselli's lawyer called upon Robert Maheu. Johnny needed his CIA go-between to back up his adventurous story about fighting Castro's forces in the Caribbean. But Maheu acted dumbfounded.

"I don't know what you're talking about," Maheu testified. He had already agreed with CIA director Richard Helms and other agency brass not to help Roselli, wary of more top-secret details leaking out.

The judge gave no sympathy or lenience to Roselli.

Regardless of the story's veracity about the CIA, the judge said, "I don't think Mr. Roselli is entitled to brownie points . . . I am not going to concede that a court should give credit to a person who attempts the assassination of anybody."

Much of the next year would be spent appealing his case in vain.

There was still a wildcard. Johnny could threaten to expose publicly all he knew about the CIA's plans to assassinate Castro unless the agency intervened on his behalf. Roselli had promised never to reveal his life as a spy but his situation now left him desperate.

Without that last-minute reprieve, Johnny knew he was soon headed to jail.

CHAPTER 43:

SOLDIERS OF FORTUNE

Unlike her sisters, Francine Giancana got married in a small, modest ceremony without her father in attendance.

The previous weddings for Sam Giancana's two older daughters were lavish Mafia affairs, presided over by the don himself. Years earlier, the nuptials for first-born Antoinette boasted one of the largest receptions ever seen in Chicago, while second-oldest Bonnie's party featured more than two hundred guests at Miami's Fontainebleau Hotel.

But with Sam out of the country, living in exile in Mexico, his youngest daughter Francine decided against a big wedding. She invited only a handful of immediate family members to witness her happy day in August 1967, without her father there to walk her down the aisle.

It was another reminder how much Sam Giancana's criminality had affected his family and his own personal life.

Giancana's lawlessness had undermined his relationship with lovers like Phyllis McGuire and several other women who floated in and out of his life. Over the past fifteen years, since the death of his wife Angeline, Sam seemed "a lost cause," as one friend described him. He seemed in search of one special woman without resolve.

On a surveillance tape recorded before he left Chicago, Giancana could be heard thinking wistfully about finding someone like Angeline but, as an FBI memo summarized, "he doesn't think he will find the woman to fit the bill."

"The FBI report unknowingly bared Sam's soul . . . and his loneliness," explained Antoinette, whose violent teenage confrontations with her father extended into a troubled adulthood of alcoholism, broken marriage, and suicide attempts. "He was searching for someone he would never find and, in an moment of candor, he admitted it."

Sam's extravagant lifestyle outside the country glossed over his inner turmoil. He continued to travel around the world, negotiating casino deals and trading in stolen jewels and some narcotics trafficking. And on occasion, using a phony passport, he managed to sneak into the United States for brief visits like the one with Johnny Roselli sometime before 1970.

By that point, Sam and Johnny were distant friends unified only by fading ties to the same Mafia family in Chicago, their CIA history in attempting to kill Castro, and their many good times together in darkened saloons with beautiful women and celebrities.

Eventually, the two gangsters caught up with each other at the home of Joe Shimon, the knavish former Washington, DC, policeman who'd befriended them. At this meeting, Sam and Johnny displayed their stoic, devil-may-care attitude with each other, the kind of macho frivolity they once enjoyed in Vegas or at the Boom-Boom Room in Miami.

Johnny seemed enlivened by Sam's tough-guy presence.

"This guy's having a ball," Roselli later explained about Sam to his mob pal, Jimmy Fratianno. "He's been to Europe, the Middle East, thinking of getting an apartment in Beirut, one in Paris, and planning a trip to Africa. As far as he's concerned, he never wants to go back to Chicago. He told me straight out he was through for good. 'My investments are sound,' he told me. 'I'm enjoying this new life. Let the cocksuckers back there knock each other off all they want, who cares?' Jimmy, I have to agree with him. I wish my investments were that sound, I'd take off too."

Roselli still had several pressing matters of his own, however.

For many months in Los Angeles, he struggled to find out who had tipped law-enforcement authorities to his alias as "Johnny Roselli" and his real family back in Boston. When Johnny finally learned through the grapevine, he requested Giancana's permission to have Sal Piscopo executed as a double-crosser. Johnny had known Piscopo for years, but his betrayal was unforgiveable.

In his weakened state politically, however, Giancana couldn't just snap his fingers to make Piscopo disappear. The protocol of such hits required the approval of the local don where Piscopo lived. By the time the ruling Los Angeles Mafioso granted their okay, Piscopo managed to evade any consequences. He died years later of natural causes.

The situation in Las Vegas was even more complex for Roselli. After the much-publicized Friars Club arrest, Chicago boss Tony Accardo demanded a sit-down meeting with Johnny and ordered him to keep away from the casinos.

"With Sam [Giancana] in Mexico, out of it completely now, [Accardo is] back in power," Roselli complained. "They've cut my balls off. He calls me into Chicago to tell me . . . to stay away until I get straightened out. Not only have they stripped me of my power but they've cut off my income."

Only Roselli's stake in the Stardust casino's gift shop—selling *tchotchke* to the "low rollers"—provided any money to him.

Along with freezing out Roselli, Accardo replaced Giancana's man in Vegas, Marshall Caifano, who had happily shared his wife Darlene's affections in return for the assignment. During his tenure out west, Caifano proved himself a very able killer. He took care of "Russian Louie" Strauss and the Outfit's biggest snitch of all, Willie Bioff, from the Hollywood extortion case. (Caifano apparently would make good on his threat against Indiana oilman Ray Ryan whose extortion testimony sent him away to prison in October 1966. Soon after Caifano's prison release in the 1970s, Ryan was blown to bits. He turned on the ignition to his Lincoln Continental and the car exploded. No one was charged.)

But on money matters, "John Marshall"—Caifano's alias in Vegas—was a poor caretaker of the Outfit's interests. He was severely outclassed in financial maneuvering by men like Howard Hughes, Moe Dalitz, and even Roselli (whom Accardo always suspected of pocketing Chicago's revenues for himself). In particular, Accardo had been incensed when Caifano sued the Nevada Gaming Control Board over its "black book," barring gangsters like Giancana and himself from casinos. Caifano's losing legal battle once again put the unwanted spotlight on the Outfit, endangering millions from its hidden interests in lucrative casino licenses. Caifano was another wise guy—like his mentor Sam Giancana—who didn't know when to keep his mouth shut.

By 1970, Accardo had had enough of Giancana's pals. Their decisions were as questionable and indiscreet as those of their former boss.

After Caifano was sent to jail in the Ray Ryan extortion case—followed by Roselli with the Friars Club conviction—Accardo decided on new management for Vegas. He dispatched an even more violent Chicago enforcer, Tony Spilotro, as the Outfit's local envoy.

At five feet four inches, Spilotro didn't engender fear unless you looked into his cold eyes or examined his lengthy rap sheet—full of atrocities but free of notable convictions. Bill Roemer, the braggadocious FBI agent, mocked Spilotro by nicknaming him "The Ant," short for "piss*ant*." But Spilotro wasn't so easily dismissed.

During his mob apprenticeship in the 1960s, Spilotro took part in a string of brutalities with Giancana's top enforcer, "Mad Sam" DeStefano, and his crew. Their crimes included the M&M torture murders in which they squeezed a victim's head in a metal vise. Equally impressive to Accardo, Spilotro successfully managed the Outfit's gambling operation in northwest Chicago, earning him a chance to move up rapidly in the ranks.

Spilotro was installed quietly but not gently into Las Vegas, where he soon made his presence felt. He became a suspect in five unsolved murders of Vegas loan collectors, delinquent on paying the Outfit. Contrary to Roselli, who shied away from unnecessary violence, Spilotro was likened to young Giancana for his fearless brutality. He set up a ring of thieves, called "The Hole in the Wall" gang, to steal jewels from the hotel rooms of rich casino guests or drugs from big-time dealers.

But one year after arriving in Vegas, Spilotro was brought back to Chicago in 1972 to face murder charges for killing Leo Foreman nine years earlier. The Foreman murder had been a launching pad in Spilotro's criminal career, earning him enough consideration to become a "made" member of the Outfit. The case was also a reminder of how violent and craven Giancana's associates could be.

This homicide case went unsolved for years. Then the FBI flipped Chuckie Crimaldi, an accomplice, who implicated Spilotro, "Mad Dog" DeStefano, and his brother Mario.

"I've broken arms, and I've broken legs, and I've watched a man die with a knife in his throat—but most of them had it coming, so what's the difference?" Crimaldi philosophized as he entered a witness protection program. "I have no regrets."

Flipping became an increasingly popular option for beleagured mobsters in America, even if they were more persuaded than inclined to confess. Since the televised apostasy of New York's Joseph Valachi in 1963, a steady number of Mafiosi had become turncoats. They opted for leniency from the feds rather than follow a stoic code of honor in jail. Traditionally, made men did the time—telling their children, as Giancana once did, that he was going away to "school." By the 1970s, as the FBI became more serious about organized crime, modern thugs looked out for themselves by pointing the finger at others. It slowly eroded away the Mafia's collective power.

A murder rap, with strong forensic evidence, now loomed over the heads of Spilotro and the DeStefano brothers. Paint chips found on Foreman's corpse matched those taken from Mario DeStefano's basement, backing up Crimaldi's account. The Outfit searched for ways to undermine the case, like bribing cops or jurors. But the greatest danger of incarceration stemmed from "Mad Sam" DeStefano and his erratic behavior.

Sporting long greasy hair and a wild gaze, DeStefano insisted on defending himself publicly and making oddball comments to the press. His brassiness seemed reminiscent of Giancana's bluster before he fled town for Mexico.

Chicago newspaperman Mike Royko appealed to DeStefano's "big ego" by inviting him to offer movie criticism of *The Godfather*, the classic 1972 gangster film then newly released. "I assured him that the nation's moviegoers would be fascinated by his expertise," Royko later remembered. "It was all set up, but at the last minute the deal fell through when Tony Accardo sent word that Sam should keep his fat mouth shut."

In the courtroom, "Mad Sam" refused to stay silent. Acting as his own attorney at pretrial hearings, DeStefano gave rambling, disjointed speeches or harassed the judge with barbed comments.

After Crimaldi gave his damning testimony, "Mad Sam" followed him menacingly to the courthouse elevator surrounded by guards. As FBI agent Bill Roemer remembered, DeStefano mumbled "something about fish, which indicated to Chuckie that Sam was going to feed him to the fishes."

Mad Sam's bizarre, psychopathic behavior—generally an attribute for a vicious mob enforcer—was now dooming the whole murder case against the Outfit. It became clear to boss Tony Accardo that something needed to be done quickly while the mob defendants were still out on bail.

Despite his claims to madness, DeStefano was lured to his death by a trap that depended upon two steadfast Mafia beliefs—in the tradition of killing key witnesses before trial, and that the code of loyalty between brothers was inviolate.

The trap was set when Spilotro and DeStefano's brother, Mario, told Mad Sam that they'd discovered the hideaway for key witness Crimaldi in Lake Geneva, about eighty miles outside of Chicago. They invited Mad Sam to join them in a weekend trip to kill their traitorous accuser.

Before leaving town, the three met at Mad Sam's garage. Acting friendly, Spilotro pulled out a double-barreled shotgun and then blasted Mad Sam. One shot ripped his arm off. Another blast tore open his chest.

Mario watched his brother die, convinced it was the only way to save himself.

Little loyalty existed between the DeStefano brothers, as Roselli with his good memory noted. "Ironic as hell, because twenty years ago, [Mad] Sam killed his own brother Mike when he became a junkie," recalled Johnny. "Giancana gave him the contract."

Similarly, Accardo insisted on this method to permanently end Mad Sam's antics and rescue the other two defendants.

As expected, the murder of Mad Sam weakened the Foreman case sufficiently so that a jury acquitted Spilotro. But Mario DeStefano was found guilty of killing Foreman. He was given a sentence of up to forty years. His appeals lawyer overturned the conviction. While awaiting a retrial, Mario died of a heart attack.

On the day of his "not guilty" verdict, Spilotro raised his arm in victory as he walked out of the courtroom. He scowled at the FBI agents who haunted him. Only Roemer, ever the avenging angel with hot doggish impulses, dared confront him in an open courtroom.

"You're still just a pissant, Tony—we'll get you yet," Roemer said, barely above a whisper.

Headed back to Vegas, Spilotro smiled defiantly. "Fuck you!" he laughed.

Roemer and the FBI had better luck with Richard Cain.

Giancana's aide-de-camp returned to Mexico after release from prison in 1971. Despite his poor eyesight requiring thick glasses, Cain worked as a "chauffeur" for the boss, driving his Mercedes-Benz around the Cuernavaca countryside.

Cain's real role was more as a financial adviser and companion, just as he'd done for Giancana before being sent so rudely to prison. Now Cain helped Giancana with big-time gambling deals and other high-risk international ventures that bordered on criminality. To hide their wealth, some Giancana rental properties in Mexico were listed under "Richard Scalzetti," an alias used by Cain based on his mother's maiden name.

Before he left Chicago, Cain told a friend, "I can't make any money here." But secretly, he did find a way. He met privately with Roemer and agreed to become a confidential FBI informant while he was working for Giancana in Mexico.

Spying was in his blood, Cain said. "He started considering himself an intelligence officer, no matter who he was working for," Roemer recalled. "When working for Giancana, he said, he did not consider himself a hoodlum but an intelligence agent."

Each piece of information Cain provided came with a pricetag. For example, the report about Giancana putting gambling casinos on cruise ships off the coast of Cozumel earned Cain $750. He considered it a bargain for the government.

"How much money would you have spent—assuming you knew enough to even think about it—to send an FBI agent or two to Cozumel and uncover what I just told you?" Cain said to Roemer. Later in this dangerous game, Cain provided information about other gangsters in Giancana's world. These reports included intelligence on Johnny Roselli, Marshall Caifano, and where Tony Spilotro stayed in Chicago when visiting from Vegas. Cain signed them all with the alias "Marquis."

Roemer insisted he kept a strict confidentiality around this arrangement. He wanted to ensure no harm would befall Cain as it did another person perceived to be an informant for Roemer—the late William "Action" Jackson. Ever the secret agent, Cain understood the peril he'd placed himself in as an FBI informer.

"Bill, if anything ever happens to me," Cain told Roemer, "I hope you will let those cocksuckers know that I was one of you—an intelligence officer working undercover in the mob. I want them to know that I doubled."

Cain's relationship with Giancana—likened by some as filial—proved grating over time. The tensions were provoked by money and ambition, and perhaps jealousy as well.

During secret surveillance in Mexico, US investigators once witnessed Cain kissing actress Phyllis McGuire alone in a car without Sam present. And during a Christmas 1972 holiday trip to Honolulu, with Cain accompanying Sam and Phyllis, a quarrel between the two men erupted. The reasons why never became clear. Cain later said he became so angry he wanted to shoot Sam. Instead he decided to get even in another way.

Cain soon called Roemer and said he wanted to reveal everything about Giancana's nefarious activities abroad. Roemer arranged for him to meet with the legal attaché in Mexico City. Records show little coordination with the CIA or awareness by Roemer about Giancana's still-secret role in the Castro assassination plot. For Cain, it was purely an act of vengeance designed to get Sam thrown out of Mexico—the country where he'd sought refuge and escape from American authorities.

"He never revealed his motivation for turning on the mob, except to say that Sam Giancana had done something to him so foul he had lost respect for Sam and wanted to bring down the whole organization," recalled his half-brother, Michael J. Cain.

In autumn 1973, Cain returned to Chicago for a visit. For several months, he'd been in regular contact with FBI agent Roemer, either in person, by telephone, or in letters signed with his codename "Marquis."

Over time, the FBI agent and his informant had learned to trust and respect one another. They now both shared the same goal of bringing down Sam Giancana and his criminal empire. In a moment of candor, Roemer later described Cain as "one of my closest friends, believe it or not." He didn't seem bothered by official warnings about Cain, including a 1968 FBI memo describing him as "a very vicious man who allegedly has killed four or five people."

To the FBI, Cain claimed that he'd been working with Giancana on setting up a gambling ship in Malta, and that the exiled boss promised Cain he could run gambling operations in Chicago if he returned to town. Cain didn't believe Sam. It sounded like a fatal setup. Rather than rejoice about the Chicago assignment, Cain worried for his safety.

Out of the blue on November 17, Cain contacted Roemer again. He asked if shadowy unknown figures following him recently in Chicago were FBI agents.

"Tires screeched, cars raced, somebody was after me," Cain recounted. "Was it you guys?"

Roemer assured him those weren't FBI agents, not to the best of his knowledge. Cain was upset but eventually he simmered. Roemer then left for a long-awaited vacation.

A few days later, Cain sat down for lunch at Rose's Sandwich Shop, a favorite in the

Chicago section known as Little Sicily. Witnesses saw Cain talking with a group of four men before they departed.

Soon after, two assailants in ski masks rushed into the luncheonette. They ordered the patrons against the wall. Then they fired two shotgun blasts at Cain, tearing away his face.

At home, Roemer heard a news alert on the radio—Dick Cain, his informant and friend, was dead.

"I was initially worried that it had been caused by a leak somewhere, that Tony [Accardo] and his guys had found out Dick was a double agent for me inside their Outfit," Roemer admitted.

Authorities later concluded that Marshall Caifano, an old friend of Giancana and Johnny Roselli's compatriot in Vegas, had killed Cain for his betrayal. Lacking sufficient evidence, however, Caifano was never charged.

Like the demise of "Mad Sam" DeStefano and so many other mob soldiers, Cain's death was another shocking reminder of how precarious life had become for Giancana, Roselli, and their gangster friends.

With so many forces now closing in, there was an undeniable sense that time also was short for Sam and Johnny.

CHAPTER 44:

KEEPING THE LID ON

"There is something about intelligence that seems to get in the blood."

—ALLEN DULLES

Cool and analytic, CIA director Richard Helms resembled his president, Richard Nixon, both physically and strategically. Both men possessed a head of slick black hair with a receding widow's peak and an equally dark view of the world always kept in mind.

They knew Cold War *realpolitik* practiced by the Russians could be harsh and cruel. In early 1973, the two men deemed the only way for democracies to resist Communism's evils was to be equally tough.

"Espionage is not played by the Marquess of Queensberry rules," Helms explained, "and the only sin in espionage is getting caught."

As a lifelong CIA organization man, Helms believed deeply in the powers of espionage. He'd grown up in America's intelligence system. He began as a spy in the Office of Strategic Services (OSS) during World War II, and worked his way up through the fledgling CIA, following a path set by his mentor, Allen Dulles.

Helms, like Dulles, shared a love of James Bond novels, with their over-the-top heroics and an institutional loyalty to those 007-like agents risking their lives in the field. Some spies enjoyed these Bond movies the way Mafioso adored gangster films.

Conversely, Helms "detested" John le Carre's spy tales of East-West struggles. He found them cynical and dispiriting to the real spies out in the cold who "have only each other on whom to lean."

Since becoming director in 1966, Helms' sense of loyalty to the CIA—and his own instinct for bureaucratic self-preservation—compelled him to keep a lid on the agency's Castro assassination plots, particularly those involving the Mafia.

One biographer described Helms as a "gentlemanly planner of assassinations." In fact, Helms preferred discreet spying and counterintelligence rather than the "boom and bang' of covert operations, such as the secret war against Cuba in the early 1960s. He'd been dubious initially of the CIA's deal with Roselli and Giancana, which he considered not worth the risky trade-offs.

"Aside from a romantic, if transient, glow of patriotism, the underworld invariably expected to be rewarded with an unwritten hunting license—in effect, an informal federal tolerance for some level of ongoing criminal activity," Helms observed. "If this doesn't suffice, a bundle of $100 notes might be expected to seal the bargain."

Nevertheless, Helms felt an institutional obligation to keep quiet about the agency's recent history and bury its secrets.

Many key players from the past were now dead. Desmond FitzGerald collapsed in 1967 on a tennis court. Dulles died in 1969 after publishing a book called *Great True Spy Stories*, recounting all his favorites. While running for president in 1968, Robert Kennedy was killed by an assassin angry about the Middle East. His involvement in the CIA's Castro plans remained largely unknown. And his brother JFK as well as President Dwight Eisenhower—who both presided over the CIA during its anti-Castro crusade—were long gone.

Only Fidel, their intended target, was still alive and in power. Castro had kept Cuba's violent atrocities from the world with the help of his imposing G-2 spy agency. Within a few days alone in 1964, eight Cubans were executed for being CIA spies. Political admirers and friendly Western journalists looked the other way at his brutal tactics.

Giancana, from his hideaway in Mexico, was also intent on wiping away his Castro past. In the early 1970s, Sam encouraged Robert Maheu to keep their secrets by sending girlfriend Phyllis McGuire to Maheu's front door.

"He [Giancana] wanted to know if you needed any help," McGuire explained, after multimillionaire Howard Hughes had sacked Maheu.

The knock on the door implicitly carried an ominous message—talk to the feds and we know where you live. Maheu preferred to interpret it as a sign of Giancana's friendship. "I was touched," Maheu recalled. "I know they say there's no honor among thieves, but you have to admit that's amazing loyalty."

Johnny felt differently. Increasingly, Roselli believed neither Maheu nor the CIA had been loyal to him.

At the glamorous Perino's restaurant on Wilshire Boulevard, where both movie stars and mobsters rubbed elbows, Johnny invited his former CIA buffer to dinner. Maheu said he "stupidly" agreed.

Though no longer retained by Howard Hughes, Maheu was still an influence peddler with both parties in Washington. He'd even hosted a political cocktail party featuring Sen. Ted Kennedy at the Sands in Las Vegas. Wanting to keep a low profile, Maheu strongly supported the CIA's decision to remain silent on the whole Castro affair. But at this dinner with Johnny, Maheu never got the chance to discuss it.

Roselli complained about his mounting legal bills from the Friars Club case and other problems instigated by his CIA work. He suggested Maheu's old boss, Howard Hughes, pick up his legal tab as a courtesy for engineering the very lucrative Desert Inn sale from the mob.

"You guys owe me," Roselli said. When Maheu said a Hughes payment wouldn't be possible, Roselli insisted, "You've got plenty."

The intense conversation between these one-time friends—who began their association a decade earlier with CIA agents sharing a beer at Maheu's backyard clambake—now turned bitter. They never touched their food.

At another point in Johnny's life, Maheu's refusal to fork over cash might have gotten him killed. But now, in his sixties, Roselli no longer had the clout of Giancana behind him, nor much of an affiliation with the Los Angeles mob. Maheu, a former G-man still with agency ties, possessed a certain invulnerability to Johnny's demands. If he wound up dead, the feds would consider Roselli the most likely suspect.

Eventually, Maheu got up from the table and walked away. The two unlikely spies, confederates in the covert war against Castro, would never speak to nor see each other again.

In his desperation, Johnny kept complaining about money. He made a similar plea for help to Moe Dalitz at the Brown Derby restaurant. Dalitz was out of power at the Desert Inn in Vegas but still the frontman for the mob-controlled Stardust. This Stardust arrangement, crafted by Roselli, allowed Dalitz "a position to continue skimming of money," according to an FBI report. This account came from an unidentified FBI informant who sat inside the Brown Derby with the two men.

When Johnny claimed he was owed sixty thousand dollars a month for the Stardust arrangement, Dalitz balked. He said he wouldn't allow a "shake down" by Roselli. He'd been "100 percent straight" with Johnny and expected the same.

But Moe was surprised by this desperate plea for cash. Dalitz admitted that "he always considered Roselli to be a millionaire." He told Johnny "if money meant keeping him out of jail, it was a different story and he would assist him but again stressed the fact that he was not going to be the victim of a shakedown."

The prospect of going to jail underlined how much Johnny's criminal career had taken a terrible toll. His dreams of becoming a movie producer or a successful businessman were now in the past. Whatever his wealth and charm, he couldn't shake his notoriety as a mobster.

At this late stage of life, there also seemed a deeper yearning. After courting so many beautiful women, Roselli had hoped, just before his indictment, to get married again. He proposed to vivacious torch singer Helen Grayco, the redheaded widow of zany popular entertainer Spike Jones. "He was really nuts about her," recalled Betsy Duncan, a mutual friend who had dated Johnny in the past.

Grayco enjoyed her own showbiz career in Vegas. She recorded albums and appeared on Dean Martin's television show in 1968. But her large Italian American Catholic family, the Grecos (she changed her stage name to "Grayco"), strongly objected to Johnny's presence. Friends wondered how a forty-year-old woman with three children could consider marrying a Mafioso. Her late husband Spike Jones, with musical gags and funny plaid suits, had always made people smile. ("When that Jones boy picks up a pistol—everybody laughs" declared a *New York Daily News* feature headline). Instead Roselli's presence evoked fear, knowing that his gunplay was no joke.

Johnny offered Helen a sapphire engagement ring encased in diamonds. Grayco, a kind-hearted woman who'd dated Roselli years before she met Jones, apparently gave him some consideration. Perhaps she found Johnny too enticing to say no, or perhaps he promised reform.

Ultimately, though, she turned him down. Marriage, and the chance for a missing happiness, eluded Johnny once again.

In February 1971, Roselli's name was linked publicly for the first time with the Castro assassination scheme. The news spread just as he went behind bars for his Friars Club conviction. Johnny hated every minute of hard time inside the McNeil Island, Washington, federal prison. He was eager to get out as soon as he could.

Hoping to gain sympathy from the courts, Roselli's attorney arranged with columnist Jack Anderson, the successor to Drew Pearson, to write a highly favorable portrayal of Johnny's efforts as a CIA spy a decade earlier. The column revealed "the terrible secret" of "six assassination attempts against Cuba's Fidel Castro" in the early 1960s (Anderson didn't know of other CIA attempts involving different figures such as AMLASH's Rolando Cubela.)

In pulpish prose, Anderson's column detailed the meetings of "ruggedly handsome gambler" Roselli with Maheu and CIA officials James "Big Jim" O'Connell and William Harvey on the "hush-hush murder mission." It didn't mention Giancana or Trafficante. But it did reprise the column's 1967 rumblings that CIA-sponsored assassination attempts against Castro might have played a revenge factor in JFK's death.

In this rendition, Johnny came off as an American hero, riding across the seas with Cuban exile sniper squads in the middle of the night—all in the name of freeing Cuba from Fidel's tyranny.

"The full story reads like the script of a James Bond movie, complete with secret trysts at glittering Miami Beach hotels and midnight powerboat dashes to secret landing spots on the Cuban coast," Anderson enthused. "Once, Roselli's boat was shot out from under him."

Johnny didn't talk directly to Anderson, but rather to his lawyer. The columnist sat in the same room listening to their conversation. It was Roselli's own brand of "plausible deniability," so he could say he never talked to the press.

Maheu refused comment for the story. But in a short interview with Anderson, Bill Harvey mentioned his "high regard" for his friend Johnny without acknowledging the CIA's killing scheme.

"This is a long story," Harvey told the columnist, "I don't think it ought to be printed."

With Dulles dead, Anderson sought comment from former CIA director John McCone who claimed the CIA-Mafia arrangement "could not have happened." His denial was a lie. McCone still seemed kept in the dark by Helms and others inside the CIA.

Anderson's column didn't spring Roselli from prison. However, Johnny's good conduct—and persistent pressure from his lawyer—got him released on parole by October 1973, after more than two years behind bars. However, there was another reason why Roselli was released early. He became a confidential government informant, convinced that no one would ever find out.

Flipping for Roselli didn't come easy. He'd always rebuffed such offers. While in prison, Roselli was compelled to appear before a federal grand jury looking into Mafia control of the Frontier hotel and casino in Vegas. At first Johnny declined to give any statements but then was given immunity, forcing him to testify. If he still refused to answer, Roselli faced more time in dreaded prison.

Eventually, Roselli's confidential grand jury testimony set off a chain reaction of events. It led prosecutors to his Friars pal, Maurice Friedman, the Frontier's front-man. In turn, Friedman's testimony helped convict three top Mafia figures from St. Louis and Detroit who actually controlled the Frontier. Federal prosecutors promised Johnny his grand jury testimony would remain a secret and he'd be safe from any harm.

When he finally was let go, Roselli spent his first night of freedom at the Beverly Hilton Hotel, relaxing and floating adrift in its heated sky-blue pool. To his surprise, FBI agents no longer tracked him as they had for more than a decade.

Trouble kept following him, however. A few months later, in February 1974, Roselli was dragged into the Senate's ongoing Watergate investigation of embattled President Richard Nixon.

Johnny's appearance, mandated by subpoena, was a lingering consequence from the Jack Anderson exposé.

At the time, a mystery existed about the underlying reasons for the 1972 burglary of the Democratic Party headquarters at the Watergate. Defendants in the case—including former CIA agent E. Howard Hunt, CIA operative Frank Sturgis and former Cuban exiles such as Bernard L. Barker—had anti-Castro histories, traceable to 1961's Bay of Pigs invasion.

Senate investigators asked Johnny what he knew about the Watergate burglars and their anti-Cuban past. As Roselli's lawyer Leslie Scherr surmised from their questions, the prosecutors felt "the reason why the break-in occurred at the Democratic Party headquarters was because Nixon or somebody in the Republican Party suspected that the Democrats had information as to Nixon's involvement with the CIA's original contract with Roselli [and] felt that a document existed showing Nixon was involved."

In this scenario, the Watergate burglars were supposedly looking for an explosive dossier detailing the CIA-Mafia attempts against Castro, which began in the Eisenhower administration. It might embarrass Nixon if made public. Instead these bunglers were caught by police, sent to jail, and prompted a cover-up by Nixon that cost him the presidency.

During the Senate Watergate questioning, Johnny did his best to resist. When staffers tried to ask Roselli about the CIA-Mafia plots, he refused, citing "national security" on the advice of his attorneys.

Johnny wasn't the only one avoiding the truth. In 1972, Helms tried to keep quiet about the prior Mafia recruiting by his agency. This stonewalling by the nation's spy master was applauded by his boss, Richard Nixon.

In a rambling tape-recorded White House conversation, the president underlined the dangers from publicly revealing the Mafia-CIA plot against Castro. Nixon worried it would make "the CIA look bad, it's going to make [E. Howard] Hunt look bad, and it's likely to blow the whole Bay of Pigs thing, which we think would be very unfortunate for the CIA, and for the country at this time."

Besides Roselli, another freelance Castro conspirator was under scrutiny. Robert Maheu had already privately revealed everything he knew about the CIA-Mafia plots to Nixon's Attorney General John Mitchell. But Watergate investigators were intrigued by Maheu's claim that he gave a hundred thousand in cash from Howard Hughes to Nixon for his 1968 presidential campaign. Eventually Maheu testified four times to the Watergate investigators.

With these sleuths, Johnny wasn't treated like a patriot but rather as a mere snitch. They didn't seem to recognize the dangers he might face on the street. For any Mafioso, testifying was a precarious position. Invariably, other mobsters would view Johnny as violating their deadly codes of *omerta*.

Before taking the Senate witness stand, Roselli sought approval from the Mafia's hierarchy. With his old boss Sam Giancana still in Mexico, Roselli apparently received the sanction to appear from mob boss Santo Trafficante in Florida. From available records, it appears no other top Mafia leader knew of Roselli's cooperation with government investigators.

For years, Trafficante had treated Johnny like a friend, recently watching out for his interests when he was in jail. They'd worked together since the Sans Souci and the mob's halcyon days in Havana's casinos. Although others wondered if the Florida gangster might be a double agent for Castro, Roselli was reluctant to believe such suspicions. Perhaps out of necessity in dealing with the Cuban exiles—or simply for old time's sake—Johnny trusted Trafficante far more than Sam ever did.

Yet over the next two years, keeping a lid on the Castro assassination story would prove impossible. The damaging leaks from Jack Anderson and Watergate investigators invariably led to more Congressional examinations of America's spy agency.

Increasingly, Roselli and Giancana were at the heart of this probe—and neither the CIA nor the president could do anything to stop it. Even the militant Cuban exiles in Florida, still devoted to Castro's demise, were upset about the disclosures surrounding this once top-secret US operation.

At the Fontainebleau Hotel in Miami, Roselli accidentally bumped into Tony Varona, the shady politician who'd been his one-time vital contact with the Cuban exiles. Roselli hadn't seen Varona in years, not since his CIA missions in Key Largo.

The old friends agreed to have lunch. Soon their conversation turned to the CIA.

Varona "felt very bitter toward the Agency," recalled Roselli, and vowed to never do business again with the spy agency. One gripe stood out above all others. "The basic complaint was that there were too many leaks."

CHAPTER 45:

SILENCERS

"I knew that just before a guy was going to be hit, the thing to do was to be very friendly with him, so as not to put him on guard."

—JOE VALACHI, QUOTED IN

THE VALACHI PAPERS BY PETER MAAS

For eight years in Mexico, Sam Giancana lived as an invisible man.

The famous Chicago gangster came and went as he pleased from San Cristobal, his heavily fortified compound, as he traveled the world in search of gambling bonanzas. Sam sometimes played golf or entertained friends. But he deliberately kept a low profile.

For this splendid isolation, away from arrest or persecution, Giancana could thank attorney Jorge Castillo. This politically influential Mexican provided the right papers and favors to protect Giancana from any government scrutiny.

As a sign of his appreciation, Giancana attended the June 1974 wedding of Castillo's son at an elegant country club in Mexico City. Sam was a conspicuous American guest among numerous local dignitaries.

Giancana no longer looked like those newspaper photos from the early 1960s, when he dressed like Frank Sinatra with a snakeskin suit, narrow tie, and a fedora. Instead, he adopted flared pants and other modish clothes of the 1970s with a graying goatee, just the way his new Hollywood girlfriend, Carolyn Morris, liked it.

Now in his mid-sixties, Sam contemplated getting married as well. Following several months of courtship, including an excursion along the Greek isles, he'd given Carolyn a large diamond engagement ring worth fifty thousand dollars.

Morris, a fashionable blonde divorcee from Palm Springs, California, was nearly twenty years Sam's junior. She counted actress Lauren Bacall as her best friend, the same widow of Humphrey Bogart who dated Sinatra in the 1950s. Carolyn was another beautiful woman, like Phyllis McGuire before her, who seemed inexplicably attracted to Sam, a tough guy constantly evading the law.

Several days after the Castillo wedding, Morris was staying as a guest at Sam's mansion when an early morning noise compelled Giancana to come outside to his front gate. He would never return again. Mexican immigration authorities quickly grabbed and handcuffed him. They demanded his name. Then they took Giancana into custody and prepared to deport him the next day, regardless of Castillo's efforts to prevent it.

After years of ignoring him, Mexican authorities were now determined to throw out this notorious criminal from their country as an "undesirable person."

Still in pajamas, Sam left his Mexican mansion without any possessions.

At first, it seemed someone at the Castillo wedding apparently noticed the American gangster's presence and decided to act on it. But in reality, Giancana's ouster was set in motion much earlier by Richard Cain, as a form of posthumous revenge for something that deeply offended him. Before his unsolved December 1973 murder in Chicago, Cain had complained to authorities about his former mentor's many criminal activities inside Mexico.

For months, Castillo's friend, Mexican President Luis Eccheverria Alvarez, received US inquiries about Giancana's "temporary resident" status but did nothing.

However, the Mexican government became alarmed by rumors linking Giancana to a CIA assassination plot against Castro, their neighbor in the Caribbean. Latin America leaders were well aware of the CIA's activities abroad, including its part in the 1967 capture and execution of Castro's guerilla comrade Ernesto "Che" Guevara inside Bolivia.

As Mexico's leader, Eccheverria wanted good relations with Castro. He would visit Cuba in a year. Thus, Giancana became suddenly expendable.

With Sam given the boot in July 1974, a US prosecutor in Chicago quickly issued a grand jury subpoena for Giancana. The FBI's Bill Roemer was there to greet Giancana, with a group of armed cops and agents, when he arrived at O'Hare airport.

After more than a decade of following this mobster's exploits, Roemer couldn't believe his eyes. Sam had "aged tremendously," he thought, with a white beard and no toupee.

"Roemer, I should have known you're behind all this," sighed Giancana, giving him more prosecutorial credit than he deserved.

Giancana wore an oversized work shirt that made him look scrawny. He needed both hands to hold up his pants without a belt.

"You guys started bugging me again and brought Carolyn into it," he complained.

His voice was no longer the booming arrogant Rush Street honk of yesterday but a quieter, more subdued tone of—as he described himself—"a broken down old man."

Detectives brought him downtown, where Giancana insisted he had nothing to do with the Cain murder. He disavowed any contacts with the Outfit and didn't plan to resume a life of crime in Chicago.

"I'm out of it," he pleaded contritely to Roemer. "So, please, just leave me alone. Nothin' personal like it was between us before. If it takes an apology, then this is it. Let's just forget what had been before."

Roemer, a witness to many crimes heard on FBI listening devices, realized his long-time pursuit of Giancana might be over. He, too, talked of his manhunt like a game.

"At that moment, I realized that I had won," Roemer later wrote in his memoir about seeing Giancana vanquished. "It had been a long, hard struggle to neutralize this mob boss—arguably the most powerful in the country during his heyday in the early and mid-sixties—but with the help of some great partners and fellow agents I had mastered the game and truly became his nemesis. This shell of a man before me now was but a shadow of the great godfather."

The eight-year odyssey of Sam Giancana away from home left a gaping hole in the emotional life of his family.

For more than a year, he had refused to speak to his oldest daughter Antoinette, after she decided to divorce her husband for his alleged beatings and physical abuse.

In her father's eyes, Antoinette had made a mess of her life with both alcoholism and adultery. No reason was good enough to break up a family, he contended, without any sense of irony about his own male behavior. Both the traditions of the Mafia as well as the church forbade it.

"You made your bed, goddammit, now you lie in it!" Sam yelled at her. "No god-dam daughter of mine is gonna get a divorce . . . . You're not going to make a fool of me that way too."

Sam's notoriety as a mobster also affected the life of his middle daughter Bonnie. She had married Anthony Tisci, an aide to Congressman Frank Annunzio, who was handpicked by Chicago machine politicians beholden to Giancana's Outfit. In 1965, Tisci quit his job for "health reasons" after he took the Fifth before a federal grand jury investigating organized crime.

Eventually, Bonnie and her husband moved to Tucson, Arizona, where her father's reputation followed them. In July 1968, shotgun fire blasted through the Tisci home's front window. The attack seemed like the handiwork of rival mob boss, Joe Bonanno, who had moved nearby in Arizona. Investigators later discovered David Hale, a rogue FBI agent, had perpetrated the shooting, trying to foment a gang war among Mafia members.

Back in Chicago, Sam managed to stay out of jail, as if he might be serious about retirement. His fiancé Carolyn Morris invited him to visit her southern California home, though their relationship seemed increasingly improbable. She found out association with a real-life gangster carried unforeseen consequences.

In February 1975, the same federal grand jury investigating Sam in Chicago called Carolyn to testify. She took the Fifth, invoking her privilege against self-incrimination, just as Giancana had done in the past. But it was hardly a performance to impress Carolyn's tony friends back in Palm Springs.

When Sam appeared in the federal courthouse in Chicago, an excited flock of reporters and photographers surrounded him, as if his fame and clout hadn't changed.

Despite what he told Roemer, Giancana still held out hope of re-establishing himself as a crime boss in Chicago. He deferred to Tony Accardo's authority over the Outfit but, as a point of contention between the two, Sam still maintained the international gambling deals he'd arranged while in Mexico.

Accardo wanted to make sure the Outfit got its fair share of those payments. Reminded again of all the trouble Sam had caused while running the Outfit, Accardo would not be denied in this request for money owed south of the border.

―――――――――

By May 1975, Sam and Johnny were still friends, linked by their criminal conspiracies, though no longer young and powerful. The showgirls, the Hollywood celebrities, the millions in gambling revenue from Vegas casinos they oversaw for the

Outfit—arguably the most formidable Mafia organization America had ever seen—were now mostly a memory.

Jail, foreign exile, and the constant drumbeat of government surveillance had kept Giancana and Roselli apart. Their few conversations usually took place on random pay phones to avoid wiretaps.

Despite all these late-in-life difficulties, however, Sam and Johnny remained loyal pals upon whom each could depend.

Virtually broke, Roselli needed Giancana's help in paying his lawyer's fees. To their great chagrin, both men had been subpoenaed by the Senate Intelligence Committee investigating the CIA's plans to assassinate Fidel Castro and other foreign leaders. Johnny had little money left for a defense attorney.

The dark secret kept hidden for years—the agency's recruitment of Mafia hitmen to pursue Cuba's Communist leader—was coming to light officially. Roselli's prominent role detailed in the Jack Anderson columns—as well as the investigative fallout from the Watergate investigation and reports of domestic spying by the CIA—prompted the US Senate hearings planned by Frank Church, a Democrat from Idaho.

Both Giancana and Roselli were expected to testify about the CIA sometime in summer 1975. Sam generously offered money to Johnny if he needed it for a lawyer. Roselli accepted through a mutual friend, conceding he wasn't above Giancana's financial assistance.

"Let me figure out what my next (attorney's) tab will be," Johnny gratefully told the unidentified mutual friend, as later recounted by the *Miami Herald*. The Senate hearings were still a few weeks away. Both men would need the best lawyers' advice possible.

Since leaving prison, Roselli had talked about getting involved again in casino gambling. Only this time, he wanted a place in the Middle East, where the governments would not ban him as in Vegas. Johnny desperately needed financial backers. Acceptance of money from Giancana may have included this dream of faraway casinos as well.

Giancana advised Johnny to be careful with associates. He worried Roselli and Santo Trafficante Jr. had become "too close." Sam now believed the Florida don, with his murky ties to both the Cuban exiles and Castro's narcotics trafficking, could not be trusted. He knew Trafficante—for all his business savvy and ability to translate Spanish—was a murderer at heart.

Perhaps the only alliance worthy of loyalty was between themselves as buddies in crime. A decade earlier, Sam and Johnny had generated millions together, with an ambitious vision that traditional bosses like Accardo could never imagine. Maybe if all went well, they could become crime partners again, overseeing the skim at some casino in Tehran or gambling ship off the coast of Belize.

But that same month, Giancana became terribly ill during a visit to Carolyn Morris in California. Doctors said he needed gall bladder surgery right away. An operation with Dr. Michael E. DeBakey, one of the nation's best surgeons, was arranged in Houston.

Sam recuperated for days in a Texas hospital bed, visited by Carolyn and his daughter Bonnie. He returned home to Oak Park, Illinois, yet he soon worsened. Giancana was sent back to Houston with a blood clot and other problems.

After several days in the hospital, where Houston police monitored him, Sam bolted out the back door. He secretly made his way back to Chicago with the help of his daughter Francine's husband, Jerome DePalma, who flew to Houston to assist him.

———————

Two days later, on June 19, 1975, Francine, her husband, and their daughter visited Sam at his Oak Park home. Together, they shared some dinner. Carolyn Morris was no longer around.

As the youngest of Angeline's babies, Francine had always been Sam's favorite. She calmed his nerves without complaint, rather than caused him grief. His surgical wounds were still very tender. He had lost a lot of weight.

Weakly, Sam chatted with his family and two old friends from the Outfit—Chuckie English and Butch Blasi—until they all departed near eleven o'clock. Undercover Chicago detectives—who'd been sitting in an unmarked car, watching who came in and out of Giancana's house—had left by that point.

Earlier that day, Senate Intelligence staffers arrived in Chicago, aware that Sam had "little taste for a grilling by a congressional committee." The next morning, they intended to escort Giancana safely to Washington, to answer the Church committee's questions about the CIA's homicidal schemes.

After his dinner guests departed, Sam said goodnight to the couple who were his housekeepers and lived upstairs. To lull themselves asleep, the couple turned on their television. *The Tonight Show Starring Johnny Carson* provided a muffled hum of laughter in the distance. Sam retired to his basement den with a little snack that Francine had left for him.

All around his well-decorated den, Sam's knickknacks—cigar humidor, paintings and hobbies like golf and photography—were on display. So was his collection of favorite movies, which included *The Manchurian Candidate*, starring his friend Frank Sinatra, with its Cold War plot of double agent spies and assassination conspiracy.

Sam pulled out the sausages in Francine's doggie bag. Atop a small stove, he started to grill them in a pan.

A knock at the basement entrance drew Sam's attention. He opened the steel door to allow in a recognizable face, apparently a trusted friend, whom he invited to share his meal.

After a little discussion, Sam turned his head to continue cooking. Along with the heated sausage, he boiled escarole and ceci beans in another pan.

Suddenly, the late-night friend became an attacker. He pulled out a .22 pistol affixed with a silencer and fired it into the back of Sam's head. A burst of blood sprayed the room.

Giancana's body collapsed to the floor. This was no random murder. The killer wanted to send a message in the way Giancana's life was taken.

As Sam's bleeding body landed on his back, with his face looking upwards, his assassin placed the pistol's silencer into Giancana's mouth. He fired away six more times, rhythmically and quietly. The stove burners were still aflame as the unknown killer escaped into the night.

Bullets into the mouth were a Mafia signature gesture, designed to show that someone suspected of squealing to authorities had been stopped dead in their tracks. It also was a warning to anyone else who might think of talking to the feds or a Congressional committee in the future.

"The Mob knew the odds were Sam wouldn't keep his mouth shut this time," surmised Robert Maheu. "So it silenced him for good."

Expressing the shock of the nation, the *New York Times* columnist William Safire called Giancana "the only person in American history to be murdered just before he was to appear in front of a congressional committee."

Local law-enforcement theorized Sam's murder wouldn't have taken place without the approval of Tony Accardo. There had been many grievances between the two.

But Giancana's family believed he'd been killed because of his work with Roselli on the CIA assassination plots against Castro.

"I always felt very strongly that the subpoena requiring Sam to appear before the [Church Senate] committee was the death warrant that led to his murder," insisted Antoinette Giancana. She rushed to his house when she heard of Sam's murder.

"He's gone—he's dead!" screamed Antoinette at his body still on the floor. She was overcome with regrets.

At the time of his death, her father still had been refusing to speak with her.

———

On June 23, 1975, a flock of reporters swarmed Giancana's funeral, just as they once did at his court appearances. A hundred mourners attended his memorial service. Young toughs threatened to beat up photographers if they snapped Sam's casket passing by.

None of the top members of Chicago's Outfit paid their respects, as though they'd been warned in advance. Neither Accardo nor any other out-of-town Mafioso showed their faces, including Johnny Roselli scheduled to testify before the Senate in a few days.

Law-enforcement observers noticed Carolyn Morris didn't attend Sam's funeral. Absent also were familiar faces from Hollywood and Las Vegas, including his Rat Pack pal and Cal-Neva partner, Frank Sinatra.

But Phyllis McGuire, his beautiful former lover, did appear. "I give her [McGuire] credit," said William Roemer, the FBI agent most familiar with Sam's personal life as well as his criminal history. "She had the guts to be seen at his funeral. . . . Almost nobody cared."

At age sixty-seven, Giancana was laid to rest at Mount Carmel Cemetery, the same place where another notorious Chicago gangster, Al Capone, was buried. Sam's remains were placed in a mausoleum, entombed next to his beloved wife Angeline. For family and friends, it was a sad reminder how Angeline's early death changed everything in Sam's life.

Hauntingly, Giancana's murder would remain unsolved. Police rummaged through his possessions and discovered numerous curious artifacts, including a framed photograph of Giancana with Pope Pius XII at the Vatican. How did this gangster, after a lifetime of murder and mayhem, arrange for his picture to be taken with the holy pontiff? For this question, like so many other circumstances surrounding his death, there were no definitive answers.

Eventually the assassin's black automatic pistol with a homemade silencer was found in a park, two miles from Giancana's home. Municipal employees stumbled upon it while cutting the grass.

Ballistic tests proved the gun was the same that killed Giancana two months earlier. Police theorized the assassin drove away swiftly from Sam's house, heard sirens and flashing lights of squad cars responding to the shooting, and ditched the murder weapon out the window of a getaway car.

Both the FBI and local authorities weighed in with their own homicide theories and motives of who might want Sam dead. But in tracing serial numbers to find out where the murder weapon had been purchased, detectives found one more suggestive clue:

The gun came from Miami, purchased in a gun shop located in the heart of Florida's Cuban exile community, the place where Trafficante was king.

CHAPTER 46:

CHURCH CONFESSIONS

"The confession of evil works is the first beginning of good works."

—St. Augustine

The two faces of Johnny Roselli, both personal and public, were on display with the death of his friend Sam Giancana.

"They fucking killed a dead man," Roselli raged to fellow gangster Jimmy Fratianno, with a private grief he didn't show others. A few days after the killing, Johnny bitterly blamed the Chicago Outfit for sanctioning such treachery against one of its own. Giancana was ill and ready to retire. He threatened no one. "Sam could barely climb a short flight of stairs."

Furiously, Roselli promised revenge on Butch Blasi, the Chicago mobster he initially suspected of murdering Giancana. "I'd like to cut his fucking balls off and shove them up his ass," Roselli snarled with disgust.

On the morning Giancana's death became known, however, Johnny showed little emotion. Roselli was in Washington, preparing to meet with staffers from the Senate Intelligence Committee investigating the CIA. The same panel had planned to call Giancana as a witness.

Overnight, Roselli stayed at the Watergate apartment of his friend Fred B. Black Jr., a corrupt lobbyist who knew Johnny from Vegas. At six that morning, a telephone call arrived about Sam's murder. When his lawyer showed up later that morning, Johnny was still in his silk pajamas and a smoking robe, ordering breakfast from room service.

Both his lawyer, Thomas Wadden, and the Senate staffers were visibly stunned by Giancana's homicide. Johnny kept his emotions to himself. He wore the cold unflappable mask of a professional killer.

The investigators decided to take a statement from Roselli immediately and to move up his scheduled appearance before the full committee by a few days.

Without luck, they also tried to subpoena Florida don Santo Trafficante Jr.— the third Mafia player in the CIA's assassination troika—but he couldn't be found. Senate investigators now suspected Trafficante or some of his well-armed Cuban exile friends might be behind Giancana's murder, rather than Blasi or some local Chicago hitman.

Johnny didn't flinch about testifying. "They're not going to do anything to me," he assured. "If they want to kill me they're going to kill me, but they're not going to scare me."

Heavy security surrounded the crowded Senate hearing room when Roselli finally testified about his life as a CIA spy. His appearance on June 24, 1975 would be the first of three times before the panel over the next year. Outside the Capitol that initial day, Johnny hustled past reporters, refusing their inquiries. But inside, under oath, he answered questions dutifully without saying much.

Johnny's guarded account would be a mix of fact and fabrication (enough so that the FBI later considered perjury charges). In testimony, he confirmed the essence of the Castro conspiracy, without revealing more than was already in the Jack Anderson columns.

Like some *Mission Impossible* television fantasy, Roselli mentioned adopting an alias "John Rawlston" when he began the CIA spy caper. His Cuban exile conspirators, such as Tony Varona, were referred to numerically—"Cuban Number 1," "Cuban Number 2," and "Cuban Number 3"—rather than by name.

Mafia partner Trafficante was called "X," adding to the mystery surrounding his sudden disappearance.

During this discussion of deadly business, Johnny exuded a gritty enigmatic charm. When one Senator inquired if he thought Giancana was motivated by jealousy for Phyllis McGuire in the Dan Rowan wiretap case, Johnny answered sagely, "I don't know how a man feels."

After another inquisitor—Sen. Barry Goldwater, former GOP presidential candidate and one-time friend of the late Willie Bioff—asked about Roselli's fuzzy memory for details, Johnny replied, "Senator, in my business, we don't take notes."

When Sen. Walter Mondale, another aspirant to the White House, asked who in higher authority wanted Castro dead, Johnny wrapped himself in the flag.

"I don't ask any questions how high," Roselli professed. "I was satisfied that I was a doing a duty for my country . . . I did it for honor and dedication."

Johnny made a point of saying his deceased friend Sam felt the same way.

While the Church panel seemed initially pleased by his testimony, Roselli's account was full of contradictions and omissions, enough to build up doubts.

Johnny seemed to be protecting his old CIA friend, William Harvey. For example, he said the assassination attempts "came to a screeching halt" after the October 1962 Cuban Missile Crisis, even though they continued for months afterwards. Johnny also denied any late-night excursions in armed high-speed boats along the Cuban coastline, despite what he told Jack Anderson and others, including his attorneys. Presumably admitting to these illegal attacks wouldn't have helped his effort to avoid deportation.

Roselli's testimony appeared so coached that Harvey was asked about it eventually when the former CIA agent appeared before the panel.

"I told him very simply—'John, please tell the Committee the truth,'" Harvey insisted. "I know what your sense of loyalty is. Under no circumstance do I want you to again jeopardize yourself because of that sense of loyalty in the mistaken impression that you may embarrass me."

In the mid-1970s, Americans no longer had the same unquestioning Cold War acceptance of the CIA, particularly after the Vietnam conflict. Yet given the gravity of the October 1962 crisis—with Soviet nuclear missiles hiding in Cuba and millions of lives at stake—Harvey had no intention of apologizing to the Senate Intelligence panel for relying on Mafia hitmen as spies or assassins.

If the president handed down the order, Harvey said it was proper for the CIA "to eliminate a threat to security of this country by any means whatever—whether it's a nuclear strike or a rifle bullet, if I may be that blunt."

Unlike higher-ups in the CIA's chain of command who dissembled or engaged in euphemisms, Harvey never minced words.

While still loyal to Harvey and Sam's memory, Johnny had no desire to protect Maheu, his first CIA contact.

In retrospect, Roselli portrayed the oily Maheu as a kind of double agent, taking public money from the CIA while working privately for Howard Hughes. There was no question of Maheu's first loyalty whenever they worked together. "He [Maheu] was always on call for Mr. Hughes," Roselli explained. "He was very careful about that."

No longer friends or business associates in Vegas, Roselli deeply resented Maheu—especially for drawing upon government officials to get himself out of a jam, while leaving him out in the cold. Roselli was keenly aware such favors didn't apply to his own criminal matters or deportation battle.

When asked if he ever tried to trade on his CIA service for personal gain, Johnny replied sarcastically, "My name is not Maheu."

A month later, under a grant of immunity, Maheu appeared before the Senate panel, defending his actions. Over the next two days, he detailed how he worked as a CIA intermediary with the Mafia figures. Maheu also admitted that he privately told Hughes about the top-secret scheme to "dispose of Mr. Castro in connection with a pending invasion."

Instead of wrapping himself in the American flag, Maheu justified his assassination activity as part of a holy war against Communism.

"Being a Jesuit trained college graduate, I understand, I believe, what a just war is," explained the Holy Cross man. "And I truly thought, and still do, that we were involved in a just war, and that we were doing, whatever we did—for the benefit of the U.S. Government."

Giancana and Roselli never sought compensation for their service, Maheu added, and, "these gentlemen appeared like angels" compared to Hughes, a man incapable of loyalty other than to himself.

After testifying, Maheu went outside and held his own press conference.

In front of some one hundred reporters from around the world, Maheu decried how his government had betrayed him and the top-secret Cuban mission. Maheu said Frank Church and other senators were merely grandstanding at the expense of America's security. He resented being compelled by these politicians to reveal long-held secrets.

"I still feel we should have never disclosed the mission," Maheu said of the Castro assassination plot, which he then proceeded to explain in detail to reporters. "I'm very bitter," he said of his Senate testimony. "When your country pledges you into secrecy . . . and 16 years later they decide to throw you in front of a bus. I had held up my part of the bargain. That was hard to swallow."

For Johnny Roselli, the most difficult question of loyalty involved Judy Campbell. She was the next one asked by the Senate for her secrets. And Roselli had no easy way to prevent her testimony.

In sifting through government documents about the Castro plots, Senate investigators discovered Campbell's relationship in the early 1960s with Giancana and Jack Kennedy. A subpoena was sent out for her testimony.

The Church committee wanted to know if Campbell's sensational love triangle between the president and the nation's top mobster might shed some light on the CIA's assassination plans against Castro.

More than a decade later, Judy had taken measures to separate herself from those early Rat Pack days of JFK and Sinatra, Giancana and Roselli, and her life as an aimless party girl. She no longer shuttled back and forth between LA, Vegas, Chicago, and the White House. She was now married to a professional golfer, a dozen years her junior. She preferred to sleep late in their motor home while they were on tour in Florida.

Searching through telephone directories, Senate investigators had trouble finding her. Once again, she was defined by a man, using her new husband's surname—Judith Exner.

To Judy, news of Giancana's death—and the Senate's desire for testimony about the CIA and Castro—seemed incredibly distant. "I felt sorry for Sam but I never even dreamed that it could involve me," she recalled.

Several weeks later, investigators issued her subpoena papers to appear in Washington. On the day of her closed-door testimony in September 1975, Senate lawyers explained they "could not tell me exactly what it was they were going to discuss, but that it had something to do with President Kennedy, John Roselli and Sam Giancana," she recalled.

Under oath, Judith Campbell Exner, as she identified herself, was asked whether these men were "friends" and about the nature of their relationship. This roster included Frank Sinatra too.

"Every time they asked me about someone, the questioner would say, 'Was he also a friend?'" she explained, "and the manner in which it was said left no doubt of the inference—*friend* was their euphemism for lover."

Exner acknowledged making a number of telephone calls to Kennedy at the White House through the first year of his presidency. She described meeting Roselli for the first time and being later introduced to Giancana by Sinatra in early 1960.

"Did either Mr. Giancana or Mr. Roselli ever ask you to communicate messages to the President?" asked one Senate inquisitor.

"No," said Exner with a one-word reply, just as her lawyer suggested. (She later claimed to the press that this was a lie and that she'd served as a kind of courier between the two men.)

The Senate panel asked about mutual friends, like Betsy Duncan whom Johnny once dated, and how she met Peter Lawford at a Fontainebleau party with Sam Giancana in Florida. She testified Kennedy's White House secretary Evelyn Lincoln arranged some of her trips to Washington. White House records and telephone logs seemed to corroborate her story.

Before their star witness left the stand, the Senate lawyers—who carefully danced around her relationship with the murdered president—asked Exner to keep her testimony "confidential." The hearing transcript indicates she'd been asked several questions in a prior executive session.

One person was especially off-limits. The panel asked that she not talk to this other special witness. The committee's Republican minority counsel requested "in particular that this matter not be discussed with Mr. Johnny Roselli, who will be appearing subsequent to this session."

Three days later, Roselli was deeply upset about Exner's testimony when he reappeared for more Senate questioning. He didn't understand why Judy needed to be dragged into a debate about the CIA and Cuba.

"I do not know what Judith Campbell has to do with this thing," complained Roselli, who claimed he wasn't present when Judy called the White House from his Los Angeles apartment. "It is a little disgusting to me because I do not really like to talk about these things, women—You are talking about the White House and Judith Campbell and all this. This is none of my affair. If it was so, I was not present, so it would be hearsay on my part if I did hear it."

Johnny was still trying to protect her, as if she was still the young Elizabeth Taylor lookalike of his memory. When asked specifically about Judy and the late president, Roselli feigned the high road.

"I could answer some of these questions, but I do not think I want to get into it," he declared. "I do not think it is relevant."

Roselli denied giving Judy any information about Cuba to pass along to Giancana. "I would not give my mother a message to give to Sam," he joked.

The Senate's promise of confidentiality surrounding Judith Campbell Exner's testimony didn't last very long.

In its huge report about the CIA's assassination plots, released around Thanksgiving 1975, the Church panel never mentioned Judy by name. In good old boy fashion, Democrats had tried to cover over the slain president's sexual affair. They later insisted staffers sign agreements that they had not leaked to the media and kept Judy's comments confidential.

In the long report, there was just a little footnote mentioning a "close friend" of JFK and the two mobsters. Only a careful reader, squinting on the bottom on page 129, could find an oblique description.

"Evidence before the committee indicates that a close friend of President Kennedy had frequent contact with the President from the end of 1960 through mid-1962," the footnote said in tiny agate type. "F.B.I. reports and testimony indicate, the President's friend was also a close friend of John Roselli and Sam Giancana and saw them often during this same period."

The Church committee said presidential telephone logs revealed seventy calls between the Kennedy White House and "the President's friend." And while Roselli and this "close friend' were interviewed, it noted somberly that "Giancana was killed before he was available for questioning."

This political bombshell detonated on a slow fuse. After several days, the *Washington Post* and other media figured out the identity of the mysterious "close friend." The sexual affairs of Judy with the president and two mobsters became front-page news.

"While straining to show that President Kennedy did not know that the C.I.A. had hired Mafia chiefs John Roselli and Sam Giancana to arrange the assassination of Fidel Castro, the committee report reluctantly and guardedly revealed a Kennedy-Mafia connection," chastised *New York Times* columnist William Safire, a former Nixon speechwriter.

Everything that Judy hoped to forget about her past was now dredged up in sordid detail. Like Maheu, she called her own press conference.

"I can at this time emphatically state that my relationship with Jack Kennedy was of a close, personal nature and did not involve conspiratorial shenanigans of any kind," said Exner, now forty-one, with her golf pro husband by her side. "My relationship with Sam Giancana and my friendship with Johnny Roselli were of a personal nature and in no way related to or affected my relationship with Jack Kennedy. Nor did I discuss either of them with the other."

Old-time Kennedy loyalists rallied around the popular Camelot image of their fallen president. They denied both the allegations of a sordid affair and that JFK knew of a Castro assassination plan.

Dave Powers, one of JFK's most trusted aides, claimed "the only Campbell I know is chunky vegetable soup." Historian and former JFK adviser Arthur M. Schlesinger Jr. blamed Allen Dulles for the CIA-Mafia conspiracy and for keeping the Kennedys out of the loop. "The record shows that the only assassination plot disclosed to Robert Kennedy involved Sam Giancana—and that Kennedy did his best thereafter to put Giancana behind bars," Schlesinger wrote.

In front of the Church committee, JFK's former top aide Ted Sorensen disavowed any idea of a Castro plot by President Kennedy. "Particularly ludicrous is the notion that one of his background would have ever knowingly countenanced the employment for these purposes of the same organized crime elements he had fought for so many years," testified Sorensen. "It is nonsense to assert that President Kennedy was obsessed with the problem of Fidel Castro . . . Any off-hand references to 'getting' Castro or deposing, removing, undermining or 'doing something' about him, never included and could not have included assassination."

Nevertheless, Camelot had taken a serious blow. For millions of Americans who loved the martyred president—a television memory burnished by home movies of Kennedy children playing joyously with him—the Church panel's revelations raised disturbing questions. Many blamed the pretty woman, who was then in her twenties, rather than the older married president whom she claimed to have adored.

"People who loved Jack felt if they could degrade me, then he was just a bad boy," Exner explained years later. "On the other side, [Republicans] felt they could destroy Jack by destroying me, by making me as bad as possible."

Judy felt betrayed by the Senate investigators who promised her confidentiality, but also by those intimates she once trusted like Sam Giancana. She realized mobsters could use "honey traps" as much as spies.

"As I look back, it's possible that Sam got exactly what he wanted from our relationship," she concluded. "Now that I know of his involvement with the Central Intelligence Agency, it is possible that I was used almost from the beginning . . . It never occurred to me that Sam's interest in me was simply because of my association with Jack Kennedy. Of course there were people who wanted to be my friend because of my relationship with Jack, backslappers who wanted 'little favors,' but Sam never asked me for anything, and so I never connected Sam with any of that."

Once more, Johnny had tried gallantly to shield Judy from harm, including the hurtful consequences of her own poor decisions. But now, with his own name splashed across the nation's headlines, Roselli realized he was more in danger than any other witness. As a Justice Department memo later underlined, Roselli "expressed fear for his life as a result of his having testified."

That dread would become especially so in the months ahead, as the Church committee prepared to call Roselli back for a third time. They wanted Johnny to testify about another highly-charged topic that the senators believed might be related to the CIA's Castro operation—JFK's assassination.

CHAPTER 47:

MISSING IN ACTION

"We, at the CIA, had gone through some considerable suffering on the exposure of the Family Jewels in 1975 . . . The Company has never been quite the same since the exposure of the Family Jewels."

—NORMAN MAILER, HARLOT'S GHOST

O ut of luck with little money, Johnny Roselli moved away from his posh lifestyle in Beverly Hills to the simpler pleasures of his sister's modest home in Plantation, Florida. Golfing, fishing, long lunches, and hanging out poolside with good-looking women kept Roselli in motion, like a man without a care in the world.

"He was the one guy who could see humor in anything," recalled one of his lawyers, Leslie Scherr. "He was a very vital man as far as women were concerned. He hadn't gotten into the celibacy stage."

Throughout early 1976, Roselli found refuge with his sister, Edith Daigle, and her husband Joe, while he kept in contact with his lawyers in Washington and friendly wise guys in Vegas and LA. Despite his search for escape in Florida, the fallout from his Senate appearances in Washington was far from over.

Following Roselli's much-publicized testimony, word spread that the Mafia's national commission was upset. Neither Roselli nor Giancana had ever informed the nation's top mobsters about their secret arrangement with the CIA. Some warned Johnny that he was in mortal danger.

As he travelled across South Florida, Roselli remained cool as ever. Mindful of assassins in the hedgerow, he carefully avoided playing the same golf course twice in a row. The Daigles lent him their Chevy Impala to get around and avoid trouble.

"If I'm ever missing, check the airports," Johnny deadpanned, "because that's where they usually leave the car."

Roselli had reached an age when a man appraises the carnage in his life and tries to make amends. He valued loyalty more than most. He particularly missed his murdered friend Sam Giancana, his clout within Cosa Nostra, and all the good times they once shared. But Johnny recognized that he had no chance of going back to Vegas with the blessing of Tony Accardo and the Chicago Outfit. They were killing members of Giancana's old crew, not promoting them.

Roselli showed his own brand of loyalty when Bill Harvey, his burly quick-to-anger former CIA handler, suddenly dropped dead of a heart attack. Despite his bluster and impulsiveness, Harvey always seemed a patriot at heart, a straight-shooter within an agency known for its deception. As a true friend, Johnny called Harvey's widow to offer more than condolences.

"Any help you need—anything—you just tell me," Roselli assured her. "You need money? You let me know, no matter how much."

In Washington, Roselli found no official loyalty for his actions as a spy. He appealed both his illegal alien conviction and the government's deportation order, without much hope of success. Getting rid of Johnny, however, wouldn't be easy. In documents, US immigration officials said the government was "having difficulty finding a country who will accept Roselli."

To forestall his ouster, Roselli's lawyers let it be known that he had more to tell about the mysteries of JFK's assassination. They floated the "blowback" theories of Cuban death squads sent to the United States in retaliation for the CIA's assassination attempts on Castro. Roselli's camp wanted to trade his explosive comments for some kind of immunity, a fresh start if possible.

"There was never the slightest doubt in John's mind that Castro was responsible for the assassination of Kennedy," said Edward P. Morgan, his Washington lawyer. Roselli "was certain that the people he (Roselli) put around Castro in the CIA plot turned right around and killed Kennedy. The people he still knew did it."

Morgan, once counsel to the Senate Foreign Relations Committee, was always bothered that the 1964 Warren Commission never learned of the Castro plot.

"I was an admirer of Earl Warren," Morgan explained. "(His) report said that . . . Oswald alone killed Kennedy. It kept bugging me, after so gruesome a detail from Roselli, that the Chief Justice could put his name on a report which didn't assess the most significant piece of evidence bearing on the killing of Kennedy."

The dark and ominous "blowback" theory—first mentioned in Drew Pearson's

1967 column with Jack Anderson but largely ignored by official Washington—now resonated with Senate panel members such as Republican Richard Schweiker and Democrat Gary Hart.

"You don't have to be a genius to believe that they [Giancana and Roselli] knew something about the coincidence of events—Cuba, Mafia, CIA and Kennedy—that somebody didn't want that out in the public 12 years later," Hart later explained.

The Senate Intelligence Committee decided to call Roselli back for a third time in April 1976. Only by putting this gangster under oath could investigators expect to find out what he knew about President Kennedy's murder.

Allen Dulles was long dead but his legacy overshadowed much of the Church Committee's investigation into the CIA's covert assassination campaign against Castro. As a grand spymaster, Dulles left no incriminating memos or telex messages. There were no definitive directives from those above him, like Eisenhower and Kennedy, nor traceable words to underlings below.

The CIA men still alive had a hard time defending themselves and the agency from the damning evidence collected by the Senate.

On television's *Face the Nation*, then-Director of Central Intelligence William Colby, a bookish, Ivy League-trained career spy with thick glasses, declined to tell the nation what he knew about the CIA's assassination past. He called it "very murky, and I really don't believe this subject is an appropriate one for an official to be talking about."

Before the Senate panel, Richard Bissell, once the CIA wunderkind now in private industry, defended his old boss Dulles. "I went on the assumption that, in a matter of this sensitivity, the Director would handle higher level clearances," he said, confident that Dulles told the White House. "By clearance, I mean authorization . . . .I left the question of advising senior officers of the government and obtaining clearances in Allen Dulles' hands."

Bissell fell on the grenade, admitting he'd seconded the involvement of Mafia figures in the ill-fated Castro conspiracy. He claimed Dulles told JFK about the Bay of Pigs invasion plans, but not armed assassins against Castro. "I think that in hindsight it could be regarded as peculiar, yes," Bissell conceded about this upside-down chain of command.

Maj. General Edward Lansdale, a one-time Kennedy favorite involved with "Operation Mongoose," denied any White House conversations about killing Castro. "I am very certain, Senator, that such a discussion never came up, that—neither with the

Attorney General nor with the President," Lansdale testified. "I didn't know anything on the assassination of Castro, any orders or anything like that. They were not
given to me."

Former CIA chief Richard Helms, crouched in a defensive posture, took a pass on
truth-telling. He dodged some questions, misled on others, when asked about the
higher-ups who knew about the Castro killing plan.

Privately, Helms had told then-Secretary of State Henry Kissinger that Robert Kennedy had "personally managed the operation on the assassination of Castro." But
under oath, Helms dissembled constantly before the dreaded Church inquisitors.
The Senate panel concluded Helms showed "a grave error in judgment" by keeping
the scheme with the two mobsters a secret from his earlier boss, John McCone.

As more top-secret CIA information became known, Helms fell into deeper trouble. He eventually pled guilty ("*nolo contendere*," to be precise) in 1977 to lying to
another Senate panel about the CIA's plans to kill Castro and funding the overthrow
of Chile's leader Salvadore Allende, killed by a military coup in 1973.

"I had sworn my oath to protect certain secrets," explained Helms to his sentencing
federal judge about his own "plausible deniability" rationale. "I didn't want to lie. I
didn't want to mislead the Senate. I was simply trying to find my way through a difficult situation in which I found myself."

Under his plea, Helms got off with a two-year suspended sentence—which meant
no jail time—and a two thousand dollar fine that sympathetic CIA comrades helped
pay by passing the hat. (His plea deal was arranged by defense lawyer Edward Bennett
Williams—the same Washington powerhouse attorney who first introduced Robert
Maheu to Johnny Roselli and later represented Judith Campbell when she was called
to testify about Sam Giancana.)

Outside the courtroom, Helms, a true believer, told reporters he wore his conviction "like a badge of honor . . . I don't feel disgraced at all. I think if I had done anything else I would have been disgraced."

Helms later published a ghostwritten apologia about his life as a spy with no mention of the Mafia figures. But his most startling admission was to historian Tim
Weiner when he asserted President Kennedy wanted Castro dead. "There is nothing
on paper, of course," Helms was quoted saying in Weiner's 2007 book. "But there is
certainly no question in my mind that he [JFK] did."

The rationale was simple to Helms, who expressed it as bluntly as a gangster like Giancana or Roselli. "If you kill someone else's leaders, why shouldn't they kill yours?"

In April 1976, the Senate panel's wishful thinking that Roselli, in his third round of testimony, would be forthcoming came up empty. Staff investigator Michael Epstein wanted their cooperative mobster to tell as much about an outside conspiracy with the JFK assassination as he testified previously about the CIA's planned demise of Castro. Some thought Roselli might be the key to unraveling a conspiracy, if one truly existed.

But as this new secret hearing began, with different lawyers by his side, Johnny would have none of it.

EPSTEIN: Mr. Roselli, the main reason why we have asked you to come back before the Committee is to give testimony that relates to information that the Cuban Government, or persons connected with Premier Castro, planned to assassinate President Kennedy in retaliation for the United States Government's plot to assassinate him. And I would like to put that issue to you in an open-ended way, and ask you to share whatever facts you can that bear on the subject.

ROSELLI: That is not true—it has never happened.

After this stunning start, Roselli admitted he did have an opinion about who shot Kennedy—just like "200 million different views that the American public has." He acknowledged talking to Bob Maheu about the possibility that Castro might be behind JFK's death but then quickly added he had "no facts," no firsthand knowledge. Just an opinion, he stressed.

Johnny clearly had a change of heart. He was now much more circumspect about his testimony. When asked about Pearson's 1967 column, Roselli claimed, "I never read it, and that's the first I heard of it"—even though he obviously was its main source.

Under oath, he had no insight about why his good friend Sam Giancana was killed. He claimed not to have spoken to Giancana in years.

EPSTEIN: Do you have any information bearing upon whether or not his death related in any way to these plots?

ROSELLI: I wouldn't know that.

As if he had been scared or warned, Roselli's testimony was full of obvious lies and deceptions. One whopper was his claim he'd never met a Cuban exile upset with JFK after the Bay of Pigs fiasco. Indeed, nearly everyone in South Florida—from Tony Varona to the CIA gringos like Bill Harvey—was upset with Kennedy when Roselli conducted anti-Castro missions there in 1962.

Slowly, the Senate inquiry provided glimpses of Roselli's divided loyalties as a spy and a mobster. His carefully parsed answers revealed how far he was willing to go in providing information to his country—a man who claimed to be a patriotic spy without being considered a snitch.

If Roselli did have proof of a conspiracy against the president, he testified, "I would have gone to the CIA immediately . . . . I would know my obligations and I would do it because I still feel for, you know, [wouldn't] stand for a thing like this."

Yet Roselli's ultimate loyalty was to the Mafia, especially Santo Trafficante, his main connection to *La Cosa Nostra's* national commission now that Giancana was dead. In testimony, Roselli minimized their involvement and swore he used Trafficante only as a Spanish interpreter "once or twice" during his CIA tenure.

Previously, Johnny had referred to Trafficante as "X," as a way of not dragging the Florida don into this fray. But during the course of these Senate hearings, other witnesses mentioned Trafficante's name—which undoubtedly made him unhappy.

Despite Roselli's sworn responses to the US Senate, Johnny gave a far different answer in private about Trafficante. To his hitman pal Jimmy Fratianno, Roselli wondered if Trafficante had been a conniving double agent for Castro all along, sabotaging the CIA's assassination attempts. Roselli said both Giancana and their mutual friend, Joe Shimon, had harbored the same doubts.

"Remember when Santo was jailed and they grabbed his money when Castro came into power, then suddenly he was released with all his money?" Roselli told Fratianno, recalling Trafficante's brief imprisonment after the 1959 Cuban revolution, when he somehow evaded the firing squad. "Shimon thinks he's a Castro agent spying on Cubans in Florida. Sam shared that suspicion. That's why Santo sat on his ass and did nothing with all that shit we gave him. He was probably reporting everything to Castro's agents, and Miami's full of them."

Giancana's doubts about Trafficante were voiced to Johnny when they talked about his Senate subpoena in 1975, just before Sam's murder. (This too was contrary to Roselli's testimony that they'd not spoken in years.)

"I remember Sam telling me when he got his subpoena," Johnny told Fratianno. "He said, 'Santo's shitting in his pants, but you can't keep his name out of it. I introduced the guy to the CIA, for Christ's sake. Everybody knows it. Maheu, Shimon, you, the whole FBI and CIA. This Santo's crazy to think we can stop his name from surfacing.'"

These Trafficante warnings increasingly made sense to him. With Giancana's ghostly words ringing in his ears, Johnny wrapped up his Senate testimony.

Back in the oppressive humid air of Florida's summer, Roselli tried to convince family, friends, and himself that everything would be fine, light, and breezy.

"Will you stop worrying? I'm all right," he assured. "Everything's under control."

In Washington, Johnny never got his deal. There would be no governmental grace, no reprieve from the trumped-up deportation order against him in exchange for his testimony full of lies and half-truths. Church told his dubious bipartisan Senate panel that no special arrangements were made with the gangster "other than a reasonable accommodation for his own personal safety."

On his way out, Roselli guaranteed to Senate investigators that his testimony would be kept top-secret. They said his mob tormentors would never find out.

Roselli knew such promises were worthless. He'd already learned that lesson the hard way. Somehow, his 1972 grand jury testimony in the Frontier Casino Hotel case had leaked, enough so that the nation's top Mafia leaders, particularly Tony Accardo, were aware of his snitching. Detroit mobster Anthony Zerilli was still in federal prison, furious about his Frontier case conviction.

Johnny also knew his attempt to keep Santo Trafficante's name out of the assassination talk in the Senate had failed miserably. "It's no secret in the underworld that Trafficante detests publicity," Jack Anderson later explained.

Though initially identified as "X," the cumulative Senate testimony put a spotlight on Trafficante, exposing his extensive network of armed Cuban exiles in Florida and treacherous double agents in Fidel Castro's Cuba.

Word went out about Trafficante's intent for revenge.

"Get out of Miami—you're in serious danger," Johnny's lobbyist friend, Fred Black, warned in a call from Los Angeles. "The Cubans are after you."

Contrite and now extremely cautious, Johnny attempted to put his affairs in order. He philosophized about life, looking for redemption. He seemed desperate for an escape clause from organized crime and a looming fate that seemed unavoidable.

"If I had known as a kid what I was getting into, I wouldn't have come close to this thing [La Cosa Nostra]," he said with remorse. "The less I see of our [Mafia] guys the better I like it, you know. I don't want to be seen with them."

Memories of Hollywood were stirred in Florida when Roselli accidentally bumped into producer Bryan Foy, his old friend who gave him a job as a B-movie "producer" after Johnny left prison in the 1940s extortion case. Foy's last film had been *PT-109*, the 1963 Kennedy-approved drama about JFK's heroic Navy time in the Pacific.

Roselli tried to interest Foy in a new film. The plot would revolve around a patriotic gangster in a CIA plot to kill Castro who gets caught up in the Kennedy assassination. Foy dismissed the idea as too fanciful for an audience.

For a short visit, Johnny flew to California, attending a Palm Springs testimonial hosted by Frank Sinatra. During this trip, he also met with another old friend, a Catholic priest named Joseph Clark, who ran LA-based charities to which Foy and Roselli once contributed, back when Johnny had money. Now Roselli had even deeper concerns.

For the first time as an adult, Roselli offered his confession to a priest. During his life of crime, all the killings and heinous acts he committed seemed to carry no moral consequence, as if he subscribed to a "just war" theory among Mafioso—a "kill-or-be-killed" approach in which murder was just part of the job.

At the Friars Club, Roselli told an acquaintance that "he would like to go back to the church" and would "like to make his peace with God," according to a FBI memo otherwise obsessed with Johnny's earthly schemes.

There seemed an odd contradiction about a lifelong gangster now asking for absolution, wiping clean his catalogue of his horrendous sins in the eyes of God, so he wouldn't face punishment in an afterlife.

Historically, the connection of Mafia figures to the Roman Catholic Church was both traditional and tribal, a bridge between the sacred and profane. Sam Giancana, who understood the accoutrements of power, paid for a fancy altar at the parish where his deceased wife Angeline once worshipped. Giancana even arranged for his photo to be taken with Pope Pius XII during a private papal audience in Rome. The gunman who took Sam's life presumably didn't allow for any sacrament of penance.

But to friends of Roselli, this last attempt at atonement was sincere. He often attended mass and was known for small acts of charity. Although a hoodlum, Johnny had been always capable of surprising moments of tenderness and empathy. Confession seemed fitting for a man who, during an earlier existential crisis, renamed himself for Cosimo Rosselli, the Italian painter who helped beautify the walls of the Vatican's Sistine Chapel.

There would be no absolving of sins in the secular world, however. Unlike those government bureaucrats with their homicidal schemes, there was no "plausible deniability" for Johnny. He either took the Fifth and went to jail or, as rumored among the mob, he became a reluctant informer and took his chances with the consequences.

Upon his return to Florida, Roselli decided to see Trafficante once more.

For two decades, Santo had treated him as a friend. Their rapport started in the 1950s at the luxuriant Sans Souci in Havana, when the Chicago Outfit with Trafficante and his Miami ally, Meyer Lansky, made a fortune running the tropical casinos together.

In his own stoic way in the early 1960s, Trafficante seemed committed to the anti-Castro plot. He helped arrange the poison pills transported by their Cuban exile friends, such as Tony Varona in Miami. Even when Giancana later expressed doubts about Trafficante's allegiances, Johnny considered Santo a reliable friend. Most notably, Trafficante generously offered financial help to Roselli's sister, Edith Daigle, when he was in prison.

On July 16, 1976, Johnny went to dinner at a Fort Lauderdale seafood restaurant with Trafficante and his wife Josie. Roselli's sister, Edith, and their visiting nephew from New Jersey joined them. The mood was pleasant and respectful. The two older men chatted but, as Edith later recalled, "there was no business discussed."

Johnny evidently felt he could make amends with Trafficante. After all, it seemed unlikely the Florida don would invite his wife to a dinner with a man he intended to murder.

For several months, Trafficante had gone into hiding in Costa Rica to avoid the Senate hearings. If he was still angry with Roselli, though, Trafficante's bravura performance gave no hint of it.

Several days later, on June 28, Johnny borrowed Edith's car in the afternoon, apparently to go play a round of golf before sunset. When he didn't return that evening, Edith alerted her husband.

Joe Daigle drove around the Fort Lauderdale area, searching for Roselli and the car. He remembered Johnny's joke ("If I'm ever missing, check the airports"). Daigle drove to the Fort Lauderdale airport without any luck.

However, Johnny's brother-in-law then went to Miami International, where Daigle discovered the family's silver Impala parked on the third-floor parking lot.

When he looked into the car, he found golf clubs—but no sign of Johnny.

CHAPTER 48:

THE LAST ONE STANDING

"Find out who's still alive and you'll find the killer."

—SAM GIANCANA

Howard Baker was shocked by the lethal consequences of the Senate's CIA hearings.

The soft-spoken Tennessee Republican had become famous as the conscientious voice of the Senate's 1973 Watergate hearings. His questions helped lead to the ouster of the most powerful man in the world, President Richard Nixon, without any violence or bloody revolution.

Yet with the Senate's CIA probe, what happened with two key witnesses—the murder of Sam Giancana *before* he could testify and now the disappearance of Johnny Roselli *after* he did—left Baker dumbfounded.

At first, Baker assumed Roselli fled the country, to avoid any further questioning. "I got the impression he was not telling us all he knew," Baker explained about Roselli's previous testimony. "He was visibly shaken by (Giancana's) murder, hence all the security precautions." Johnny told the Senator that he feared for "his safety and his life" by testifying.

Shortly after Roselli was reported missing, Baker alerted the FBI and US attorney general, asking for federal intervention. He said the Senate had "a continuing interest" in Roselli and "felt there may be a possible Obstruction of Justice" charge because of his disappearance, according to an August 3, 1976, FBI memo.

Something more sinister was afoot, however.

After interviewing Johnny's family in Florida, FBI agents sent a memo to Washington headquarters, indicating Roselli may have been killed rather than taken flight, as the Chevy Impala parked at Miami International suggested. It said the Daigles "felt that Roselli's previous hoodlum activities, plus being publicly identified with an alleged plot to assassinate Fidel Castro, could have been a contributing factor to Roselli's disappearance." Everyone worried where Johnny might be.

Finally, on August 7, the remains of Roselli came gurgling up in Dumfoundling Bay—not far from the Fontainebleau Hotel where he and Sam Giancana began their CIA murder scheme against Castro more than a decade earlier.

Johnny's body was found in a leaky fifty-five-gallon oil drum, washed up along the shallow waterways in North Miami. The silver-haired Mafioso had been strangled and stabbed. His legs were sawed off.

Assassins stuffed his remains inside the barrel, weighed down by heavy chains. They dumped it into the murky waters, assumedly never to be seen again. Gases from his decomposing body, though, caused the buried barrel to rise to the surface.

The floating drum was spotted by fishermen, aghast at the sight of human limbs hanging out of its gaping holes. Local police immediately launched a homicide investigation, eventually aided by the FBI. Try as they might, however, authorities never found Roselli's killers.

The long journey of Filippo Sacco—an Italian immigrant who renamed himself as "Johnny Roselli," becoming a powerful Mafia figure in Hollywood and Las Vegas, and whose CIA espionage case caused tremors throughout the American and Cuban governments—had ended in a most ignominious way. He died as a patriot, at least by his own estimate, on the run from his enemies.

Roselli's sister decided on a small funeral. Few were in attendance to say good-bye to "Handsome Johnny," the life of the party. Unlike Giancana, his remains were placed in a cardboard coffin rather than some granite mausoleum, hoping to draw as little attention as possible. Nevertheless, the gruesome, sensational circumstances surrounding Roselli's murder attracted national headlines.

"Deep Six for Johnny," blared a *Time* magazine headline. A front-page *New York Times* story declared Roselli had been killed "as a direct result of his testimony before the Senate committee" about the CIA as well as President Kennedy's death. Jack Anderson, who had been preparing a column about Johnny's disappearance when his body bobbed up in the bay, lamented: "Mafia mobster John Roselli may have taken the secret of the John F. Kennedy assassination with him to his death."

Roselli's killing also compounded the mystery surrounding the death of Giancana.

In dealing with other murder mysteries, Giancana's brother later recalled, Sam would invoke the old Mafia adage to "find out who's still alive and you'll find the killer." Using this "last one standing" logic, Chuck Giancana pointed at Santo Trafficante Jr., the other Mafioso in the CIA scheme.

But while the underworld was a likely suspect, Sam's eldest daughter, Antoinette, also suggested others. "Was it the Central Intelligence Agency?" she wondered in her memoir. "Had they sent an assassin, someone close to Johnny Roselli, whom Dad did like and trusted enough to work with him in the plots to eliminate Fidel Castro? Were they afraid that Sam might say too much?"

One thing was certain. By the time of their unsolved homicides, most of Sam and Johnny's associates were already dead or muttering good riddance to them.

"All I know is that Roselli used a lot of people for his own advantage—there's no way to know how far he'd go," said Robert Maheu. In an act of apparent self-preservation, Maheu had long ago distanced himself from the two mobsters.

Unlike other CIA figures whose careers or reputations were severely damaged by the Cuban operation—notably William Harvey, Richard Helms, John McCone, Richard Bissell, and the ultimate spymaster Allen Dulles—Maheu had prospered as a kind of double agent, working for the agency while looking out for the private interests of Howard Hughes.

"I am one of the last people left who knows what really went on during the operation to assassinate Fidel Castro," Maheu boasted in his own ghostwritten book two decades later. "A lot of people involved died pretty suddenly. Maybe just a co-incidence . . . maybe not. They decided to cut him [Roselli] in pieces. They stuck his foot in his mouth, wrapped his legs around his head, and then sank him in a steel drum. I'm not sure how I want to go, but I am certain that I want my body to be in one piece when I do."

Maheu managed to be one of the last ones standing, dying at the ripe old age of ninety in 2008. He, too, considered himself a patriot, a well-intentioned go-between for America's spy agency, though with lingering regrets. "I wish to God I'd never been involved in it [the Castro assassination plot]," he concluded. "It was the right choice at the time . . . but the wrong choice looking back. The truth is buried in a lot of graves."

Despite many unanswered questions, the Senate revelations about Giancana and Roselli's covert work for the CIA did expose one undeniable fact—political assassination as the darkest tool of spycraft for America.

The Church panel examined the CIA lab's handiwork in creating all sort of poisons, guns, exploding cigars and seashells, contaminated scuba gear, and lethal James Bond-like gadgets designed to liquidate Castro. This tawdry display of murderment was apparently what Helms meant when he forewarned, "A lot of dead cats will come out."

Frustrated Senate investigators quizzed the CIA about why "pertinent files do not contain more documents dated during the 1960 through 1963 period relating to the Castro assassination attempt." But the agency offered a compelling rationale for safeguarding its deepest secrets.

"There were a lot of Cubans who worked with the Americans to free Cuba," the CIA explained in a 1977 memo. "They carried their plans to desperate extremes, risking their lives at the Bay of Pigs and in hundreds of smaller incursions. Some were associated with scheming to assassinate Castro himself; some did this on their own as patriots; and some, also as patriots, did it with the support of representatives of the United States government. Right or wrong, the identity of those people constitute [sic] a trust of the American Government. If betrayed it would be a breach of honor and a demonstration to our allies today, and to those individuals around the world who work with us, that they must review the risk they take in our association."

Those on the Senate Intelligence Committee, such as Howard Baker, prized for his judiciousness, came away with strong suspicions that both Eisenhower and John F. Kennedy approved of these killing plans. "It is my personal view that on balance the likelihood that presidents knew of the (Castro) assassination plots is greater than the likelihood that they did not," Baker concluded.

In its final report, the Church committee couldn't say for sure how high the Mafia-CIA murder scheme went within the US government. But evidence of "get Castro" campaigns and questionable legal tactics caused historians to reassess JFK and Robert Kennedy—the hawkish attorney general who became a liberal Senator from New York, assassinated during his 1968 run for the presidency. Violence played such a fateful deciding factor in the Kennedy family history that it seemed hard to imagine, in retrospect, that the two Kennedy brothers were in power during America's first known assassination scheme against a foreign leader.

While friends and former colleagues, like Arthur Schlesinger, vigorously defended the fabled Camelot legacy, other admirers were at a loss to excuse Robert Kennedy's covert actions against Cuba. "Knowledge of the links among his brother, the Mafia and the CIA's Castro assassination plans would forever stain John Kennedy's reputation," judged historian Ronald Steel. "Exactly how directly involved the Kennedys were in these activities remains a matter of contention. But there is a compelling trail of circumstantial evidence."

For a half-century, this shroud of "plausible deniability" extended to virtually all top decision-makers in the Castro murder plot.

Finally, with the 2007 release of its top-secret "Family Jewels" documents, the CIA admitted Allen Dulles "was briefed and gave his approval" for the Mafia's homicidal hand with Castro. The agency described Giancana and Roselli as "assets" in its "sensitive mission requiring gangster-type action" against Castro. Yet the "Family Jewels" never clarified exactly what Eisenhower, JFK, and his brother knew about the Castro assassination plans either.

This lack of definitive proof blurred an even larger American debate about killing political opponents abroad.

In the wake of the Church hearings, President Gerald Ford issued a 1976 executive order banning political assassination, condemning the practice. Over time, however, such White House absolutes would prove malleable. Indeed, history would reveal Ford's then-aide, Richard Cheney, had prevented an earlier CIA commission, looking at domestic spying, from disclosing the same assassination plans against Castro eventually revealed by the Church panel.

Even among some Kennedy liberals, a realpolitik debate existed about political assassination. "If somebody had knocked off Hitler in 1936 or 1937, I think it would have been a big help," conceded Nicholas deB. Katzenbach, a former top Justice Department official in the Kennedy administration, in 1975.

For a generation, subsequent presidents abided by this ban on foreign assassination until the terror attacks of September 11, 2001. Like the Cold War fears of the 1960s, America suddenly placed security concerns above all. The CIA created an assassination squad against Al-Queda leaders at the urging of a familiar White House figure, Vice President Dick Cheney. Eight years passed until this hit squad's existence was revealed publicly in 2009.

Once more, America debated political assassination. Its leaders were now armed with ever more sophisticated high-tech killing devices—such as drones, spray devices, and biological and radiological elements that can kill without a trace.

"Does the United States want to return to this era of uncertainty?" wrote former presidential advisers Mark Medish and Joel McCleary in 2010, recalling the CIA's Castro murder scheme. "Do democratically elected leaders wish to open this bloody door again, when in fact their own protection is as porous and precarious as ever? Technology has made assassination, as well as escalatory and asymmetrical reprisals, easier than ever for both the geese and the ganders."

In the mind of the American public, however, the most lasting impact of Giancana and Roselli and their CIA conspiracy involved the nagging doubts about JFK's assassination.

During the 1970s, the national post-Watergate mood of paranoia and distrust in government contributed to well-publicized fears that Kennedy hadn't been killed by a lone assassin named Lee Harvey Oswald but rather by an orchestrated conspiracy. (A 2013 Gallup poll showed 61 percent still rejected the lone gunman theory.)

For months, Congress debated whether to reexamine the Warren Commission's findings. Shortly after Roselli's shocking murder, the House agreed to create a Select Committee on Assassinations, looking at questions of a criminal conspiracy surrounding both President Kennedy's 1963 murder and the killing of Rev. Dr. Martin Luther King in 1968. "It is awfully unusual for these people (Giancana and Roselli) to be erased before anyone has a chance to interview them," said Rep. Thomas N. Downing, the House committee's initial chairman.

Over the next several months, the House committee called numerous witnesses. The names of Giancana and Roselli, *in absentia*, came up repeatedly.

Former CIA chief Richard Helms conceded he never told the Warren Commission about the two mobsters recruited for the Castro plot. "I didn't inform them of those things, but they had among them as members Mr. Allen Dulles, who was certainly aware of what had been going on with respect to Cuba," Helms explained.

Katzenbach testified he didn't know about the Mafia-Castro plot when he relayed Bobby Kennedy's suggestion that Dulles be placed on the Warren Commission. "Perhaps naively, but I thought that the appointment of Allen Dulles to the Commission would ensure that the Commission had access to anything that the CIA had,"

Katzenbach admitted. "I am astounded to this day that Mr. Dulles did not at least make that information available to the other commissioners."

Even former President Gerald Ford, once a Warren commissioner, seemed astonished that Dulles never revealed to the panel what he knew.

"He certainly should have because of his previous responsibilities," Ford recalled in 2003 about the Castro subterfuge. "At the time we thought we did a thorough job. Whether we slipped up on this particular aspect, history can only come up to its own conclusion."

In its final report, the House panel claimed JFK "was probably assassinated as a result of a conspiracy" and that evidence showed "a high probability that two gunmen fired at" Kennedy—as if confirming the public's long-held nightmare about its martyred president.

But the House committee had a hard time finding any concrete proof or putting a finger on any culprits beyond Oswald who fatally wounded the president. The panel ruled out as suspects both the Cuban and Russian governments as well as, for that matter, the CIA.

Rather than finding clear-cut answers, the House panel was better at finding fault—particularly with the subsequent murder investigation and the security surrounding Kennedy in Dallas. Perhaps the biggest flaw it found was the decision by both the CIA and FBI to keep a lid on the multiple Castro assassination attempts by Johnny, Sam, and their Cuban exile conspirators.

"The plots, in short, should have been made known to the Warren Commission," the report said. "If they had been investigated in 1964, they might have provided insights into what happened in Dallas and resolved questions that have persisted."

If ever an answer emerged to 'Who killed JFK?" the report suggested, it would likely start by looking at individual anti-Castro Cubans or individual members of organized crime. And the living nexus of those two groups was another last man standing—Santo Trafficante Jr.

After their frightening demise, the star-crossed conspiracy of Sam Giancana and Johnny Roselli against Cuban leader Fidel Castro, once wrapped in flag-waving and CIA intrigue, now seemed like the kiss of death for others in their orbit.

Chuckie Nicoletti, a Chicago associate of the two mobsters, faced a similar fate. In March 1977, he was called by the House Select Committee on Assassinations, looking to quiz him about JFK's murder. Nicoletti, a seasoned Windy City hitman nicknamed "The Butcher," helped plan logistics against Castro in the early 1960s.

Over time, though, Nicoletti became upset with his business partners, the "Cuban Mafia"—a term he used for the exiles associated with Trafficante in gunrunning and drug trade. The Cuban mobsters slowly displaced Giancana's Chicago hoodlums in this illegal trade while the CIA supposedly looked the other way in the interest of stopping Communism.

House investigators wanted Nicoletti to explain more on the witness stand, hoping for possible leads to a JFK conspiracy. But "The Butcher" never showed up.

Sitting in his Oldsmobile, a vehicle customized with special places to hide guns and switches to cover its rear lights, Nicoletti was shot three times in the head outside a Chicago restaurant. It happened the same day the House was arranging for Nicoletti's testimony.

With the gunfire, Chuckie's husky body fell onto the car's accelerator. It caused the Olds to catch fire and explode, eliminating all clues. His murder remained unsolved.

"It seems like every time somebody important turns up," a House staffer complained, "he turns up dead."

Those in the Chicago Outfit, glad to be rid of Giancana as boss, laughingly referred to another unsolved murder—the floating Florida barrel with Roselli's body in it—as "Johnny in a drum." Police detectives said Chicago mob bosses had authorized Trafficante to get rid of Roselli, but his henchmen proved incompetent. Overheard later on an approved government listening device, Chicago hitman Joey Aiuppa summed up Roselli's botched liquidation in purely professional terms: "Trafficante had the job and he messed it up."

Trafficante, however, was far from a bungler. Like a master spy, he acted as a double agent "playing both sides" between the CIA and the Mafia, government investigators eventually determined.

During the CIA's 1960s attempts against the Cuban leader, Trafficante never exposed his conflicting loyalties. He also never upset the bolita business or narcotics trafficking that depended upon Castro's cooperation.

Throughout the 1970s, Trafficante worked hard to avoid testifying with a House appearance, just as he'd done with the Senate subpoena. Eventually, federal agents found him at home.

When they knocked on his door, a grumpy voice could be heard inside the house, asking warily about the visitors' intent. The feds explained they were serving a subpoena. Trafficante accepted it but instructed them to leave the court papers on a bench near his front door.

Reluctantly the feds did so and then watched from a distance on the street. The Mafia don emerged cautiously. He slowly picked up the papers, and then went inside again and closed the door.

House investigators wanted to cross-examine Trafficante about his CIA activities with Giancana and Roselli, but also his purported threat toward President Kennedy.

The most sensational information came from Jose Aleman, a well-connected anti-Castro Cuban turned FBI informant. Aleman remembered Trafficante's ominous threat in 1962. "Mark my words, this man [John] Kennedy is in trouble, and he will get what is coming to him. . . . He is going to be hit," Trafficante warned, according to a statement Aleman gave privately to investigators.

As an assassination witness, Aleman brought impressive credentials. He'd collaborated with Roselli, Maheu, and Trafficante on the plot to kill Castro in 1961 and held a rallying meeting for their killing plans at his Miami residence. Aleman was also a close friend of Rolando Cubela Secades, the would-be Castro assassin codenamed AMLASH who in 1963 received the makeshift CIA poison pen weapon on the same day JFK was shot.

But when called to testify publicly before the House, Aleman offered a very different version. According to the House report, Aleman said he feared for his life—"afraid of possible reprisal from Trafficante or his organization"—and asked for government protection. He also backed off about the JFK threat by Trafficante. On the stand, Aleman now claimed it was "his impression that Trafficante may have only meant the President was going to be hit by 'a lot of Republican votes' in the 1964 election, not that he was going to be assassinated."

Aleman would be haunted by fear for the rest of days. "He was convinced the Mafia was after him," recalled his friend Eugenio Martinez, later arrested as one of the Watergate burglars. "He trusted very few people." Five years later, Aleman killed himself during a wild police shootout at his home.

When Trafficante finally appeared before the House in September 1978, he gave a carefully staged performance under immunity, a potpourri of lies and deception that left House investigators wondering what might really be the truth.

For starters, Trafficante refuted Aleman's claim that he spoke about the JFK assassination before it happened or had any hand in that event.

"I never made the statement that Kennedy was going to get hit, because all the discussion I made with Mr. Aleman, as sure as I am sitting here, I spoke to him in Spanish," Trafficante claimed. "There was no reason for me to tell him in English that Kennedy is going to get shot. I deny that I made that statement."

Careful not to perjure himself, Trafficante downplayed his part in the CIA's Castro assassination plans and said he had no idea why Giancana and Roselli were killed. He hazily admitted going to dinner with Johnny—along with Trafficante's wife and Roselli's sister—two weeks before his murder.

"I don't remember what we discussed," Trafficante said, barely taxing his memory. "We didn't discuss nothing about Castro, that's for sure."

By always being guarded—staying in the shadows, tending to his money, travelling under an alias and never being flashy—Trafficante prospered in a world full of risk until 1987, when his heart gave out at age seventy-two. "I've been a gambler all my life," he told investigators. "I'm used to taking chances."

His own lawyer, Frank Ragano, later admitted Trafficante's "unilluminating" House testimony was "a recital of evasive answers." With so many dead witnesses and dead-end leads, investigators found little to link Trafficante to the murders of Giancana and Roselli or to the JFK assassination.

"One fact, however, was indisputable: Santo Trafficante was the only survivor of the three mobsters recruited by the CIA to kill Fidel Castro," Ragano said about his still-standing client.

In their later years, when Frank Sinatra visited Florida to perform, it was Trafficante whom the FBI spotted in the audience, just like they once did with Sam and Johnny. During the 1970s Congressional investigations, Sinatra had managed to avoid testifying about his '60s fling with Judy Campbell and nocturnal activities with Sam, Johnny, and the president.

"We are left to ponder what might have been learned if only 'Old Blue-Eyes' could have been required to sing," lamented New York Times columnist William Safire. In the 1980s, by denying any past contacts with the Mafia, Sinatra not only survived but also regained his Nevada gaming license with support from his new presidential friend, Ronald Reagan.

Despite his voluminous FBI file, Sinatra claimed his friendships with mobsters like Sam Giancana and Johnny Roselli were more rumors than fact. "Sure, I knew some of those guys," Sinatra said, before he passed away in 1998. "And it doesn't matter anymore, does it? Most of the guys I knew, or met, are dead."

The sexual intrigue exuding from the Castro assassination plot became a permanent part of the American dialogue. Upon the 1999 passing of Judith Campbell Exner, Safire couldn't help thinking about the old Camelot scandal amidst a new controversy involving the existing president, Bill Clinton, with a starry-eyed young woman interning at the White House.

"This nexus of politics, covert action, show biz and organized crime was indisputably news," Safire said of the Jack, Judy, Sam, and Johnny affair. "Its unfortunate long-term fallout: Because sex was central to the story, the coverage opened the door to later intrusions into the private lives of public figures, whether involving crimes or not."

Indeed, many of these shady themes—from spies to sexual compromises—would be later reprised during the Trump administration in all its tawdry spectacle.

With more than a little irony, the target of the CIA's wrath, Fidel Castro, lasted the longest.

The number of assassination attempts on Castro—America's bête noire for more than a half century and the despot responsible for the deaths of thousands of his own countrymen—varies according to who's doing the counting. They range from at least eight officially (including the Mafia escapade acknowledged by the CIA) to more than six hundred attempts unofficially, alleged by Castro's partisans.

The fundamental reason why Castro survived was counterespionage—first learned at the hand of Soviet master spies and enforced domestically with a brutality that would make a killer like Giancana blush. Many CIA double agents inside Cuba found their fate at the end of a gun, in a hellacious prison, or were left in a ditch. Even those agency "moles" who survived were not as they seemed.

Starting in 1961, Cuba's intelligence service ferreted out and flipped thirty-eight CIA spies within Cuba—virtually every double agent planted within its borders.

These disloyal informers served up a steady diet of disinformation to Washington. It was a stunning feat of counterespionage that top CIA officials didn't realize until a Cuban defector revealed it in June 1987.

The defecting spy, Maj. Florentino Aspillaga Lombard of the Cuban Directorate of Intelligence (DGI), described how Castro, a self-proclaimed Marxist socialist, had accumulated a secret private fortune like any greedy Russian kleptocrat. He said Castro's treasures included a $4.2 million Swiss bank account as well as yachts and luxurious family homes in Cuba and Russia. (Castro was so angered by this betrayal he ordered an assassination of Aspillaga in London. The gunman fired but didn't kill him.)

However, the defector's biggest embarrassment was detailing how the CIA had been "penetrated" by Castro moles since the Bay of Pigs fiasco in 1961. Aspillaga's list of names all checked out. Somehow Dulles and a long line of American agents, often blind or patronizing to the ways of Cuban culture, had been seriously outfoxed.

But most remarkable was Castro's spying within the United States. He sent "hundreds of spies" into Florida and "infiltrated" nearly every anti-Castro exile group over the next three decades. From these agents, the Cuban dictator learned much of what his enemies planned to do against him.

"They operate as diplomats and cab drivers, dealers of guns and drugs and information," observed CIA expert Tim Weiner in 1996. "They thrive in embassies—a sizable contingent of the Cuban delegation to the United Nations do cloak-and-dagger work, United States officials say—and in the bars and restaurants of the Little Havana section of Miami."

Bill Harvey, the intuitive CIA spy who handled Roselli and the Cuban exiles based in Florida, told the Senate panel it was "quite conceivable" that the whole Castro assassination plot had been "infiltrated" by double agents all the time. After all, whose side was Juan Orta, Rolando Cubela, Marita Lorenz, Tony Varona, or even Trafficante really on? As historian and Kennedy aide Arthur M. Schlesinger later concluded, "If Trafficante was indeed a double agent, one can see why Castro survived so comfortably the ministrations of the CIA."

Late in life, Castro denied any "blowback" conspiracy theories against President Kennedy in retaliation for the assassination plots by Giancana and Roselli and other CIA operatives. Instead he slipped a few more drops of paranoia into the American psyche.

"I have reached the conclusion that Oswald could not have been the one who killed Kennedy," declared Castro, then eighty-seven years old in November 2013, the fiftieth anniversary of JFK's death. "We tried to recreate the circumstances of this shooting, but it wasn't possible for one man to do. The news I had received is that one man killed Kennedy in his car with a rifle, but I deducted that this story was manufactured to fool people."

America's obsession with Castro lasted until November 25, 2016, when he died at age ninety. The ending came not from an assassin's bullet or poison, but asleep in his bed. Just as Castro in life had ignited fierce debate within the United States, he did so once again in death.

Departing US President Barack Obama expressed sympathy, careful not to offend the Cuban government now run by Castro's brother Raul, while president-elect Donald Trump condemned Castro as "a brutal dictator," recalling the firing squads and human rights abuses. In Miami, generations of Cuban exiles—especially the Bay of Pigs veterans and their families—cheered Fidel's demise.

Obituaries and remembrances of Castro dutifully mentioned the assassination attempts against him as a maniacal pursuit that failed. Forgotten in these final tallies were the names of Johnny Roselli, Sam Giancana, and their other CIA spy co-conspirators.

"Beyond anything else, it was Mr. Castro's obsession with the United States, and America's obsession with him, that shaped his rule," concluded the *New York Times*, which originally heralded him as a liberator. The worldwide coverage was a reminder of how Castro could hold up a mirror to some of America's worst instincts as well as his own.

By then, Castro's beautiful tropical nation of Cuba seemed frozen in time. Its atrophied streets and mid-century cars appeared just as they did on New Year's 1959, when a young Fidel seized power and the Yankee gangsters soon were told to leave.

The resulting killing games between the superpower nation and the former Soviet satellite carried on for years until the Cold War crumbled and President Obama, not even born when it began, opened the door once again to American visitors.

In the end, Castro survived at a terrible cost—to his impoverished people, and to a nation ninety miles to the north that engaged in assassination attempts and moral deceit to get rid of him.

With blood on so many hands, he was truly the last one standing.

AFTERWORD

Despite its dark nature, *Mafia Spies* was a joy to research, write, and help produce as the companion book for a television project with the same name. During the research, my wife Joyce joined me in checking out locales in Las Vegas and Miami, including "Little Havana," the Fontainebleau Hotel, and former CIA facilities in Southern Florida. My sons, Taylor, Reade, and Andrew, read drafts and shared their own insights. As millennials, they wondered why Cuba was still a backward land and how Castro had managed to survive repeated assassination attempts like a "whack-a-mole" amusement park game. I am most grateful for an early reading by Rev. Raymond A. Schroth, S.J., an inspiration to a generation of Fordham journalism students. Many thanks also to author Gay Talese, who shared his old notes of a conversation with Judith Campbell Exner, and my *Newsday* colleague Mark Harrington, who edited an early draft.

In the sources cited in the Notes section, I relied on court testimony, Congressional hearing transcripts, and other available documents from the John F. Kennedy and Lyndon B. Johnson presidential libraries, the National Archives and Records Administration, the National Security Archive at George Washington University, the Mary Ferrell Foundation, the FBI's Freedom of Information Library known as "The Vault," and the online archives of the CIA. Many thanks to editors Mark Gompertz and Caroline Russomanno—as well as senior publicist Johanna Dickson—for all their help and guidance. I'm also indebted to my New York literary agent John W. Wright for his support and to my attorney Scott E. Schwimer in Beverly Hills who has worked with me for twenty years and championed the development of my previous nonfiction book *Masters of Sex* into an award-winning Showtime drama series.

In a similar vein, *Mafia Spies* began as a nonfiction book serving as the inspiration for a proposed dramatic television series with Emmy-winning showrunner Kirk Ellis. This Hollywood project started over lunch with Peter Roth, President and Chief Content Officer of Warner Bros. Television Group, and his gifted Senior Vice

President, Jennifer Littlehales. With a proverbial handshake, we agreed on a television project based on a book that I wanted to write. Both Peter and Jennifer were a constant source of great support and encouragement along the way. Warner executives Leigh London Redman, Jennifer Robinson, Clancy Collins White, and Stephanie Groves were also tremendously gracious.

All of the people mentioned above deserve to have this book dedicated in their names. But for their many years of love and encouragement, "Joyce and her boys, the best gang of all" seems the most fitting.

—Thomas Maier, Long Island, New York, April 2019

NOTES

ABBREVIATIONS

NARA—National Archives and Records Administration.
HSCA—House Select Committee on Assassinations
SSCI—Senate Select Committee on Intelligence.
FBI—Federal Bureau of Investigation, "Vault" of Files Released Under Freedom of
    Information Act.
CREST—CIA Records Search Tool
JFK2017—documents released in part or in full under JFK Assassination Records
        Collection Act, added to NARA's public database in 2017.
NYT—The New York Times.
WP—The Washington Post.
CT—Chicago Tribune.

PHASE I: PLAN OF ACTION

"There is nothing more necessary than good intelligence": Washington, George.
"The Writings of George Washington: pt. I. Official letters relating to the French war,
and private letters before the American revolution: March, 1754 May, 1775." Cambridge:
Folsom, Wells, and Thurston, 1834–1837, p. 122. "There are a lot of killers": Tatum,
Sophie. "Trump Defends Putin: 'You think our country's so innocent?'" CNN Politics,
February 6, 2017.

CHAPTER 1

"When everyone is dead": Kipling, Rudyard. "Kim". New York: Penguin Books, 1994,
p. 192. "Congressional hearing": Martin, David C., "Rosselli Arrives to Testify," The Associated Press, June 24, 1975. "Poison pills:": In 2007, the CIA released a series of reports,
compiled in the early 1970s and known as "The Family Jewels," detailing various covert
activities, including "gangster-type action" and assassination plots against Fidel Castro.
CREST: 0001451843. In 2017, another extensive account was released, detailing the
activities of Roselli, Giancana, and associates, contained in the May 23, 1967, CIA Inspector General's "Report on Plots to Assassinate Fidel Castro," JFK2017:104-10213-10101.
"To assassinate Castro": Testimony of John Roselli, June 24, 1975, NARA: 157-10014-
1000, p. 12. "Who'd want to kill an old man like me?": Gage, Nicholas. "Mafia Said to
Have Slain Rosselli Because of His Senate Testimony; Mafia Reported to Have Murdered
Rosselli Because He Testified Without Its Approval," NYT, February 25, 1977. "A damned
Murder Inc." and "It will all come out one day": Holland, Max. "The Assassination
Tapes," The Atlantic, June 2004. "The documents show": Kessler, Glenn. "Trying to Kill
Fidel Castro, The Washington Post, June 27, 2007.

CHAPTER 2

"Intelligence is probably the least understood": Dulles, Allen. The Craft of Intelligence: America's Legendary Spy Master on the Fundamentals of Intelligence Gathering for a Free World." Guilford, Connecticut: Lyons Press, 2016, p. 39. **"Here is one of the most peculiar types"**: Lathrop, Charles. "The Literary Spy," New Haven: Yale University Press, 2004, p. 111. **"Its mystery and folk wisdom"**: Grose, Peter. "Gentleman Spy: The Life of Allen Dulles," Boston: University of Massachusetts Press, 1996, p. 18. **"There are few archbishops in espionage"**: Weiner, Tim. "Legacy of Ashes: The History of the CIA" New York: Knopf Doubleday, 2008, p. 632. **"Dulles was a master of bureaucratic infighting"**: Powers, Thomas. "The Man Who Kept the Secrets: Richard Helms and the CIA," New York: Knopf, 1979, pp. 82–83. **"Allen was genial in the extreme"**: Weiner, Tim. "Legacy of Ashes: The History of the CIA," New York: Doubleday, p. 26. **"I don't feel I deserve as good a wife as I have"**: Kinzer, Stephen, "The Brothers: John Foster Dulles, Allen Dulles, and Their Secret World War," New York: Times Books, 2013, p. 44. **"We can let the work cover the romance"**: Bancroft, Mary. "Autobiography of a Spy," New York: Morrow, p. 137. Also in, Hodgson, Godfrey. "Obituary: Mary Bancroft," The Independent in London, February 17, 1997. **"bomber gap"**: Divine, Robert A. "The Sputnik Challenge" Oxford University Press, USA, 1993, pp. 174, 44, 66. **"if Castro was a Communist or not"**: Ambrose, Stephen. "Eisenhower: Soldier and President" New York: Simon & Schuster, 1991, p. 516. **"The President observed that spying seems to be nothing new"**: "Foreign Relations of the United States, 1958-1960, Volume VI: Cuba," Current Section: 593. 10/17/60 - Memorandum of a Conference with the President, White House, Washington, p. 1090. **"We believed the world was a tough place"**: Slotkin, Richard. "Gunfighter Nation: The Myth of the Frontier in Twentieth-Century America," Norman: University of Oklahoma Press, 1998, p. 740.

CHAPTER 3

"Condemn me": Castro, Fidel. "The Prison Letters of Fidel Castro". New York: Nation Books, 2009. p. ix. **"The young man is larger than life"**: Editorial, NYT, April 25, 1959, p. 20. **"This man has spent the whole time scolding me"**: Official History of the Bay of Pigs Invasion, Vol III, p. 243. http://www.foia.cia.gov/sites/default/files/document_conversions/4186/bop-vol3.pdf **"We are prepared to take counter-measures"**: NYT, October 17, 1959, p. 9. **"could outfight, outrun, outswim, outride and outtalk any man in Cuba"**: Hinckle, Warren and William W. Turner, "The Fish Is Red: The Story of the Secret War Against Castro," New York: Harper & Row, 1981, pp. 8–9. **"Everyone I ever talked to about it believed it was Fidel"**: Latell, Brian. "Castro's Secrets: Cuban Intelligence, The CIA and the Assassination of John F. Kennedy," New York; Palgrave Macmillan, pp. 44–48. **"a highly effective machinery of repression"**: DeCosse, Sarah A. "Cuba's Repressive Machinery: Human Rights Forty Years After the Revolution," June 1999, summary p. 1. **"Castro will fall within six months"**: "Castro Fall Predicted," NYT, August 21, 1960, p. 4. **"Gentlemen do not read each other's mail"**: Stimson, Henry L. "On Active Service in Peace and War," New York: Harper & Brothers, 194, p. 188. **"For the first time in our history"**: Lawrence, W. H. "Kennedy Assails Castro as Enemy," The New York Times, August 27, 1960. **"thorough consideration be given to the elimination of Fidel Castro"**: Weiner, Tim. "Legacy of Ashes: The History of the CIA," New York: Doubleday, p. 216. **"Castro's regime must be overthrown"**: Bissell, Richard Jr. and Jonathan E. Lewis. "Reflections of a Cold Warrior: From Yalta to The Bay of Pigs," New Haven, Conn: Yale University Press, 1996, p. 153. **"The great problem is leakage and breach of security"**: Ibid. **"I have always felt the director should naturally assume"**: Weber, Ralph. "Spymasters: Ten CIA Officers in Their Own Words" Landham, Md.: Rowman & Littlefield, 2002, p. 35. **"Throughout Eisenhower's** period in office": Bissell, Richard. Speech given by Bissell at CIA Headquarters, 12 October 1965. (CIA approved for release on January 9, 2014). http://www.governmentattic.org/11docs /CIA-1965Bissellspeech_2014.pdf. **"gangster-type action"**: Maheu memo to Deputy Director of Central Intelligence, June 24, 1966, JFK2017:104-10133-10091, p. 1. Also, NYT. "A Plot to Assassinate Castro Was Approved by C.I.A. Director Allen Dulles," June 26, 2007. http:// washington.blogs.nytimes.com/2007/06/26/a-plot-to-assassinate-castro-was-approved-by -cia-director-allen- dulles/. **"I hoped the Mafia would achieve success"**: Bissell, Richard Jr. and Jonathan E. Lewis. "Reflections of a Cold Warrior: From Yalta to The Bay of Pigs," Yale University Press, 1996, p. 157. **"If they could do away with Castro, they would have won"**: Testimony of James P. O'Connell, US Senate Select Committee on Intelligence, NARA: 157-10002-10148, May 30, 1975, p. 94. **"The thing was to get rid of Mr. Castro"**: Ibid., p. 95. **"Get in touch with Bob Maheu"**: Ibid., p. 95.

CHAPTER 4

"Deadly poisons are often concealed under sweet honey": Douglas, Charles Noel. "Forty thousand quotations, prose and poetical; choice extracts on history, science, philosophy, religion, literature, etc. Selected from the standard authors of ancient and modern times, classified according to subject." New York: G. Sully and Co., 1917, p. 450. **"Over the years"**: CIA Inspector General's Report on Plots to Assassinate Fidel Castro, May 23, 1967, declassified 1994, p. 33. **"procurement of feminine companionship"**: CIA Biography of Robert Mahue, Oct 4, 1973, NARA:104-10122-10279, p. 3. **"honey trap"**: Maheu, Robert and Richard Hack. "Next to Hughes": New York: HarperCollins, 1992, pp. 71–75. **"We want you to go to bed with him"**: JFK2017:157-10004-10270; also, Locker, Ray and Ed Brackett, "JFK Files: CIA lined up actress to date with Jordan's King Hussein during visit to United States," *USA Today*, January 9, 2018. **"Though I'm no saint, I am a religious man"**: Maheu, Robert and Richard Hack. "Next to Hughes": New York: HarperCollins, 1992, pp. 114–115. **"In my mind, justified or not"**: Ibid., pp. 114–115. **"I considered myself a reasonably good Catholic"**: Smith, Bryan. "How the CIA Enlisted the Chicago Mob to Put a Hit on Castro," *Chicago* magazine, Oct. 22, 2007, p. 2.

CHAPTER 5

"There are moral as well as physical assassinations": Voltaire quoted in Ballou, Maturin M. "Edge-tools of speech." Boston: Houghton, Mifflin, 1899, p. 26. **"his eyes, his ears, and his mouthpiece"**: Maheu, Robert and Richard Hack. "Next to Hughes," New York: HarperCollins, 1992, p. 3. **"The whole thing probably took me an afternoon"**: Ibid. p. 66. **"But it was his eyes that people remembered best"**: Rappleye, Charles and Ed Becker. "All-American Mafioso: The Johnny Rosselli Story," New York: Doubleday, 1991, p. 7. **"We built a solid friendship over the years"**: Maheu, Robert and Richard Hack. "Next to Hughes": New York: HarperCollins, 1992, p. 134. **"They independently learned that Johnny"**: Ibid., p. 138. **"Bob was a pretty sharp guy"**: Testimony of James P. O'Connell, United States Senate Select Committee on Intelligence, NARA: 157-10002-10148, May 30, 1975, p. 104. **"If it saved even one American life"**: Maheu, Robert and Richard Hack. "Next to Hughes": New York: HarperCollins, 1992, p. 115. **"This was a story that Shef and I conjured up"**: Testimony of James P. O'Connell, United States Senate Select Committee on Intelligence, NARA: 157-10002-10148, May 30, 1975, p. 111. **"clients of an international nature"**: Ibid., p. 111. **"the international investors were quite unhappy"**: Ibid., p. 111. **"I am not kidding"**: Russo, Gus. "The Outfit: the role of Chicago's underworld in the shaping of modern America," New York: Bloomsbury, 2003, p. 386. **"Me? You want me to get involved with Uncle Sam?"**: Ibid., p. 386. **"It's up to you to pick whom you want"**:

Jones, Howard. "The Bay of Pigs," New York: Oxford University Press, 2008, p. 208. **"I won't ever reveal the content of any private conversations"**: Maheu, Robert and Richard Hack. "Next to Hughes," New York: HarperCollins, 1992, p. 140. **"I would have to be satisfied that this is a government project"**: Smith, Bryan. "How the CIA Enlisted the Chicago Mob to Put a Hit on Castro," *Chicago* magazine, October 23, 2007. **"It comes from high level sources"**: Ibid. **"Many people have speculated that Johnny"**: Maheu, Robert and Richard Hack. "Next to Hughes," New York: HarperCollins, 1992, p. 140.

CHAPTER 6

"The Outfit, as you should know": Royko, Mike. "Mike Royko: The Chicago Tribune Collection 1984–1997," Chicago: Agate Publishing, p. 87. **"Sam Giancana is the chief executive"**: Demaris, Ovid. "Captive City," New York: Lyle Stuart, 1969, p. 4. **"For years, the Mafia has thrived in Chicago"**: Royko, Mike. "Mike Royko: The Chicago Tribune Collection 1984–1997," Chicago: Agate Publishing, p. 91. **"Shit, I knew Sam (Giancana) when he was driving for Jack McGurn"**: Demaris, Ovid. "The Last Mafioso," New York: Times Books, 1981, pp. 100–101. **"It gives him a little more leverage"**: Ibid., p. 101. **"constitutional psychopath"**: Demaris, Ovid. "Captive City," New York: Lyle Stuart, 1969, p. 8. **"Who wouldn't pretend he was nuts to stay out of the army?"**: Giancana, Antoinette and Thomas C. Renner. "Mafia Princess: Growing Up in Sam Giancana's Family," New York: William Morrow, 1984, p. 107. **"I know they're going to kill me"**: *Chicago Tribune*, "Study Motives in Killing That Roe Expected," Aug. 6, 1952. **"He denied knowing Roe"**: *Chicago Tribune*, "Seize Caifano's Brother in Roe Killing Inquiry," July 3, 1951, p. 7. **"Keep your head down"**: Roemer, William F. Jr. "Accardo: The Genuine Godfather," New York: Donald I. Fine, 1995, p. 214. **"A man's got to marry a virgin, not a slut"**: Giancana, Sam and Chuck Giancana, "Double Cross: the explosive, inside story of the mobster who controlled America," New York: Warner Books, 1992, p. 58. **"say with all sincerity that Mooney had treasured Ange more than any other woman,"**: Ibid., p. 219 **"Sam was morose, disconsolate"**: Giancana, Antoinette and Thomas C. Renner. "Mafia Princess: Growing Up in Sam Giancana's Family." New York: William Morrow, 1984, p. 128.

CHAPTER 7

"Sam asked me to concentrate on Vegas": Demaris, Ovid. "The Last Mafioso," New York: Times Books, 1981, p. 106. **"quicker than you could hum a few bars of 'Anything Goes'"**: Giancana, Sam and Chuck Giancana, "Double Cross: the explosive, inside story of the mobster who controlled America." New York: Warner Books, 1992, p. 73. **"I stopped talking Italian"**: Rappleye, Charles and Ed Becker. "All-American Mafioso: The Johnny Rosselli Story," New York: Doubleday, 1991, pp. 17–18. **"When Christ died on the cross"**: Ibid., p. 38. **"I was a young fellow with very little education"**: Harris, Kathyrn. "John Roselli," *St. Petersburg Times*, August 25, 1976. **"You either click with people"**: Bartlett, Donald L. and James B. Steele. "Empire: The Life, Legend, and Madness of Howard Hughes": New York, W. W. Norton & Co., 1981, p. 281. **"To this very day, she"**: Harris, Kathyrn. "John Roselli," St. Petersburg Times, August 25, 1976. **"It was Johnny who made June quit"**: Ibid. **"bodyguard for Harry Cohn"**: Wiedrich, Bob. "CIA's 'Mobster' Cut Filmland Swath," *Chicago Tribune*, March 14, 1975, section 2, p. 4. **"I have a foolproof device for judging a picture"**: Kael, Pauline. "For Keeps: 30 Years At the Movies," New York, Dutton, 1994, p. 264. **"Harry, that's 'No sire' and 'Yes sire'"**: Gabler, Neal. "An Empire of Their Own: How the Jews Invented Hollywood," New York: Random House, Knopf Doubleday, 2010, p. 180. **"It only proves what they always say,"**: Ibid. p. 153. **"I represented, we might say, the picture industry"**: Hearings before the Special

Committee to Investigate Organized Crime in Interstate Commerce, Part 5, Illinois, September 9, 1950-January 19, 1951, Roselli testimony, p. 394. **"I had Hollywood dancing to my tune"**: Friedrich, Otto. "City of Nets: A Portait of Hollywood in the 1940s," Oakland: University of California Press, p. 66. **"I think you are trying to give this testimony of yours"**: Testimony of John Rosselli (sic). Hearings before the Special Committee to Investigate Organized Crime in Interstate Commerce, Part 5, Illinois, September 9, 1950-January 19, 1951, p. 394. **"Harry, I need your help"**: Mahoney, Richard. "Sons & Brothers: The Days of Jack and Bobby Kennedy," New York: Arcade Publishing, p. 63. **"Nothing happens without my say so"**: Demaris, Ovid. "The Last Mafioso," New York: Times Books, 1981, p. 107. **"I'll pay when Russian Louie hits town"**: Rappleye, Charles and Ed Becker. "All-American Mafioso: The Johnny Rosselli Story," New York: Doubleday, 1991, p. 140. **"Bioff seemed a pleasant individual"**: Goldwater, Barry M. with Jack Casserly. "Goldwater," New York: Knopf Doubleday, 2013, p. 197. **"There is no doubt in my mind that Willie Bioff was repaid"**: Giancana, Antoinette and Thomas C. Renner. "Mafia Princess: Growing Up in Sam Giancana's Family," New York: William Morrow, 1984, p. 104. **"This goddamn town is in my blood"**: Russo, Gus. "The Outfit," New York: Bloomsbury, 2008, p. 331. **"Chicago got that stoolie Willie Bioff, who testified against us"**: Demaris, Ovid. "The Last Mafioso," New York: Times Books, 1981, p. 107.

CHAPTER 8

"It's like stepping into a movie set of what Hollywood thinks": Mullin, Jay. "Cuba's Carefree Cabaret," By Jay Mallin, http://cuban-exile.com/doc_176-200/doc0193.html. **"Scholarly looking"**: JFK2017:124-10195-10346. **"A very unusual personality"**: JFK2017:124-10206-10145. **"Down there, when Santo wants to clear anything, he goes to Chicago"**: Demaris, Ovid. "The Last Mafioso," New York: Times Books, 1981, p. 105. **"as a 'gambling reform' advisor"**: Moruzzi, Peter. "Havana Before Castro: When Cuba Was a Tropical Playground," Utah Smith, Gibbs Publishers, 2009, p. 174. **"For gamblers, particularly the high rollers"**: Ibid., p. 120. **"price is no object"**: Wells, Pete. "Murder, Mayhem and the Mafia," 34 Street, September 20, 1984, p. 4. **"The point is that these bosses"**: Demaris, Ovid. "The Last Mafioso," New York: Times Books, 1981, p. 18. **"I ran like I was doing the 100-yard dash"**: Giancana, Antoinette and Thomas C. Renner. "Mafia Princess: Growing Up in Sam Giancana's Family," New York: William Morrow, 1984, pp. 196–197. **"Louis Santo"**: "Police List of Hoodlums; The Scene of Gangsters International Convention Near Binghamton," NYT, November 16, 1957, p. 10. **"I tore up a $1,200 suit"**: Jacob, Mark. "10 Things You Might Not Know About the Outfit," The Chicago Tribune, August 26, 2007. **"further proof of the existence of a criminal syndicate"**: Smith, Dwight C. Jr. "The Mafia Mystique," New York: Basic Books, 1975, p. 162. **"Are you going to tell us anything or just giggle?"**: Goldfarb, Ronald L. "Perfect Villians, Imperfect Heroes: Robert F. Kennedy's War Against Organized Crime," New York: Random House, p. 65. **"With the exposure of this new menace"**: Roemer, William F. "Accardo: The Genuine Godfather," New York: Donald I. Fine, 1995, p. 194. **"We are not only disposed to deport"**: Denton, Sally and Roger Morris. "The Money and the Power," New York: Knopf, 2001, p. 207. **"The murder of hostages by the government is an almost daily occurrence"**: Greene, Richard. "Graham Greene: A Life In Letters," New York: Vintage, 2008, p. 238. **"They're going to execute me"**: English, T.J. "Havana Nocturne: how the Mob owned Cuba . . . And then lost it to the revolution," New York: William Morrow, 2007, p. 313. **"That rotten bastard, he stole millions of dollars from us"**: Cain, Michael J. "The Tangled Web: The Life and Death of Richard Cain," New York: Skyhorse, 2007, p. 71. **"You give me a couple of guys with machine guns"**: Russo, Gus. "The Outfit," New York: Bloomsbury, 2008, p. 385.

CHAPTER 9

"pulling any punches": Maheu, Robert and Richard Hack. "Next to Hughes," New York: HarperCollins, 1992, p. 139. "We may know some people": Smith, Bryan. "How the CIA Enlisted the Chicago Mob to Put a Hit on Castro," *Chicago* magazine, Oct. 22, 2007. "Roselli made it clear": Osborn, Howard J. "Family Jewels," Memo to CIA Management Committee, May 16, 1973, (top secret document released publicly in 2007), pp. 12–17. "He was going with this young lady in New York": Testimony of John Roselli, September 22, 1975, US Senate Select Committee on Intelligence, NARA: 157-10002-10387, p. 18. "Give Johnny a flag": Russo, Gus. "The Outfit," New York: Bloomsbury, 2008, p. 387. "We were just trying to find somebody who was tough enough": Testimony of James P. O'Connell, United States Senate Select Committee on Intelligence, NARA: 157-10002-10148, May 30, 1975, pp. 7–11. "The objective clearly was the assassination of Castro": CIA Inspector General's Report on Plots to Assassinate Fidel Castro, May 23, 1967, declassified 1994, p. 32. "His extraordinary mind was fatally flawed": Powers, Thomas. "The Man Who Kept the Secrets: Richard Helms and the CIA," New York: Knopf, 1979, pp. 93–95. "There had to be a piece of him": Sambides, Nick. "A Spymaster's Son, Bangor man seeks traces of his CIA dad," Bangor Daily News, August 25, 2013. "Bissell got calls from the Mafia": Thomas, Evan. "The Very Best Men: The early years of the CIA," New York: Simon and Schuster, 1995, p. 234. "I had no desire to become personally involved": Bissell, Richard Jr. and Jonathan E. Lewis. "Reflections of a Cold Warrior: From Yalta to The Bay of Pigs," Yale University Press, 1996, p. 157. "bad words": Oral Interview Richard Bissell, October 17, 1975, National Security Archive, George Washington University, p. 17. "tacit approval to use his own judgment": CIA Inspector General's Report on Plots to Assassinate Fidel Castro, May 23, 1967, declassified 1994, p. 34. "I knew it was serious. I knew these were Mafia leaders": Interview with Richard Bissell contained in Hearings Before the Select Committee on Assassinations of the US House of Representatives, Volume X, March 1979, Washington: US Government Printing Office, p. 179. "I thank God to this day that I had competent associates": Roemer, William F. "Roemer: Man against the Mob," New York: Random House, 1989, p. 70. "Finally a deal was made": Roemer, William F. "Accardo: The Genuine Godfather," New York: Dutton, 1995, pp. 90–92. "Had my colleagues and I been caught": Roemer, William F. "Roemer: Man Against the Mob," New York: Random House, 1989, p. 70. "a pretty good idea": Higham, Charles. "Howard Hughes: The Secret Life," New York: Macmillan, 2004, p. 203.

CHAPTER 10

"James Bond, with two double bourbons inside him": Fleming, Ian. "Goldfinger," South Yarmouth, Mass.: Curley, 1959, p. 1. "In that moment, Sinatra is welcoming Presley": Kaplan, James. "Sinatra: The Chairman," New York: Doubleday, p. 319. "Giancana was on location": Frank Sinatra FBI file, Part 22 of 30, Chicago teletype to Director, dated 4-21-61. "People would fall over themselves": Giancana, Antoinette and Thomas C. Renner. "Mafia Princess: Growing Up in Sam Giancana's Family," New York: William Morrow & Co., p. 138. "John Rawlston": Testimony of John Roselli, June 24, 1975, US Senate Select Committee on Intelligence, NARA: 157-10014-10001, p. 49. "He didn't come off as thuggish," and "a courier to Cuba": Smith, Bryan. "How the CIA Enlisted the Chicago Mob to Put a Hit on Castro," Chicago Magazine, Oct. 22, 2007, p. 2. "potent pill which could be placed in Castro's food": Stockton, Bayard. "Flawed Patriot: The Rise and Fall of CIA Legend Bill Harvey," Washington, DC: Potomac Books, 2006, p. 173. "something lethal that could be done without any fanfare": Testimony of James P. O'Connell, United States Senate Select Committee on Intelligence, NARA: 157-10002-10148, May 30, 1975, p. 115.

"The thing that I got": Testimony of Santo Trafficante, House Select Committee on Assassinations, NARA: 180-10118- 10137, p. 29. "Look Jim, I know who you are": Testimony of James P. O'Connell, United States Senate Select Committee on Intelligence, NARA: 157-10002-10148, May 30, 1975, p. 114. "He [Roselli] never took a nickel": Ibid., pp. 26–27. "the Chicago chieftain of the Cosa Nostra and successor to Al Capone": Osborn, Howard J. "Family Jewels" Memo to CIA Management Committee, May 16, 1973, (top secret document released publicly in 2007), p. 13. "Maheu claimed that this was the first time": Hearings before the Select Committee on Assassinations of the US House of Representatives, Volume 5, Washington: US Government Printing Office, 1979, p. 248. "Cryptically"and "They are Johnny's close friends": Testimony of James P. O'Connell, United States Senate Select Committee on Intelligence, NARA: 157-10002- 10148, May 30, 1975, p. 30. "This is probably what we could have expected": Hearings before the Select Committee on Assassinations of the U.S. House of Representatives, Volume 5, Narration by G. Robert Blakey, Chief Counsel and Staff Director, Washington: US Government Printing Office, 1979, pp. 248–249. "You have to consider the perspective of the times": Testimony of James P. O'Connell, United States Senate Select Committee on Intelligence, NARA: 157-10002-10148, May 30, 1975, p. 42. "in the company of a good-looking girl": John Roselli FBI file, February 1961 report. "I didn't know then that Sam was the Chicago Godfather": Kelley, Kitty, "The Dark Side of Camelot," Int. with Judith Exner, People, February 29, 1988. "hanging around the studios": Gage, Nicholas. "Link of Kennedy Friend to Mafia Is Still a Puzzle," NYT, April 12, 1976. "Beautiful - Looks like Liz Taylor": Demaris, Ovid. "The Last Mafioso," New York: Times Books, 1981, p. 109. "I used to think he [JFK] was more interested in gossip than in Russian missiles": Fisher, Eddie and David Fisher. "Been There, Done That," New York: Macmillan, 2000, p. 274. "What'd you say his name was?": Levy, Shawn. "Rat Pack Confidential," Doubleday, 1998, p. 109. "When you talked to Jack" and "They seemed to have a genuine": Kelley, Kitty. "The Dark Side of Camelot," Int. with Judith Exner, People, February 29, 1988. "I own Chicago. I own Miami": Hilty, James. "Robert Kennedy: Brother Protector," Temple University Press, 2000, p. 206. "I feel like I was set up to be the courier": Kelley, Kitty. "The Dark Side of Camelot," Int. with Judith Exner, People, February 29, 1988.

PHASE II: COVERT OPERATIONS

"Covert operations can rarely achieve": Weiner, Tim. "Legacy of Ashes: The History of the CIA," New York: Knopf Doubleday, 2008, p. 340. "The modern patriotism": Rasmussen, R. Kent. "Mark Twain: His Words, Wit and Wisdom," New York: Gramercy, 2001, p. 208.

CHAPTER 11

"He was shot and killed after being tortured": Court papers in lawsuit, Lynita Fuller Caskey, as Personal Representative of the Estate of Robert Otis Fuller, Deceased, on behalf of Lynita Fuller Caskey, surviving daughter, and The Estate of Robert Otis Fuller Vs. The Republic of Cuba; 11th Judicial Circuit, Miami-Dade County, Florida, General Jurisdiction Division, Case No. 02-12475, May 13, 2002. "I learned of hundreds of people, labeled as agitators": Hunt, E. Howard and Greg Aunapu. "American Spy: My Secret History in the CIA, Watergate and Beyond," Hoboken, N.J.: John Wiley & Sons, 1967, p. 117. "We have the conviction that it was the imperialistic United States": Phillips, R. Hart. NYT, March 5, 1961, p. 33. "He completely believed": Beschloss, Michael. "The Crisis Years: Kennedy and Khrushchev, 1960–1963," New York: HarperCollins, 1991. "Do you have a sport?": Arlen Specter, Congressional Record-Senate, February 27, 2002, p. 2133. "All week long Havana rang with feverish alarms": Time, "Cuba: Invasion Jitters," November 7, 1960. "received a

thorough education in the difficulty": Bissell, Richard Jr. and Jonathan E. Lewis. "Reflections of a Cold Warrior: From Yalta to The Bay of Pigs," Yale University Press, 1996,
pp. 154–155. **"Everyone must be prepared"**: Ibid. p. 153. **"Cubans don't know how to keep
secrets"**: Thomas, Evan. "The very best men: the early years of the CIA," New York: Simon
and Schuster, 1995, p. 242. **"I am quite certain he [Shef Edwards] said, 'This has the
approval of the DCI',"**: Testimony of James P. O'Connell, United States Senate Select Committee on Intelligence, NARA: 157-10002- 10148, May 30, 1975, p. 33. **"a Wall Street guy out
for Castro"**: Testimony of John Roselli, April 23, 1976, US Senate Select Committee on
Intelligence, NARA: 157-10014-10000, (released in 1998), p. 10. **"They would lose men
there"**: Ibid., p. 25. **"I was sort of holding Roselli's hand"**: Testimony of James P. O'Connell,
United States Senate Select Committee on Intelligence, NARA: 157-10002-10148, May 30,
1975, p. 45. **"That's Joe, our courier"**: CIA Inspector General's Report on Plots to Assassinate
Fidel Castro, May 23, 1967, (declassified 1994), p. 36.

CHAPTER 12

"The cops played Bolita and so did priests": Ragano, Frank and Selwyn Raab. "Mob Lawyer," New York: Scribner, 1994, p. 21. **"More than a million"**: FBI Memo, September 22,
1960, JFK2017:124-10195-10346, p. 19. **"Fidel Castro has operatives in Tampa and Miami"**:
Crile, George III, "The Mafia, the CIA, and Castro," The Washington Post, May 16, 1976.
"At the time I think that it [the assassination plan] was a good thing": Deitch, Scott M.
"The Silent Don: The Criminal Underworld of Santo Trafficante Jr.," Barricade Books, 2007,
p. 139. **"Santo Trafficante Jr. was perhaps the most important of the three"**: Crile, George
III, "The Mafia, the CIA, and Castro," The Washington Post, May 16, 1976. **"I don't know
why—it didn't seem strange at all"**: Testimony of Santo Trafficante, House Select Committee on Assassinations, NARA: 180-10118-10137, p. 28. **"Hell, we would not care if they went
to the devil himself"**: Testimony of John Roselli, September 22, 1975, US Senate Select
Committee on Intelligence, NARA: 157-10002-10387, p. 15. **"I spoke the language, he
didn't"**: Testimony of Santo Trafficante, House Select Committee on Assassinations, HSCA
Report, Volume V, NARA: 180-10118-10137, p. 359. **"If I knew about him, knew that kind of
man he was"**: Ibid., p. 357. **"Informant [Aleman], who is a Cuban exile"**: House Select
Committee on Assassinations , FBI-HSCA subject file: Jose Aleman, NARA: 124-10305-
10003, pp. 1–18. **"efforts were being made by U.S. racketeers"**: CIA Inspector General's
Report on Plots to Assassinate Fidel Castro, May 23, 1967 (released in 1993), p. 29. **"clients
who wanted to do away with Castro"**: Testimony of Santo Trafficante, House Select Committee on Assassinations, HSCA Report, Volume V, NARA: 180-10118-10137, p. 360.

CHAPTER 13

"I've got a little more than luck" and **"The government wants us to clip Fidel Castro"**:
Demaris, Ovid. "The Last Mafioso," New York: Times Books, 1981, p. 108. **"Fuck the
commission"**: Ibid., p. 107. **"The way he told it—which was vaguely"**: George Bliss and
John R. Thomson. "Momo's Man: Cain played Mob game and lost big," Chicago Tribune,
December 21, 1973, p. 8. **"a practice Giancana may have promoted"**: House Select Com-
mittee on Assassinations, Staff Report on the Evolution and Implications of the CIA-
Sponsored Assassination Conspiracies Against Fidel Castro, NARA: 180-10147-10192,
p. 75. **"Several of Cain's activities during the fall of 1960"**: Hearings before the Select
Committee on Assassinations of the U.S. House of Representatives, Ninety-fifth Congress,
second session, Volume 10, Washington: U.S. Government Printing Office, 1979, p. 172.
"This was a golden opportunity for Dick": Cain, Michael J. "The Tangled Web: The Life
and Death of Richard Cain," New York: Skyhorse, 2007, pp. 72–73. **"a mistress of Castro"**:

Hearings Before House Select Committee on Assassinations, Volume X, March 1979, pp. 175–76. "**I am Cuba**": Geyer, Georgie Anne. "Guerrilla Prince: The Untold Story of Fidel Castro," Kansas City, Mo: Andrews McMeel, 2001, p. 216. "**Because of his [Castro's] reaction**": JFK2017:104-10062-10044. "**She was pure gold**": Skierka, Volker. "Fidel Castro: A Biography," New York: John Wiley & Sons, 2014, p. 167. "**I met (Johnny) Roselli at the Fontainebleau**": Ann Louise Bardach. "The Spy Who Loved Castro," *Vanity Fair*, November 1993. "**I couldn't find the capsules**": Schlesinger, Arthur M. Jr. "Robert Kennedy and His Times," New York: Houghton Mifflin, 1978, p. 482. "**Did you come here to kill me?**": Ann Louise Bardach, "The Spy Who Loved Castro," *Vanity Fair*, November 1993.

CHAPTER 14

"**Without even looking at the punk**": Smith, Bryan. "How the CIA Enlisted the Chicago Mob to Put a Hit on Castro," Chicago Magazine, Oct. 22, 2007, p. 2. "**Someday I'll explain it to you . . .**": Ibid. "**He could not bring himself to get rid of anything that was hers**": Giancana, Antoinette and Thomas C. Renner. "Mafia Princess: Growing Up in Sam Giancana's Family," New York: William Morrow, 1984, p. 177. "**He had been running around with other women since Momma's death**": Ibid., p. 259. "**When I met him I did not know who he was**": Phillis McGuire Interview with Barbara Walters on ABC television's "20/20" program, September 8, 1989. "**we didn't want him to leave**": Smith, Bryan. "How the CIA Enlisted the Chicago Mob to Put a Hit on Castro," Chicago Magazine, Oct. 22, 2007, p. 3. "**has a vicious temperament**": Giancana, Antoinette and Thomas C. Renner. "Mafia Princess: Growing Up in Sam Giancana's Family," New York: William Morrow, 1984, p. 224. "**I got a call from Bob Maheu**": Testimony of James P. O'Connell, United States Senate Select Committee on Intelligence, NARA: 157-10002-10148, May 30, 1975, pp. 66–67. "**Well, can Bob [Maheu] get somebody to do it?**": Ibid, p. 67. "**Giancana felt that he was being cuckholded**": March 15, 1979 letter from House Select Committee on Assassinations to CIA Director, JFK2017:104-10067-10134, p. 6. "**He (Maheu) was doing it to see if any loose conversation was going on**": Testimony of John Roselli, September 22, 1975, US Senate Select Committee on Intelligence, NARA: 157-10002-10387, p. 14. "**It became like a Keystone [Kops] comedy**": Testimony of James P. O'Connell, United States Senate Select Committee on Intelligence, NARA: 157-10002-10148, May 30, 1975, pp. 68–71. "**That was the first mistake**": Smith, Bryan. "How the CIA Enlisted the Chicago Mob to Put a Hit on Castro," *Chicago* Magazine, Oct. 22, 2007, p. 3. "**I was in love with her**": Interview with Dan Rowan, The Milwaukee Journal - Apr 22, 1975. "**I remember his expression, smoking a cigar**": Hinckle, Warren and William W. Turner. "The Fish Is Red: The Story of the Secret War Against Castro," New York: Harper & Row, 1981, p. 38. "**could have prompted Giancana to direct Maheu**": Hearings Before House Select Committee on Assassinations, Volume X, March 1979, pp. 172–174. "**I just blew my top**" and "**When I confronted him with that**": Testimony of John Roselli, September 22, 1975, US Senate Select Committee on Intelligence, NARA: 157-10002-10387, pp. 16–17, 24–25.

CHAPTER 15

"**Above all, do not get into any trouble**": The Memoirs of Jacques Casanova, Volume 5, New York, G. P. Putnam's Sons, 1945, p. 78. "**It is difficult to understand**": Roemer, William F. Jr. "Accardo: The Genuine Godfather," New York: Donald I. Fine, 1995, p. 223. "**You see that fucking fish?**": Brashler, William. "The Don: The life and death of Sam Giancana," New York: Ballantine Books, 1976, p. 227. "**command post**": Inserra, Vincent L. "C-1 and the Chicago Mob," Xlibris, 2014. p. 47. "**Very soon we learned why Sam had been so knowledgeable**": Roemer, William F. "Roemer: Man Against the Mob," New

York: Random House, 1989, p. 149. **"He [Teeter] remarked that Phyllis McGuire is a headstrong know-it-all type"**: Dark, Tony. "The FBI Files of Sam Giancana," Hosehead Productions, 2009, pp. 134–137. **"to be done away with very shortly"**: FBI Vault File of Fidel Castro, Part 03 of 04, pp. 28–30, Castro1c.pdf, p. 181. **"everything had been perfected for the killing"**: Giancana, Antoinette and Thomas C. Renner. "Mafia Princess: Growing Up in Sam Giancana's Family," New York: William Morrow, 1984, pp. 1–2. **"identity of the person who allegedly met with Giancana"**: Ibid., p. 17. **"Read lips from any distance"**: JFK2017:124:10226-10399. **"Hoover's rivalry with the CIA was one of long standing"**: Powers, Thomas. "The Man Who Kept the Secrets: Richard Helms and the CIA," New York: Knopf, 1979, p. 342. **"I am sure I referred it to Mr. Edwards"**: Testimony of Richard Bissell, July 22, 1975. Hearings of the Senate Select Committee on Intelligence, NARA: 157-10011-10017, (released in 1993). **"Under Project Johnny"**: Memo for Chief, Security Analysis Group, June 24, 1975, JFK2017: 104-10133-10027, pp. 1–2. **"If mobsters were bragging about knocking off"**: Thomas, Evan. "The Very Best Men: the early years of the CIA," New York: Simon and Schuster, 1995, p. 227. **"He [DuBois] said Maheu's operations often smack of the 'cloak and dagger' type of affair"**: FBI Vault File of Fidel Casto, Part 01 of 04, Castro1a.pdf, pp. 28–32. **"It was obvious a criminal investigation had begun"**: Maheu, Robert and Richard Hack. "Next to Hughes," New York: HarperCollins, 1992, p. 147. **"The big problem was keeping the [FBI] surveillance a secret"**: Ibid., p. 147.

CHAPTER 16

"Everyone had to face the reality": Bissell, Richard Jr. and Jonathan E. Lewis. "Reflections of a Cold Warrior: From Yalta to The Bay of Pigs," Yale University Press, 1996, p. 159. **"It is not my practice to give interviews"**: Rasenberger, Jim. "The Brilliant Disaster: JFK, Castro, and America's Doomed Invasion of Cuba's Bay of Pigs," New York: Scribner, 2011, p. 79. **"this tour of Mr. Dulles' carefully concealed world"**: Loftus, Joseph A. "Kennedy is Given a Secret Briefing by CIA," NYT, July 24, 1960, p. 1. **"I know this outfit"**: Collier, Peter and David Horowitz. "The Kennedys: An American Drama," New York: Summit Books, 1984, p. 234. **"Allen Dulles came down to visit Palm Beach"**: Letter from Joseph P. Kennedy to J. Edgar Hoover, April 12, 1957, FBI Vault File, Joseph P. (Joe) Kennedy Sr., Part 4 of 8, p. 36. **"I remember at the time that Jack Kennedy was working"**: Oral History Interview with Allen W. Dulles, December 5–6, 1964, Washington, DC, Interview by Thomas Braden for the John F. Kennedy Library, p. 1. **"Ridicule, chiefly"**: Thomas, Evan. "The very best men: the early years of the CIA," New York: Simon and Schuster, 1995, p. 207. **"a publicity gag"**: Schlesinger, Arthur M. "Letters: Presidential Libraries," NYTimes, February 4, 2001. **"Allen admitted that the flamboyant Bond bore"**: Kinzer, Stephen. "The Brothers: John Foster Dulles, Allen Dulles, and Their Secret World War," New York: Times Books, 2013, p. 274. **"Some of the professionals working for me"**: Robert G. Weiner, ed. "James Bond in World and Popular Culture: The Films are Not Enough," Newcastle upon Tyne: Cambridge Scholars, 2011, p. 209. **"When a new Bond movie was released"**: Ibid, p. 212. **"I found Kennedy to be bright"**: Bissell, Richard Jr. and Jonathan E. Lewis. "Reflections of a Cold Warrior: From Yalta to The Bay of Pigs," Yale University Press, 1996, pp. 159–160. **"I was in the ironic position"**: Nixon, Richard. "The Six Crises," New York: Doubleday, p. 355. **"Luckily, the CIA gave me time off"**: Maheu, Robert and Richard Hack. "Next to Hughes," New York: HarperCollins, 1992, p. 143. **"The fact that all this hoopla"**: Ibid., p. 119.

CHAPTER 17

"What's this?": Breslin, Jimmy. "Money Hungry Men Continue to Bug CIA," Fort Lauderdale, Fla. Sun-Sentinel, January 14, 1987. **"Okay, smart-ass"**: Maheu, Robert and

Richard Hack. "Next to Hughes," New York: HarperCollins, 1992, pp. 114–115. **"Borgia of the CIA"**: Escalate, Fabian, "The Cuba Project: the secret war: CIA covert operations against Cuba 1959-62," Australia: Ocean Press, 1995, p. 51. **"the Health Alteration Committee"**: Hinckle, Warren and William W. Turner. "The Fish Is Red: The Story of the Secret War Against Castro," New York: Harper & Row, 1981, p. 30. **"He fancied himself a technological promoter"**: Thomas, Evan. "The Very Best Men: Four Who Dared: The Early Years of the CIA," New York: Simon & Schuster, 1996, p. 212. **"unquestionably a patriot"**: Weiner, Tim. "Sidney Gottlieb, 80, Dies; Took LSD to CIA," NYT, March 10, 1999. **"The cigars were so heavily contaminated"**: CIA Inspector General's Report on Plots to Assassinate Fidel Castro, May 23, 1967, (declassified 1994), pp. 36–37. **"I gave it to Roselli"**: Testimony of James P. O'Connell, United States Senate Select Committee on Intelligence, NARA: 157-10002-10148, May 30, 1975, p. 87. **"I was with Sam at the Fontainebleau"**: Testimony of John Roselli, September 22, 1975, US Senate Select Committee on Intelligence, NARA: 157-10002-10387, p. 5. **"We're going to have to see him sometime"**: Levy, Shawn. "Rat Pack Confidential," Doubleday, 1998, p. 138. **"I heard you hadn't been wearing the ring"**: Ibid., p. 138. **"I do recall something about Maheu saying"**: Testimony of John Roselli, September 22, 1975, US Senate Select Committee on Intelligence, NARA: 157-10002-10387, p. 11. **"opened up his briefcase and dumped a whole lot of money on his lap"**: Stockton, Bayard. "Flawed Patriot: The Rise and Fall of CIA Legend Bill Harvey," Washington, DC: Potomac Books, 2006, p. 173. **"As far as I can remember, they couldn't be used in boiling soup"**: Smith, Bryan. "How the CIA Enlisted the Chicago Mob to Put a Hit on Castro," Chicago Magazine, Oct. 22, 2007, p. 4. **"Johnny's going to handle everything"**: Escalate, Fabian. "The Cuba Project: the secret war: CIA covert operations against Cuba 1959–62," Australia: Ocean Press, 1995, p. 83. **"Did you see the paper?"**: Rappleye, Charles and Ed Becker. "All-American Mafioso: The Johnny Rosselli Story," New York: Doubleday, 1991, p. 192. **"El Caballo"**: Bardach, Ann Louise. "Fidel Castro, The Vanity Fair Interview," *Vanity Fair*, March 1994. **"After several weeks of reported attempts"**: JFK2017:104-10133-10091.

CHAPTER 18

"This world is the will to power": Anderson, Mark. "Plato and Nietzsche: Their Philosophical Art," London: Bloomsbury, 2014, p. 89. **"Accardo always tries to maintain a low profile"**: Roemer, William F. Jr. "Accardo: The Genuine Godfather," New York: Donald I. Fine, 1995, p. 201. **"She's the toughest one in that family"**: O'Brien, John. "Mob Saga on Target," The Chicago Tribune, October 24, 1990, Section 5, p. 1. **"Command performance"**: Leen, Jeff. "A K A Frank Sinatra," *The Washington Post* Magazine, March 7, 1999, p. M6. **"They were starting to call Mooney and Johnny"**: Russo, Gus. "The Outfit: the role of Chicago's underworld in the shaping of modern America," New York: Bloomsbury, 2003, p. 388. **"The scene smacked of a grade B movie"**: FBI Vault File - Sam Giancana, File 92-3171, report quotes an article appearing in the "Chicago American" dated April 5, 1959, p 1. **"Why bother us this way?"**: "Covering the Mob," *Time* magazine, April 20, 1959. **"Who wouldn't pretend he was nuts to stay out of the Army?"**: Giancana, Antoinette and Thomas C. Renner. "Mafia Princess: Growing Up in Sam Giancana's Family," New York: William Morrow, 1984, p. 107. **"Had Jackson been our source"**: Roemer, William F. Jr. "Roemer: Man Against the Mob," New York: Donald I. Fine, 1989, p. 280. **"You shoulda seen the guy"**: "The Conglomerate of Crime," Time magazine, Feb. 28, 2002. **"He was floppin around on that hook"**: Ibid. **"I got nothin' to say to you guys"**: Roemer, William F. Jr. "Roemer: Man Against the Mob," New York: Donald I. Fine, 1989, p. 147. **"Why aren't you investigating the Communists?"**: Thomas, Evan. "Robert Kennedy: His Life,"

New York: Simon & Schuster, 2000, p. 162. **"I love this country and I would sacrifice my life for it"**: FBI Vault File, Sam Giancana, Report dated July 18, 1961 after Giancana interviewed at O' Hare International Airport, Chicago, 7/12/61, by Bureau Agents. **"was asked to clarify the last remark"**: Ibid. **"I heard about you being a fairy"**: Roemer, William F. Jr. "Roemer: Man Against the Mob," New York: Donald I. Fine, 1989, p. 141. **"I know all about the Kennedys"**: FBI File of Fidel Castro, Part 02 of 04, pp. 37–43, Castro1b.pdf. **"I thought we were all on the same side"**: Roemer, William F. Jr. "Roemer: Man Against the Mob," New York: Donald I. Fine, 1989, p. 157. **"passed over our heads"**: Ibid., p. 150.

CHAPTER 19

"There's money pouring in like there's no tomorrow": Denton, Sally and Roger Morris. "The Money and the Power," New York: Knopf, 2001, p. 224. **"It is his purpose to settle minor difficulties"**: FBI Vault Files- John Roselli. Part 3 of 12, p. 132. **"Admonished" and "indiscreet actions"**: FBI Vault Files- John Roselli. Part 6 of 12, Report about Roselli by Los Angeles bureau office dated September 26, 1960, p. 126. **"never liked me"**: Demaris, Ovid. "The Last Mafioso," New York: Times Books, 1981, p. 220. **"Well, yes, I knew him as Joe Kennedy"**: Testimony, of John Roselli, September 22, 1975 (morning session), US Senate Select Committee on Intelligence, NARA: 157-10002-10386, p. 62. **"Was very close to Frank Sinatra"**: FBI Vault File on Frank Sinatra, August 8, 1968 summary memo outlines Giancana "close" connections to Sinatra in business and social ventures starting from early 1960s. **"I'd rather be a don of the Mafia"**: Russo, Gus. "The Outfit: the role of Chicago's underworld in the shaping of modern America," New York: Bloomsbury, 2003, p. 369. **"hoodlum complex"**: FBI Vault File on Frank Sinatra, File #92-3171. **"Proposition" and "Sinatra feels he can do some good"**: Leen, Jeff. "A K A Frank Sinatra," The Washington Post Magazine, March 7, 1999, p. M6. **"Frank was particularly pleased"**: Exner, Judith. "My Story," New York: Grove Press, 1977, p. 62. **"Everybody's too busy being dazzled"**: Giancana, Sam and Chuck Giancana. "Double Cross: the explosive, inside story of the mobster who controlled America," New York: Warner Books, 1992, p. 195. **"a wizard, a business mastermind"**: Jacobs, George. "Mr. S.: My Life with Frank Sinatra," New York: Macmillan, 2003, p. 102. **"afloat when he was drowning"**: Ibid, p. 102. **"Since antiCatholic sentiment ran high"**: Sinatra, Nancy. "Frank Sinatra: An American Legend." Santa Monica, CA: General Publication Group, 1995, p. 146. **"Joe Kennedy couldn't be trusted"**: Russo, Gus. "The Outfit: the role of Chicago's underworld in the shaping of modern America," New York: Bloomsbury, 2003, p. 372. **"He was a guy on the inside"**: Giancana, Sam and Chuck Giancana. "Double Cross: The Explosive, Inside Story of the Mobster Who Controlled America," New York: Warner Books, 1992, p. 318. **"no vision, no imagination"**: Demaris, Ovid. "The Last Mafioso," New York: Times Books, 1981, p. 100. **"I could see everybody jockeying"**: Ibid., p. 100. **"We thought we were causing trouble"**: Roemer, William F. Jr. "Roemer: Man Against the Mob," New York: Donald I. Fine, 1989, p. 39. **"actually very pleased that Darlene"**: Roemer, William F. Jr. "The Enforcer: Spilotro: The Chicago Mob's Man over Las Vegas," New York: Ballantine Books, 1994, pp. 3–4. **"John Marshall"**: Ibid., pp. 72–73.

CHAPTER 20

"Dulles gave them a foreign policy with one hand": le Carre`, John. "The Spy Who Came in from the Cold," New York: Walker Books, 2005 (reprint of 1964), p. 55. **"I knew we were getting close to action"**: Maheu, Robert and Richard Hack. "Next to Hughes," New York: HarperCollins, 1992, p. 149. **"cold feet"**: Testimony of John Roselli, April 23, 1976, US Senate Select Committee on Intelligence, NARA: 157-10014-10000, (released in

1998), p. 28. **"The go signal never came"**: Smith, Bryan. "How the CIA Enlisted the Chicago Mob to Put a Hit on Castro," *Chicago* magazine, Oct. 22, 2007, p. 5. **"Do you people realize how desperate"**: Jones, Howard. "The Bay of Pigs," New York: Oxford University Press, 2008, p. 118. **"Golden Boy"**: Hearings before the President's Commission on the Assassination of President Kennedy, Volume 21, Washington, DC: US Printing Office, 1964, p. 610. **"You can't beat brains"**: Reeves, Richard. "President Kennedy: Profile of Power," New York: Simon & Schuster, 1993, p. 72. **"I've always felt that intelligence ought"**: Lathrop, Charles. "The Literary Spy," New Haven: Yale University Press, 2004, p. 111. **"As I moved forward with plans for the brigade"**: Bissell, Richard Jr. and Jonathan E. Lewis. "Reflections of a Cold Warrior: From Yalta to The Bay of Pigs," Yale University Press, 1996, p. 157. **"I've got to do something about those CIA bastards"**: Reeves, Richard. "President Kennedy: Profile of Power," New York: Simon & Schuster, 1993, p. 103. **"Though the assassination plan was confided to Robert Maheu"**: Schlesinger, Arthur M. Jr. "Robert Kennedy and His Times," New York: Houghton Mifflin, 1978, p. 488. **"Although Bissell testified that Allen Dulles never told him"**: "Alleged Assassination Plots Involving Foreign Leaders: An Interim Report of the Select Committee to Study Governmental Operations with Respect to Intelligence Activities, Volume 13098, United States Senate, Washington, DC: US Government Printing Office, 1975, p. 117. **"Allen Dulles had reason to believe that JFK knew"**: Reeves, Richard. "President Kennedy: Profile of Power," New York: Simon & Schuster, 1993, p. 714. **"What do you think if I ordered Castro to be assassinated?"**: Alleged assassination plots involving foreign leaders: An Interim Report of the Select Committee to Study Governmental Operations with Respect to Intelligence Activities, Volume 13098, United States Senate, Washington, DC: US Government Printing Office, 1975, p. 138. **"We don't know if we are your allies or your prisoners"**: Schlesinger, Arthur M. "A Thousand Days: John F. Kennedy In The White House," Houghton Mifflin Harcourt, 2002 (reprint of 1965 edition), p. 282. **"One of my CIA contacts alerted me"**: Maheu, Robert and Richard Hack. "Next to Hughes," New York: HarperCollins, 1992, p. 150. **"it was imperative I talk with the president"**: Maheu, Robert and Richard Hack. "Next to Hughes," New York: HarperCollins, 1992, p. 125. **"This is the worst day of my life"**: Matthews, Chris. "Kennedy and Nixon," New York: Simon & Schuster, 1997, p. 198. **"He said, 'If this were a parliamentary government"**: Oral Interview Richard Bissell, October 17, 1975, National Secruity Archive, George Washington University, pp. 3–4. **"Bureau of Public Roads"**: Marchetti, Victor and John D. Marks. "The CIA and the Cult of Intelligence," New York: Alfred A. Knopf, 1974, p. 275. **"Dulles never worked in the building he created"**: "The CIA Campus: The Story of Original Headquarters Building," www.cia.gov, May 22, 2008. **"Our friend Sam asked me"**: Maheu, Robert and Richard Hack. "Next to Hughes," New York: HarperCollins, 1992, p. 125.

CHAPTER 21

"I confess, it is my nature's plague": Shakespeare, William. "Tragedy of Othello, the Moor of Venice," New York: Harper, 1890, p. 91. **"Don't ask me where I am"**: Anthony Ramirez, "You Want Jokes?" NYT August 3, 2003. **"We never paid Johnny or Sam Gold a cent"**: Testimony of Col. Sheffield Edwards, Hearings of U.S. Senate Select Committee on Intelligence, NARA: 157-10002-10048, May 30, 1975 (released 1994), p. 16. **"might reveal information relating to the abortive Bay of Pigs"**: Stockton, Bayard. "Flawed Patriot: The Rise and Fall of CIA Legend Bill Harvey," Washington, DC: Potomac Books, 2006, p. 174. **"I wouldn't have told him anything about Sam"**: Exner, Judith. "My Story," New York: Grove Press, 1977, p. 192. **"Stupid"**: Gage, Nicholas. "2 Mafiosi Linked to CIA Treated Leniently by U.S." NYT, April 13, 1976, p. 1. **"I knew that Bob Maheu had given**

the FBI some information": Testimony of John Roselli, April 23, 1976, US Senate Select Committee on Intelligence, NARA: 157-10014-10000, (released in 1998), p. 9. "sources and contacts in Cuba which perhaps could be utilized successfully": FBI Vault File of Fidel Casto, Part 01 of 04, p. 189, Castro1a.pdf. "dirty business": FBI Vault File of Fidel Casto, Part 01 of 04, p. 189, Castro1a.pdf, FBI memo dated June 21, 1963, uses term based on interview with William Harvey. "Giancana gave every indication of cooperating": FBI Vault File of Fidel Casto, Part 01 of 04, p. 189, Castro1a.pdf, FBI memo dated May 21, 1961, based on int. with Sheffield Edwards. "expressed great astonishment": Alleged Assassination Plots Involving Foreign Leaders: An Interim Report of the Select Committee to Study Governmental Operations with Respect to Intelligence Activities, Volume 13098, United States Senate, Washington, DC: US Government Printing Office, 1975, p. 133. "materialized to date": Ibid., p. 330. "I hope this will be followed up vigorously": FBI Vault File of Fidel Casto, Part 01 of 04, Justice Dept. memo dated June 3, 1961, with directive from Attorney General Robert F. Kennedy, p. 225, Castro1a.pdf. "Mr. Babcock stated that it could conceivably cause embarrassment": FBI Vault File of Fidel Castro, Part 02 of 04, pp.52–66, Castro1b.pdf. "chief gunman for the group that succeeded the Capone mob": Investigation of Improper Activities in the Labor or Management Field: Hearings before the Select Committee on Improper Activities in the Labor or Management Field, Eighty-fifth Congress, First Session, Volume 47, Washington DC: US Government Printing Office, 1959, p. 17042. "Our relationship with [the informant] has been most carefully guarded": Gentry, Curt. "J. Edgar Hoover: The Man and the Secrets," New York: W. W. Norton & Co., 2001, p. 489.

CHAPTER 22
"A review of telephone calls of Judith E. Campbell": FBI Vault File on Frank Sinatra, File # 62-83219, Section 3, FBI memo dated February 26, 1962. "prettier than Elizabeth Taylor": Exner, Judith. "My Story," New York: Grove Press, 1977, p. 205. "What are you trying to do – turn her head?": Ibid., p. 215. "Now that I knew Johnny Roselli, he began calling me quite regularly": Ibid., p. 224. "Wall of Roselli's apartment": JFK2017:124-10291-10060. FBI memo, July 19, 1963. "Christ, with the both of us living here": Ibid., p. 256. "Coming to my front door, stopping me in parking lots": Testimony of Judith Campbell Exner, Senate Select Committee to Study Governmental Operations with Respect to Intelligence Activities, September 20, 1975, p. 12. "I adored getting flowers": Exner, Judith. "My Story," New York: Grove Press, 1977, p. 125. "Judy was pushy and reckless": Gage, Nicholas. "Link of Kennedy Friend to Mafia Is Still a Puzzle," NYT, April 12, 1976. "To be perfectly honest about it, I think I was caught up a little with the intrigue": Exner, Judith. "My Story," New York: Grove Press, 1977, pp. 128–131. "If you want to know anything about Judy Campbell": Ibid., p. 273. "his name 'Johnny Roselli' was an alias": FBI Vault File on John ("Handsome Johnny") Roselli, Part 8 of 12, FBI memo detailing Roselli aliases, p. 105. "Come on, let's get some fresh air": Exner, Judith. "My Story," New York: Grove Press, 1977, p. 236.

PHASE III: THE PATRIOTIC ASSASSIN
"Marked for the knife of the patriotic assassin": Machiavelli, Niccolo. "The Discourses," New York: Penguin, 1970, p. 32. "In a wilderness of mirrors": Martin, David C. "Wilderness of Mirrors," New York: Harper & Row, 1980, p. 216.

CHAPTER 23
"a front": House Select Committee on Assassinations, HSCA Report, Volume X Current Section: VI. Brigade 2506—Manuel Artime—Movimiento de Recuperacion Revolucionaria

(MRR), p. 11. **"We cannot, as a free nation, compete"**: Schlesinger, Arthur M. Jr. "Robert Kennedy and His Times," New York: Houghton Mifflin, 1978, p. 492. **"gambling elements"**: JFK2017: 157-10002-10015. **"Bobby felt even more strongly about it than Jack"**: Branch, Taylor and George Crile III, "The Kennedy Vendetta: How the CIA waged a silent war against Cuba," Harpers, July 1975, p. 52. **"Operation Mongoose"**: JFK2017:178-10002-10473. **"It was run as if it were a foreign country"**: Ibid., p. 51. **"a kind of action about which everybody in Miami"**: Didion, Joan. New York: Simon & Schuster, 1987, p. 89. **"A red-faced, pop-eyed"**: Martin, David. "The CIA's Loaded Gun," The Washington Post, October 10, 1976. **"Executive action"**: Testimony of William K. Harvey, U.S. Select Committee on Intelligence, June 25, 1975 (released 1994), NARA: 157-10002-10106, pp. 77–79. **"One of the first things that John Kennedy"**: JFK2017: 104-10324-10002, Secret Interview with Samuel Halpern, p. 99. **"My belief is that he"**: NARA157-10011-10020, Bissell testimony, June 9, 1975, pp. 55–58, also JFK157-10011-10020. **"to establish contacts with the underworld"**: Memo from Walter Elder, Review Staff to CIA Task Force, August 28, 1975, JFK2017:104-10303-10001, p. 2. **"Rocky Fiscalini," "shady characters," and "I had never engaged"**: Ibid. **"Time, effort, manpower"**: JFK2017:178-10002-10479. **" 'the Magic Button,' or the 'last resort beyond last resort,"**: Jones, Howard. "The Bay of Pigs," New York: Oxford University Press, 2008, p. 49. **"America's James Bond"**: Thomas, Evan. "The very best men: the early years of the CIA," New York: Simon and Schuster, 1995, p. 69. **"So you're our James Bond?"**: Martin, David C. "Wilderness of Mirrors," New York: Harper & Row, 1980, p. 129. **"had been fully approved"**: Jones, Howard. "The Bay of Pigs," New York: Oxford University Press, 2008, p. 49. **"Bill Harvey is going to take over Roselli"**: Testimony of James P. O'Connell, United States Senate Select Committee on Intelligence, NARA: 157-10002-10148, May 30, 1975, p. 108. **"the operation was off"**: CIA Inspector General's Report on Plots to Assassinate Fidel Castro, May 23, 1967, declassified 1994, p. 33. **"After the Bay of Pigs, Bob Maheu was not around anymore on"**: Testimony of John Roselli, September 22, 1975, US Senate Select Committee on Intelligence, NARA: 157-10002-10387, p. 7. **"I am not saying this in any denigrating way"**: Testimony of James P. O'Connell, US Senate Select Committee on Intelligence, NARA: 157-10002-10148, May 30, 1975, p. 50. **"I do not want anything to do with these two men"**: Testimony, of John Roselli, September 22, 1975, US Senate Select Committee on Intelligence, NARA: 157-10002-10387, pp. 11–12. **"You don't have to worry about that"**: Ibid., p. 12. **"not a radical"**: "Cuba's Perennial Rebel: Manuel Antonio de Varona," NYT, April 8, 1961, p. 2. **"We were going to see who picked it up"**: CIA Inspector General's Report on Plots to Assassinate Fidel Castro, May 23, 1967, declassified 1994, pp. 56–57. **"At that point he [Roselli] told me, 'Harvey isn't all that bad a guy'"**: Testimony of James P. O'Connell, US Senate Select Committee on Intelligence, NARA: 157-10002-10148, May 30, 1975, p. 56. **"Nothing's happening"**: CIA Inspector General's Report on Plots to Assassinate Fidel Castro, May 23, 1967, declassified 1994, p. 55.

CHAPTER 24
"The Mafia, some protestors said, was only a small part of organized crime": Talese, Gay. "Honor Thy Father," New York: World Publishing, 1971, p. 460. **"Might have learned concerning Johnny and Sam's 'business ventures'"**: Maheu, Robert and Richard Hack. "Next to Hughes," New York: HarperCollins, 1992, p. 37. **"Needless to say, my position did not please Hoover"**: Ibid., p. 37. **"Showcase Enterprises"**: FBI Vault File of Frank Sinatra, Part 23 of 29, p. 93. **"oral commitments"**: Ibid, FBI memo dated April 13, 1962, p. 93. **"Investigation indicates Roselli may be handling various matters in Las Vegas for Sam Giancana"**: "Showcase Enterprises," FBI Vault File of Frank Sinatra, Part 23 of

29, p. 93. **"I'm the only entertainer who has ten percent of four gangsters"**: Denton, Sally and Roger Morris. "The Money and the Power," New York: Knopf, 2001, p. 262. **"I'm gonna get my money out of there"**: Giancana, Antoinette and Thomas C. Renner. "Mafia Princess: Growing Up in Sam Giancana's Family," New York: William Morrow, 1984, p. 282. **"Made such demands that the start of the filming"**: FBI Vault File of Frank Sinatra, Part 23 of 29, p. 95. **"The Untouchables"**: Demaris, Ovid. "The Last Mafioso," New York: Times Books, 1981, p. 123. **"Sam and I go back a long way"**: Ibid., p. 122. **"Jimmy, what I'm about to tell you has been decided by our family"**: Ibid., p. 123. **"Stop getting your nose in where it doesn't belong"**: Kelley, Kitty. "His Way: The Unauthorized Biography of Frank Sinatra," New York: Bantam, 2010, p. 320. **"I just couldn't hit him"**: Ibid., p. 320. **"He was a runty, bald and big-nosed gentleman"**: Roemer, William F. Jr. "Roemer: Man Against the Mob," New York: Donald I. Fine, 1989, p. 146. **"very much in love"**: FBI Vault File of John ("Handsome Johnny") Roselli, Part 12 of 12, roselli5b.pdf, pp. 8, 38. **"McGuire was observed"**: JFK2017:124-10226-10374. **"If Sam said something, Sinatra was on his feet"**: Kelley, Kitty. "His Way: The Unauthorized Biography of Frank Sinatra," New York: Bantam, 2010, p. 296. **"You better believe that when the word got around town"**: Ibid., p. 300. **"Here I am, helping the government"**: Mahoney, Richard D. "Sons & Brothers: The Days of Jack and Bobby Kennedy," Arcade Publishing, 1999, pp. 195–196. **"That rat bastard, sonofabitch"**: Ragano, Frank and Selwyn Raab. "Mob Lawyer," New York: Scribner, 1994, p. 218. **"Bobby liked Frank"**: Gage, Nicholas. "Ex-Aides Say Justice Dept. Rejected a Sinatra Inquiry," NYT, p. 1. **"Bobby would always tell us, 'Peel the banana"**: Ibid., p. 1. **"The Compound"**: Wilson, Earl. "Sinatra: An Unauthorized Biography," New York: Macmillan, 1976, p. 310. **"This is my buddy"**: Giancana, Antoinette and Thomas C. Renner. "Mafia Princess: Growing Up in Sam Giancana's Family," New York: William Morrow, 1984, p. 281. **"He's got an idea that you're mad at him"**: "The Mob," Life magazine, May 30, 1969, p. 46. **"If he [JFK] had lost this state here"**: Kuntz, Tom and Phil Kuntz. "The Sinatra Files: The Secret FBI Dossier," New York: Three Rivers Press, 2000, p. 156. **"After all, if I'm taking somebody's money"**: Ibid., p. 153. **"One minute he says he's talked to Robert"**: Kelley, Kitty. "His Way: The Unauthorized Biography of Frank Sinatra," New York: Bantam, 2010, p. 294. **"If he can't deliver, I want him to tell me"**: "The Mob," Life magazine, May 30, 1969, p. 46. **"You got the right idea, Mo"**: Mahoney, Richard D. "Sons & Brothers: The Days of Jack and Bobby Kennedy," Arcade Publishing, 1999, p. 126. **"I'm fucking Phyllis, playing Sinatra songs in the background"**: Kaplan, James. "Sinatra: The Chairman," New York: Doubleday, p. 413. **"Too fucking bad"**: Kelley, Kitty. "His Way: The Unauthorized Biography of Frank Sinatra," New York: Bantam, 2010, p. 295. **"When he says he's gonna do a guy a little favor"**: "The Mob," Life magazine, May 30, 1969, p. 46. **"Let's show 'em"**: Kelley, Kitty. "His Way: The Unauthorized Biography of Frank Sinatra," New York: Bantam, 2010, p. 329.

CHAPTER 25

"A secret is seldom safe in more than one breast": Swift, Jonathan. The Prose Works of Jonathan Swift, Volume 10, London: Bell, 1914, p. 93. **"If you ever know as many secrets as I do"**: Schlesinger, Arthur M. Jr. "Robert Kennedy and His Times," New York: Houghton Mifflin, 1978, p. 478. **"Not knowing him from Adam at that point"**: Testimony of William K. Harvey, US Select Committee on Intelligence, June 25, 1975 (released 1994), NARA: 157-10002-10106, pp. 130–132. **"Harvey was having periodic meetings with someone in Miami"**: Shackley, Ted and Richard A. Finney. "Spymaster: My Life in the CIA," Dulles, Virginia: Potomac Books, 2005, p. 56. **"I saw no reason at that time to charge him"**: Testimony of William K. Harvey, US Select Committee on Intelligence, June 25,

1975 (released 1994), NARA: 157-10002-10106, pp. 65–68. "I think it is highly improper": Reeves, Richard. "President Kennedy: Profile of Power," New York: Simon & Schuster, 1993, p. 337. "He's sending me stuff on my family and friends": Ibid., p. 298. "efforts to obtain intelligence information in Cuba through the hoodlum element": FBI memo dated March 23, 1962, from J. Edgar Hoover to CIA, "CIA targets Fidel: secret 1967 CIA Inspector General's report on plots to assassinate Fidel Castro," Melbourne: Ocean Press, 1996, p. 64. "I thought you would be interested in learning of the following information": Mahoney, Richard D. "Sons & Brothers: The Days of Jack and Bobby Kennedy," New York: Arcade Publishing, 1999, p. 156. "prominent underworld figures Sam Giancana of Chicago and John Roselli of Los Angeles": Reeves, Richard. "President Kennedy: Profile of Power," New York: Simon & Schuster, 1993, p. 289. "referred to Campbell as the girl": Ibid., p. 289. "He didn't have the guts to tell his brother": Thomas, Evan. "Robert Kennedy: His Life," New York: Simon & Schuster, 2000, p. 168. "If you could have seen Mr. Kennedy's eyes get steely": Schlesinger, Arthur M. Jr. "Robert Kennedy and His Times," New York: Houghton Mifflin, 1978, p. 493. "The Attorney General had thought that Roselli was doing the job": Investigation of the Assassination of President John F. Kennedy: Hearings Before the Select Committee on Assassinations of the U.S. House of Representatives, Ninety-fifth Congress, Second Session, Volume 4, Washington, DC: U.S. Government Printing Office, 1979, p. 143. "was not true and Colonel Edwards knew it was not true": Alleged Assassination Plots Involving Foreign Leaders: An Interim Report of the Select Committee to Study Governmental Operations with Respect to Intelligence Activities, United States Senate: Together with Additional, Supplemental and Separate Views, p. 134.

CHAPTER 26

"We penetrated deeper and deeper into the heart of darkness": Conrad, Joseph. "Heart of Darkness and Other Tales," New York: Oxford University Press, 2002, p. 138. "Colonel Roselli" and his band of exile marauders: Details about Roselli's excursion, including the boat shot out from under him, were outlined in Anderson, Jack, "The Washington Merry-Go-Round—6 Attempts to Kill Castro Laid to CIA," The Washington Post, January 18, 1971, and in Anderson, Jack, "The Washington Merry-Go-Round—Castro Stalker Worked for the CIA," The Washington Post, February 23, 1971. An earlier account appeared in Peterson, Morton, "The CIA Plots to Kill Castro," Man's Magazine, January 1967. Both Anderson columns were later included in the confidential CIA "Family Jewels" memo, prepared by the Agency's Director of Security in 1973, that was eventually released publicly in June 2007. More details about the Texana III boat appeared in St. George, Andrew, "The Attempt to Assassinate Castro," Parade, April 12, 1964. "the dapper American agent in charge": Ayers, Bradley Earl. "The War That Never Was: An Insider's Account of CIA Operations against Cuba," Indianapolis:Bobbs-Merrill, 1976, p. 95. "knew all the help by their first name, tipped hugely": Stockton, Bayard. "Flawed Patriot: The Rise and Fall of CIA Legend Bill Harvey," Washington, DC: Potomac Books, 2006, p. 179. "I said that every time I had to meet anyone connected with these": Testimony of John Roselli, September 22, 1975, US Senate Select Committee on Intelligence, NARA: 157-10002-10387, p. 13. "At that time, I was beginning to feel that this was a pressure on the FBI's part": Ibid., p. 13. "more of a pro": Ibid., p. 11. "Sorry for the poor bastards": JFK2017:157-10014-10236, p. 44. "the biggest flag-waving SOB in the country": LaBrecque, Ron. "Could Roselli Have Linked Castro Plot to JFK Death?" Miami Herald, September 19, 1976, p. 1. "It's not hard to imagine Harvey admiring Johnny for": Stockton, Bayard. "Flawed Patriot: The Rise and Fall of CIA Legend Bill Harvey," Washington, DC: Potomac Books,

2006, pp. 180–181. "**They looked like they wouldn't even float**": JFK2017:178-10002-10091. William Sturbitts testimony, p. 48. "**What do you hear from Johnny?**": JFK2017: 151-10014-10087, Testimony of Joseph Shimon, Senate Select Committee to Study Governmental Operations with Respect to Intelligence Activities, September 12, 1975, p. 37. Also, see Anderson, Jack and Joseph Spear, "Witness Tells of CIA Plot to Kill Castro," The Washington Post, November 1, 1988.

CHAPTER 27

"**Castro Agent in US Informing**": JFK2017:111-10004-10000. "**You never know when a worm goes into someone's head**": Latell, Brian. "Castro's Secrets: Cuban Intelligence, The CIA and the Assassination of John F. Kennedy," New York: Palgrave Macmillan, p. 4. "**What would the Brits do in Cuba?**": Holzman, Michael. "James Jesus Angleton, the CIA, and the Craft of Counterintelligence," Amherst: University of Massachusetts Press, 2008, p. 191. "**We're developing a new capacity in the Company**": Ibid., p. 191. "**had been penetrated**": Stockton, Bayard. "Flawed Patriot: The Rise and Fall of CIA Legend Bill Harvey," Washington, DC: Potomac Books, 2006, p. 186. "**good friend**": Ragano, Frank and Selwyn Raab. "Mob Lawyer," New York: Scribner, 1994, p. 210. "**I looked at Johnny and I thought he must be some kind of idiot**": Ibid., p. 209. "**deeply involved in narcotics trafficking**": Deitche, Scott M. "The Silent Don: The Criminal Underworld of Santo Trafficante Jr," New York: Barricade Books, 2007, pp. 86–88. "**The implication was that he [Trafficante] had sabotaged**": Ibid., p. 146. "**Personal secretary**": The Associated Press, "Orta Denies Plot," NYT, March 30, 1960, p. 14. "**kept Santo Trafficante Jr. in jail to make it appear**": Schlesinger, Arthur M. Jr. "Robert Kennedy and His Times," New York: Houghton Mifflin, 1978, p. 484. "**patriotic duty**": Phillips, R. Hart. "Castro's Repressive Acts Awaken Cubans to Reality," NYT, June 12, 1961, p. 1. "**The Cubans' skill at keeping their own double-cross system secure**": Latell, Brian. "Castro's Secrets: Cuban Intelligence, the CIA and the Assassination of John F. Kennedy," New York: Palgrave Macmillan, p. 13. "**Donna**": Fletcher, Pascal. "Fidel Castro still blocking Cuba changes: sister," Reuters, Oct. 27, 2009. "**Did I feel remorse about betraying Fidel**": "Castro's sister 'spied for CIA'": BBC News, October 26, 2009. http://news.bbc.co.uk/2/hi/8327163.stm. "**Fidel's radical conversion**": Carroll, Rory and Giles Tremlett, The Guardian, October 26, 2009. "**Obtained Juanita's agreement**": JFK2017:178-10002-10469. "**If you needed somebody to carry out murder**": Hinckle, Warren and William W. Turner. "The Fish Is Red: The Story of the Secret War against Castro," New York: Harper & Row, 1981, p. 31. In Martin's book, "A Wilderness of Mirrors," this Helms quote referred to another potential assassin candidate. "**While brave and dedicated to the cause of defeating Castro**": Shackley, Ted and Richard A. Finney. "Spymaster: My Life in the CIA," Dulles, Virginia: Potomac Books, 2005, p. 57.

CHAPTER 28

"**It's been like old times to see the crowds**": Leonard, Will. "Rusty Warren, off the record, still packs 'em in!" The Chicago Sunday Tribune, Part 5, p. 10. "**Practically all of Chicago's top hoodlums, with the exception of Giancana, were present**": FBI report based on November 27, 1962, surveillance of Villa Venice, in FBI Vault File of Frank Sinatra, Part 24 of 29, p. 7, http://foia.fbi.gov/sinatra/sinatra09c.pdf. "**Hold the noise down**": Fishgall, Gary. "Gonna Do Great Things: The Life of Sammy Davis, Jr.," New York: Simon & Schuster, 2010, p. 184. "**Baby, let me say this**": Ibid., p. 185. "**I love Chicago, it's carefree and gay; I'd even work here without any pay**": Kaplan, James. "Sinatra: The Chairman," New York: Doubleday, p. 494. "**You know, as much as I like Frank, I can't go there**": Schlesinger, Arthur M. Jr. "Robert Kennedy and His Times," New York: Houghton Mifflin,

1978, p. 496. **"Frank—How much can I count on the boys in Vegas?"**: Hersh, Burton. "Bobby and J. Edgar Revised Edition: The Historic Face-Off between the Kennedys and J. Edgar Hoover that Transformed America," New York: Basic Books, 2007, p. 281. **"What is this shit?"**: Kaplan, James. "Sinatra: The Chairman," New York: Doubleday, p. 438. **"There was an endless silence"**: Jacobs, George. "Mr. S.: My Life with Frank Sinatra," New York: Macmillan, 2003, p. 164. **"Frank didn't buy that for a minute"**: Kelley, Kitty. "His Way: The Unauthorized Biography of Frank Sinatra," New York: Bantam, 2010, p. 336. **"They [the Kennedys] used him [Sinatra] to help them raise money"**: Hilty, James. "Robert Kennedy: Brother Protector," Temple University Press, 2000, p. 208. **These tapes were played back"**: JFK20017: 157-10014-10087, Shimon's Senate testimony, September 12, 1975, p. 66. **"stopped and picked up a blonde woman"**: FBI Vault File of John ("Handsome Johnny") Roselli, Part 8 of 12, roselli3b.pdf, p. 13. **"He was just trying to discredit me"**: Testimony of John Roselli, September 22, 1975, US Senate Select Committee on Intelligence, Vol 1 of 2, noon session, NARA: 157-10002-10387, pp. 46–47. **"He trusted no one, not Phyllis"**: Giancana, Antoinette and Thomas C. Renner. "Mafia Princess: Growing Up in Sam Giancana's Family," New York: William Morrow, 1984, p. 272. **"Here I am!"**: Russo, Gus. "The Outfit: the role of Chicago's underworld in the shaping of modern America," New York: Bloomsbury, 2003, p. 336. **"As far as I know, this is the first PGA-sponsored golf tournament"**: Demaris, Ovid. "Captive City," New York: Lyle Stuart, 1969, p. 63. **"At the golf course, I'd follow him to the men's room"**: Royko, Mike. "Golf Chicago-Style," Chicago Tribune, June 10, 1990. **"He was most knowledgeable about the Chicago mob"**: Mahoney, Richard D. "Sons & Brothers: The Days of Jack and Bobby Kennedy," Arcade Publishing, 1999, p. 103. **"This is like Nazi Germany"**: Roemer, William F. Jr. "Roemer: Man against the Mob," New York: Donald I. Fine, 1989, p. 189. **"Tell everyone that everything is off"**: Thomas, Evan. "Robert Kennedy: His Life," New York: Simon & Schuster, 2000, p. 165. **"You can't go giving these [FBI] guys abuse"**: Giancana, Antoinette and Thomas C. Renner. "Mafia Princess: Growing Up in Sam Giancana's Family," New York: William Morrow, 1984, p. 333. **"I know that it was Paul (Ricca) who guided Sam along"**: Ibid., p. 163. **"When you talk about heat, you're talking to a man"**: Demaris, Ovid. "The Last Mafioso," New York: Times Books, 1981, p. 128.

CHAPTER 29

"And they tell me you are crooked and I answer": Sandburg, Carl. "Chicago Poems," New York: Henry Holt, 1916, p. 3. **"We finally got so pissed off we put his head in a vise"**: Griffin, Dennis N. and Frank Culotta, "Cullotta: The Life of a Chicago Criminal, Las Vegas Mobster, and Government Witness," Las Vegas: Huntington Press, 2007, p. 62. **"Find Torture Angle"**: The Chicago Tribune, "Find Torture Angle in Auto Trunk Deaths – Two Beaten beyond Recognition," May 16, 1962, p. 37. **"Every thief in Chicago knew that Elmwood Park"**: Roemer, William F. Jr. "The Enforcer: Spilotro: The Chicago Mob's Man over Las Vegas," New York: Ballantine Books, 1994, p. 27. **"He would later become Sam Giancana's closest confidant"**: Roemer, William F. Jr. "The Enforcer: Spilotro: The Chicago Mob's Man over Las Vegas," New York: Ballantine Books, 1994, p. 51. **"He [Dick Cain] knew that if he was able to get in tight with the Cubans"**: Cain, Michael J. "The Tangled Web: The Life and Death of Richard Cain," New York: Skyhorse, 2007, p. 83. **"modest beginnings for a grandiose scheme by my father"**: Giancana, Antoinette and Thomas C. Renner. "Mafia Princess: Growing Up in Sam Giancana's Family," New York: William Morrow, 1984, p. 248. **"Lukewarm"**: Ibid., p. 255. **"It was just conversation that meant nothing to me"**: Interview with Judith Campbell Exner, Hearings before Senate Select Committee on Intelligence.

September 20, 1975, p. 29. "**Cain is believed to have been Giancana's contribution to the CIA attempt**": Wiedrich, Bob. "CIA tried to use mob's Giancana," Chicago Tribune, December 31, 1973, p. 10. "**The suspicion is that Cain**": JFK2017:180-10145-10205, p. 14. "**looking into communism in Central America**": FBI HSCA Subject: Richard Cain, Main File 105-93264, p. 2. "**If you find me in a trunk, DeStefano is the man who put me there**": Demaris, Ovid. "Captive City," New York: Lyle Stuart, 1969, p. 301. "**I told you I would get you**": Herion, Don. "The Chicago Way," Xlibris Corp., 2010, p. 17.

CHAPTER 30

"**I never saw a dark side of him**": Fessier, Bruce. "Gangsters in Paradise: Behind the Rich Legend and Lore of the Mafia in the Coachella Valley Is a Very Real and Violent Reality," The Desert Sun, November 30, 2014. "**I was singing at the Desert Inn and the FBI came in**": Ibid. "**Some guys are squeamish like little girls**": Demaris, Ovid. "The Last Mafioso," New York: Times Books, 1981, p. 121. "**Now Accardo decided enough was enough**": Roemer, William F. Jr. "The Enforcer: Spilotro: The Chicago Mob's Man Over Las Vegas," New York: Ballantine Books, 1994, pp. 72–73. "**I met Roselli with Marilyn a couple of times**": Slatzer, Robert F. "The Marilyn Files," New York: SP Books, 1992, p. 52. "**could bestow a Judy Campbell**": Jacobs, George. "Mr. S.: The Last Word on Frank Sinatra," New York: Macmillan, 2003, p. 136. "**You sure get your rocks off fucking the same broad as the brothers**": Roemer, William F. Jr. "Roemer: Man against the Mob," New York: Donald I. Fine, 1989, p. 184. "**Engaged in an orgy**": Ibid., p. 175. "**probable suicide**": Schumach, Murray. "Marilyn Monroe's Death Is Called Suicide," NYT, August 18, 1962, p. 10. "**I heard the phone ring and I thought it was Marilyn**": Jeanne Carmen Interview, CNN "Larry King Live," Panel Discusses Marilyn Monroe, August 5, 2003, http://www.cnn.com /TRANSCRIPTS/0308/05/lkl.00.html. "**Tony Accardo at this time had let Giancana have his head**": Roemer, William F. Jr. "Accardo: The Genuine Godfather," New York: Donald I. Fine, 1995, p. 260. "**private showing**": FBI Vault File of Frank Sinatra, Part 24 of 29, p. 14. http://foia.fbi.gov/sinatra/sinatra09c.pdf. "**Unsocial Register**": Oulahan, Richard and Thomas Thompson, *Life*, September 27, 1963, p. 93. "**Frank called me every name in the book**": Ibid., p. 95. "**This is Frank Sinatra! You fucking asshole!**": Thompson, Douglas. "The Dark Heart of Hollywood: Glamour, Guns and Gambling – Inside the Mafia's Global Empire," New York: Random House, 2012, p. 26. "**This place was so busy**": Oulahan, Richard and Thomas Thompson, *Life*, September 27, 1963, p. 95. "**This is a way of life and a man has to lead his own life**": Levy, Shawn. "Rat Pack Confidential," Doubleday, 1998, p. 264. "**Aren't you people being a little hard on Frank out here?**": Goldstein, Norm. "Frank Sinatra, Ol' Blue Eyes," New York: Holt, Rinehart and Winston, p. 72. "**Well Mr. President, I'll try to take care of things here in Nevada**": Burbank, Jeff. "Las Vegas Babylon: The True Tales of Glitter, Glamour, and Greed," Lanham, Md.: M. Evans & Co, 2008, p. 150. "**When Victor made a move, Sinatra jumped on him**": Roemer, William F. Jr. "Roemer: Man against the Mob," New York: Donald I. Fine, 1989, pp. 270–271. "**What do you mean, your money**": Kelley, Kitty. "His Way: The Unauthorized Biography of Frank Sinatra," New York: Bantam, 2010, p. 356. "**Sam couldn't get over the fact that Frank had done that**": Ibid., p. 365. "**Advise that Giancana in extremely tenuous situation**": Giancana, Antoinette and Thomas C. Renner. "Mafia Princess: Growing Up in Sam Giancana's Family," New York: William Morrow, 1984, pp. 139–140.

CHAPTER 31

"**Phase Two**": Prados, John. "Safe for Democracy: The Secret Wars of the CIA," Chicago: Ivan R. Dee, 2006, p. 308. "**said he took the occasion to express his personal**

appreciation to Roselli": CIA Inspector General's Report on Plots to Assassinate Fidel Castro, May 23, 1967, declassified 1994, p. 113. **"the top priority of the United States government"**. Weiner, Tim. "Legacy of Ashes: The History of the CIA," New York: Doubleday, p. 212. **"I trust that if you ever try and do business with organized crime again"**: Schlesinger, Arthur M. Jr. "Robert Kennedy and His Times," New York: Houghton Mifflin, 1978, p. 493. **"exploiting the potential of the underworld in Cuban cities"**: "Foreign Relations of the United States, 1961-1963," Volume X, Cuba, 1961–1962. **"He [Varona] was running his own little army"**: Testimony of James P. O'Connell, United States Senate Select Committee on Intelligence, NARA: 157-10002-10148, May 30, 1975, p. 54. **"DeVarona was understandably pleased"**: House Select Committee on Assassinations, CIA Collection (staff notes), NARA: 180-10144-10027, (released 1997), p. 11. **"I am not in favor of Cubans breaking with Washington"**: The Associated Press, "Cuban Exile Chief Accuses the U.S. of Defaming Him," NYT, April 18, 1963, p. 1. **"I was very, very dubious A"**: Testimony of William K. Harvey, U.S. Select Committee on Intelligence, June 25, 1975 (released 1994), NARA: 157-10002-10106, pp. 103–105. **"Why can't you get things cooking like 007?"**: JFK2017: 157-10011-10053. Also, Comentale, Edward P. , Stephen Watt and Skip Willman. "Ian Fleming & James Bond: The Cultural Politics of 007," Bloomington: Indiana University Press, 2005, p. 196. **"What would you teach them – babysitting?"**: Corn, David. "Blond Ghost: Ted Shackley and the CIA's Crusades," New York: Simon & Schuster, 1994, p. 82. **"came down to Miami every four to six weeks, mostly to see Johnny Roselli"**: Stockton, Bayard. "Flawed Patriot: The Rise and Fall of CIA Legend Bill Harvey," Washington, DC: Potomac Books, 2006, p. 127. **"the fucker"**: Corn, David. "Blond Ghost: Ted Shackley and the CIA's Crusades," New York: Simon & Schuster, 1994, p. 82. **"I ran across a lot of soldiers of fortune looking for a fast buck"**: Gleichauf, Justin F. "A Listening Post in Miami," CIA Library, cia.gov. **"cowboy"** and **"He [Robertson] was always trying to crank us up for the missions"**: Branch, Taylor and George Crile III. "The Kennedy Vendetta: How the CIA waged a silent war against Cuba," Harpers, July 1975, pp. 57–58. **"Through his Cuban contacts, attempt to verify"**: Roselli: Chronology of Events, JFK2017: docid-32423624, pp. 44–46. **"young and hot-headed"**: Latell, Brian. "Castro's Secrets: Cuban Intelligence, The CIA and the Assassination of John F. Kennedy," New York: Palgrave Macmillan, 2012, pp. 49–54. **"If the war had begun"**: Ibid. **"You're dealing with people's lives in a half-assed operation"**: Mahoney, Richard D. "Sons & Brothers: The Days of Jack and Bobby Kennedy," Arcade Publishing, 1999, p. 215. **"If you fuckers hadn't fucked up the Bay of Pigs"**: Stockton, Bayard. "Flawed Patriot: The Rise and Fall of CIA Legend Bill Harvey," Washington DC: Potomac Books, 2006, p. 141. **"Harvey has destroyed himself today"**: Corn, David. "Blond Ghost: Ted Shackley and the CIA's Crusades," New York: Simon & Schuster, 1994, pp. 92–93. **"There was never a time a halt was called"**: Testimony of John Roselli, September 22, 1975, US Senate Select Committee on Intelligence, NARA: 157-10002-10387, p. 5. **"to find out certain intelligence that was going on."**: Ibid., pp. 4–9. **"They were assured of an audience with him"**: Ibid., p. 8. **"a man at least half as brave as the members of Brigade 2506"**: Didion, Joan. "Miami" New York: Simon & Schuster, 1987, p. 89. **"Artime and his group were supported by the CIA"**: NARA: 1993.07.20.14:36:34:680620, John Roselli - OGC Files not Made Available to HSCA Staffers, p. 25. **"Very frankly at that stage, and with the deep concern"**: Testimony of William K. Harvey, US Select Committee on Intelligence, June 25, 1975 (released 1994), NARA: 157-10002-10106, p. 74. **"Termination fee"**: Stockton, Bayard. "Flawed Patriot: The Rise and Fall of CIA Legend Bill Harvey," Washington, DC: Potomac Books, 2006, p. 184.

CHAPTER 32

"Volunteer": Kornbluh, Peter. "US-Cuban Diplomacy, 'Nation' Style," The Nation, April 10, 2013. "I've already done the loaves and fishes": Ibid. "Ringleader": Bracker, Milton, "Three Cubans Sezied with Arms Here in Sabotage Plot," NYT, November 18, 1962, p. 1. "devised a plan to have Donovan be the unwitting purveyor": CIA Report "John McCone as Director of Central Intelligence 1961-1965," marked "secret" and declassified in 2015 and posted by George Washington University National Security Archive, excerpts pp. 99–102, 137–140. "Castro is crazy like a fox": The Associated Press, "Castro Tactics Prove His Skill, Donovans Says," The Washington Star, April 11, 1964. "in the hope that the Justice Department's drive": Hinckle, Warren and William W. Turner, "The Fish Is Red: The Story of the Secret War against Castro," New York: Harper & Row, 1981, p. 189. "This is the earliest date": CIA Inspector General's Report on Plots to Assassinate Fidel Castro, May 23, 1967, declassified 1994, pp. 71–72. "Well, this didn't happen": Hinckle, Warren and William W. Turner, "The Fish Is Red: The Story of the Secret War against Castro," New York: Harper & Row, 1981, p. 189. "Project Johnny": JFK2017:104-10133-10027. "Identified the team as his own": Kaiser, David E. "The Road to Dallas," Harvard University Press, 2008, p. 154. "Gangster elements in the Miami area were offering $150,000": HSCA, Segregated CIA Collection, Box 36, NARA: 104-10103-10346, "New Considerations in CIA Syndicate Operation," p. 5. Also, "Bissell committed $150,000," Maheu Memo to Depurty Director of Central Intelligence, June 24, 1966, JFK2017:104-10133-10091, p. 18. "Johnny's involved": Mahoney, Richard. "Sons & Brothers: The Days of Jack and Bobby Kennedy," New York: Arcade Publishing, p. 270. "J. Ralston": FBI file from Los Angeles office to Director, dated June 21, 1963, identifies this name as an alias of John Roselli. FBI-HSCA Subject File: John Roselli, NARA: 124-10282-10250. "Do you know who your dinner guest is?": CIA Inspector General's Report on Plots to Assassinate Fidel Castro, May 23, 1967, declassified 1994, JFK2017:104-10213-10101, p. 59. "Very early I did make it clear that I couldn't understand": Stockton, Bayard. "Flawed Patriot: The Rise and Fall of CIA Legend Bill Harvey," Washington, DC: Potomac Books, 2006, p. 230. "If the Attorney General told me to jump through a hoop": Latell, Brian. "Castro's Secrets: Cuban Intelligence, the CIA and the Assassination of John F. Kennedy," New York: Palgrave Macmillan, pp. 92–94. "We were told they were going to do the same with our children": Bates, Daniel. "Revealed: How Robert Kennedy feared Mafia would blind his children in acid attack," Daily Mail, January 23, 2012. "The President was obviously serious": Bradlee, Benjamin C. "Conversations with Kennedy," New York: Norton, 1975, p. 98. "That fucking Bobby Kennedy is making life miserable": Ragano, Frank and Selwyn Raab. "Mob Lawyer," New York: Scribner, 1994, p. 135. "Livarsi na pietra di la scarpa! (Take the stone out of my shoe!)": Posner, Gerald. "Case Closed: Lee Harvey Oswald and the Assassination of JFK," New York: Random House, 1993, p. 215. "Bobby Kennedy is stepping on too many toes": Ragano, Frank and Selwyn Raab. "Mob Lawyer," New York: Scribner, 1994, p. 135. "Mark my words": Schlesinger, Arthur M. Jr. "Robert Kennedy and His Times," New York: Houghton Mifflin, 1978, p. 549. "stepping up its activities against Cuba": Beschloss, Michael R. "The Crisis Years: Kenmnedy and Khrushchev, 1960–1963," New York: Edward Burlingame Books, 1991, p. 658. "We are prepared to fight them and answer in kind": Latell, Brian. "Castro's Secrets: Cuban Intelligence, the CIA and the Assassination of John F. Kennedy," New York: Palgrave Macmillan, pp. 174–175. "I am sure glad the Secret Service didn't catch us bringing this gun in here": Helms, Richard and William Hood. "A Look Over My Shoulder: A Life in the Central Intelligence Agency," New York: Random House, 2003, p. 227. "Bobby was as emotional as he could be [about Cuba], and he always talked like he was the President": Martin, Ralph G., "Seeds of Destruction: Joe Kennedy and His Sons," New York: G. P. Putnam's Sons, 1981, p. 338.

CHAPTER 33

"Like many CIA people, in love with the subtle and the artful": Powers, Thomas. "The Man Who Kept the Secrets. Richard Helms and the CIA," New York: Knopf, 1979, p. 150. "I thought he was crazy at the time": Int. with Samuel Halpern, CNN. "The Cold War, Episode 10, Cuba," November 29, 1998. http://nsarchive.gwu.edu/coldwa/interviews/episode-10/halpern4.html. "Sure, Sam, we can make anything blow up": Ibid. p. 4. "So I went and told Des": Ibid. "The real pay-off": Thomas, Evan. "The Very Best Men: The early years of the CIA," New York: Simon and Schuster, 1995, p. 292. "man inside Cuba": CIA Inspector General's Report on Plots to Assassinate Fidel Castro, May 23, 1967, declassified 1994; mention of Juan Orta as spy inside Cuba on March 28 1961, p. 33. "It was not the act that he objected to": Crile, George III. "The Riddle of AMLASH," Washington Post, May 2, 1976. "indignantly refused to be polygraphed": CIA Inspector General's Report on Plots to Assassinate Fidel Castro, May 23, 1967, declassified 1994, mention of Cubela refusal to be polygraphed in August 1962, p. 84. "for assurances of US moral support": CIA Inspector General's Report on Plots to Assassinate Fidel Castro, May 23, 1967, declassified 1994, pp. 82–85. "Dangle": Clark, Robert M. "Intelligence Collection," Washington, DC, CQ Press, 2013, p. 54. "While Cubela was anxious to do away with Castro": CIA Inspector General's Report on Plots to Assassinate Fidel Castro, May 23, 1967, declassified 1994, p. 92. "high power rifles w/scopes": Ibid., p. 90. "needle was so fine that the victim would hardly feel it": Ibid., p. 93. "but didn't want to know": Ibid., p. 95.

CHAPTER 34

"like I was in a giant maze . . . sick": Summers, Anthony and Robbyn Swan, "Sinatra: The Life," New York: Knopf, 2005, p. 293. "Did you ever see John Roselli and so-and-so together?": Investigation of Organized Crime in Interstate Commerce: Hearings before a Special Committee to Investigate Organized Crime in Interstate Commerce, United States Senate, Eighty-first Congress, Second Session, Washington, DC: US Government Printing Office, p. 124. Also, Exner, Judith. "My Story," New York: Grove Press, 1977, p. 284. "You would have to know the nature of the beast": Testimony of John Roselli, September 22, 1975, US Senate Select Committee on Intelligence, NARA: 157-10002-10387, p. 15. "I would be loyal to Sam and Johnny": Exner, Judith. "My story," New York: Grove Press, 1977, p. 279. "I was 26 and in love": The Chicago Tribune, "Kennedy Mistress Reveals Abortion in Magazine Story," December 11, 1996. This claim also was repeated in Judith Campbell Exner's 1999 obituary in The New York Times. "She also said she had an abortion after becoming pregnant with Kennedy's baby, almost a year before Kennedy was assassinated," the Times reported in September 27, 1999, story, "Judith Exner Is Dead at 65; Claimed Affair with Kennedy," by Eric Pace. Three days later, the Times ran an "Editor's Note" saying that the obituiary of Exner's "assertions" and a denial by Kennedy's aide Dave Power should have included a broader context. "It should also have reflected what is now the view of a number of respected historians and authors that the affair did in fact take place," said the Times. "The evidence cited by various authorities in recent years has included White House phone logs and memos from J. Edgar Hoover." "You know I can't keep this child": Smith, Liz. "The Exner Files," Vanity Fair, January 1997. "Do you think Sam would help us?": Exner, Judith. "My Story," New York: Grove Press, 1977, p. 193. "Damn him!": Ibid., p. 194. "at the request of the Attorney General": Mahoney, Richard D. "Sons & Brothers: The Days of Jack and Bobby Kennedy," Arcade Publishing, 1999, p. 97. "Otash, you know, you're going to have some serious problems": Rappleye, Charles and Ed Becker. "All-American Mafioso: The Johnny Rosselli Story," New York: Doubleday, 1991, p. 210. "looking for dirt": JFK2017:124-10285-10332; also, Miller,

Michael E. "Strippers, surveillance and assassination plots: The wildest JFK Files," The Washington Post, October 27, 2017. **"associated with prominent underworld figures"**: March 26, 1962, FBI memo, NARA:124-10225-10037. **"I want to ask you something"**: Exner, Judith. "My Story," New York: Grove Press, 1977, p. 193. **"Sam, you don't want to marry me"**: Smith, Liz. "The Exner Files," Vanity Fair, January 1997. **"We were intimate that night, although I certainly wasn't in love with him"**: Ibid.

CHAPTER 35

"I didn't believe it at first because I was in a sound sleep": Testimony of John Roselli, April 23, 1976, US Senate Select Committee on Intelligence, NARA: 157-10014-10000, (released in 1998), p. 5. **"That was the first thing that came to my mind"**: Testimony of John Roselli, April 23, 1976, US Senate Select Committee on Intelligence, NARA: 157-10014-10000, (released in 1998), pp. 5–6. **"Gina" and "Arlene" and "urgent"**: JFK2017:124-10222-10400. **"I'm going to Hickory Hill to be with Bobby"**: Robarge, David. "DCI John McCone and the Assassination of President John F. Kennedy," David Robarge, Studies in Intelligence Vol. 51, No. 3 (September 2013), Approved for Release: September 29, 2014, p. 2. **"There's so much bitterness"**: Schlesinger, Arthur M. Jr. "Robert Kennedy and His Times," New York: Houghton Mifflin, 1978, p. 609. **"I asked him in a way he couldn't lie to me"**: Robarge, David. "DCI John McCone and the Assassination of President John F. Kennedy," David Robarge, Studies in Intelligence Vol. 51, No. 3 (September 2013), Approved for Release: September 29, 2014, p. 5. **"Kennedy may very well have thought there was some connection"**: DCI John McCone and the Assassination of President John F. Kennedy," David Robarge, Studies in Intelligence Vol. 51, No. 3 Part 2 of 2, Approved for Released: April 10, 2015, Chapter 14, "Death of the President," p. 334. **"personal feelings of guilt"**: Robarge, David. "DCI John McCone and the Assassination of President John F. Kennedy," David Robarge, Studies in Intelligence Vol. 51, No. 3 (September 2013), Approved for Release: September 29, 2014, p. 5. **"Do you have any angles"**: Bugliosi, Vincent. "Reclaiming History: The Assassination of President John F. Kennedy," New York: W. W. Norton & Co., 2007, p. 1158. **"Now they'll get off my back, off Carlos' [Marcello] back"**: Ragano, Frank and Selwyn Raab. "Mob Lawyer," New York: Scribner, 1994, p. 359. **"He was a marksman who knew how to shoot"**: Investigation of the Assassination of President John F. Kennedy: Hearings before the Select Committee on Assassinations of the U.S. House of Representatives, Ninety-fifth Congress, Second Session, Volumes 8–9, Washington: U.S. Government Printing Office, 1978, p. 42. **"I will tell you something, in another two months from now"**: Final Report of House Selection Committee on Assassinations, Summary of Findings, January 1979, p. 169. **"Maybe if you had clipped him"**: Moldea, Dan. E., "The Flip Side of the Underworld," The Washington Post, February 8, 1981. **"I couldn't believe it"**: Exner, Judith. "My Story," New York: Grove Press, 1977, p. 288. **"I didn't want to see him, but he patiently resisted me"**: Ibid., p. 288. **"Frank was pretty broken up"**: Kelley, Kitty. "His Way: The Unauthorized Biography of Frank Sinatra," New York: Bantam, 2010, p. 371. **"Come on, now, don't get so mad"**: Newton, Michael. "Mr. Mob: The Life and Crimes of Moe Dalitz," Jefferson, NC: McFarland & Co., 2009, p. 218. **"You know something"**: Exner, Judith. "My Story," New York: Grove Press, 1977, p. 289. **"Your show is ending"**: JFK2017:124-10200-10052. **"Jack was dead"**: Exner, Judith. "My Story," New York: Grove Press, 1977, p. 292.

CHAPTER 36

"Truth has a hard time once legends are established": Lathrop, Charles. "The literary Spy," New Haven: Yale University Press, 2004, p. 150. **"I hope not"**: Grose, Peter.

"Gentleman Spy: The Life of Allen Dulles," Boston: University of Massachusetts Press, 1996, p. 539. **"I'm just a patsy"**: Bugliosi, Vincent. "Reclaiming History: The Assassination of President John F. Kennedy," New York: W. W. Norton & Co., 2007, p. 842. **"We had thousands and thousands of hours of tape recordings"**: Posner, Gerald. "Case Closed: Lee Harvey Oswald and the Assassination of JFK," New York: Random House, 1993, p. 354. **"It was so tantalizing to go over that record"**: Oral History Interview with Allen W. Dulles, December 5-6, 1964 Washington, DC, Interview by Thomas Braden for the John F. Kennedy Library, p. 33. **"He looked like the ghost of his former self"**: Katzenbach, Nicholas DeB., "Some of It Was Fun: Working with RFK and LBJ," New York: W. W. Norton, 2008, p. 134. **"As for the makeup of the rest of the commission"**: Johnson, Lyndon Baines. "The Vantage Point: Perspectives of the Presidency, 1963-1969," New York: Holt, Rinehart and Winston, 1971, p. 27. **"I suggest that you and I might have a word together before I put anything on the tape"**: Letter dated January 28, 1964, from Allen Dulles letter to RFK, JFK Library. **"I bet you any amount of money"**: Demaris, Ovid. "The Last Mafioso," New York: Times Books, 1981, p. 193. **"there was still argument"**: Schlesinger, Arthur M. Jr. "Robert Kennedy and His Times," New York: Houghton Mifflin, 1978, p. 615. **"the possibility that someone associated with the underworld"**: Final Report of House Selection Committee on Assassinations, Summary of Findings, January 1979, p. 168. **"That the CIA hid its operation to murder the Cuban leader"**: Posner, Gerald. "Case Closed: Lee Harvey Oswald and the Assassination of JFK," New York: Random House, 1993, p. 453. **"benign cover-up"**: Robarge, David. "DCI John McCone and the Assassination of President John F. Kennedy," David Robarge, Studies in Intelligence Vol. 51, No. 3 (September 2013), Approved for Release: September 29, 2014, p. 20. **"Neither frank nor accurate"**: Ibid., p. 12. **"He [Edwards] said something about, well, we never briefed McCone"**: Testimony of James P. O'Connell, United States Senate Select Committee on Intelligence, NARA: 157-10002-10148, May 30, 1975, p. 39. **"Do we have an application of morality"**: Int. with Allen Dulles from "The Science of Spying," NBC network documentary narrated by John Chancellor, May 4, 1965. **"All I can say is that I am a parson's son"**: Ibid.

CHAPTER 37

"Anytime I would go to Chicago, I'd have been at his home": Testimony of John Roselli, September 22, 1975, US Senate Select Committee on Intelligence, NARA: 157-10002-10387, p. 20. **"Sam didn't realize I could hear"**: Giancana, Antoinette and Thomas C. Renner. "Mafia Princess: Growing Up in Sam Giancana's Family," New York: William Morrow, 1984, p. 324. **"In Chicago we were never able to establish"**: Roemer, William F. "Roemer: Man against the Mob," New York: Random House, 1989, p. 157. **"He never mentioned organized crime to me again"**: Caro, Robert A. "The Passage of Power," New York: Vintage, 2013, p. 577. **"When I received word of Johnson's executive order"**: Roemer, William F. "Roemer: Man against the Mob," New York: Random House, 1989, p. 224. **"The publicity Giancana got at the Cal-Neva Lodge earlier"**: FBI memo dated April 9, 1964 in FBI File Vault- Frank Sinatra, File #9-11775, http://foia.fbi.gov/sinatra/sinatra02a.pdf. **"used strong language in response"**: Wiedrich, Robert. "Police Find Juice Loan Mob Grabs Take of Independents," The Chicago Tribune, July 27, 1964, p. 3. **"If Bobby Kennedy wants to talk to me"**: Schlesinger, Arthur M. Jr. "Robert Kennedy and His Times," New York: Houghton Mifflin, 1978, p. 495. **"For Chrissakes, that's a cardinal rule"**: Roemer, William F. Jr. "Accardo: The Genuine Godfather," New York: Donald I. Fine, 1995, pp. 262–265. **"died of unnatural causes–a heart attack"**: Russo, Gus. "The Outfit: The role of Chicago's underworld in the shaping of modern America," New York: Bloomsbury, 2003, p. 459. **"If he lied, we could get him for perjury"**: Roemer, William F. Jr. "The

Enforcer: Spilotro: The Chicago Mob's Man over Las Vegas," New York: Ballantine Books, 1994, p. 73. **"I didn't need you to get where I am, and don't forget it"**: Giancana, Antoinette and Thomas C. Renner. "Mafia Princess: Growing Up in Sam Giancana's Family," New York: William Morrow, 1984, p. 288. **"I'm going to give him up"**: Demaris, Ovid. "Captive City," New York: Lyle Stuart, 1969, p. 12. **"You fellows have been writing bad stories about me and Sam"**: Ibid., p. 12. **"Sam loved Phyllis in his own way"**: Giancana, Antoinette and Thomas C. Renner. "Mafia Princess: Growing Up in Sam Giancana's Family," New York: William Morrow, 1984, p. 292. **"It was felt that Bergit might prove to be a psychological weapon"**: Vincent Inserra. "C-1 and the Chicago Mob," USA: Xlibris, 2014, p. 108. **"I wish I could get out of here"**: Wiedrich, Robert. "Giancana Mum Before Jury, Blabs at Bar," The Chicago Tribune, May 31, 1965, p. 5. **"You have the key to your own cell"**: The Federal Reporter, second series - Volume 352, West Publishing Company, 1966, p. 923. **"Sam chose the only course he could choose"**: Giancana, Antoinette and Thomas C. Renner. "Mafia Princess: Growing Up in Sam Giancana's Family," New York: William Morrow, 1984, p. 334.

CHAPTER 38

"Dave was very selective": Fonzi, Gaeton and Marie Fonzi. "The Last Investigation," New York: Skyhorse Publishing, 2013, p. 376. **"get out of the cloak and dagger business"**: JFK2017: 177-10001-10445. **"boom and bang operations"**: Shackley, Ted and Richard A. Finney. "Spymaster: My Life in the CIA," Dulles, Virginia: Potomac Books, 2005, p. 76. **"Zenith"**: HSCA Report, Volume X Current Section: VI. Brigade 2506—Manuel Artime—Movimiento de Recuperacion Revolucionaria (MRR), p. 11. **"The bearded devil had won the war"**: Shackley, Ted and Richard A. Finney. "Spymaster: My Life in the CIA," Dulles, Virginia: Potomac Books, 2005, p. 76. **"The Kennedy administration had completed extensive top-secret plans"**: Hinckle, Warren and William W. Turner, "The Fish Is Red: The Story of the Secret War against Castro," New York: Harper & Row, 1981, pp. 20–21. **"harassment, sabotage and psychological warfare"**: CIA Files, Office of General Counsel, NARA: 1993.07.20.14:36:34:680620, JOHN ROSSELLI - OGC files not made available to HSCA staffers, p. 44. **"when Bobby Kennedy separated from the Johnson administration"**: Investigation of the assassination of President John F. Kennedy: hearings before the Select Committee on Assassinations of the U.S. House of Representatives, Ninety-fifth Congress, second session, Volume 10, Washington DC: US Government Printing Office, p. 68. **"it seemed something always went wrong during these sabotage operations"**: Shackley, Ted and Richard A. Finney. "Spymaster: My Life in the CIA," Dulles, Virginia: Potomac Books, 2005, p. 73. **"No one knows how we know"**: Latell, Brian. "Castro's Secrets: Cuban Intelligence, The CIA and the Assassination of John F. Kennedy," New York: Palgrave Macmillan, p. 101. **"The report from the Mexico City station"**: Weiner, Tim. "Legacy of Ashes: The History of the CIA," New York: Knopf Doubleday, 2008, p. 261. **"believed the only solution to the problems in Cuba"**: "Alleged Assassination Plots Involving Foreign Leaders: An Interim Report of the Select Committee to Study Governmental Operations with Respect to Intelligence Activities, Volume 13098, United States Senate, Washington, DC: US Government Printing Office, 1975, p. 90. **"heard that Trafficante could have been a double agent"**: FBI-HSCA subject file: John Roselli, NARA: 124-10289-10035, p. 59. **"was killed at the direction of the Castro regime"**: CIA File dated March 7, 1968, titled "Garrison and the Kennedy Assassination: Cubans and Other Latin Americans Allegedly Involved," NARA: 1993.06.29.19:33:56:210480, p. 1.

PHASE IV: THE PRICE OF EVERYTHING

"Once you've lived the inside-out world of espionage": Ayers, Pip. "John LeCarre Reflects," July 15, 2011 (Mail Online version).

CHAPTER 39

"I can buy any man in the world": Bartlett, Donald L. and James B. Steele. "Empire: The Life, Legend, and Madness of Howard Hughes," New York, W. W. Norton & Co., 1981, p. 448. "definitely of the new school": Reid, Ed and Ovid Demaris. "The Green Felt Jungle," New York: Trident Press, 1963, p. 224. "There was a flash on the TV that Castro was dead": Testimony of John Roselli, April 23, 1976, US Senate Select Committee on Intelligence, NARA: 157-10014-10000, (released in 1998), pp. 32–33. "I guess it is still working": Ibid., p. 33. "Roselli was a like a key to the city": Maheu, Robert and Richard Hack. "Next to Hughes," New York: HarperCollins, 1992, p. 159–161. "We roped Hughes into buying the D.I.": Drosnin, Michael. "Citizen Hughes," New York: Holt, Rinehart and Winston, 1985, p. 120. "for many years": Bartlett, Donald L. and James B. Steele. "Howard Hughes: His Life and Madness," New York: W. W. Norton & Co., 2011, p. 285. "I found him sexless": Porter, Dawn. "Howard Hughes: Hell's Angel," New York: Blood Moon, 2004, p. 250. "Facilitator": Maheu, Robert and Richard Hack. "Next to Hughes," New York: HarperCollins, 1992, pp. 159–161. "I had found a person fitting the background": Hinckle, Warren and William W. Turner, "The Fish Is Red: The Story of the Secret War against Castro," New York: Harper & Row, 1981, p. 28. "finder's fee": Ibid., p. 267. "I just split four hundred big ones with Sam": Demaris, Ovid. "The Last Mafioso," New York: Times Books, 1981, p. 166. "Howard wanted every casino": Schumacher, Geoff. "Sun, Sin & Suburbia: An Essential History of Modern Las Vegas," Las Vegas: Stephens Press LLC, 2010, p. 102. "the skim": Denton, Sally and Roger Morris. "The Money and the Power," New York: Knopf, 2001, p. 242. "Now I want to tell you who the casino manager is going to be here": Maheu, Robert and Richard Hack. "Next to Hughes," New York: Harper-Collins, 1992, p. 162. "Welcome to Las Vegas—Howard Hughes' Monopoly set": Bartlett, Donald L. and James B. Steele. "Empire: The Life, Legend, and Madness of Howard Hughes," New York: W. W. Norton & Co., 1981, p. 303. "the Xanadu of Rat Pack lore": Wolcott, James. "When They Were Kings," Vanity Fair, May 1997. "Frank has gotten Ava completely out of his system": Kaplan, James. "Sinatra: The Chairman," New York: Doubleday, p. 19. "red carpet": Ibid., p. 535. "My job was to find out if any men visited her": Maheu, Robert and Richard Hack. "Next to Hughes," New York: HarperCollins, 1992, p. 67. "to woo and coo, and talk Ava out of getting a divorce": Ibid., p. 58. "I built this hotel from a sandpile": Garrison, Omar V. "Howard Hughes in Las Vegas," New York: Lyle Stuart, 1970, p. 56. "You make one move": Summers, Anthony and Robbyn Swan. "Sinatra: The Life," New York: Knopf, 2005, p. 332. "active in LCN [La Cosa Nostra] matters": FBI Vault File on Frank Sinatra, File #92-3171, p. 25. "Informant did not believe this was planned": Ibid., p. 25. "Hughes made the nation think Las Vegas was now clean": Moe, Albert Woods. "Nevada's Golden Age of Gambling," Angel Fire, NM: Puget Sound Books, 2001, p. 104. "You can't steal $100,000 a month and pay dividends": Congressional Record: Proceedings and Debates of the . . . Congress, Volume 115, Part 12, Washington, DC: US Government Printing Office, 1969, p. 15698.

CHAPTER 40

"Instead of the cross, the Albatross": Coleridge, Samuel Taylor. "The Rime of the Ancient Mariner and Other Poems," New York: HarperCollins, 2016, p. 72. "There were no colored lights or sparkling trees": Giancana, Antoinette and Thomas C. Renner. "Mafia Princess:

Growing Up in Sam Giancana's Family," New York: William Morrow, 1984, p. 335. "**Vitu-perous**": Roemer, William F. Jr. "Accardo: The Genuine Godfather," New York: Donald I. Fine, 1995, p. 286. "**Giancana was as adamant as ever**": Ibid., p. 286. "**My situation with 'Batters' is piss poor**": Demaris, Ovid. "The Last Mafioso," New York: Times Books, 1981, p. 244. "**a posh castle near Cuernavaca**": Smith, Sandy. "The Fix," *Life*, September 12, 1967, p. 43. Also, JFK2017: 124-10195-10249. "**extended vacation**": Giancana, Antoinette and Thomas C. Renner. "Mafia Princess: Growing Up in Sam Giancana's Family," New York: William Morrow, 1984, p. 338. "**Cain was not the average, old-neighborhood thug**": Brashler, William. "The Don: the life and death of Sam Giancana," New York: Ballantine Books, 1976, p. 39. "**Anything that Sinatra does, Giancana is a part of it**": Montgomery, David and Jeff Leen. "The Sinatra Files: Forty Years of the FBI's Frank Talk," The Washington Post, December 9, 1998 (online). "**alleged Mafia connections**": CIA memo dated January 10, 1974, on name check on Salvatore (sic) Giancana and Richard Cain. NARA: 104-10133-10404. "**Oh what a tangled web we weave**": Cain, Michael J. "The Tangled Web: The Life and Death of Richard Cain," New York: Skyhorse, 2007, p. 157. "**Shamus, here**": Demaris, Ovid. "The Last Mafioso," New York: Times Books, 1981, p. 120. "**See my attorney**": FBI memo May 12, 1966, FBI Vault File - John ("Handsome Johnny") Roselli, Part 8 of 12, p. 109, http://foia.fbi.gov/roselli/roselli3b.pdf. "**Filippo Sacco**": Ibid. "**Giovanni Roselli**": JFK2017: 124-10291-10058. "**We know where you were born**": Ibid. "**Compro-mised themselves by dealing with Roselli**": Justice Dept. memo to FBI dated May 23, 1966, FBI Vault File - John ("Handsome Johnny") Roselli, Part 8 of 12, p. 91, http://foia.fbi .gov/roselli/roselli3b.pdf. "**top echelon criminal informant**": Ibid., p. 92. "**capitalize on his inner turmoil to develop**": Ibid., p. 92. "**is very good looking and all the girls go for him**": FBI memo dated April 29, 1963, FBI-HSCA Subject file: John Roselli, NARA: 124-10225-10219, p. 78. "**a person's own telephone is the biggest stool pigeon**": Ibid., p. 78. "**This has nothing to do with you personally, John**": Rappleye, Charles and Ed Becker. "All-American Mafioso: The Johnny Rosselli Story," New York: Doubleday, 1991, p. 261. "**I did not ask him to get the FBI off my back**": Ibid., p. 304. "**they had a big feud going on between the FBI and the CIA**": Testimony of John Roselli, September 22, 1975, US Senate Select Commit-tee on Intelligence, NARA: 157-10002-10387, p. 48. "**the child was himself at that age**": FBI memo May 12, 1966, FBI Vault File - John ("Handsome Johnny") Roselli, Part 8 of 12, p. 112, http://foia.fbi.gov/roselli/roselli3b.pdf. "**Blackmail**": FBI Vault File of Fidel Castro, Part 03 of 04, p. 28-30, Castro1c.pdf, pp. 18–20. "**open the door**": FBI Vault File of Fidel Castro, Part 02 of 04, p. 212-214, Castro1b.pdf.

CHAPTER 41

"**Let's put it this way: Is that the freeway?**": John Kobler, "The (Million-Dollar) Sting at the Friars Club," New York Magazine, July 21, 1975, p. 28. "**my friend Johnny**": Ibid., p. 32. "**There were other members who had served sentences**": "Crime: Deep Six for Johnny," Time magazine, August 23, 1976. "**Roselli's master coup was muscling in**": John Kobler, "The (Million-Dollar) Sting At the Friars Club," New York Magazine, July 21, 1975, p. 28. "**The most important thing**": Rappleye, Charles and Ed Becker. "All-American Mafioso: The Johnny Rosselli Story," New York: Doubleday, 1991, p. 229. "**Forget it–the first guy they want him to inform on**": Demaris, Ovid. "The Last Mafioso," New York: Times Books, 1981, pp. 191–196. "**Look Ed, number one, I'm not going to snitch on nobody**": Ibid., pp. 191–196. "**I want the name of the prick that turned me in**": Ibid., p. 170. "**because I owe it a lot**": Testimony of James P. O'Connell, United States Senate Select Committee on Intelligence, NARA: 157-10002- 10148, May 30, 1975, pp. 26–27. "**it's the one thing in my life**": "Mob Conned CIA in Castro Assassination Plot," St. Louis

Post-Dispatch, January 13, 1981, p. 37. **"One of our assassination teams was captured"**: Demaris, Ovid. "The Last Mafioso," New York: Times Books, 1981, p. 196. **"in strictest confidence"**: FBI memo dated February 26, 1976, FBI - HSCA Subject File: John Roselli, NARA: 124-10289-10035, p. 195. **"Listen Ed, as far as I know"**: Demaris, Ovid. "The Last Mafioso," New York: Times Books, 1981, p. 196. **"Hero"**: Testimony of William K. Harvey, U.S. Select Committee on Intelligence, June 25, 1975 (released 1994), NARA: 157-10002-10106, p. 142. **"serious enough"**: Powers, Thomas. "The Man Who Kept the Secrets: Richard Helms and the CIA," New York: Knopf, 1979, p. 120. **"President Johnson is sitting on a political H-bomb"**: Weiner, Tim. "Legacy of Ashes: The History of the CIA," New York: Doubleday, p. 314. **"Blowback"**: Ibid., p. 313. **"He had clients (unnamed) who knew that Castro was aware"**: FBI File of Fidel Castro, Part 03 of 04, p. 28-30, Castro1c.pdf, p. 168. **"a high type individual of the Catholic faith"**: Mahoney, Richard D. "Sons & Brothers: The Days of Jack and Bobby Kennedy," Arcade Publishing, 1999, pp. 338–339.

CHAPTER 42

"You know [there's] this story going around about the CIA": Holland, Max. "The Assassination Tapes," The Atlantic, June 2004. **"reputable people"**: Beschloss, Michael. "Taking Charge: The Johnson White House Tapes 1963-1964," New York: Simon & Schuster, 1998, p. 563. **"It sounded just so [wild] . . . just like you're telling me that Lady Bird was"**: Ibid., p. 563. **"I'll tell you something [about John Kennedy's murder] that will rock you"**: Holland, Max. "The Assassination Tapes," The Atlantic, June 2004. **"It will all come out one day"**: Ibid. **"Bobby Kennedy understood that public revelation of the materials"**: Hersh, Seymour M. "The Dark Side of Camelot," Boston: Little, Brown, 1997. **"I do not know whether he suspected how much vital information both the FBI"**: Schlesinger, Arthur M. Jr. "Robert Kennedy and His Times," New York: Houghton Mifflin, 1978, p. 644. **"unwilling to criticize it and thereby reopen"**: Ibid., p. 644. **"I was unaware of the efforts by the CIA to assassinate Castro"**: Katzenbach, Nicholas DeB., "Some of It Was Fun: Working with RFK and LBJ," New York: W. W. Norton, 2008, p. 133. **"badly frightened Bobby Kennedy"**: Weiner, Tim. "Legacy of Ashes: The History of the CIA," New York: Knopf Doubleday, 2008, p. 314. **"Robert Kennedy as attorney general knew about the CIA plot"**: Ibid., p. 314. **"I didn't start it. I stopped it"**: Schlesinger, Arthur M. Jr. "Robert Kennedy and His Times," New York: Houghton Mifflin, 1978, p. 494. **"We cannot over emphasize the extent"**: Weiner, Tim. "Legacy of Ashes: The History of the CIA," New York: Knopf Doubleday, 2008, p. 315. **"If one left the criminal aspects of Roselli's activities out of the picture"**: FBI memo dated May 8, 1967, HSCA segregated CIA collection, Box 48, "Johnny Roselli" file. NARA: 104-10133-10080. **"Harvey questioned [the] characterization of Roselli as a tool"**: Ibid. **"could hardly be regarded favorably"**: Summary memo dated December 27, 1968, by Howard Osborn. FBI File of Fidel Castro, Part 03 of 04, pp. 28–30, Castro1c.pdf, p. 45. **"The worse thing"**: FBI Vault File of Fidel Castro, Part 03 of 04, pp. 28–30, Castro1c.pdf. **"would never 'pull the string' on us"**: HSCA segregated CIA collection, Box 42, NARA: 1993.07.20.14:27:51:590280, File marked "Harvey, William King - OS/SAG Files for HSCA staff, p. 150. **"knew all about the operation"**: Ibid., p. 150. **"would be his neck"**: HSCA segregated CIA collection, Box 1, file marked "Luncheon Meeting with William K. Harvey," NARA: 1993.07.01.10:05:48:530800, p. 3. **"his full realization of the hazard to him personally"**: Ibid., p. 4. **"Damn it, you guys were sitting on your asses"**: Testimony of James P. O'Connell, United States Senate Select Committee on Intelligence, NARA: 157-10002- 10148, May 30, 1975, p. 154. **"Sell anyone down the river"**: File marked "Luncheon meeting with William K. Harvey," HSCA segregated CIA collection, Box 1, NARA: 1993.07.01.10:05:48:530800. **"a very selfish life"**:

Rappleye, Charles and Ed Becker. "All-American Mafioso: The Johnny Rosselli Story," New York: Doubleday, 1991, p. 230. **"I don't know what you're talking about"**: FBI File dated May 12, 1966. FBI Vault File, Johnny Roselli, Part 8 of 12, p. 109. **"I don't think Mr. Roselli is entitled to brownie points"**: Kobler, John. "The (Million-Dollar) Sting at the Friars Club," New York Magazine, July 21, 1975, p. 34.

CHAPTER 43

"a lost cause": Giancana, Antoinette and Thomas C. Renner. "Mafia Princess: Growing Up in Sam Giancana's Family," New York: William Morrow, 1984, p. 292. **"The FBI report unknowingly bared Sam's soul"**: Ibid., p. 293. **"This guy's having a ball"**: Demaris, Ovid. "The Last Mafioso," New York: Times Books, 1981, p. 220. **"With Sam [Giancana] in Mexico"**: Ibid., p. 220. **"Pissant"**: Roemer, William F. Jr. "Accardo: The Genuine Godfather," New York: Donald I. Fine, 1995, p. 311. **"The Hole in the Wall"**: Farrell, Ronald and Carole Case. "The Black Book and the Mob: the Untold Story of the Control of Nevada's Casinos," Madison, Wisc.: University of Wisconsin Press, 1995, p. 70. **"Kill me, get it over with"**: Roemer, William F. Jr. "The Enforcer: Spilotro: The Chicago Mob's Man over Las Vegas," New York: Ballantine Books, 1994, pp. 39–41. **"I've broken arms, and I've broken legs"**: Koziol, Ronald. "Hit Man's Job Hardly Glamorous," The Chicago Tribune, December 3, 1989. **"School"**: Brashler, William. "The Don: the life and death of Sam Giancana." New York: Ballantine Books, 1976, p. 77. **"I assured him that the nation's moviegoers"**: Royko, Mike. "Dr. Kookie, you're right!" New York: Plume Books, 1990, p. 106. **"something about fish"**: Roemer, William F. Jr. "The Enforcer: Spilotro: The Chicago Mob's Man over Las Vegas," New York: Ballantine Books, 1994, p. 91. **"Ironic as hell, because twenty years ago"**: Demaris, Ovid. "The Last Mafioso," New York: Times Books, 1981, p. 276. **"You'll still just a pissant, Tony"**: Roemer, William F. Jr. "The Enforcer: Spilotro: The Chicago Mob's Man over Las Vegas," New York: Ballantine Books, 1994, p. 92. **"I can't make any money here"**: Wiedrich, Bob. "Tower Ticker," Chicago Tribune, Janaury 31, 1972, p. 18. **"He started talking about his being a soldier of fortune"**: Roemer, William F. "Roemer: Man against the Mob," New York: Random House, 1989, p. 387. **"How much money would you have spent"**: Ibid., p. 229. **"Bill, if anything ever happens to me"**: Ibid., 230. **"He never revealed his motivation for turning on the mob"**: Cain, Michael J. "The Tangled Web: The Life and Death of Richard Cain," New York: Skyhorse, 2007, p. 223. **"one of my closest friends, believe or not"**: Roemer, William F. Jr. "The Enforcer: Spilotro: The Chicago Mob's Man over Las Vegas," New York: Ballantine Books, 1994, p. 51. **"a very vicious man"**: Dark, Tony. "The FBI Files of Sam Giancana," Hosehead Productions, 2009, p. 479. **"Tires screeched, cars raced, somebody was after me"**: Roemer, William F. "Roemer: Man against the Mob," New York: Random House, 1989, p. 235. **"I was initially worried that it had been caused by a leak"**: Roemer, William F. Jr. "Accardo: The Genuine Godfather," New York: Donald I. Fine, 1995, p. 307.

CHAPTER 44

"There is something about intelligence that seems to get in the blood": Powers, Thomas. "The Man Who Kept The Secrets: Richard Helms and the CIA," New York: Knopf, 1979, p. 342. **"Espionage is not played by the Marquess of Queensberry rules"**: McManus, Doyle and Don Shannon. "Israel Apologizes to U.S. in Spy Case: Shultz Welcomes Promised Probe in Pollard Affair," Los Angeles Times, December 2, 1985. **"Detested"**: Powers, Thomas. "The Man Who Kept the Secrets: Richard Helms and the CIA," New York: Knopf, 1979, p. 55. **"have only each other on whom to lean"**: Robarge, David. "Richard Helms: The Intelligence Professional Personified," CIA Historical Document, April 14, 2007, https://www.cia.gov/library/center-for-the-study-of-intelligence/csi-publications/csi-studies/studies/vol46no4/article06.html. "gentlemanly planner of assassinations": Morley, Jefferson. "The Gentlemanly Planner of Assassinations," Slate, November 1, 2002. "Aside from a romantic, if transient, glow of patriotism, the underworld": Helms, Richard and William Hood. "A Look over My Shoulder: A Life in the Central Intelligence Agency," New York: Random House, 2003, p. 201. "He [Giancana] wanted to know if you needed any help": Maheu, Robert and Richard Hack. "Next to Hughes," New York: HarperCollins, 1992, p. 125. "Stupidly": Ibid., p. 125. "You guys owe me": Ibid, p. 126. "a position to continue skimming of money": FBI-HSCA Subject File - John Roselli, NARA: 124-10288- 10230, p. 3. "he always considered Roselli to be a millionaire": Ibid., p. 3. "He was really nuts about her": Rappleye, Charles and Ed Becker. "All-American Mafioso: The Johnny Rosselli Story," New York: Doubleday, 1991, p. 290. "When that Jones boy picks up a pistol—everybody laughs": Okon, Mary. "Spike to the Guns!," New York Daily News, Sunday News magazine, October 3, 1954, p. 12. "the terrible secret": Anderson, Jack. "6 Attempts to Kill Castro Laid to CIA," The Washington Post, January 15, 1971. "The full story reads like the script of a James Bond movie": Ibid. "high regard": Anderson, Jack. "Castro Stalker Worked for the CIA," The Washington Post, February 23, 1971, also contained in "Family Jewels" report, p. 18. "This a long story": Ibid. "could not have happened": Rappleye, Charles and Ed Becker. "All-American Mafioso: The Johnny Rosselli Story," New York: Doubleday, 1991, pp. 297–299. "the reason why the break-in occurred at the Democratic Party": Ibid., p. 307. "The CIA look bad, it's going to make Hunt look bad": Rasenberger, Jim. "The Brilliant Disaster: JFK, Castro, and America's Doomed Invasion of Cuba's Bay of Pigs," New York: Scribner, 2011, p. 398. "felt very bitter toward the Agency": HSCA segregated CIA collection (staff notes)/ NARA: 180-10145-1021, p. 4.

CHAPTER 45

"undesirable person": Inserra, Vincent L. "C-1 and the Chicago Mob" Xlibris, 2014, p. 253. "aged tremendously": Roemer, William F. "Roemer: Man Against the Mob," New York: Random House, 1989, p. 336. "Roemer, I should have known": Ibid., p. 336. "You guys started bugging me again": Inserra, Vincent L. "C-1 and the Chicago Mob" Xlibris, 2014, p. 252. "I'm out of it": Roemer, William F. "Roemer: Man Against the Mob," New York: Random House, 1989, p. 336. "At that moment, I realized that I had won": Ibid., p. 336. "You made your bed, goddammit, now you lie in it!": Giancana, Antoinette and Thomas C. Renner. "Mafia Princess: Growing Up in Sam Giancana's Family," New York: William Morrow, 1984, p. 298. "Let me figure out what my next (attorney's) tab will be": LaBrecque, Ron. "Could Roselli Have Linked Castro Plot to JFK Death?" The Miami Herald, September 19, 1976, p. 1A. "too close": Giancana, Sam and Chuck Giancana. "Double Cross: The Explosive, Inside Story of the Mobster Who Controlled America," Warner Books, 1992, p. 493. "The Mob knew the odds": Maheu, Robert and Richard Hack. "Next to Hughes," New York: HarperCollins, 1992, p. 132. "the only person in American history to be murdered": Safire, William. "Murder Most Foul," NYT, December 22, 1975, p. 28. "I always felt very strongly that the subpoena": Sifakis, Carl. "The Mafia Encyclopedia," Facts On File, 2005, p. 346. "I give her [McGuire] credit": Roemer, William F. Jr. "Roemer: Man against the Mob," New York: Donald I. Fine, 1989, p. 358.

CHAPTER 46

"The confession of evil": Day, Malcolm. "1,001 pearls of Bible wisdom: insights and inspirations from the biblical tradition," San Francisco: Chronicle Books, 2008, p. 154. "They fucking killed a dead man": Demaris, Ovid. "The Last Mafioso," Times Books,

1981, pp. 293–294. **"They're not going to do anything to me"**: Rappleye, Charles and Ed Becker. "All-American Mafioso: The Johnny Rosselli Story," New York: Doubleday, 1991, p. 310. **"I don't know how a man feels"**: Testimony of John Roselli, June 24, 1975, US Senate Select Committee on Intelligence, NARA: 157-10014-10001, p. 53. **"Senator, in my business, we don't take notes"**: Rappleye, Charles and Ed Becker. "All-American Mafioso: The Johnny Rosselli Story," New York: Doubleday, 1991, p. 313. **"I don't ask any questions how high"**: Testimony of John Roselli, June 24, 1975, US Senate Select Committee on Intelligence, NARA: 157-10014-10001, pp. 57–59. **"I told him very simply—'John, please tell"**: Testimony of William K. Harvey, US Select Committee on Intelligence, June 25, 1975 (released 1994), NARA: 157-10002-10106, p. 142. **"To eliminate a threat to security of this country by any means whatever"**: Ibid., p. 22. **"He [Maheu] was always on call for Mr. Hughes"**: Testimony of John Roselli, June 24, 1975, US Senate Select Committee on Intelligence, NARA: 157-10014-10001, p. 83. **"My name is not Maheu"**: Ibid., p. 90. **"dispose of Mr. Castro in connection"**: Drosnin, Michael.. "Citizen Hughes: The Power, the Money and the Madness of the Man Portrayed in the Movie, 'The Aviator'," New York: Crown, 2008, p. 70. **"Being a Jesuit trained college graduate, I understand"**: Maheu, Robert and Richard Hack. "Next to Hughes," New York: HarperCollins, 1992, p. 23. **"I still feel we should have never disclosed the mission"**: Smith, Bryan. "How the CIA Enlisted the Chicago Mob to Put a Hit on Castro," Chicago Magazine, Oct. 22, 2007, p 2. **"I felt sorry for Sam but I never even"**: Exner, Judith. "My Story," New York: Grove Press, 1977, p. 298. **"could not tell me exactly what it was they were going to discuss"**: Ibid., p. 298. **"Every time they asked me about someone, the questioner would say"**: Ibid., p. 299. **"Did either Mr. Giancana or Mr. Roselli ever ask you"**: Church, US Senate committee boxed files/Interview with Judith Campbell Exner, NARA: 157-10002-10384, September 20, 1975, p. 9. **"I do not know what Judith Campbell has to do with this thing"**: Testimony of John Roselli, September 22, 1975, US Senate Select Committee on Intelligence, NARA: 157-10002-10387, pp. 23–25. **"I could answer some of these questions"**: Summers, Anthony and Robbyn Swan, "Sinatra: The Life," New York: Knopf, 2005, p. 268. **"close friend"**: Testimony of James P. O'Connell, United States Senate Select Committee on Intelligence, NARA: 157-10002-10148, May 30, 1975, p. 30. **"Evidence before the committee indicates that"**: US Senate Select Committee to Study Governmental Operations with Respect to Intelligence Activities, Church Committee Report, Cuba section, p. 129. **"Giancana was killed before he was available for questioning"**: Ibid., p. 129, contained in second footnote. **"While straining to show that President Kennedy did not know"**: Safire, William. "The President's Friend," The New York Times, December 15, 1975, p. 31. **"I can at this time emphatically state that my relationship"**: The Associated Press, "JFK's 'Close Friend' Promises More Details on Relationship," The Nashville Tennessean, p. 8. **"the only Campbell I know is chunky vegetable"**: Morrison, Patt. "Judith Campbell Exner Dies; Had Affair With JFK; History: L.A. socialite was vilified for her relationship with the president and Chicago mobster Sam Giancana," The Los Angeles Times, September 26, 1999. **"The record shows that the only assassination plot disclosed to Robert Kennedy"**: Schlesinger, Arthur M. Jr. "Robert Kennedy and His Times," New York: Houghton Mifflin, 1978, p. 496. **"Particularly ludicrous is the notion that one of his background would have ever knowingly"**: Testimony & Affadavit of Theodore C. Sorensen before Church Committee, July 21, 1975, NARA: 157-10005-10253, pp. 5–7. **"People who loved Jack felt if they could degrade me"**: Morrison, Patt. "Judith Campbell Exner Dies; Had Affair With JFK; History: L.A. socialite was vilified for her relationship with the president and Chicago mobster Sam Giancana," The Los Angeles Times, September 26, 1999. **"As I look back, it's possible that Sam got exactly what he wanted from our relationship"**: Exner, Judith. "My Story," New York: Grove Press, 1977, p. 142. **"expressed fear for** his life as a result of his having testified": August 13, 1976, letter from US Attorney General Richard Thornburgh to the FBI Director. John ("Handsome Johnny") Roselli Part 8 of 12, FBI Vault file hltp://foia.fbi.gov/roselli/roselli3b.pdf.

CHAPTER 47

"We, at the CIA, had gone through some considerable suffering": Mailer, Norman. "Harlot's Ghost," New York: Random House, p. 30. "He was the one guy who could see humor in anything": Harris, Kathryn. "John Roselli," St. Petersburg Times, August 25, 1976, p. 1D. "If I'm ever missing, check the airports": Rappleye, Charles and Ed Becker. "All-American Mafioso: The Johnny Rosselli Story," New York: Doubleday, 1991, p. 321. "Any help you need – anything—you just tell me": Stockton, Bayard. "Flawed Patriot: The Rise and Fall of CIA Legend Bill Harvey," Washington, DC: Potomac Books, 2006, p. 170. "having difficulty finding a country who will accept Roselli": FBI Vault File of Fidel Castro, Part 03 of 04, pp. 28–30, Castro1c.pdf, p. 88. "There was never the slightest doubt in John's mind": LaBrecque, Ron. "Could Roselli Have Linked Castro Plot to JFK Death?" Miami Herald, September 19, 1976, p. 1. "I was an admirer of Earl Warren": Ibid. "You don't have to be a genius": Mohamed, Farah and Ryan Grim. "Senator Who Investigated JFK Assassination: 'American Journalism Never Followed Up on That Story'," The Huffington Post, November 22, 2013. "very murky, and I really don't believe this subject is an appropriate one": The Associated Press, "3 Presidents Not Linked to Castro Murder Plots," Ocala Star-Banner, October 6, 1975, p. 12A. "I went on the assumption": Testimony of Richard Bissell, June 9, 1975 (Marked Top Secret until declassified in May 1994), Senate Select Committee to Study Governmental Operations with Respect to Intelligence Activities, Church Committee Boxed Files, NARA: 157-10011-10020, pp. 24–26. "I think that in hindsight it could be regarded as peculiar, yes": Ibid., p. 35. "I am very certain, Senator, that such a discussion never came up": Testimony of General Edward Lansdale Re: Cuban Operation, July 8, 1975, (Marked Top Secret until declassified in April 1994), Senate Select Committee to Study Governmental Operations with Respect to Intelligence Activities, Church Committee Boxed Files, NARA: 157-10005-10236, p. 18. "personally managed the operation on the assassination of Castro": Holland, Max. "The Assassination Tapes," The Atlantic, June 2004. "a grave error in judgment": Marquis, Christopher. "Richard M. Helms Dies at 89; Dashing Ex-Chief of the C.I.A." NYT, October 23, 2002. "nolo contendere": Marro, Anthony. "Helms, Ex-C.I.A. Chief, Pleads No Contest to 2 Misdemeanors," NYT, November 1, 1977. "I had sworn my oath to protect certain secrets": Barnes, Bart. "Richard Helms Dies," The Washington Post, October 24, 2002. "like a badge of honor . . . I don't feel disgraced at all": Marquis, Christopher. "Richard M. Helms Dies at 89; Dashing Ex-Chief of the C.I.A." NYT, October 23, 2002. "There is nothing on paper, of course": Weiner, Tim. "Legacy of Ashes: The History of the CIA," New York: Knopf Doubleday, 2008, p. 216. "If you kill someone else's leaders, why shouldn't they kill yours?": Ibid., p. 216. "Mr. Roselli, the main reason why we have asked you to come back": Testimony of John Roselli, April 23, 1976, US Senate Select Committee on Intelligence, NARA: 157-10014-10000, (released in 1998), p. 7. "I never read it, and that's the first I heard of it": Ibid., p. 31. "Do you have any information bearing upon whether or not his death": Ibid. "I would have gone to the CIA immediately": Testimony of John Roselli, April 23, 1976, US Senate Select Committee on Intelligence, NARA: 157-10014-10000, (released in 1998), p. 54. "Remember when Santo was jailed and they grabbed his money": Demaris, Ovid. "The Last Mafioso," New York: Times Books, 1981, p. 328. "I remember Sam telling me when he got his subpoena": Ibid., p. 329. "Will you stop worrying? I'm all right": Ibid., pp. 388–392. "It's no secret in the underworld that Trafficante detests publicity": Stockton, Bayard. "Flawed Patriot: The Rise and Fall of CIA Legend Bill Harvey," Washington, DC: Potomac Books, 2006, p. 310. **"Get out of Miami—you're in serious danger"**: Rappleye, Charles and Ed Becker. "All-American Mafioso: The Johnny Rosselli Story," New York: Doubleday, 1991, p. 319. **"If I had known as a kid what I was getting into"**: Demaris, Ovid. "The Last Mafioso," New York: Times Books, 1981, p. 110. **"he would like to go back to the church"**: JFK2017:124-10277-10167. **"there was no business discussed"**: Rappleye, Charles and Ed Becker. "All-American Mafioso: The Johnny Rosselli Story," New York: Doubleday, 1991, p. 319.

CHAPTER 48

"Find out who's still alive and you'll find the killer": Giancana, Sam and Chuck Giancana. "Double Cross: the explosive, inside story of the mobster who controlled America," New York: Warner Books, 1992, p. 464. **"I got the impression he was not telling us all he knew"**: Tucker, William. "Roselli got final drink," Miami News, August 10, 1976. **"His safety and his life"**: JFK2017: 157-10014-10236. Madigan memo, p. 17. **"a continuing interest"**: FBI Vault File of John ("Handsome Johnny") Roselli, Part 8 of 12, roselli3b.pdf, pp. 148–150. **"felt that Roselli's previous hoodlum activities, plus being publicly identified"**: FBI Vault File of Fidel Castro, Part 03 of 04, pp. 28–30, Castro1c.pdf, pp. 103–105. **"Deep Six for Johnny"**: *Time* magazine. "Crime: Deep Six for Johnny," August 23, 1976. **"as a direct result of his testimony before the Senate committee"**: Gage, Nicholas. "Mafia Said to Have Slain Rosselli because of His Senate Testimony," NYT, February 25, 1977, p. 1. **"Mafia mobster John Roselli may have taken the secret"**: Anderson, Jack with Les Whitten. "Washington Merry-Go-Round," syndicated column, The Anniston Star, September 7, 1976, p. 14. **"the only person in American history to be murdered"**: Safire, William. "Murder Most Foul," NYT syndicated column, The Dispatch, Lexington, NC, January 3, 1976, p. 2. **"Was it the Central Intelligence Agency?"**: Giancana, Antoinette and Thomas C. Renner. "Mafia Princess: Growing Up in Sam Giancana's Family," New York: William Morrow, 1984, p. 346. **"All I know is that Roselli used a lot of people for his own advantage"**: Maheu, Robert and Richard Hack. "Next to Hughes," New York: HarperCollins, 1992, p. 133. **"I am one of the last people left who knows"**: Ibid., p. 131. **"I wish to God I'd never been"**: Ibid., p. 134. **"A lot of dead cats will come out"**: Weiner, Tim. "Legacy of Ashes: The History of the CIA," New York: Knopf Doubleday, 2008, p. 392. **"Pertinent files"**: JFK2017:104-10133-10276. **"There were a lot of Cubans"**: JFK2017:104-10106-10013. **"It is my personal view that on balance"**: LaBrecque, Ron. "Could Roselli Have Linked Castro Plot to JFK Death?" Miami Herald, September 19, 1976, p. 1. **"Knowledge of the links among his brother"**: Steel, Ronald. "In Love with Night: The American Romance with Robert Kennedy," New York: Simon & Schuster, 2000, p. 91. **"was briefed and gave his approval"**: Washington-The New York Times Blog, "A Plot to Assassinate Castro Was Approved by C.I.A. Director Allen Dulles," NYT, June 26, 2007. **"Assets"**: Ibid. **"If somebody had knocked off Hitler in 1936 or 1937"**: Daniel, Clifton. "The Assassination-Plot Rumors," NYT, June 6, 1975, p. 66. **"Does the United States want to return to this era of uncertainty?"**: Medish, Mark and Joel McCleary. "Assassination Season Is Open," NYT, April 14, 2010. **"It is awfully unusual for these people (Giancana and Roselli) to be erased"**: "Deaths Called 'Unusual'," NYT, March 31, 1977, p. 14. **"I didn't inform them of those things"**: HSCA Report, Volume IV, Current Section: Testimony of Richard Helms, September 22, 1978, (Resumed), p. 121. **"Perhaps naively, but I thought that the appointment of Allen Dulles"**: HSCA Report, Volume III. Current Section: Testimony of Nicholas Katzenbach, Former Attorney General of the United States, September 1978, pp. 699–703. **"He certainly should have**

because of his previous responsibilities": Gerald R. Ford Oral History Interview, July 8, 2003, John F. Kennedy Library, p. 15. "**was probably assassinated as a result of a conspiracy**": HSCA Report, Summary of Findings, March 29, 1979, p. 97. "**The plots, in short, should have been made known to the Warren Commission**": HSCA Report, Summary of Findings, March 29, 1979, p. 117. "**It seems like every time somebody important turns up**": Deitche, Scott M. "The Silent Don: The Criminal Underworld of Santo Trafficante Jr.," Barricade Books, 2007, p. 212. "**Johnny in a drum**": Rappleye, Charles and Ed Becker. "All-American Mafioso: The Johnny Rosselli Story," New York: Doubleday, 1991, p. 8. "**Trafficante had the job and he messed it up**": Ibid., p. 8. "**Playing both sides**": JFK2017: 104-10066-10060. "**Mark my words, this man [John] Kennedy is in trouble**": Rappleye, Charles and Ed Becker. "All-American Mafioso: The Johnny Rosselli Story," New York: Doubleday, 1991, p. 549. "**afraid of possible reprisal from Trafficante or his organization**": HSCA Report, pp. 174–175. "*his impression that Trafficante may have only meant the President was going to be hit*": Ibid. "**He was convinced the Mafia was after him**": Powell, Robert Andrew. "Rough Diamond," Miami New Times, August 15, 1996. "**I never made the statement that Kennedy was going to get hit**": HSCA Hearings, Testimony of Santo Trafficante, September 28, 1978, pp. 375–377. "**I don't remember what we discussed**": Ibid., pp. 367–368. "**I've been a gambler all my life**": HSCA Hearings, Testimony of Santo Trafficante, September 28, 1978, p. 367. "**a recital of evasive answers**": Ragano, Frank and Selwyn Raab. "Mob Lawyer," New York: Scribner, 1994, p. 326. "**One fact, however, was indisputable**": Ibid., p. 325. "**We are left to ponder**": Summers, Anthony and Robbyn Swan, "Sinatra: The Life," New York: Knopf, William Safire NYT column quoted in, 2005, p. 293. "**Sure, I knew some of those guys**": Hamill, Pete. "Sinatra: The Legend Lives," New York magazine, April 28, 1980, p. 34. "**This nexus of politics, covert action, show biz and organized crime**": Safire, William. "The President's Friend," NYT, October 4, 1999. "**more than 600 attempts**": Hughes, Trevor. "Assassins repeatedly tried and failed to kill Castro over the decades," USA Today, November 26, 2016. "**penetrated**": Weiner, Tim and Julia Preston. "Mexico Ends Asylum Case, Sends Officials Back to Cuba," NYT, October 5, 2000. Also, CREST #CIA-RDP89(;01371R000700360012-1. "**hundreds of spies**": Weiner, Tim. "Castro's Moles Dig Deep (Not Just among Exiles)," The New York Times, March 1, 1996. "**They operate as diplomats and cab drivers**": Ibid. "**quite conceivable**": Stockton, Bayard. "Flawed Patriot: The Rise and Fall of CIA Legend Bill Harvey," Washington, DC: Potomac Books, 2006, p. 18. "**infiltrated**": United Press International, "Analysts Say All Anti-Castro Groups in U.S. Infiltrated by Cuban Spies," Sarasota Herald-Tribune, June 20, 1983, p. 5A. "**If Trafficante was indeed a double agent**": Schlesinger, Arthur M. Jr. "Robert Kennedy and His Times," New York: Houghton Mifflin, 1978, p. 484. "**I have reached the conclusion that Oswald could not have been the one**": Goldberg, Jeffrey. "Castro: Oswald Could Not Have Been the One Who Killed Kennedy," The Atlantic, Novermber 20, 2013. "**a brutal dictator**": Wootson, Cleve R. Jr. "How Donald Trump responded to the death of Fidel Castro, 'a brutal dictator'," The Washington Post, November 26, 2016. "**Beyond anything else, it was Mr. Castro's obsession**": DePalma, Anthony. "Fidel Castro, Cuban Revolutionary Who Defied U.S., Dies at 90," NYT, November 26, 2016, p. 1A. "**In the end, Castro survived at a terrible cost**": Garvin, Glenn. "Red Ink: The high human cost of the Cuban revolution," Miami Herald, December 1, 2016. This story tallies the number of deaths attributed to the Castro regime, including those murdered, those killed by firing squads, and the thousands who drowned trying to escape their island nation.

INDEX